PKI: Implementing and Managing E-Security

PKI: Implementing and Managing E-Security

Andrew Nash
William Duane
Celia Joseph
Derek Brink

Osborne/**McGraw-Hill**
New York   Chicago   San Francisco
Lisbon   London   Madrid   Mexico City
Milan   New Delhi   San Juan
Seoul   Singapore   Sydney   Toronto

Osborne/**McGraw-Hill**
2600 Tenth Street
Berkeley, California 94710
U.S.A.

To arrange bulk purchase discounts for sales promotions, premiums, or fund-raisers, please contact Osborne/**McGraw-Hill** at the above address. For information on translations or book distributors outside the U.S.A., please see the International Contact Information page immediately following the index of this book.

PKI: Implementing and Managing E-Security

1234567890 CUS CUS 01987654321
ISBN 0-07-213123-3

Publisher
Brandon A. Nordin

**Vice President &
Associate Publisher**
Scott Rogers

Executive Editor
Steven Elliot

Project Manager
Mark Karmendy

Acquisitions Coordinator
Alex Corona

Technical Editors
Brian Breton
Kathrin Winkler
John Linn

Copy Editor
Lunaea Weatherstone

Proofreader
Susie Elkind

Illustrator
Michael Mueller

Production and Indexing
MacAllister Publishing Services, LLC

Contents at a Glance

Contents

Foreword

PKI: Implementing and Managing E-Security

If you've done any e-commerce on the Web, then you've most likely exchanged data securely with a number of Web sites—your name, passwords, credit card number, order information—all safely delivered over the Internet, encrypted with a secret key your computer shares with the Web site so that no one else can read the information.

How did that key get there?

Unless your computer came pre-installed with a secret key for every Web site you might want to reach (it didn't), or at least with a secret key for a central key server (there isn't one), you need some way to set up that shared secret key with the Web site. Your computer can't send the secret key, or someone else might intercept it. Somehow, by exchanging messages, your computer and the Web site need to arrive at the secret key, in such a way that none else can figure it out—which seems difficult, because your computer and the Web site don't have any common secrets.

Twenty-five years ago, scientists in the academic community, and thirty years ago, researchers in the classified arena, made the remarkable discovery that you don't need to share any secrets to encrypt messages. Instead of the traditional approach where you encrypt and decrypt with the *same* key, they showed that you could encrypt with one key and decrypt with a different one. The encryption key can then be made public, like a phone number. The decryption key stays private, like someone's phone. Anyone can call you; only you (hopefully!) get to answer the call.

This discovery, called *public key cryptography*, answers the question of how your computer sets up a shared secret key with a Web site. The computer, in essence, looks up the Web site's public encryption key and encrypts a randomly generated secret key with the Web site's public key. The Web site then decrypts with its private decryption key and recovers the secret key your computer generated. The rest of your messages are encrypted with the shared secret key.

One essential question remains, however: How does your computer know it's looked up the Web site's, and not someone else's, public key? (Imagine that the phone book listed someone else's phone number after your name!) This is the issue addressed by *public key infrastructure (PKI)*: matching public keys with their owners.

Public key cryptography is the easy part. Public key infrastructure, or PKI, is the challenge today. Just like phone numbers, people's public keys change occasionally; and just like phone books, there are many publishers, for different communities and purposes. Which publishers should be trusted and for which purposes? What if a publisher can no longer be trusted? How do you know if someone's public key is still the right one? All of these issues are particularly important as digital signatures—a major application of PKI—become more widely adopted.

This book guides you through the basic building blocks and major issues involved in PKI, the problems to be solved, and the solutions that are available. The authors' practical, accessible approach—benefiting from their years of experience architecting other technologies such as computer networking—introduces PKI in a meaningful and readable manner. We hope you enjoy reading this book—and the next time you send data securely over the Internet, encrypted with a shared secret key, you'll know exactly how that key got there, and much more.

Scott T. Schnell
Senior Vice President of Marketing & Corporate Development
RSA Security Inc.

About the Authors

Andrew Nash is Director of PKI Standards and Technologies at RSA Security. He was one of the architects for the Koen® Advanced PKI product line and is co-chair of the PKI Forum Technical Working Group.

William Duane is a Technical Director at RSA Security Inc. He is one of the architects behind RSA's Keon® PKI solution and is responsible for new token form factors, including Smart Cards and emerging cryptographic devices.

Celia Joseph is Chief Consulting Architect in RSA's Professional Services organization, where she builds and deploys enterprise security solutions. She is the lead consultant in RSA's Security Assessment and Design service, and her custom development work at RSA emphasizes cryptography and PKI.

Derek Brink is a Director in RSA's Product Marketing organization. His work has included market and competitive analysis, strategic planning, and product marketing for the company's public-key infrastructure, authentication, services, and intrusion detection products. He also chairs the Executive Board of the PKI Forum.

About the Reviewers

As the leading publisher of technical books for more than 100 years, McGraw-Hill prides itself on bringing you the most authoritative and up-to-date information available. To ensure that our books meet the highest standards of accuracy, we have asked a number of top professionals and technical experts to review the accuracy of the material you are about to read.

We take great pleasure in thanking the following reviewers for their insights:

Brian Breton is currently a Senior Product Marketing Manager at RSA Security Inc., responsible for RSA Keon®, RSA's suite of public key infrastructure products. Brian has over 15 years of industry experience in engineering, product management, and product marketing positions at companies offering products in the areas of PKI, DCE authorization, Kerberos, system security auditing and operating systems.

John Linn, Principal Architect at RSA Laboratories, has been involved with security technologies for networks, distributed systems, and messaging since 1980. He is an active participant and working group chair within the Internet Engineering Task Force (IETF) security area, and has authored several Internet standards-track specifications and conference papers on aspects of security technology, including security service interfaces, cryptographic protection for messaging, distributed authentication, and attribute certification.

Kathrin Winkler has over 20 years of experience in analysis, design, and engineering of network software. She has held positions as a principal consultant and industry analyst at Renaissance Worldwide, and as a Consulting Software Engineer in Digital Equipment Corporation's Networks and Windows NT engineering groups. Ms. Winkler is currently Vice President of Engineering at Practicity, Inc., a knowledge management application software provider.

Preface

Public Key Infrastructure (PKI) is a tremendously exciting area to work in. It enables many of the new technologies that are used to build electronic commerce solutions.

The current state of development of PKI needs to be put into perspective. In many ways, it is similar to the state of Networking infrastructure in the early 1980s. That means that there are constantly new developments; people are coming up with new ways to use the technology and there are lots of ways for creative engineers, product people, and implementers to come up with solutions.

What makes PKI fun as a technologist is that although there are lots of really cool things you can do with it, it is not complete yet. There are still plenty of rough edges on PKI and problems that need to be solved—just as Networking infrastructure took many years to overcome its usability problems. This should not discourage anyone from using PKI, as it is a workable solution now and getting progressively better.

One of the most popular talks I [Andrew] used to give was called "Pragmatic PKI." This described the values of PKI, but I spent a lot of time identifying the problems with PKI that people were not aware of. Questions like, "How do you really know the identity of the individual who is using the public key to sign that transaction?" or "How secure is the storage for the private key?" or "How do you support mobile users if your keys are in a Web browser key store?". There were a whole raft of issues that people buying PKI needed to be aware of—and of course we supplied products that addressed these issues (if I had only talked about problems we couldn't solve, the product managers would have been really annoyed with me).

At the time, when pressed, I would admit that there was a list of problems longer than my arm that I could talk about. The reason they never came up was that before people could understand the potential problems, it was necessary to spend so much time setting up the description of the environment that people could not appreciate the solution. There were way too many more immediate problems to deal with.

Today, many of the issues I used to talk about are becoming widely recognized as issues that need to be addressed by a PKI solution. Many more vendors provide solutions to these problems. Early proprietary solutions are giving way to implementations based on a growing body of proven standards. Interoperability issues are being resolved in test labs in many different parts of the world. Organizations like the PKI forum (www.PKIForum.org) create an opportunity for PKI vendors, customers, users, and implementers to resolve the deployment issues with PKI.

New opportunities for PKI and related fields continue to develop. Attribute certificates and Privilege Management Infrastructure are addressing the problems of authorizing users (after their identity has been established using PKI) and conveying rights to access systems in a standard fashion. Wireless devices and support for services that require identification of huge, highly mobile user populations as well as privacy for the transactions find support from public keys and its associated infrastructure.

We seem to have passed the point where more hype than content has been associated with PKI. Now the fun part starts—where we can eliminate the complexity of the user's experience and make PKI a "really useful" infrastructure.

This book is intended to introduce you to the concepts and technology of cryptography and PKI and then show how PKI can be deployed and used to support the rapidly expanding world of electronic commerce and information delivery. Along the way we want to show how PKI relates to the other important security technologies like authentication, and deal with pragmatic issues like how you show an economic return on your PKI investment.

Have Fun!

CHAPTER 1

Introduction

Public Key Infrastructure has caused considerable excitement over the last couple of years. All new technologies tend to follow an "S" curve that describes their acceptance and usefulness. As with any new technology during its honeymoon phase (the initial upswing of the curve), PKI has seen significant amounts of media hype. The reasons are clear. Public/private keys when combined with other encryption technologies enable all aspects of the security services we need for electronic commerce. When this is combined with the capabilities of Public Key Infrastructure for creating and managing vastly scalable sets of digital identities, we have the opportunity to see rich and secure electronic commerce solutions developed.

As with other technologies in this early phase, the promise of PKI as a technology has outstripped many of its early capabilities. The result has been disappointment in the usability and integration of PKI. The good news is that, as with other technologies, while we are on the down slope (of the S curve) after the initial crest of enthusiasm, the whole PKI industry has made major leaps forward in applying the technology to solving electronic commerce solutions. We still have a considerable way to go before PKI achieves the same level of integration and ease of use as computer networks, but networking was much more badly integrated, non-interoperable, and painful to use for much of its early career than PKI.

Security Trends

The trend toward electronic commerce of all types, varieties, and flavors has caused substantial changes in the attitudes that organizations have toward security. Until relatively recently, security for most organizations was a matter of protecting access to corporate data. The biggest issue was how to stop people getting into your systems who wanted to trash them or to view proprietary information.

Broad availability of networked systems within corporations, beginning in the early 1980s, created a new environment in which information could be shared. As entry points using dialup connections and acoustic couplers allowed access to these networks, we created the opportunity for a whole new industry to grow up dedicated to protecting those entry points. As we began to interconnect remote sites using dedicated lines and then tie them into the Internet, we also created the potential for broad access by all sorts of undesirable characters.

With the increased availability of network access, security became a matter of how to create the hardened outer wall around your soft and squishy inner systems. We all knew that security of individual systems was way too hard to manage and control, but controlled perimeters was a manageable concept (until someone created their own private connection to the Internet for their internal system). Security was primarily about how to stop the barbarian hordes from ravaging the civilized cultures huddling within the corporate network. Beware if you were a traveling network message crossing the hostile wastes between walled cities.

A whole new language of defense strategies was created, and we constructed models based on fortress mentalities and perimeter defenses. Authentication products were created to identify the townsfolk to the guards at the gates. We constructed demilitarized zones (DMZs) to distinguish those areas where we would allow external access to less sensitive machines or those we were prepared to fight to the death for (bastion hosts). We built firewalls to separate the regions within our network cities to limit the damage that invaders could cause when they ravished our systems and burned our data. We built intrusion detection systems (battlements) and mantraps (baileys). The corporate inner citadel had to be maintained.

Electronic Commerce and Security Today

Security challenges are now significantly different. Networking has moved from its medieval roots to a renaissance period. The massive adoption of the Internet as a basis for electronic commerce has moved the whole security model from one of a small community huddling within a medieval keep to a walled city with an open marketplace. Possibly, we are on the way to an environment where we can have open cities without walls that allow major commercial interactions.

We are certainly concerned with keeping the corporate data safe—those barbarians are still out there—but the emphasis has shifted to the need to maximize free trade. Yesterday, security was primarily about how to limit access. Today, it is about how to maximize access—to the right people.

Many of the traditional (only on the Internet does it take less than ten years to establish a tradition) security mechanisms are still essential, but there is a significant difference. There is no strongly guarded perimeter. You allow access to your corporate data by partners (to share strategy and technology to develop products), by customers (to access online remedial information instead of using a helpdesk and to place orders), and by contractors and consultants (who are now indistinguishable from your own employees). You outsource your data centers to companies who perform facilities management halfway across the country. Your network connectivity and management are provided by Internet service providers, and even some of your applications are being run for you by application service providers. The one thing it is impossible to spot here in all this mess is where the perimeter might lie.

Security Services

Our view of security is rapidly becoming much more sophisticated. Instead of limiting our security thinking to firewalls and routers, we are now starting to think much more about the underlying principles that need to be applied to the information and services we need to protect and to which we want to grant access. Can access to some services be opened to anyone? Do some messages need to be encrypted to maintain privacy or signed to prevent change and authenticate their origin?

Electronic security relies on fundamental processes or services that allow construction of a secure solution for delivery of business information and services across a network. These services include

▪ Identification

▪ Authentication

▪ Authorization

▪ Integrity

▪ Confidentiality

▪ Non-repudiation

Identification is the process of recognizing a particular individual. You identify people by recognizing physical properties about them, such as their face, height, and build. In a cryptographic sense, you would like to associate some unique information with a person or other entity that only they can reproduce. Ideally, you want to allow the presentation of this information in such a way that it cannot be captured by an eavesdropper.

Authentication is any process by which you prove and verify certain information. Providing your mother's maiden name when asking an organization to provide access to your account information qualifies as an (albeit weak) authentication. The act of signing a form and comparing the signature to a previous record of your signature before accessing your security vault is authenticating that you are the valid holder of the safe deposit box key. Cryptographically, you can also sign electronic documents—this allows an authentication process to run that identifies who you are.

Just for the record, identification and authentication are different. Identification requires that the verifier check the information presented against all the entities it knows about to verify which one is being dealt with, while authentication requires that the information be checked for a single, previously identified, entity. While identification must uniquely identify a given entity, authentication does not necessarily require uniqueness. For instance, someone logging into a shared account is not uniquely identified, but by knowing the shared password, she is authenticated as one of the users. This has the interesting property of allowing privacy (hiding your identity) while authenticating your access to the system—something that is important when you want to engage in a transaction, but not allow other people to know it was you.

Authorization is the process of determining what you are allowed to do. After you have been authenticated (and possibly identified), you may be allowed to do anything you want. It is more likely, however, that only some people are allowed to do some things. For example, only your supervisor is likely to be authorized to grant your leave request—your workmates will not be able to sign your request. In our electronic world, authorization depends on authentication (and possibly an identity) used in conjunction with a rule set to determine if you are allowed access to certain systems or functions within that system. For example, if you subscribe to a satellite or cable TV system, you will only be authorized to watch the channels you have paid for.

Integrity in this context is the process of ensuring that information is unchanged. When you sign a message or a document, you not only authenticate the origin of the message, you also ensure that the contents cannot be modified. This is a highly desirable feature when you wish to establish an agreement between two parties.

Confidentiality (or privacy) is simply keeping information secret. It is what you hope will happen when you share information with a lawyer or doctor. It is probably not what happens when you share private information with your yappy friend. This is the area that most people associate with the terms "cryptography" and "encryption." When you want to keep the contents of a note private, you place it in an envelope that hides the information. When you encrypt information, you prevent unintended people from seeing the contents of your message.

Non-repudiation is a big word that means you cannot deny doing something. If your friend needs to borrow five dollars, and you are worried she might forget she borrowed the money, you can have her sign and date an IOU note. In that way, you have a document that can be proven to be correct at a certain time and date, and which is bound to your friend. If you and your friend get into a "Yes you did, no I didn't" type of argument, the IOU can be shown to another friend, who will advise your deadbeat friend to pay up. For security services, this usually requires the use of a digital signature and a secure digital timestamp to establish the identity of the signer and when it was signed. Practically, this may require additional services before it becomes a workable feature.

All of these services are employed in one form or another in our daily lives. The challenge is how to reproduce similar services in an electronic commerce world. The techniques that are used to create electronic analogs to these services are based on cryptography.

Public Key Infrastructure

Public Key Infrastructure provides the framework that allows you to deploy security services based on encryption. Other infrastructures using purely symmetric (secret key) encryption have been attempted and failed due to the management, scalability, and life cycle issues they encountered. PKI allows you to create the identities and associated trust you need for identification and authentication processes, and to manage the public/private key-based encryption that provides an infinitely more scalable solution than previous encryption and security infrastructures.

When we first started with networking, most of the implementations were created by companies like IBM (SNA) and Digital Equipment Corporation (DECnet), and then there were a few defense organizations and universities using the ARPAnet. Networking was fun, but required a lot of arcane knowledge (just like operating systems) and could not be explained or configured by the man on the street. It also did not scale very well—a couple of hundred networked computers was a big deal in those days. Interoperability between these network implementations was spotty at best, using weird gateways, and you had to know how to form network addresses where you specified how to route through the gateways by hand (ahh, those were the days—sigh!). Things did not really heat up in the networking space until standards were developed and adherence became pervasive. (Believe me, we learned that having a standard did not mean the same thing as interoperable implementations a long time ago.)

In the PKI technology space, huge strides have been made in the last few years in the area of standardization. In addition to X.509 recommendations from the International Telecommunications Union (ITU) and the PKCS standards from RSA Laboratories, the most significant body of work has been achieved in the Internet Engineering Task Force (IETF) through the PKI X.509 (PKIX) working group. Other industry and government groups have worked to define profiles and operational models that tailor broader PKI specifications to the needs of their communities for security and electronic commerce. Don't let all of the standards and standards purveyors bother you—we will ease you into all of this and tell you about them later when you need them.

Applications

While many PKI vendors are making strides in dealing with the usability and deployment aspects of PKI, one area is lagging significantly. Integration of PKI into applications is poorly done at best.

A fundamental that we should establish up front is this: infrastructures are useless. At least infrastructures are useless until you have applications that are effectively integrated with them and that make good use of the services provided.

PKI, as its name implies, is an infrastructure. As with any other good infrastructure, it works best when it is seen least. The use of public/private keys and certificates for signing e-mail, authenticating to Web sites, validating transactions, and the myriad of other functions will only be successful when the applications hide (preferably completely) the PKI mechanisms used to perform these activities.

One significant area where PKI success has been demonstrated is in the use of SSL server side certificates. Many applications rely on the privacy and integrity derived from an SSL session established with a Web server for secure electronic commerce transactions. The reason for the success of this application of certificates is that it is almost entirely transparent to the end user, and most of the functionality required to support it is built directly into the Web browsers. Use of more sophisticated aspects of PKI such as authentication of clients has not been as well integrated and the result has been to limit the use of client side certificates.

If anything will slow the deployment of PKI and delay the returns that can be made, it is the poor integration of PKI with applications. While new toolkits, Web plug-ins, Java applets and servlets, mobile credential stores, and new PKI services are all needed to simplify this environment, application providers need to take advantage of these options if practical electronic commerce solutions are to emerge.

Audience

This book is targeted at anyone who wants to learn about the technology associated with PKI—particularly if they are involved in deployment, planning, or operation of a Public Key Infrastructure. It is also applicable to anyone considering building electronic commerce systems and wanting to learn about the underlying technology when integrating PKI into applications. We have specifically provided information on areas such as authentication technology, smart cards, and biometrics. This is where many implementers will see integration between the cryptographic needs of applications and authentication of the PKI identities that will support them.

About this Book

You will be pleased to hear that you do not need to read all of this book—although some of the authors may be heartbroken that you skipped their content.

For general readers wanting a short introduction to PKI, I would suggest you read Chapters 1 through 4 and Chapter 7.

For readers interested in PKI concepts, particularly for the purposes of purchasing and deploying a PKI, I would suggest you read Chapters 1 through 4, Chapter 7, and Chapter 10. Then come back and read Chapter 8 when you need to build a more complex PKI within your own organization or between organizations. Read Chapter 9 when you want to launch into the world of authentication (don't leave this one out).

For readers who have already had an introduction to cryptography and PKI and do not need any training wheels, but who would like to know more about the technology, I would suggest you read Chapter 1 and Chapters 4 through 9.

Appendix A is useful reference material for anyone wanting the details on X.509 certificates and CRLs. It's information that can be accessed whenever you are inquisitive—after all, inquiring minds want to know.

You will notice that in all the cases discussed above, you are required to read Chapter 1. That is because it is my [Andrew's] chapter and as I have already given you permission to skip some of the other chapters I wrote, it is only fair you should read this one.

Chapter 1 is the general introduction to the book, which you have nearly completed by the time you have read this far.

Chapter 2, "Introduction to Cryptography," examines the principles involved in cryptographic techniques based on symmetric and public/private keys. It discusses the shortcomings of symmetric key and public key systems and shows how the techniques may be combined to create effective solutions. Don't worry, you will not need a degree in mathematics to understand this section.

Chapter 3, "Public Key Infrastructure Basics," begins by asking why cryptographic techniques alone are not enough and introduces the concepts of digital identities and certificates. The components that are implemented in a PKI are introduced.

Chapter 4, "PKI Services and Implementations," discusses the services that are offered in a PKI and examines such issues as key storage and security. It also looks at the implementation options for organizations considering a PKI.

Chapter 5, "Key and Certificate Life Cycle," looks at the processes associated with creation and management of keys and certificates within a PKI.

Chapter 6, "A PKI Architecture—The PKIX Model," examines the protocols and standards used to define a particular PKI architecture as defined in the ITEF PKIX working group.

Chapter 7, "Application Use of PKI," investigates how applications use PKI to implement secure services and protocols. This chapter also discusses the various standards that define PKI and how applications use it.

Chapter 8, "Trust Models," discusses how trust relationships are established between groups within an organization or between organizations. A variety of trust models are described, starting with simple bilateral trust and working through to complex trust networks.

Chapter 9, "Authentication and PKI," looks at the processes associated with authentication and evaluates various authentication techniques and devices, including tokens, smart cards, and biometrics.

Chapter 10, "Deployment and Operation," considers the practical aspects of how a PKI should be planned, deployed, and operated.

Chapter 11, "PKI and Return on Investment," considers the financial aspects of owning a PKI. It examines the business case for investing in a PKI.

Appendix A, "X.509 Certificates," is a detailed description of the content and use of the fields and extensions to X.509 certificates and certificate revocation lists.

Appendix B, "Solution to the Test," is the answer to the test posed in Chapter 2.

Appendix C, "Privilege Management Infrastructure," is a discussion on attribute certificates.

A glossary of terms is found at the end of the appendixes.

About the Authors

In working with a group of authors who do the writing directly, rather than using a ghost writer, many of the aspects of the writers' personal styles and personalities become evident. Rather than try to homogenize all writing styles, we chose to let the individual authors speak in their own voice. In those places where first-person usage occurs, the writers have included their name [in brackets]. We felt that this would allow the innocent not to be tainted by scurrilous storytelling.

CHAPTER 2

Introduction to Cryptography

My Mom

My [Bill's] mother makes a great peppermint stick pie.

It has a thick, chocolate graham cracker crust and is filled with a sweet peppermint filling. Mom's peppermint stick pie is hard to miss. You'll immediately know if you are in the same room as one of these wonderful pies, because the mint fragrance fills the air, and the wonderful red-speckled pie rimmed in deep chocolate fills the eye. At least that is the way it will be temporarily, because Mom's pie does not last long. I always associate Mom's peppermint stick pie with the holidays—probably because that is the only time of year she makes them. While some people's heads are filled with visions of dancing sugarplums during the holidays, mine is filled of visions of spoons laden with Mom's gooey, chocolaty, minty pie.

This description of the contents of my cranium will no doubt come back to haunt me.

You might be wondering why I am talking about Mom's peppermint stick pie in a book that is focusing on public key systems and security. Well, unfortunately, it seems that my sister has the only remaining copy of Mom's precious peppermint stick pie recipe. To complicate matters further, my sister and I do not live in the same state, so getting the recipe to me will require some doing. As if these problems were not enough, I suspect that someone is trying to steal Mom's wonderful recipe. If I didn't know Mrs. Fields to be the honorable chocolate chip cookie meister that she is, I would suspect her of trying to steal Mom's recipe in order to branch her massive cookie kingdom into new directions!

Before the application of cryptographic techniques to standard Internet applications such as e-mail and the Web, it would have been difficult to see how my sister could securely transfer Mom's recipe to me. In the context of this discussion, secure means:

- I can guarantee that my sister is the source of the recipe.
- I can guarantee that the recipe was not modified as it was sent to me via the Internet.
- Nobody will be able to see Mom's recipe as it is sent to me, thereby preventing the theft of the recipe.
- My sister cannot claim later that she never sent me the recipe.

Before we get into the process of getting Mom's special recipe from my sister, let's explore the general need for cryptography.

Is Cryptography Really Needed?

As we saw in the previous chapter, the initial Internet applications were very weak when it came to security. In fact, most applications, Internet based or not, do not support much security. Many applications have some sort of password-based authentication, while many others do not. Some applications have some sort of encryption, usually of the database associated with that application, but most do not. Very few applications support digital signatures or non-repudiation.

This situation might lead you to the conclusion that security enhancements are therefore not needed. Nothing could be further from the truth.

As a generalization, security enhancements like these are needed in most applications, because in most applications the data being processed has some value or there would be some repercussions if the information were exposed. I'd like to take a few minutes to give some well-known examples of where cryptographic techniques could have been applied to improve electronic commerce. Let's look specifically at some well-known attacks related to credit cards on the Internet, where encryption could have helped prevent the attack.

Everyone has heard discussions of the risks surrounding the use of credit cards for online Internet purchases. As you will see in a minute, the application of cryptography has protected the transmission of credit card information over secure Web sessions. Unfortunately, that only protects your credit card number in transit over the Internet to your online merchant. Once the merchant has received the credit card number, it is stored in a database on the merchant site. These databases are frequently connected to the merchant's internal network. As a result, almost all online credit card thefts occur when an attacker finds a way through the merchant's firewall and copies the credit card database.

One spectacular example of this was the compromise of the CD Universe credit card database in January 2000. An attacker, purportedly in Russia, was successful in copying CD Universe's database of 300,000 credit card numbers across the Internet, and then attempted to extort protection money from CD Universe. CD Universe refused to pay, and the hacker then published 25,000 of the credit card numbers on the Web. In this situation, the various issuing banks (the banks which send out credit cards) reacted in a variety of ways. Some banks reissued all involved credit cards at a cost of about $20 per card. Other issuing banks just warned their customers to monitor their statements closely for unusual transactions.

For the customers of CD Universe, the risk was small because credit cards have protection, which limits the risk of using a credit card, usually to $50 or less. Increasingly, credit card companies are reducing this customer risk to zero. Unfortunately for CD Universe, confidence in the company eroded and caused a significant impact to their business. Also, unknown to most people is the fact that the merchants are liable for online fraud. As a result, the cost of any purchases made with the stolen credit cards (before they were revoked) is borne by the merchants who sold the goods. This fraud cost is a serious issue for merchants, and most of this cost is ultimately passed on to consumers. There is also the real but unquantifiable loss of confidence by the buying public in the online use of credit cards each time one of these situations occurs. If cryptography had been used to encrypt the database of credit card numbers, the attackers would not have been able to extract the credit card numbers, even if they were able to copy the merchant database.

I would like to think that the situation with CD Universe was an exception, but I am afraid that it is more the rule. Most companies do not have adequate protection of their databases. During the year 2000, there were more cases of this type of problem. In March, it was reported that 485,000 credit card numbers stolen from an e-commerce site were discovered being stored on a U.S. government agency Web site. In September, Western Union reported that hackers attacked their Web site and extracted 15,700 credit card numbers. In October, a hacker stole 55,000 credit card numbers from Creditcards.com, and then attempted to extort money from Creditcards.com. These are just a few examples, which took only a few minutes of Web searching to locate. There are many more press articles on attacks like these and probably far more unreported attacks.

The protection of credit card databases via encryption is useful when the attack is directly against a computer as well as when the attack is mounted across the Internet.

Another example, which also illustrates the financial impact of these problems, was the theft of a single notebook computer at Visa International in November 1996. Although it was believed that the thief stole the notebook simply to get the notebook, this particular notebook unfortunately contained more than 314,000 credit card numbers. The issuing banks of the involved credit cards needed to reissue all the involved credit card numbers and deal with the loss of customer confidence. The published cost to replace a credit card is $20, and as a result, this single theft cost approximately $6.3 million. Again, the simple act of encrypting the credit card information residing on the notebook hard drive would have prevented these problems and saved millions of dollars.

When you begin to think about it, there are very few cases where digital information does not have value. Obviously things like online e-commerce need to be protected, but almost anything else does as well. More and more "content" is being sold directly over the Internet. This includes distributing software, music, e-books, images, movies, and so on over the Internet without theft. There are privacy concerns with sending e-mail or other personal information across the Internet.

When lecturing about cryptography, I like to use the example of an electronic contract between a lawyer and his client. Compared with a standard paper contract, the electronic contract loses a lot unless cryptography is used. Without cryptography, you have no assurance of the source of the contract, you have no assurance that the contract was signed, you have no assurance that the contract was modified, and you have no legal recourse against cheating. In essence, the contract is worth the paper it is printed on (and since it is an electronic contract, and therefore not printed, its worth is zero).

I hope I have given you some feeling for the importance of cryptographic techniques such as encryption to help protect critical information. Critical information comes in many forms, and thankfully, it does not know or care if the information is very important (such as credit card numbers), or really critical (such as Mom's peppermint pie recipe).

Now that you have learned a little about the importance of cryptography, let's see how it works. In the spirit of an introductory chapter, I hope to make this an educational and hopefully entertaining tour of cryptography. We will not be diving into the details of the various algorithms, but rather treat them as broad classes and examine the strengths and weaknesses of each.

Cryptography

Cryptography is the science of applying complex mathematics to increase the security of electronic transactions. Cryptography is based on really hard math problems. Harder math than you had in Mrs. Buxworth's algebra class. (Mrs. Buxworth is my son's algebra teacher. Right now my son is doing fine in algebra, but I figure that if his grades begin to slip I can inform Mrs. Buxworth that I mentioned her name in a book and maybe she will cut him some slack.)

Cryptographic Algorithms

An algorithm is the set of steps needed to solve a mathematical problem. In the field of computer science, algorithms are implemented typically as parts of a program referred to as a routine or a library. The main program usually performs the mathematical operation on various sets of data by calling the algorithm libraries repeatedly. Some particularly complex algorithms may be implemented in specialized hardware—an example would be the 3-D video acceleration chips embedded in the video cards of today's PCs.

Cryptographic algorithms are mathematical algorithms and are designed so that the cryptographic algorithm can be called with different sets of data to be operated on. For example, an encryption algorithm may be called with credit card data to be encrypted one time and a pie recipe to be encrypted another time. You may have heard the term *cryptographic service provider* (CSP). A CSP is essentially a library of cryptographic algorithms (encryption algorithms, signing algorithms, and so on) which can be called via a well-defined interface to perform a particular cryptographic function. Cryptographic algorithms are complex, and in some instances benefit from a hardware accelerator to speed up some of the math. Many Web servers use a cryptographic accelerator board that runs the complex math of cryptographic algorithms in specialized high-speed hardware. In Chapter 9 on PKI and authenticators, we will talk about smart cards and how many smart cards include hardware math accelerators to speed up cryptographic algorithm computations.

Cryptology and Cryptanalysis

Cryptography is a fascinating area. It is actually split into two disciplines, *cryptology* and *cryptanalysis*.

Cryptologists are mathematicians and researchers who expend their valuable brain cells inventing new cryptographic algorithms. After years of work, somewhat like a new proud parent, the cryptologists release their inventions to the cryptographic community for review. This is where the cryptanalysts come in. Armed with formidable tools, they analyze the algorithm for weaknesses and perform various tortures and attacks on the design in an all-out attempt to break the algorithm. They are frequently successful.

Now, you might think that at this point the cryptologists are pretty ticked off. I'm sure it's annoying to have years of work picked apart by the cryptanalysts, but in most cases the cryptologists learn something new about how to make better algorithms and head back into the lab armed with this information to engineer even more secure algorithms.

Cryptography is the only branch of computer science I can think of that has these two parallel, opposing, and symbiotic branches.

There have been several cases where someone thought it might be a good idea to invent a new cryptographic algorithm, but to try and keep it a secret rather than release it for cryptanalytic review. This is referred to as "security by obscurity." In general, security by obscurity does not work. These algorithms are complex math and probably exceed the capacity for one cranium to hold all possible aspects of the math and therefore all possible attacks. As a result, it seems to require the community of cryptanalysts to help ensure the security of the algorithm. There have been some spectacular failures of cryptographic algorithms that attempted security by obscurity.

Security by Obscurity

In November 1999, several Norwegian programmers of the group *Masters of Reverse Engineering* (MoRE) successfully cracked the *Content Scrambling System* (CSS) encryption algorithm used to encrypt DVDs. Since this cryptographic algorithm was built into every DVD player and was used to encrypt millions of DVDs sold around the world, it will be a complex task to migrate to a new DVD encryption algorithm. The CSS algorithm was an example of an algorithm developed in secret that did not undergo the open review of the cryptanalysts.

In March 1997, Counterpane Systems and UC Berkeley collaborated to crack the *Cellular Message Encryption Algorithm* (CMEA), which is used to encrypt numbers entered into a cell phone keypad (credit card numbers, for example). CMEA was designed to use keys that are 64 bits in length (64-bit keys), which would have been reasonably secure. Unfortunately, the algorithm, which was developed in secret and not subject to cryptanalytic review, had several weaknesses that reduced its effective key length from 64 to 32 (or even 24) bits. Since the strength of a cryptographic algorithm (and hence its resistance to attack) is directly related to the length of the key, this dramatically reduced the strength of the CMEA encryption. Going from 64-bit effective key length to 24-bit effective key length essentially changes CMEA from reasonably strong to very weak.

In November 2000, Adi Shamir (the S in RSA) cracked one of the series of A5 algorithms used to protect digital cell phone conversations in more than 200 million GSM-based cell phones throughout Europe and the U.S. Shamir was able to decrypt cell phone conversations using just a digital scanner and a standard PC. Again, the A5 series of cryptographic algorithms was developed in secret without cryptanalytic review.

Cryptography 101

For the purposes of this chapter, I am not going to get into the deep math behind cryptographic algorithms. I will only address cryptography at a very basic level, to give you a flavor of the various types of cryptographic algorithms and how they are used in today's applications.

Cryptography is based on the concept that some computations can be easy in one direction but extremely difficult in the opposite direction. It seems counterintuitive that a computation can run easily in one direction but be difficult in the other direction, but in fact this is quite common. A simple example may be illustrative of this fact. Pick two relatively large integers. Multiply them together. Take the product and give it to someone else. Without telling them either of the two initial numbers, ask them what the two starting integers were. Creating the product was easy; reversing it into the two starting integers is hard.

To be honest, I cheated a little. The test was a little unfair, because there could be more than one answer to the problem. In this case, there could be multiple sets of integers that produce the same product. To make this an accurate example, the integers would need to be reasonably large prime numbers. You would multiply the two prime numbers together and pass the result to your friend. You would then ask your friend to find the original prime numbers. Determining the prime factors of a number is recognized as an extremely difficult math problem.

NOTE:

Prime numbers are numbers whose whole number factors are limited to 1 and the number itself.

In addition to having the property that the computation runs easily in one direction, but is hard in the reverse direction, cryptographic algorithms also have the property that there is a "trap door." The trap door is a technique that allows you to solve the problem in the reverse direction as long as you know the secret.

RSA encryption is based on factorization into prime numbers. Other cryptographic algorithms are based on different difficult problems in math.

I was once having lunch with a luminary in the field of cryptography. During the discussions, it came out that while pursuing his doctorate, this person had done work on *Elliptic Curve Cryptography* (ECC). During various presentations I had made on cryptography, I was occasionally asked to give a simple explanation of ECC. At this point I asked this large-lobed person if he could provide me with a layperson's definition of Elliptic Curve Cryptography. He sat up straight, and his eyes twinkled. He was clearly delighted to have the chance to talk about ECC. He looked me straight in the eye and started, "Imagine a three-dimensional torus rotating in free space. Then imagine an elliptical function that bisects the torus at two points . . ." At this point I burst into laughter. This was the easiest explanation of ECC that he could muster, and I could imagine trying to use that explanation during a presentation on cryptography.

As I said, cryptography is based on really hard math.

The Characters

As you recall, I am talking about all of this with a specific objective in mind. I need to get that great peppermint stick pie recipe from my sister. To illustrate the various algorithms, I am going to use some simple graphics. Refer to Figure 2-1. This cloud represents the Internet. Rather than try and use some fancy graphics, I prefer to use a blob.

Figure 2-1

The Internet

Next is Figure 2-2. This figure represents the hacker trying to get or modify Mom's peppermint stick pie recipe. Bad hacker.

Figure 2-3 is the elusive recipe. In this example, you can see the text "Mom's secret peppermint stick pie recipe" clearly in the document. This indicates the clear-text version of the recipe, or stated another way, the version of the recipe that is not encrypted. In the case of any readable document, such as the recipe, the clear-text version of the document is the readable version as it was created.

Figure 2-2

The hacker

Bad, bad
hacker

Figure 2-3

The clear-text
recipe

Note that Mom's actual recipe is not represented here. Did you think I would actually be that foolish?

Figure 2-4 is the recipe in its encrypted form. In this form, a hacker cannot read the recipe, and in fact a good encryption algorithm would make the recipe look like a random series of bits. I have the words "Mom's secret peppermint stick pie recipe" faintly visible in this figure, but that is just so we can keep track of what is going on later. Because the encrypted recipe looks like a random series of bits, an actual encrypted document would give you no hint about what the original clear-text document was.

We will need a few more graphics as we go on, but this will be enough to get us going.

Figure 2-4

The encrypted recipe

Symmetric Cryptography

There are two main classes of cryptographic algorithm, symmetric and asymmetric. Symmetric cryptography has been in existence for a long time. It predates use by the Egyptians.

Now, you might think that because I work for RSA, the company that owns the most widely used asymmetric cryptographic algorithm, that I am about to tell you that symmetric algorithms stink and that asymmetric algorithms, especially the RSA algorithm, are great. Well, it's true!

Sorry. Actually, that's not true.

As you will see in a few minutes, both symmetric and asymmetric algorithms have strengths and weaknesses. All modern cryptographic systems use both properly to leverage the strength of each, without inheriting the problems of each.

Pick a Number, Any Number

Keys are important parts of cryptographic algorithms, both symmetric and asymmetric. A cryptographic key is somewhat like a physical key used to lock or unlock a door. For each type of lock, there is a specific shaped key that fits the lock. It must be a certain length; it must have grooves along the key in the correct position. A key for a particular manufacturer's lock will generally fit into any lock of that type, but only the correct key. The key with the proper pattern of ridges will turn and open the lock.

Cryptographic keys are similar to physical keys in many ways. Each cryptographic algorithm needs a key of the correct length (in other words, the correct number of bits). You can run a cryptographic algorithm with any key of the proper length, but only the key that has the correct bit pattern will cause the algorithm to decrypt an encrypted document.

Symmetric cryptographic algorithms take clear text as input. Then, using a *symmetric key*, they output an encrypted version of the clear text (also called the cipher text).

Symmetric keys are nothing more than a random number of the correct length. If the symmetric algorithm is a 40-bit symmetric encryption, the symmetric key will be 40 bits long. If the symmetric algorithm is a 128-bit symmetric encryption, the symmetric key will be 128 bits long.

It is vital that the symmetric key be created with a good random number generator. By good, I mean that the random number generator will randomly pick numbers evenly distributed across the full bit space of the key length, and will not be biased toward or away from certain values. Poor random number generators will tend to select certain values or skip other values within the key space, and as a result, reduce the effective number of bits in the key. This will in turn reduce the strength of the encryption.

The best sources for random numbers involve a piece of hardware designed to emit truly random numbers. Some events in nature are truly random. If one counts the time between cosmic ray hits on a Geiger counter, you can derive good random numbers. I once saw a Web site where a Lava Lamp was used to generate random numbers. In fact, bad electronics make great random number generators. One respected source for random numbers is a diode that has purposely been constructed to be a noisy diode. It turns out that noise is a good source of randomness. If noise and randomness are good, there should be a way to use geese to generate good keys for cryptographic algorithms.

You may hear someone refer to a cryptographic algorithm as "secure." This typically means that the cryptanalysts have attacked the algorithm for enough time to be confident that the algorithm is based on sound math, and that there are no significant ways of cracking data encrypted using the algorithm unless the key is known or guessed. Often the cryptanalysts will find a weakness in a cryptographic algorithm if the algorithm is used in some very specific way. Rather than throw the baby out with the bath water, the implementations of the algorithm are coded to avoid the weakness and only utilize the algorithm in ways that are secure.

If all these conditions are met, the only way to crack the encryption is to randomly try all the possible keys in the key space. This is called a *brute-force* attack. Statistically, you will need to try about half the keys within the key space in order to hit on the correct key. Key lengths are chosen so that it is computationally infeasible to try half the keys within the key space even if you use massive numbers of computers over the length of time that the data being protected must remain secure. Obviously, we cannot predict the future, so assumptions are made about the probable increase in computing power during the lifetime of a key (then a little fudge factor is usually thrown in as well just to be safe) in order to determine an appropriate key length.

To get an idea of key space sizes, let's look at a few examples. A 40-bit key means that there are 2^{40} keys, or said another way, about 1.1E12 keys. That's more than 1,000,000,000,000 possible keys. A 64-bit key is 2^{64}, or about 1.8E19 keys. That's almost 20,000,000,000,000,000,000 possible keys. Today's standard symmetric key size is 128 bits. A 128-bit key is about 3.4E38 keys. That's more than 340,000,000,000,000,000,000,000, 000,000,000,000,000 possible keys. Imagine the key ring!

By the way, I think I must mention one pet peeve of mine right here. People sometimes refer to the symmetric key as the "secret key" because it must remain a secret. Please don't refer to symmetric keys as secret keys. It gets very confusing because the private key in asymmetric cryptography must also remain secret. In conversations, it gets a little like the old Abbott and Costello "Who's on first" routine if you use the term "secret key." "Is the 'secret key' the symmetric key or the private key?" "That's right . . ." Symmetric keys are symmetric keys. Private keys are private keys. Please stick with these terms.

Why are symmetric cryptographic algorithms called symmetric? As you will see, it is because the same key is used to encrypt and decrypt.

Symmetric cryptographic algorithms come in two flavors: block ciphers and stream cipher. A cipher is another word for an encryption algorithm.

Block ciphers encrypt data in small fixed length chunks, typically 64 bits in length. There are many block ciphers, including DES, 3-DES, RC2, RC5, RC6, and Rijndael (also referred to as AES).

DES is the best known and best studied symmetric algorithm. DES was developed by IBM in the late 1970s and had significant involvement from the NSA. DES is a block cipher that uses blocks 64 bits in length. A DES key is fixed at 56 bits in length. DES has lasted a long time and has seen much use in cryptographic solutions, but due to the increasing power of computers, its 56-bit key is becoming vulnerable to brute-force attack.

3-DES is shorthand for triple DES. Because of increasing concerns around the vulnerability of DES, various techniques have evolved for increasing the strength of DES by encrypting the data three times, or combining three crypto operations based on DES to increase the effective key length.

RC2 is also a block cipher. The RC series of ciphers was developed by Ron Rivest (the R in RSA), and RC stands for *Rivest Cipher* or *Ron's Code*. RC2 was developed as a drop-in replacement for DES, but is two to three times faster than DES.

RC5 is another cipher by Rivest. RC5 typically uses 64- or 128-bit blocks and can support variable key lengths up to 2048 bits. RC5 is also a very simple algorithm to implement. Algorithms, such as RC5, that support variable-length keys have some nice features. The longer the key, the more processor power will be required to encrypt data, but the resulting encryption will be stronger. By choosing an appropriate key length, you can achieve the desired strength with the minimum necessary power. In addition to this, many governments have restrictions on the strength of the encryption that can be used. Encryption algorithms that support variable-length keys can be adjusted to meet governmental requirements as needed.

RC6 was developed as a potential replacement for DES and was a finalist in the competition for the next generation standard symmetric encryption algorithm. The next generation algorithm is named the *Advanced Encryption Standard* (AES). RC6 is a block cipher based on RC5, supporting 128-bit blocks and a key size of 128 bits. RC6 did not win the AES competition, but the open analysis of RC6 helped produce a powerful new symmetric algorithm.

The winner of the AES competition was a symmetric block cipher named Rijndael. Rijndael was submitted by Daemen and Rijmen (Belguim), and like all AES candidates, supports 128-bit key lengths.

Other AES finalists included MARS (IBM), Serpent (Anderson, Biham, and Knudsen), and Twofish (Schneier, Kelsey, Whiting, Wagner, Hall, and Ferguson).

In addition to block ciphers, which operate on fixed length chunks of data, there are stream ciphers which operate on individual bits of data. Perhaps the best known is RC4. RC4 is very fast, faster than any block cipher, and supports variable-length keys.

Once you have a good symmetric algorithm and a random number to use as a symmetric encryption key, the process is fairly straightforward. Refer to Figure 2-5.

Figure 2-5

Symmetric encryption

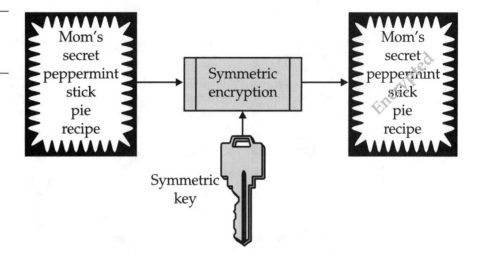

The clear-text recipe is encrypted, using the symmetric key, and the output is the encrypted recipe. Easy!

To reverse this process is equally easy. Refer to Figure 2-6.

Figure 2-6

Symmetric decryption

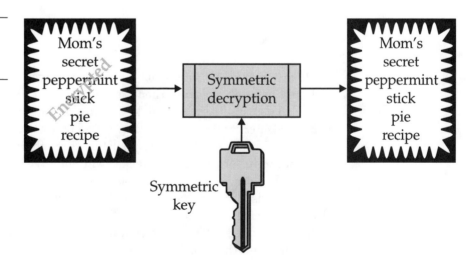

The encrypted recipe is decrypted, using the same symmetric key, and the output is the recovered clear-text recipe.

Now we're cooking! I am beginning to see how I can use cryptography to *finally* get a copy of Mom's recipe from my sister. Let's see how this could work. Refer to Figure 2-7.

Figure 2-7

Symmetric encryption and decryption

It's so . . . well, symmetric!

My sister and I will agree on a symmetric algorithm in advance. She (actually her software) will then create a random number of the correct length to use as the symmetric key. Using that key, the symmetric algorithm will encrypt the clear-text recipe and produce the encrypted cipher-text. She will then send me the cipher-text through the Internet, and even if the hacker intercepts it, the hacker will not have the symmetric key to decrypt the data. When the cipher-text is delivered to me, the same symmetric key is used to decrypt the cipher-text and recover the original clear-text recipe.

As I mentioned before, symmetric encryption has been around for quite some time, and the algorithms, which have survived the test of time, are quite secure. Symmetric algorithms are also quite fast, so the encryption of large amounts of data can proceed at a rapid pace without significant impact to the processor load. As an additional benefit, the cipher-text produced from a symmetric encryption is compact, usually about the same size as the original clear text.

Sounds too good to be true! Unfortunately, there is a problem.

Have you noticed the problem yet? If not, look at Figure 2-7 again, and read its description to see if you can figure out what the problem is.

The hacker must not get a copy of the key used to encrypt the recipe. But my sister must get a copy of the key to me so that I can perform the decryption. If she sends me the key over the Internet, the hacker will get a copy.

I've got an idea. What if I decide to meet my sister in the middle of the night in a parking lot halfway between our two homes? We can pull our cars up beside each other, roll the windows down, and she can pass the symmetric key to me through the open windows. With a knowing wink, we will roll up our windows and drive off in opposite directions.

But if we are going to go through all this intrigue, why doesn't she just pass me the recipe through the window and avoid all this trouble?

The situation is actually worse than it sounds. Once you use a symmetric key, it should be discarded and a new random key generated. This is because it is inadvisable for a symmetric key to be used repeatedly. Each time the symmetric key is reused, more data is generated, which can be used to attack the security of the symmetric key.

This means you will have to find a way to exchange a key each time you encrypt a new document. Even that isn't the end to the problems. Imagine that you are in a recipe-sharing club, where each member exchanges recipes with the other members. If there are five members in your club, each member would need to create four keys (you don't send one to yourself), so the total number of keys would be $5 \times (5-1)$ or 20 keys. If there are 20 members in your club, the total number of keys would be $20 \times (20-1)$ or 380 keys. If there are 100 members in your club, the total number of keys would be $100 \times (100-1)$ or 9,900 keys. The number of keys is roughly the square of the number of participants. And each of these keys is used once, somehow transferred to the other person, and not reused.

Additionally, if you decide to store these recipes, you may want to store them in their encrypted form for security. This implies that you will also need to retain the symmetric encryption key used to decrypt each cipher-text as needed. Of course, you would need to store the symmetric keys separately from the cipher-text. Otherwise, an attacker who was able to gain access to the cipher-texts would also get the associated decryption keys. If the symmetric keys are stored separately from the cipher-text, you will need some sort of key management system to help you figure out which of the 9,900 keys belongs to the 9,900 cipher-texts. You will need some system to figure out which keys to delete as the associated cipher-texts are deleted.

One other point about symmetric algorithms is important. Recall that earlier in the chapter I mentioned that digital signatures were a cryptographic technique used to bind information to a person. If you want to perform a digital signature on some document, there needs to be something unique associated with just the signer. If two people hold the same symmetric key (one for encryption and the other to decrypt), whatever mathematical computation one person does can also be done by the other person. For this reason, symmetric keys are not preferred to perform digital signatures or support non-repudiation.

As you can see, key distribution, key storage, key management, and lack of digital signature support are all problems with symmetric algorithms. Looks like I cannot get the recipe just yet.

Symmetric Cryptography Recap

Before we leave symmetric algorithms, I would like to capture the important points to remember:

- With symmetric cryptography, the same key is used to encrypt and decrypt.

- Symmetric encryption is fast.

- Symmetric encryption is secure.

- The cipher-text that results from a symmetric encryption is compact.

- Since the symmetric key needs to get to the recipient, symmetric encryption is subject to interception.

- The number of keys in symmetric cryptography goes up roughly with the square of the number of participants, and therefore does not scale well to very large populations.

- Symmetric cryptography requires complex key management.

- Symmetric cryptography is not suited for digital signatures or non-repudiation.

Asymmetric Cryptography

Well, if symmetric cryptography didn't work for my problem, let's have a look at asymmetric cryptography.

All the comments previously discussed about the need for good random number generators, and for well-tested algorithms apply to asymmetric cryptography as well.

When it comes to key sizes, the situation is more complex with asymmetric cryptography than symmetric cryptography. In general, it requires a longer key length in asymmetric cryptography to achieve the same level of security as you get with a symmetric algorithm using a shorter key. In addition to this, you cannot directly compare key lengths between two different asymmetric algorithms, or sometimes even between two variants of the same asymmetric algorithm.

There are fewer asymmetric cryptographic algorithms, and generally they are based on much more complex and obtuse mathematics.

Whitfield Diffie and Martin Hellman first introduced the concept of asymmetric cryptography in the mid-1970s. The Diffie-Hellman cryptographic algorithm was developed specifically to address the problems I just talked about involving the secure distribution of symmetric encryption keys. Diffie-Hellman is based upon the mathematics of discrete logarithms. Although not as popular as RSA asymmetric cryptography, Diffie-Hellman is a commonly used asymmetric algorithm.

The RSA algorithm is the most successful asymmetric algorithm. RSA is the most studied asymmetric cryptographic algorithm; it has withstood many attacks over its long lifetime. The fundamental patent on the RSA algorithm expired in September 2000, and as a result, the RSA algorithm is now being incorporated as a mandatory asymmetric cryptographic algorithm in many protocols, assuring it a long life. The RSA algorithm typically uses 1024-bit keys for individuals right now, and is probably the most computationally complex popular cryptographic algorithm in use. In low-end processor situations, such as in smart cards, a cryptographic hardware accelerator is required to perform RSA computations.

NOTE:

The RSA algorithm is the most successful public/private key cryptographic algorithm. The RSA algorithm was invented at MIT by Rivest, Shamir, and Adleman (hence the name RSA).

Elliptic Curve Cryptography (remember the three-dimensional rotating torus?) is the next most recognized asymmetric algorithm. ECC has been around a shorter time than RSA, but so far is also resisting attacks against the algorithm. In reality, there are several variants of ECC, so perhaps ECC is better described as a class of cryptographic algorithms rather than an individual algorithm. ECC is supported in many protocols as an optional cipher-suite, and is perhaps the asymmetric algorithm of choice for applications that do not require broad interoperability. This is because ECC does not require cryptographic acceleration in most applications; it runs fine with integer math units found on all processors. In addition to this, ECC is computationally less complex than RSA, and can use smaller keys and achieve the same level of security as longer RSA keys.

While we are on the topic of key lengths, I realize that all the various key lengths get confusing. As I'm sure you realize, each cryptographic algorithm needs a particular size key in order to achieve a certain level of security. In April 2000, RSA Laboratories published a bulletin by Robert Silverman discussing the comparison of various key lengths and various algorithms.[1] In that bulletin, Silverman produced a table, reproduced here as Table 2-1, which compares the relative strength of symmetric, ECC, and RSA keys.

Table 2-1 Internet Applications and Cryptography	**Symmetric Key**	**ECC Key**	**RSA Key**	**Time to Break**	**Machines**	**Memory**
	56	112	420	Less than 5 minutes	10,000	Trivial
	80	160	760	600 months	4,300	4GB
	96	192	1020	3 million years	114	170GB
	128	256	1620	10E16 years	0.16	120TB

NOTE:

RSA Laboratories is an organization within RSA Security. The charter for RSA Laboratories is basically to promote the general growth of the security industry, even if the research or standards do not benefit RSA Security itself. Many of the important standards, such as the PKCS series of standards, were developed with RSA Laboratories sponsorship.

Table 2-1 assumes that $10 million is available for purchasing computer hardware to perform the attack, and that memory is about $0.50 per megabyte. Note that the age of the universe is about $15 \times 10E9$ years old, so the last line of the table is *really* long!

By looking at Table 2-1, you can see why it was necessary to move from the DES algorithm, which had fixed key lengths of 56 bits, to the new AES algorithm (recall that AES is a symmetric algorithm) with a key length of 128 bits. In addition to this, you can see why people are moving from 768-bit RSA keys to 1024-bit RSA keys. Lastly, from the table, you can see that a symmetric key of 96 bits is roughly the same strength as an ECC key of about 192 bits, and this is roughly the same strength as an RSA key of 1020 bits. In some situations, such as when sending keys over very slow communications lines, the difference in the key lengths can be a significant issue.

If you are interested in more information about this topic, please refer to Silverman's excellent paper.

Other asymmetric cryptographic algorithms do exist, but most of these are the new kids on the block. Examples include NTRU and Arithmetica. These algorithms are based on different math problems than either RSA or ECC (NTRU is based on integer matrix computations, for example). These newer algorithms hold promise, but have not had the length of testing by cryptanalysts that ECC, never mind RSA, has had.

It is important to note that almost all vendors of asymmetric cryptography support multiple asymmetric algorithms. This is prudent, because there is always the chance that some day a method to crack one of these algorithms will be found. By having multiple algorithms, it would be easy to switch from one to another algorithm if necessary.

Public and Private Keys

Asymmetric algorithms are different than symmetric algorithms in one very important way. When you generate a symmetric key, you just pick a random number of the proper length. With asymmetric key generation, the process is more complex. Asymmetric algorithms are called asymmetric because, rather than using a single key to perform both encryption and decryption, two different keys are used: one to encrypt, the other to decrypt. These two independent, but mathematically related, keys are always generated together. The process is much more complex than just picking a random number, but it always involves a source for randomness.

When an asymmetric key generation is complete, there are two keys: a public key and a private key. You want your public key to be known by everyone. On the other hand, you must carefully keep your private key hidden. In some cases, even *you* have no way of knowing what your private key is! Asymmetric keys have the amazing property that what is encrypted with one key can only be decrypted with the other key (see Figure 2-8).

The interesting thing about public/private key pairs is that any key cannot decrypt what it encrypts.

Now I think we are getting somewhere. Let's see how this would work to help me with my problem (I mean the recipe problem). Take a look at Figure 2-9.

Figure 2-8

Public and private keys

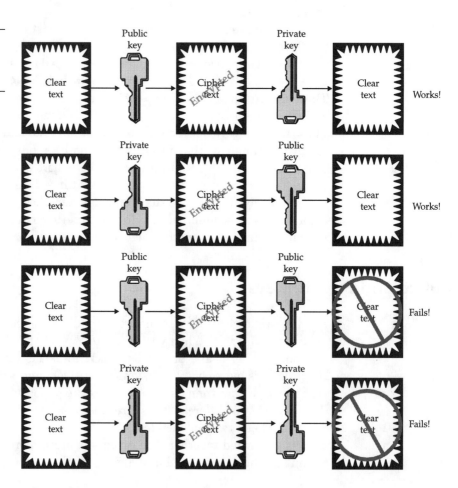

Figure 2-9

Public/private
key encryption
and decryption

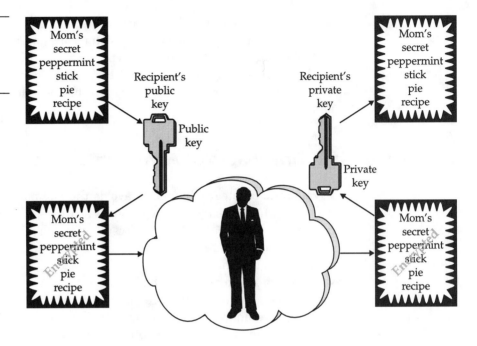

In this example, since I am the recipient, I (my software) would generate my public/private key pair in advance. I would then carefully protect
my private key so nobody else in the world knew it. I would, however,
make my public key available for everyone to use. You might imagine the
equivalent of a phone directory for public keys, where everyone would go
to look up someone else's public key.

In my example, my sister would look up my public key in that directory,
and use my public key to produce the original cipher-text. That cipher-text
would then be sent to me across the Internet. Note that if the hacker hiding in the Internet were to intercept the cipher-text, he could also look up
my public key in the directory. But as you recall from Figure 2-8, the only
thing that can decrypt a cipher-text created with a particular public key
is the matching private key. The hacker would not be able to decrypt the
cipher-text with the public key.

When the cipher-text was finally delivered to me, my private key would
be used to decrypt the cipher-text and recover the original cipher-text.

This would actually work. I finally have a way to get Mom's recipe from
my sister. Unfortunately, there are still some issues. If the hacker wanted
to be really nasty, he could take some other recipe—say, a peppermint

stick pie with a *plain* graham cracker crust—encrypt it using my public key, and send it to me instead of my sister's original recipe. The fact that my public key is public makes me vulnerable to this type of attack. We need some way to authenticate that the recipe came from my sister and was not modified or substituted by the hacker. More about this in a minute.

The Benefits and Drawbacks of Asymmetric Cryptography

Asymmetric cryptography neatly avoids the key management problems we had with symmetric cryptography. Each person only needs to share one key, his or her public key. As a result, in your recipe-sharing club, five members would share five public keys total, rather than 20 keys. Twenty members would share 20 keys rather than 380. One hundred members would share 100 keys rather than 9,900. As you can see, the key management and scaling properties are far superior with public/private key systems when compared to pure asymmetric key systems.

One additional benefit of public/private key systems which may not jump out at you is the fact that with public/private key systems, you do not need to have a prior relationship with someone before you can send them encrypted information. With symmetric key systems, you must establish some form of prior relationship so that you can exchange the symmetric key to be used for a later decryption operation. With public/private key systems, the sender need only look up the recipient's public key, encrypt the document, and send it to the recipient. The recipient already has the matching private key needed to decrypt the cipher-text.

One last benefit of public/private key systems is their asymmetric nature. This allows each holder to perform mathematical operations with his or her private key, which nobody else in the universe can perform. This is the basis for digital signatures and non-repudiation.

Unfortunately, all the news is not good. Unlike their symmetric counterparts, asymmetric algorithms are comparatively slow. How slow? They can be 10 to 100 times slower than a comparable strength symmetric algorithm. This may not be much of an issue when encrypting a recipe a few hundred bytes long, but if you were encrypting the results of the human genome project, this would be a serious problem.

In addition to the slow speed, asymmetric algorithms have another problem. When encrypting using an asymmetric algorithm, the size of the cipher-text is larger than the original clear text. This is particularly an issue when there are multiple levels of encryption going on. If you used pure asymmetric cryptography, an application would encrypt data, which expands the size, and would then send it over a secure Web session, which would again expand the size. This might run over an IPSec-encrypted tunnel, which would again expand the size.

Nuts.

Asymmetric Cryptography Recap

Before we move on to solve these issues, I wanted to reiterate the things I would like you to remember about asymmetric cryptography:

- With asymmetric cryptography, what is encrypted with one key (public or private) can only be decrypted with the other key (private or public).
- Asymmetric encryption is secure.
- Since you do not need to send a key to the recipient, asymmetric encryption does not suffer from key interception.
- The number of keys that need to be distributed is the same as the number of participants, hence asymmetric cryptography scales well to very large populations.
- Asymmetric cryptography does not have complex key distribution problems.
- Asymmetric cryptography does not require a prior relationship between the parties for key exchange.
- Asymmetric cryptography supports digital signatures and non-repudiation.
- Asymmetric encryption is relatively slow.
- Asymmetric encryption expands the cipher-text.

The Best of Both Worlds

Fortunately, there is a way out of these problems. If you compare the lists of things I wanted you to remember about symmetric and asymmetric cryptography, you will notice a curious thing. In every area where one algorithm class is weak, the other is strong. When you see this type of situation, it calls out to the engineer in you to find a way to combine the two solutions in such a way that you capture the strengths of each without inheriting the problems of either.

It is very rare that you can pull such a marriage off, but with the combination of symmetric and asymmetric cryptography you can come very close to the ideal solution that has the following properties:

- The solution must be secure.
- Encryption must be fast.
- The encrypted cipher-text must be compact.
- The solution must scale to large populations.
- The solution must not be vulnerable to key interception.
- The solution must not require a prior relationship between the parties.
- The solution must support digital signatures and non-repudiation.

The combination of symmetric and asymmetric cryptography meets every one of these requirements. You can get the speed and compact text you want from a symmetric cipher, and the scaling, simpler key management, resistance to interception, and digital signature/non-repudiation support you want from public/private key cryptography.

Take a look at Figure 2-10 to see how this process works.

Figure 2-10

Encrypting with the combination

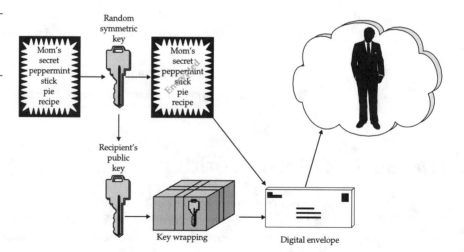

The process starts with the generation of a random symmetric key. That symmetric key is used to encrypt the clear-text recipe, producing the encrypted version of the recipe. So far, so good. The symmetric cipher is secure (the number one criteria listed previously) and fast (number two), and the resulting cipher-text is compact (number three). Now, the problem we had before with symmetric encryption was how to get the symmetric key to the recipient. This is where public/private key crypto comes in.

We look up the recipient's public key in the directory, and use it to encrypt *just the random symmetric key*. Sure, asymmetric crypto is slow, but since the size of the symmetric key is very small (typically 128 bits) the actual time spent on an asymmetric encryption is small. The result of this encryption is a random symmetric encryption key, encrypted with an asymmetric public key. (You'll probably want to read that again.) One key encrypted with another key. This is often referred to as a *key wrapping operation*.

The last step in this process is to attach the wrapped key to the cipher-text in preparation for sending to the recipient. The combination is sometimes referred to as the *digital envelope*. The digital envelope is sent to the recipient across the Internet. If a hacker intercepts the digital envelope, it is of no use to him. It may even frustrate him to know that the symmetric encryption key he needs in order to get at the recipe is actually inside the digital envelope, but it is encrypted with the recipient's public key and so remains tantalizingly just out of reach. Take that!

The use of public/private key encryption to wrap the symmetric key gives the solution scalability, protects against interception of the symmetric encryption key, does not require a prior relationship between the involved parties, and supports digital signatures/non-repudiation—thus meeting the remaining criteria in our previous list.

Before we move on to process this digital envelope at the recipient, please take a few minutes to review Figure 2-10. I will warn you right now that it looks easy when you're sitting there looking at the figure. The figures that follow will also look equally simple. Five seconds after you close this book, you will likely be unable to recall if you use the recipient's public key or private key to wrap the symmetric key. No, wait. Wasn't it the sender's public key, or was it the sender's private key . . . ?

It seems to take everyone at least three times through this material to get it right. Once you have it down, it is rather funny to watch somebody else struggle with these concepts. They are deceptively simple when you are looking at the simple figures, but they become devilishly complex when you begin to consider the number of keys and possible combinations.

There will be a test later.

Okay, now that you are an expert in encrypting with the combination of asymmetric and symmetric crypto, let's move on to the decryption step. Please refer to Figure 2-11.

Figure 2-11

Decrypting with
the combination

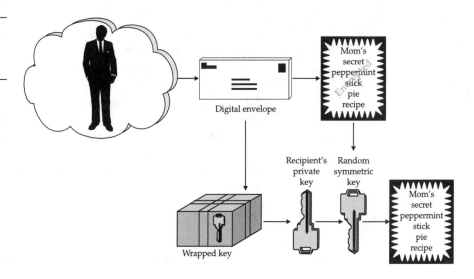

This process starts with the reception of the digital envelope. The first step is to decompose the digital envelope into its constituent parts: the cipher-text and the wrapped key. Recall that the wrapped key is the symmetric key encrypted with the recipient's public key. Since the recipient cannot access the cipher-text yet, the next step is to recover the symmetric key. The wrapped key is decrypted using the recipient's private key. The symmetric key is then used to decrypt the cipher-text, recovering the original clear-text recipe. The symmetric key is then discarded, its work done.

This solution is just plain elegant. The process just described (with some variations) is the foundation for most modern encryption solutions, from encrypted e-mail to encrypted Web sessions to encrypted virtual private networks. We have successfully grafted the benefits of symmetric cryptography (security, speed, compact text) with the benefits of asymmetric cryptography (security, scaling, no prior relationship).

Before moving on, it is worth taking a few minutes to review the purity and nobility of the solution.

As I mentioned previously, there is still a problem with public/private key systems that must be addressed. You have seen how a pure public/private key-based encryption can be used to securely move small amounts of data, and how in reality we use a combination of symmetric and public/private key encryption to move arbitrarily large amounts of data. Unfortunately, a clever hacker could look up my public key in the directory, and then encrypt some other recipe. The hacker would then encrypt (wrap) the symmetric key using my public key. The hacker would then create the digital envelope and send it to me across the Internet. I would happily decrypt the wrapped key using my private key and produce the false recipe, thinking all along that it came from my sister.

We need some way to guarantee that the recipe came from my sister; we need digital signatures. But before we can examine the digital signature process, we need to talk about hashes.

Hashes

No, I am not talking about neuro-toxic substances. Hash algorithms are fairly common in computer science. They are perhaps most commonly used to accelerate the process of indexing into large arrays or databases of information. Despite their wide use, most people don't know what the heck a hash is. Before we can talk about digital signatures, you need to understand hashes.

A hash algorithm will take a large chunk of data and compress it into a *fingerprint* or *digest* of the original data. If you are a computer scientist, I recommend that you skip the next paragraph or two, as my description of hashes will probably bore you. I struggled to think of a simple way to explain hash algorithms and came up with two examples.

If I were to give you the number 483,820, and asked you to divide that number by 4, you would get the result of 120,955. In a way, 120,955 is a fingerprint for the equation (483,820 divided by 4). No matter how many times you divide 483,820 by 4, you always get 120,955. If you changed either number in the equation by any amount, the division would not produce 120,955. Alternatively, if I handed you the number 120,955, but did not tell you any further information, you would be unlikely to tell me what the original equation was, since there are an infinite number of divisions that could have produced the same result.

In many ways, these features are the same as those associated with hash algorithms. With a hash, you take a large block of data and compute an equation across the data. The output of the hash is a value that is smaller than the original data. If you change even one bit of the original data, the output hash value will be different. Also, as with the division example, there are many different sets of data that could compute the same hash value.

Another example I like to use when talking about hashes is the *cyclic redundancy check* (CRC) value that is placed at the end of most communication messages (see Figure 2-12).

Figure 2-12

Cyclic
redundancy
checks

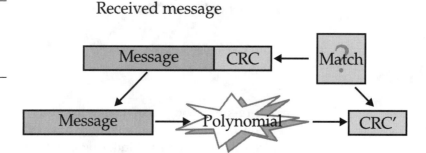

Received message

When messages are about to be sent over a communications line, it is common to run a polynomial equation across the bytes of the message. This polynomial produces a result, the CRC code, which is attached to the end of the message before it is sent. When the receiving system gets the message with the CRC attached, it essentially runs the same polynomial across the message (excluding the original CRC) and produces a second copy of the CRC (labeled CRC' in the figure). The software then compares the original CRC with the new CRC'. If both CRCs match, there is a high degree of confidence that the message was not modified as it flew through the network.

NOTE:

In reality, CRC polynomials are constructed in such a way that the receiving system will run the same polynomial across the entire message, including the original CRC. If the message has not been corrupted, the CRC will effectively "cancel" the computation and the result of the second polynomial computation will be zero. If any bits have changed in the message or the CRC during transmission, the output of the polynomial will not be zero. This allows a fast way to check the integrity of the message without having to do an explicit compare operation.

In a way, the CRC is acting like a fingerprint or digest of the message, which can be verified at the receiver of the message. There are multiple messages that will produce the same CRC, and if a single bit of the message changes, the CRC value will change. The CRC is exhibiting all the same properties we ascribed to a hash.

The hash algorithms that are used in cryptography are all designed with some special properties:

- You cannot run the hash backwards and recover any of the initial clear text.

- The resulting digest will not tell you anything about the initial clear text.

- It is computationally infeasible to create/discover clear text that will hash to a specific value. This prevents an attacker from substituting a document without causing the digest match to fail.

There are a number of cryptographic hash algorithms. MD2 is a hash from RSA that produces a 128-bit digest, and which is optimized for low-end 8-bit microprocessors. MD5 also produces a 128-bit digest, but is optimized for 32-bit processors. The SHA-1 hash is also optimized for high-end processors and produces a 160-bit digest.

Digital Signatures

Now that you are all experts in hash algorithms, let's see how to use them. In this example, I would like to change the problem a little. Let's assume for this exercise that I don't care if anyone sees Mom's recipe. In this case, it can be sent across as clear text. Allowing the recipe to remain in the clear will simplify the figures and allow us to focus on the digital signature process.

I do, however, want to be sure the recipe is coming from my sister. I would like to prevent the problem discussed previously where a hacker attempts to slip me a different recipe.

In Figure 2-13, I have represented the hash algorithm as a funnel. The large clear text goes in the funnel, and the digest pops out the bottom.

Figure 2-13

Creating a digital signature

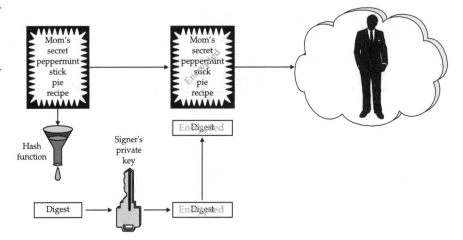

As shown in the figure, we start with the clear-text recipe. At this point, an appropriate hash algorithm is selected, and it is used to process the clear-text recipe producing the digest. Next, the sender's private key is used to encrypt the digest. The encrypted digest is attached to the original clear-text recipe and sent to the recipient across the Internet. You may be struggling to see how this process gets us anywhere. It will all make sense when you see the digital signature verification process, so let's proceed. Please refer to Figure 2-14.

The clear-text recipe with the encrypted digest attached travels across the Internet to the recipient (in this example, from my sister to me). My software would separate the clear-text recipe from the encrypted digest. My sister used her private key to encrypt the original digest. Just as we

Figure 2-14

Verifying a digital
signature

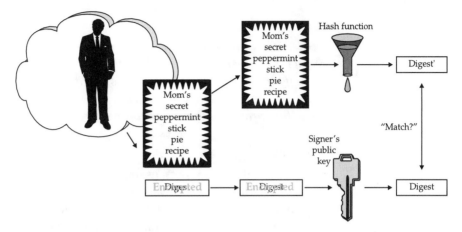

did in the previous examples, I will get her matching public key from the
directory. Using my sister's public key, I will decrypt the digest, recovering
the original clear-text digest.

Here comes the clever part. I now turn to the clear-text recipe. Using
the same hash algorithm that my sister used to create the original digest,
I will take the received clear-text recipe and create a new copy of the
digest, shown as digest' in Figure 2-14. As a last step, I will compare the
newly created digest', with the original digest I decrypted using my sister's public key. If the two copies match, I know several things.

If the two copies of the digest match, I know that my sister was the
author of the message. This is assured because I used my sister's public
key to decrypt the encrypted digest, and since I recovered the correct
plain-text digest, I know it was originally encrypted using the matching
private key. Since my sister is the only person in the universe who has the
matching private key, I can guarantee that my sister was the author of the
message. Can you see what else I know?

If the two copies of the digest match, I also know that the recipe was
not modified as it traversed the Internet. If the hacker had attempted to
modify the clear-text recipe as it passed by, the digest' version of the digest
would have a different value than the decrypted version of the digest created by my sister before she sent the message into the Internet.

Recall that if even one bit of the clear text changes, the digest resulting
from the hash algorithm will be different. This capability of hashes to
detect the smallest change in the clear text is what makes them useful for
verifying *message integrity*.

NOTE:

Occasionally in my talks on cryptography, someone will ask how the recipient knows which hash algorithm to use when computing digest'. To simplify the figures, I did not mention that along with the encrypted digest, an informational block is passed, which identifies which hash algorithm produced the original digest.

I am not quite done yet. There is one way to break this system that needs to be addressed. Let's assume that the hacker is particularly clever and decides to attack the system with some good old nonlinear thinking. Rather than attempt to find a way to defeat the hash algorithm, or perhaps defeat the private key encryption, our clever hacker might turn his attention elsewhere.

Recall that the train of logic in verifying the signature goes something like this:

1. I looked up my sister's public key in the directory.

2. I used that key to decrypt the encrypted digest.

3. The encrypted digest was created using my sister's private key.

4. My sister has the only copy of the private key in existence.

5. Therefore, if the decrypted digest and digest' match, the recipe *must* have come from my sister.

Unfortunately, our clever hacker tripped us up right at the start. If he is able to reach into the directory and substitute his public key for my sister's public key, the whole process collapses like a house of cards sitting on Jell-O in the middle of an earthquake.

Once the hacker substitutes his public key under my sister's name in the directory, he can start with his own recipe, create a digest, encrypt it with his private key, and then send the message to me. I will extract his public key from the directory under my sister's name. Assuming that I have the correct key, I will proceed to perform the signature verification. In this case, digest' will match the decrypted digest and I will smile, secure in the false knowledge that I have a cryptographically strong assurance that the recipe came from my sister!

We need some way to make sure that a particular public key belongs to a particular person. This is where digital certificates come in.

Digital Certificates

We will be spending considerably more time covering the details of digital certificates in the next few chapters, but it is important to get the basic concepts down early.

I hope that you have not heard too much about digital certificates. There is a lot of misinformation being distributed about digital certificates, and it tends to mislead people as to what they are and how they are used. Digital certificates are actually quite a simple concept (see Figure 2-15).

Figure 2-15

Digital certificate concepts

X.509 Digital Certificate

"I officially notarize the association between this particular user and this particular public key."

A digital certificate is simply a document that states, "I guarantee that this particular public key is associated with this particular user; trust me!"

In their simplest form, that's really all that digital certificates are. They list who the owner of the public key is and contain a copy of that user's public key. A trusted authority then signs the whole thing. By "signs the whole thing," I mean the digital signature process we just discussed. A hash of the whole certificate is created, and that hash is encrypted using the private key of the trusted authority.

To check the validity of a digital certificate, all you need to do is use the trusted authority's public key to validate the signature on the certificate.

If the certificate checks out okay, you can be assured that the private key contained in the certificate belongs to the person listed in the certificate.

What's that I hear? Are you accusing me of trying to pull the wool over your eyes? I can just hear people saying, "Hey, wait a minute. What's to stop the hacker from substituting his public key for the trusted authority's public key? You end up with the same mess!" Well, it's a valid question.

The way this is handled is that the trusted authority will create a certificate that has its own identity information, as well as the trusted authority's public key, and sign it. This is called a *self-signed certificate*. The software must manage these special top-level certificates carefully since they are the basis for trust for all certificates signed by that authority.

The software you use already knows the self-signed certificates of many of these trusted authorities. If you look into the security settings of your Web browser, you will discover a long list of the trusted authorities already known by the browser. The browser manufacturer loaded these certificates after verifying that the trusted authority was real.

There are ways to manage this list of trusted authorities, but (fortunately for me) this is getting beyond the scope of this chapter. Later in this book, we will discuss advanced certificate concepts and will also discuss the establishment of trust.

Assuming that we can trust certificates, let's see how they are used in the digital signing example we were working on. In the public/private key examples we have talked about so far, in almost all cases the public key is not actually sitting naked in a directory. The public key is stored in a digital certificate, and a copy of the certificate is usually stored in a directory at the trusted authority that issued the certificate. In addition, the user who is identified in the certificate and who owns the public key enumerated in the certificate has a copy of the certificate as well.

NOTE:

Actually, since certificates are public information, and you want everyone to have easy access to certificates, there can be as many copies of your certificate as needed. Any attempt to tamper with the certificate will be immediately detectable when the certificate is used. The software using the certificate will always perform signature verification on the certificate, and if the certificate has been modified, the hash values will not match. At this point, the software will refuse to use the public key in the certificate and flag an error.

In the example shown in Figures 2-13 and 2-14, the software will typically make the process easier. Since my sister's software has a copy of her certificate, and since it knows that I will need a copy of my sister's certificate to extract her public key, it will be a nice guy and send a copy of her certificate along with the encrypted digest (see Figure 2-16).

Figure 2-16

Using digital certificates

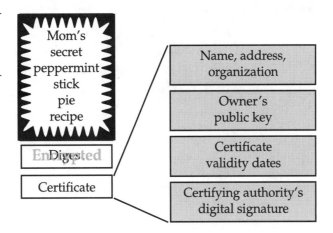

In this figure, you can see that when my sister's software attached the encrypted digest to the clear-text recipe, it also attached a copy of her digital certificate. In this picture I've added slightly more detail about what is in the digital certificate. In addition to the name of the owner, digital certificates frequently contain some additional information about the user, such as his or her company and perhaps the organization within the company where that user is.

In addition to a copy of the user's public key, certificates also contain validity dates. Certificates become valid on a certain date and expire on a certain date. Typically, certificates have a lifetime of a few years, but some certificates have lifetimes as short as a few hours in specialized applications.

Now that you have an understanding of digital certificates, we can revisit the digital signature verification process and update the figure to be a bit more accurate (see Figure 2-17).

As we discussed, in reality the sender will include a copy of the digital certificate along with encrypted hash and the clear-text recipe. The first step is to separate the three components. Next, the digital certificate is checked to see if the signature on the certificate is valid. Checking for

Figure 2-17

Really verifying a digital signature

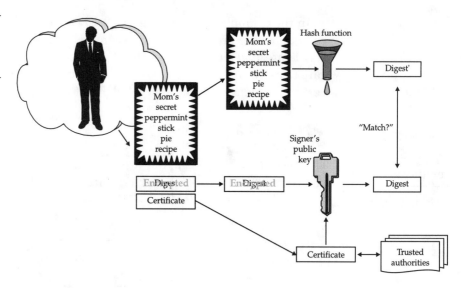

validity starts by checking if someone your software trusts signed the certificate. This is done by checking the signer of the certificate against the trusted authority list contained within the software.

If the authority that signed the certificate is not included in the trusted authority list, the verification stops with an error. In some applications, you will be prompted and asked how to proceed. You may be allowed to ignore the fact that the signer of the certificate is not known and proceed. You may be allowed to add the signer's certificate to your trusted authority list. This should not be done without careful consideration. Once the signer is added to your trusted authority list, your software will automatically trust any certificate signed by that source. If the source is the hacker, you just gave him a doorway into your system.

Assuming that a trusted authority known to your software signed the certificate, the sender's certificate itself is checked for validity. This includes comparing a new hash of the certificate data with the copy that was encrypted by the trusted authority when the certificate was created. If the certificate passes this check, the validity dates are examined. Finally, if the certificate has not expired, you will extract the sender's public key and the rest of the process will work as described in Figure 2-14.

Non-Repudiation

Non-repudiation is a seemingly straightforward extension to digital signatures. As we have seen, digital signatures can be used to bind a document to a particular person and ensure that the document has not been tampered with. Digital signatures fall short when attempting to prevent someone from cheating.

Consider the following example. Let's assume someone agrees to pay you five dollars. You could have that person digitally sign the promise to pay you the five dollars. You would think that this would be enough to stand up in a court of law and produce evidence that that person promised to pay you the money. Unfortunately, it is not quite enough.

A devious person could simply destroy their private key and claim that the private key was stolen. He would further claim that he had not promised to pay you the money, but rather it was the person who stole the private key who made the promise.

What is missing to make this work is the concept of time. To convert a digital signature into one which has the property of non-repudiation, the time at which the signature was executed must be encoded into the document before the hash is created. In that way, the time the document was signed cannot be tampered with without causing the signature verification to fail.

In addition to encoding the time within the document, you must ensure that the time source is secure. If that time source could be shown to be unreliable, the signature could be repudiated. Getting a guaranteed good time source is not a simple problem. It would seem that you need some trusted third party with an accurate clock (such as a clock synchronized to the NIST atomic clock). Since the whole point of non-repudiation is to catch cheating, you cannot send this good time to the party signing the document and trust that they will not modify the time. As a result, some sort of cosigning service where both the trusted time source and the signer of the document cosign the data is needed.

Trusted time services and associated non-repudiation go beyond what I intended to cover in this chapter and are evolving services on the market today. Nonetheless, I wanted to give you a little flavor of the issues surrounding non-repudiation.

Congratulations!

Finally I have enough support to get Mom's recipe from my sister. My sister can use the combination of symmetric and asymmetric cryptography to securely and efficiently transfer the recipe to me without the risk of the recipe being intercepted by evildoers.

My sister can digitally sign the recipe, including sending me her certificate so that I can be sure that she is the source of the recipe and that the recipe has not been tampered with.

You have finally made it to the end of basic cryptography. As I mentioned before, it will take you about three passes through this before you can close the book and draw the set of figures on your own. I don't recommend that you do all three passes through this material at the same time, lest your brain overheat.

By the way, we have seen lots of complex steps. Certificates flying here and there, trusted authority table processing, hashes, symmetric ciphers, key wrapping, digital signatures, and so on. It is easy to walk away with the impression that this stuff is really hard to use. This is not typically the case.

With most major mail packages, you cause mail to be encrypted by checking one box. You digitally sign mail by checking another box. Signature verification and decryption of encrypted messages happens automagically when the mail is received. When surfing the Web to a protected site, you simply get a warning dialog box letting you know when secure communications start and stop. All the work is done for you by the dedicated and tireless software engineers of security products.

Cryptography Recap

Before we move on to showing how these concepts are used to help secure Web transactions, I thought we should capture some of the main points I would like you to remember:

- The best applications of cryptography combine both symmetric and asymmetric algorithms to leverage the strengths of each.
- With the combination of symmetric and asymmetric cryptography, symmetric keys are typically ephemeral—used once and then discarded. Symmetric keys are used for bulk encryption.

- Asymmetric keys are typically used to wrap symmetric keys to protect them during transit, as well as to encrypt hashes of data to create digital signatures.

- Public keys are protected from tampering by encoding them in a digital certificate, along with the identity of the owner.

- Trusted authorities sign digital certificates. Most software contains preloaded lists of trusted authorities.

- Digital signatures need to include an accurate and reliable timestamp if they are to resist repudiation.

- Mom makes a great peppermint stick pie.

Securing Web Transactions

I'd like to bring these concepts together with a real-world example. When browsing the Web, there are times when you need to enter sensitive data such as personal information or credit card numbers. In these situations, it is important that you authenticate the server you are sending the information to, because it makes no sense to send sensitive information if you don't know who is getting that information. In addition to this, it is important that the communications between your Web browser and the Web server be encrypted so that attackers cannot gather the information as it flows across the Internet.

Precisely the techniques we have been examining in this chapter are used to achieve this security. Web servers support a protocol named *Secure Sockets Layer* (SSL) that utilizes cryptographic techniques that you will no doubt now find familiar. Let's go through the process step by step (see Figure 2-18).

In this figure, we see that the Web server has already been issued a digital certificate that contains the identity of the Web server, as well as the Web server's public key. Implied, but not shown, is the fact that the Web server also is holding the matching private key. Note also that the Web browser has its preloaded table of trusted authorities.

To simplify this example, I will only show what is known as "server-side SSL." As you will see, when you use server-side SSL, the Web browser authenticates the Web server, and an encrypted channel is developed between the Web browser and Web server. However, the Web server does

Figure 2-18

SSL configuration

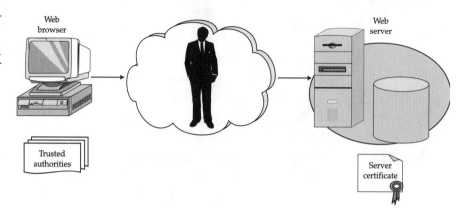

not authenticate the Web browser. This is fairly common. If you are buying something from amazon.com, you want to be sure that you are really connected to Amazon, and you want your credit card information encrypted. Amazon does not need to authenticate your Web browser, simply because you will be identifying yourself via your credit card information anyway.

There are cases where it is necessary for the Web server to authenticate the Web browser. An example might be if a company was to put all its corporate information on a company Web server. It would be important in that case to ensure that only actual employees of the company were accessing the Web server. In these cases, SSL with client-side authentication is used.

Back to our example, remember in this case we are only performing server-side SSL.

The first step in the process is for the Web server to send its digital certificate to the Web browser (see Figure 2-19). Recall that since all the information in the digital certificate is public information, it does not matter that the certificate travels between the Web server and the Web browser in the clear.

In Figure 2-20, you see the Web browser extracting the Web server's public key from the certificate. Before the Web browser can trust the public key, it must validate the Web server's certificate. The Web browser will be able to see if the certificate is signed by a source on the trusted authority list. Assuming that it is, the Web browser will then compute the hash of the certificate and compare it with hash in the certificate (decrypted using the trusted authority public key). If the hashes match, the browser

Figure 2-19

Certificate
exchange

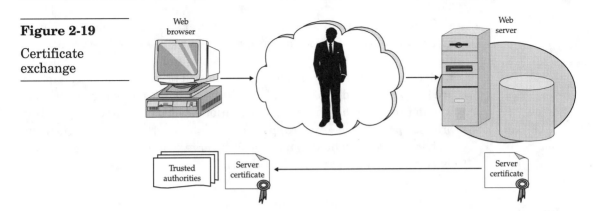

knows the certificate has not been tampered with. Next, the browser will
check the validity dates encoded in the certificate to be sure that the certificate has not expired. Assuming it has not, it will do one more special
check associated with Web server certificates. Part of the identity information in the server certificate is the URL of the Web server. The browser
will do an extra check to ensure that the node that sent the certificate has
the same URL as was encoded into the identity information. If all these
checks match, the browser will then extract the public key of the Web
server from the Web server certificate.

Figure 2-20

Public key
extraction

Once the Web browser has the Web server's public key, it then generates a random symmetric encryption key. This key will be used to encrypt the conversation between the Web browser and the Web server. Recall that a symmetric encryption algorithm is used because symmetric ciphers are fast, and they do not expand the data during the encryption operation. In order to move the symmetric encryption key to the Web server, the Web browser performs a key wrapping operation (see Figure 2-21). The symmetric key is encrypted using the Web server's public key that was just extracted from the server's digital certificate.

Figure 2-21

Key wrapping

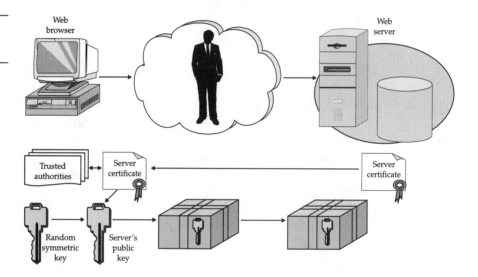

The Web browser sends the wrapped key to the Web server. Recall that since symmetric key is encrypted using the server's public key, and since the server is the only entity that has the matching private key, the hacker cannot extract the symmetric key.

Now that the Web server has the wrapped key, it can use the private key to decrypt the wrapped key (see Figure 2-22). This yields the original symmetric key that was randomly generated by the Web browser.

At this point, both the Web browser and the Web server have a copy of the same symmetric encryption key.

In Figure 2-23 you can see that both ends of the conversation have the same symmetric key. They can now start an encrypted conversation using the exchange symmetric key to encrypt and decrypt the data from each other.

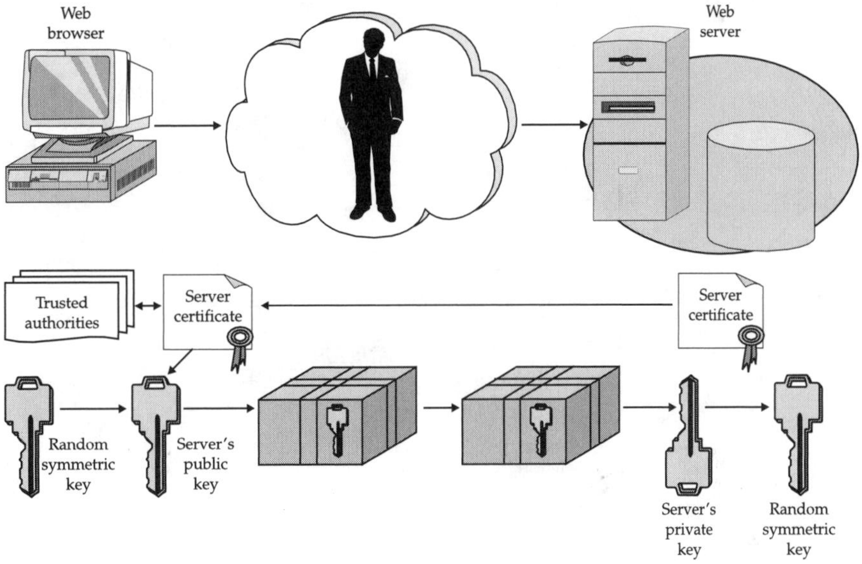

Figure 2-22

Unwrapping the key

Something else happened in this exchange as well, and it is a little subtle. As I mentioned at the start, the Web browser needs to be sure that it is talking to the correct Web server—in other words, the Web browser needs to authenticate the Web server.

The check I mentioned in the certificate processing where the Web browser verifies the URL of the Web server is not a sufficient check. This is because an evil Web site could be spoofing as the real Web site. In this case, all traffic for the real Web site will be redirected to the evil site. This type of attack is reasonably common in the Internet and is frequently accomplished when the attacker compromises a DNS server and redirects traffic to the evil site. Therefore, simply checking the URL is not sufficient. Something stronger is needed; can you see how the authentication happened?

The Web browser generated a random symmetric encryption key, and then encrypted it using the public key of the Web server. The fact that the Web server was able to engage in an encrypted conversation with the Web browser told the Web browser that the server had successfully decrypted the wrapped key and extracted the symmetric key. This in turn told the Web browser that it was in fact talking to the real Web server because the real Web server is the only node in the universe that has the matching private key needed to perform the unwrapping operation.

Figure 2-23

Let the
conversation
begin!

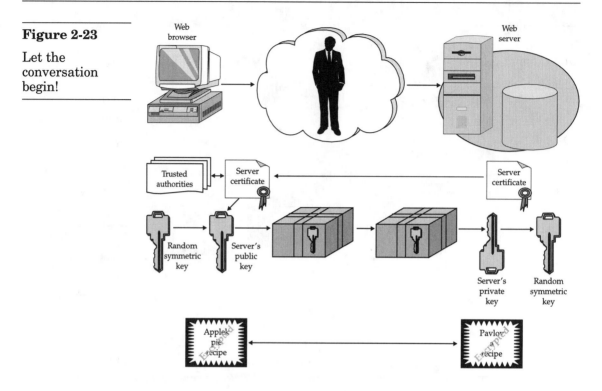

Now you are SSL experts too! Note that I simplified the SSL protocol
somewhat to demonstrate the concepts. Later in the book we will revisit
SSL in more detail.

Why Isn't Cryptography Pervasive Yet?

The need for cryptographic-based security seems compelling, and we have
now seen that cryptographic solutions based on asymmetric and symmetric cryptography exist, so it is a fair question to ask why it is not commonplace. I feel the reason is mainly due to three issues:

- Standards-based, interoperable security solutions are not yet
  ubiquitous.
- People are frequently not sensitive to security issues, at least not
  until the first time they get burned!
- The base cryptographic algorithms are in a state of migration.

Let's examine each of these issues briefly.

Standards-Based, Interoperable Solutions

For many years, the security market has been dominated by proprietary solutions from each of the vendors. This is a common situation in emerging markets. Each vendor will try to capture as much of the market as quickly as possible using a proprietary solution. In some cases, these proprietary solutions are used because a vendor has an honest belief that their technology is better and can win in the market. In other cases, the use of proprietary technology is a calculated effort by the vendor to lock as many customers into their solution as possible, making it very difficult for that customer to move to a different security vendor.

As the market begins to grow, these tactics begin to fail. This is because no vendor is large enough to address all the needs of any customer, and customers are very reluctant to get tied into a single vendor solution for anything. As a result, the market needs to evolve into a standards-based market where solutions interoperate with each other. This gives the customer the ability to purchase the needed products from multiple vendors and integrate them into a consistent framework.

This change in the market is also good for vendors, although sometimes painful. In a market consisting of multiple, proprietary, noninteroperable solutions, the various vendors end up competing with each other for the small part of the market that is willing to use the proprietary solutions. When a market evolves to embrace standards-based interoperability, this attracts more customers, and as a result the whole market grows. Each vendor can cooperate to create interoperable solutions, but compete with each other on price, performance, and functionality—all within the context of a larger market.

The security market is in the middle of just such a transition. It has been dominated by proprietary solutions that do not interoperate, but is evolving into an open standards-based market.

Getting Burned

The second point above is an interesting one. Those of us who have been in the security products business for some time have watched an interesting change take place. As recently as a few years ago, enhancements for security were usually very low on the priority of companies when it came to spending money. They viewed spending money on security in the same way people view buying insurance. You really hate to spend the money unless there is a compelling reason to do so, and even then you hate to do it.

This led to some strange behavior. It was very common to talk to companies about the need to add security to their environments; as technologists we could have great conversations about cryptography, but often it did not lead to the purchase of security products. At some unpredictable point later, we would get a call for a massive purchase of security product. That company had just been compromised and was in a panic to increase their level of security.

One example of this occurred when I was working with NASA and the *Department of Energy* (DOE) on a massive network that slightly predated the Internet. NASA, the DOE, most space science institutions, most high energy physics institutions, and many universities were connected to the SPAN/HEPnet network (Space Physics Analysis Network/High Energy Physics network). SPAN/HEPnet ran a set of protocols that were developed by Digital Equipment Corporation, and which were very similar to TCP/IP in many ways. Parts of this network ran over satellites owned by NASA.

While helping design this network with NASA, I once asked what kind of security was wanted on the satellite links. The reply was rather embarrassing. "You just don't get it, do you?" I was scolded. "The U.S. taxpayers already paid for these satellites, they are paying for the transmission lines, they paid for the routers, heck, they even paid for the robots we sent to other worlds to gather the scientific information that will flow over these communications lines. They already paid for it! As a result, we want absolutely no security. We want these links fully open. We want to be the scientific Library of Congress, open to the whole world. Get it?"

Well, you don't need to beat me with a stick twice. I decided not to ask about security again. The rest of the meeting went better.

One week later, NASA called a special meeting, and the only topic was how to secure the communication lines, including the satellite links. In the intervening week, apparently, a German hacker group had decided to take a little electronic tour of the SPAN/HEPnet network looking for scientific research related to nuclear weapons. Although SPAN/HEPnet did not carry traffic relating to weapons development, this situation shook them enough that security went from absolutely off the radar screen to the top priority in less than one week.

Until recently, this was commonly the case. Customers would talk a good game about security, but unless they had been burned by an attack, they would usually not invest in much more than a firewall. Fortunately for us all, the situation is changing. Press articles are published every day that describe hacks on databases and Web sites, as well as the corresponding impact to the bottom line of companies. Security has changed from being viewed as insurance to being viewed as a fundamental requirement. Companies are coming closer and closer to the realization that security is necessary to protect the interest of their stockholders, to protect the perception of the company by customers and the industry, to protect the privacy of their customers and partners, and to protect the intellectual property and products of the company itself.

In addition to these issues, people are beginning to realize that security is integral to increasing revenues and decreasing costs. Many companies now see the need to enhance security in order to achieve compliance with governmental or legal regulations. And last, but not least, the increasing awareness around security issues has brought demands from customers and partners that products be secure. We will cover these important issues in more detail in Chapter 11.

Migration

Until recently, most of the market was based upon proprietary, symmetric-based cryptography. As discussed earlier, this allowed vendors to create monolithic solutions that were efficient but closed.

The growth in the size of corporate networks has been amazing over the last decade, and we are now entering a time where companies are extending their networks to cover their business partners and even their customers. These business-to-business and business-to-customer communications must be secure. The combination of these factors has increased the size of the community that must participate in a common key exchange system well beyond what a simple symmetric solution can handle.

In addition to this, the proprietary symmetric-based solutions worked when one vendor provided all the components of the solution. In today's market, customers choose different parts of the solution from different vendors. This creates a drive toward open, interoperable solutions.

As a result of these pressures, the market is in the middle of an evolution toward modern cryptographic solutions that are combinations of asymmetric and symmetric crypto, and which are based upon open standards and demonstrated interoperability.

Lastly, the movement toward an open, interoperable set of solutions based upon the combination of symmetric and asymmetric crypto has been driven by the adoption of several key protocols. The movement away from client/server application deployment toward Web-based application solutions has driven the importance of the protocol stacks (including security) that are associated with the Web. Two important standards in this area are SSL and IPSec. As discussed previously, SSL is frequently (but not exclusively) used to secure Web sessions at the application level. Note that in the evolving area of the wireless Web (Web connectivity to cell phones and wireless PDAs), there are protocols similar to SSL (such as WTLS) that also incorporate the concept of symmetric encryption with asymmetric key wrapping.

IPSec is a protocol that secures communications between two nodes (rather than between two applications as is the case with SSL). IPSec is frequently used to secure corporate communications across the Internet. Often, SSL sessions are run over an IPSec session. It is somewhat wasteful to have two levels of encryption running on top of each other, but it is a practical outcome of the way in which networks are managed. The people responsible for application security cannot know if the application will always be run over an IPSec session, and as a result the application security people run their applications over SSL to protect the data. Similarly, the people responsible for the line-level security know that not all applications have embedded application-level security into the applications, and as a result IPSec is frequently used to encrypt all traffic at the line level.

SSL, IPSec, and wireless protocols such as WTLS are open, support interoperability, and are based on symmetric encryption of the data stream, with asymmetric crypto used to wrap the symmetric encryption keys.

The Test

Before we leave this chapter, you will recall that I promised you a test.

In the previous examples, I showed you how to combine symmetric and asymmetric cryptography into a practical encryption solution. I also showed you how to perform digital signatures for the purpose of verifying the source of a document, and for verifying that the document had not been modified in transit.

You may have noticed that I did not show you how to do it all. So, here is your homework. Using the same types of figures I have used in this chapter, show how my sister could send me Mom's recipe adhering to the following principles:

- The solution must be secure.
- Encryption of the recipe must be fast.
- The encrypted cipher-text must be compact.
- The solution must scale to large populations.
- The solution must not be vulnerable to key interception.
- The solution must not require a prior relationship between the parties.
- The solution must be able to guarantee the source of the recipe.
- The solution must be able to detect if the recipe was modified in transit.

Good luck. I don't grade on a curve. By the way, the answer is in Appendix B.

Reference

[1]RSA Laboratories Bulletin number 13, April 2000. "A Cost-Based Security Analysis of Symmetric and Asymmetric Key Lengths."

CHAPTER 3

Public Key Infrastructure Basics

Public Key Infrastructure Basics

Public key cryptography provides the tools that enable security operations like digital signatures and key distribution. The basic technology has been available in different forms for about twenty-five years (dating this from the original paper published by Diffie and Helleman).[1] RSA, named for its designers, Rivest, Shamir, and Adleman, was developed in 1978 and remains the most widespread public key algorithm in use today.[2]

Applications such as Lotus Notes have used public key cryptography for authentication, whereas the e-mail encryption application *Pretty Good Privacy* (PGP) used its own form of public key technology since the early 1990s. However, the widespread use of public key-based cryptography mechanisms is relatively recent.

NOTE:

PGP (Pretty Good Privacy) is an application that uses PKI to protect the privacy of users' e-mail and files.[3]

The expanding use of public key technology has been enabled by the set of services, programming interfaces, administrative tools, and user applications that form a *Public Key Infrastructure* (PKI). While PKI standards, technologies, and implementations are still evolving, as is typical of any complex infrastructure, they have a fairly standard structure that is commonly recognizable and generally accepted.

Why Isn't Public Key Cryptography Enough?

In the last chapter, you saw a rich set of encryption methods and techniques that enable you to provide any of the security services you are likely to need. Public/private keys were shown to be a significant component of the services that are used by these solutions. So why is an infrastructure for public/private keys required at all? Let's look at an example.

One of the more interesting security mechanisms based on public key cryptography is the generation of digital signatures. Electronic documents have lacked a well-accepted way to allow the author to attest to the contents of a document, or to verify that the contents have not been modified from the original. Digital signatures support both of these attributes. You might require a digital signature for simple tracking purposes, to allow an individual to verify that he has reviewed or signed-off on an expense form. Alternatively, to give an electronic form of a contract some status under law, the parties to the contract need to provide their mark in a way that is recognizable.

Recent legislation in the United States and Europe has provided the basis for legal recognition of various forms of electronic signatures. This includes digital signatures generated using systems based on public key cryptography. Let's re-examine the process of creating a digital signature.

Creating a digital signature first requires that a cryptographic hash be created for the significant content of the documents to ensure that information is not modified (see Figure 3-1). For a contract, the significant content will likely include all of the text of the document. For a Web form, the hash will include at least the data input fields, including information such as product description, user and payment information, and so on, whereas the HTML tags used for formatting may not be required. The resulting hash value or digest is then encrypted using the signer's private key.

NOTE:

The differentiation between format and content is an important principle employed in signing message content constructed with XML. This is discussed in Chapter 7 on application use of certificates.

Figure 3-1

Digital signature process

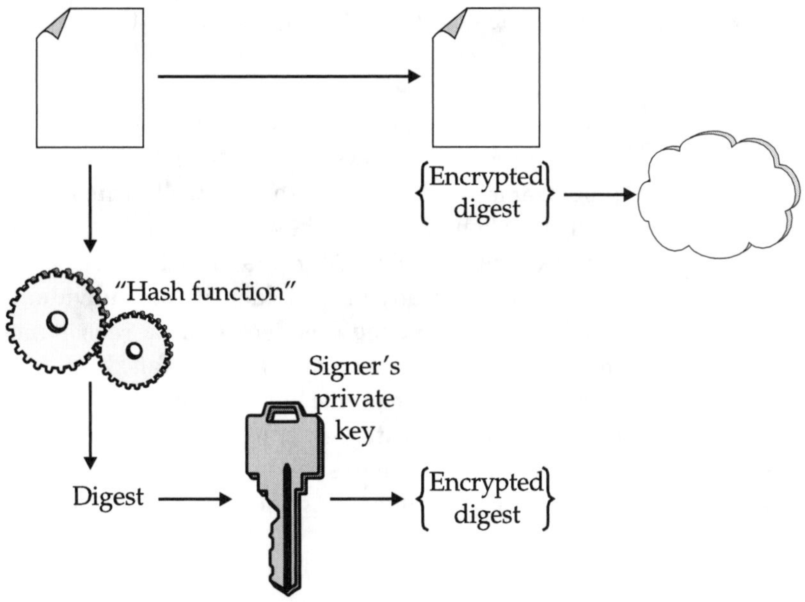

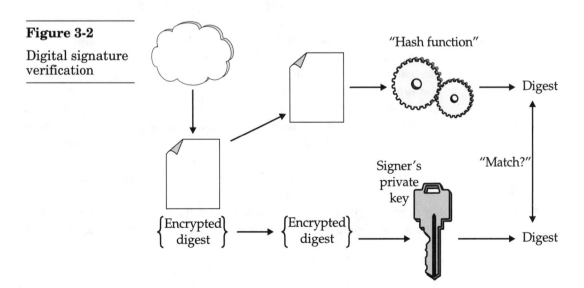

Validation of the digital signature requires regenerating the hash of the significant document content. The original hash value that was encrypted using the signer's private key must then be decrypted using the signer's public key, and then the two hash values must be compared (see Figure 3-2). If the hash values match, the signature is considered verified. What could be simpler?

Figure 3-2

Digital signature verification

The problem is this: How do you know that the key pair used to encrypt and later decrypt the hash value actually belongs to the individual you believed signed the document?

Creation of a public/private key pair is a simple operation for a user—your average Web browser can be used. (This is much more difficult for a programmer to do; at least to do it well, which is why there have been so many problems with good key generation in early versions of PKI-enabled applications.) A clever interloper may have substituted his public key for a public key already used to identify an individual—after all, the public key is public and should be located in a reasonably accessible place—or may have convinced you to take it by falsely claiming the identity in the first place. Once the public key has been published, the interloper uses the corresponding private key in his possession to generate a signature. The sequence of steps we described earlier for signature verification will render a correct result, leading the user validating the signature to trust it—incorrectly.

We have arrived at a state where simply using cryptographic techniques is not sufficient to meet the goals of a security service such as the generation of a verifiable digital signature. Possession of a public/private key pair alone is not enough to allow the establishment of a trusted identity.

The Need for Trusted Identities

The primary role of PKI is establishing digital identities that can be trusted. These identities in turn can be used in conjunction with cryptographic mechanisms to deliver a security service like authentication, authorization, or validation of a digital signature where the users of the service can have reasonable confidence that they have not been misled.

The problem with creating an identity you can trust is finding some person or institution that you are prepared to trust sufficiently to attest to the identity. Suitably trustworthy individuals might include a long-time friend, a family doctor, a court judge, or a trusted institution. Institutions that fall into this category might include a professional organization like the *American Medical Association* (AMA), which certifies doctors, or the Bar Association, which accredits lawyers.

If you can locate a suitably trustworthy individual or entity, and it can provide a reasonable level of confidence in the *process* it uses to prove the veracity of the identity it creates, and the *identification mechanism* it supplies is reasonably unforgeable, then you can place some level of trust in the name or identity it creates. In this scheme, you are allowing trust to be transferred or imputed from the originally trusted entity to some new entity.

Establishment of trusted identities is an event that takes place in many different ways every day. An example is the use of a letter of introduction from a friend or trusted business acquaintance to introduce some third party that wishes to build a relationship with you.

NOTE:

This is the kind of networking or relationship establishment that an alternate public / private key system like PGP uses to establish trust.

Although it may be possible to meet any other person on earth given enough contacts, finding someone we both trust to introduce us may be difficult. Even if we as individuals are satisfied with a personal introduction, more formal institutions such as the taxation department (or the IRS in the USA), the bank, or the immigration service in another country are not likely to agree to the use of informal networks of relationships to establish your bona fides.

In addition to personal introductions, certain authorities are recognized as having the right or ability to establish identities. Examples include the Department of Transport (or if you are American, the Registry of Motor Vehicles), which issues a license identifying that you are permitted to operate a motor vehicle, the Passport Office that provides identities that enable you to be recognized by other countries, and the credit card company that issues you an identity that enables you to make purchases on credit.

NOTE:

The passport identifies you and enables a foreign nation to trust the identity based on who issued it; it does not confer the right to enter the country.

In all of these cases, we recognize (well, most of us are prepared to accept them, anyway . . .) the right or authority of the institution to issue or authorize these identities.

NOTE:

The driver's license is actually an example of a certificate that provides an identity as well as demonstrating the permission to drive a motor vehicle. This will be examined in more detail when we look at authorization and the rights that the holder of an identity may have to perform some set of actions.

We have some expectations about how identity-issuing authorities will function. The identity issued by one authority is valid in its own domain but probably will not cross over as a valid identity in another domain. For example, you cannot use a credit card in most countries to identify yourself for the purposes of crossing a border. The methods used to establish, control, and protect credit card identities are not considered sufficient for the purposes of recognizing identities internationally.

Some forms of identity that are issued are considered stronger or more useful than others, usually based on the level of trust we place in the issuing authority and the amount of required proof to establish those identities. Some of these identities, such as passports, may in turn be used when establishing the identity of a person applying for a driver's license.

From experience, we expect that most identities will be issued for some finite period and will usually require a renewal process at the expiration of that validity period. This eminently sensible constraint on the nondigital identities we encounter prevents the identity outliving the holder and enable associated rights (such as driving a car) to be revalidated periodically. The renewal process is usually simpler than the original application process and will often use the existence of a previous version of the same identity to reduce the proof required to validate the identity being renewed.

For the consumers of an identity, such as a vendor accepting a credit card, we expect that the issuing authority will track the status or good standing of the identity, will provide some means to invalidate or revoke the identity, and will convey that information to the consumer.

Certification Authorities

Within a PKI, the *Certification Authority* (CA) is the trusted authority responsible for creating or certifying identities. This is much more than running an application that can generate digital certificates to serve as electronic identities. This is comparable to the difference between a national passport office that issues passports and a color photocopy service that may be used to reproduce them. Just because identities can be created does not mean anyone will use or trust them.

NOTE:

In this discussion, certification of identities refers to the process of proving the initial ("real") identity of the applicant for a digital identity. This function is separated out into the Registration Authority *(RA) in most CA implementations. The role of the RA is discussed in more detail later in this chapter.*

The CA implements procedures that verify the identity of an applicant registering for a certificate and issues a digital certificate that can be used as proof of that identity. Identities are issued for a specific time period, and the CA has the ability to revoke the certificate and advise users of the certificate that it has been revoked.

Identities used in everyday life have long-established historical precedents for whom we trust to issue them and the processes they use. However, questions arise about the CAs that create identities for use in an electronic world. Whom will you trust to operate a CA? How widely should the identities be used? What processes and proofs will be used to establish the identities? What mechanisms can be provided in a digital network to provide a reasonably unforgeable identity?

The first place you might look to find trustworthy operators of a CA are the previously trusted institutions with which you have always dealt. These may include banks, credit card companies, the Post Office, other government bodies like the taxation department or passport office, or possibly a professional accreditation group like the AMA.

So, are these suitable operators for a CA? In all of these cases, the answer is "Maybe," but is almost always qualified in the next breath by the clause, "for this specific purpose." It may be valid for the Department of Transport to issue an electronic certificate to use as a license, but you may not want them to have anything to do with your credit cards or credit rating.

In addition to traditional "trusted entities," new forms of issuing authorities have emerged. Many of these public CAs have had to establish a trusted reputation with no pre-existing name or reputation to trade on.

A trusted reputation has been established by public CAs by constructing very secure facilities and by carefully establishing and auditing operating procedures and personnel.

What Is a Digital Certificate?

A digital certificate forms an association between an identity and the public/private key pair possessed by the holder of the identity.

You have concluded that a particular issuing authority can be trusted to establish your identity for the purpose you need. The next step is to produce a document that can be used to certify that you have been issued a validated identity. A digital certificate is the electronic form of this document. For electronic use, you need to produce a digital document or certificate that will supply enough information to enable someone else to satisfy himself that you are the rightful holder of the identity.

The particular form of digital certificate that is described throughout this book is an X.509 digital certificate named after the standard that defines its content and use.[4]

For the purposes of this discussion, we are going to refer to the individual or other entity identified by the certificate as the *certificate owner*. The entity that is passed the certificate and wishes to use it to prove an identity is the *certificate user*. This user is sometimes referred to more formally as the *relying party*.

Real-World Certificates

Before we look at the contents of a digital certificate, let us consider a nondigital analog in the world of identities.

Your passport is the example we are going to examine. An example showing a modified version of my [Andrew's] passport is included in Figure 3-3. It contains the following types of identifying features:

- **Name**   The name identifies the holder or subject of the passport.
- **Birth date and place**   Additional identifying information describes where and when the holder was born.
- **Photograph and signature**   The photograph and signature are used for comparison purposes.
- **Issuing country**   The name of the issuer identifies the country that is certifying the identity of the subject.

Figure 3-3

Passport
information

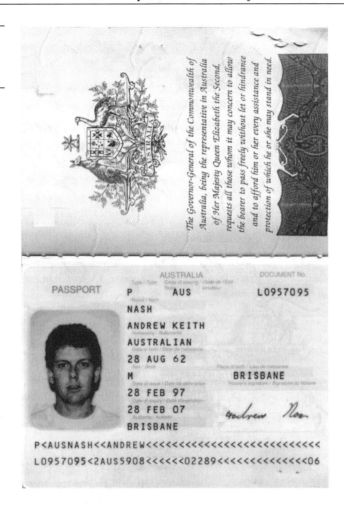

- **Unique number**   A serial number uniquely identifies this
particular passport.
- **Commencement date**   The commencement date states when the
passport was issued.
- **Termination date**   The termination date specifies the last date on
which this passport is considered valid.
- **Official insignia**   The signature of the issuer and a holographic
seal prevent forgery.

■ **Page numbers**   Pages are numbered and the serial number incised through the pages to ensure the contents remain unchanged (so pages cannot easily be added or removed from the document).

■ **Additional information**   This information may specify the type of passport or the conditions that constrain its use.

All in all, this fairly complex document provides a very sophisticated identity. The amount of effort taken to collect and verify the contents establishes this as a respected form of identification that can be used also as a primary document to establish your identity under many circumstances.

NOTE:

Other forms of identity or documentation may be derived from a primary document. Other examples of primary documents include certified birth certificates and marriage certificates.

Digital Certificates

Let us compare the digital certificate issued by a CA with the passport example we just examined. In this case, we will take a look at a certificate stored in Microsoft Internet Explorer. Figure 3-4 shows the high level view of the certificate within IE.

The fields in an X.509 digital certificate mirror the contents of a passport fairly well at this high-level view. Once we start looking at the contents in detail (in Appendix A), fields that are unique to the specification and requirements of a PKI-based digital certificate will be described.

NOTE:

Information like version numbers and issuer identifiers have been omitted for clarity at this point.

The kind of information displayed within IE under the details tab for an X.509 certificate is shown in Figure 3-5 and include the following:

■ **Subject**   The subject names the individual or entity being identified by the certificate. Additional identifying information may be included in the name of the subject or other specific fields in the certificate

Figure 3-4

Certificate
contents

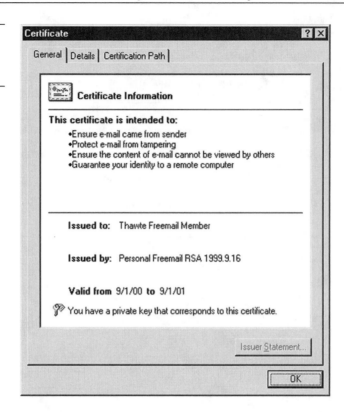

body (in Figure 3-4, the subject name includes an e-mail address of
the form *user@enterprise.com*).

- **Public key**   The public key corresponds to the subject's private key.

- **Issuer**   The issuer identifies the trusted source that generated and
  signed the certificate.

- **Serial number**   A serial number enables this certificate to be
  uniquely identified even if another certificate is issued containing
  all the same information (or substantially similar amounts of
  information).

- **Valid from**   The start date specifies the earliest time the certificate
  may be used.

- **Valid to**   The end date specifies the latest time the certificate may
  be used. Together with the start date, this defines the validity period
  for the certificate.

Figure 3-5

Certificate details

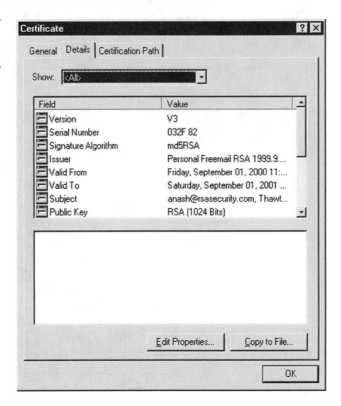

- **Key/certificate usage**   The key/certificate usage information describes the valid uses for the subject's public/private key pair. In the browser display, this is identified by the section entitled "This certificate is intended to" in Figure 3-4.

- **Digital signature**   The digital signature (not shown in this figure) of the issuer generated using the issuer's private key verifies the subject's identity. The hash value used in constructing the CA signature on the certificate enables verification that the certificate contents have not been tampered with.

NOTE:

In the example, the field named Signature Algorithm contains a value of "md5RSA." This indicates that the hashing algorithm used is MD5, and that the resulting hash is encrypted using the RSA algorithm to create the signature.

The subject and issuer names are defined using conventions defined in the X.500 standard. This allows a unique name to be established by defining a concept known as a *distinguished name*. A distinguished name may include use of distinguishing information such as the organization the individual works for, the address where he is located, or the way you would address the individual on the Internet. The information from a certificate is shown graphically in Figure 3-6.

Some Terminology

As a starting point, we will define some terminology that identifies the participants in the use of certificates.

An *end-entity* is a person or object that is the subject identified by a certificate, or a user of a certificate that identifies another end-entity. An end-entity includes people, network nodes (such as Web servers, firewalls, or routers), executable programs, and just about any object that has a unique identity and can be assigned a certificate.

The *certificate owner* is the end-entity identified in the subject field of the certificate. This end-entity may sometimes be referred to as the *certificate subject*.

Figure 3-6

General X.509 certificate format

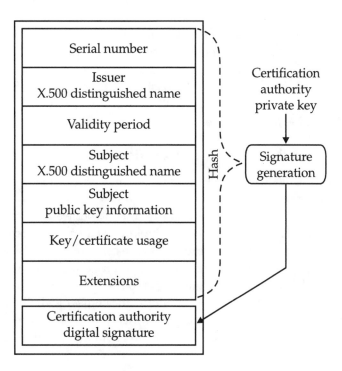

The *certificate user* is an end-entity that receives a certificate and uses it for the purposes of establishing the identity of a certificate owner. As the certificate user relies on the identity established in the certificate, they are sometimes known as the *relying party*.

Certificate Types and Attributes

In addition to the information used to directly establish the identity of the certificate owner, other information or attributes are included in certificates for use by a particular application.

Certificates used to identify e-mail senders will include the e-mail address of the sender. Usually this will take the Internet form of an e-mail address, such as **user@rsasecurity.com**. This enables the identity in the certificate to be directly compared to the originating e-mail address on a mail message.

Computers or network components such as routers must also be identified but have different naming or identity requirements than human users. For example, when creating secure network links using a virtual private network technology, it is essential that the identity of the communicating machines be authenticated. The identity in this case will usually be the TCP/IP network addresses that the cooperating machines will be using in the network packets.

Other information might identify the policy that was used to create the certificate or the policy describing where and when the certificate may be used. For example, the certificate may only be valid on a secure network, or for encrypting highly sensitive information on an unsecured network. Appendix A describing X.509 certificates will cover in detail the fields that enable additional certificate information to be provided.

Security Aspects of Certificates

Certificates have several interesting security features that are worth discussing briefly.

The certificate itself is a public structure containing public information. This includes the public key used in the process of validating the identity. As a result, the certificate can be freely published and accessed in the widest possible fashion—or can it?

Allowing widespread access to the certificate reduces issues associated with distributing the certificate to the users who need access to it. However, when planning for a certificate infrastructure you should consider the scope of use for the certificate. For example, if information such as the home address of the user were included in the Subject Distinguished Name, or the Social Security number were included in the certificate body, would you want this certificate made publicly available outside of your organization?

NOTE:

The Subject Distinguished Name is a field name within the certificate.

The privacy aspects of the information included in the certificate should be carefully considered. The use of some types of identifying information may indeed constrain where you should publish a digital certificate. Given that it may be very difficult to control access to a certificate, considerable thought should be given to the information stored in the certificate.

Certificates are self-protected structures. If the contents of a certificate are modified, or when an untrusted source has been used to issue the certificate, the certificate user will normally be warned by their application software. As a result, certificates can be sent into hostile environments without providing additional protection for the certificate and without the need for a high-security repository.

NOTE:

Other reasons may exist for protecting a repository to provide security or privacy, including preventing deletion of Certificate Revocation Lists *(CRLs)—more on this topic later.*

The presence of the signature on the certificate from an authorizing source enables the certificate user to establish trust in the certificate owners' identity. In addition, the presence of the public key in the certificate enables verification that the certificate owner possesses the corresponding private key.

Application Use of Certificates

This section serves to introduce some of the more common applications that use certificates. These applications and the services they use will be discussed in detail in Chapter 7.

Secure Sockets Layer

The *Secure Sockets Layer* (SSL) protocol will be familiar to anyone who has accessed information securely on the Web. SSL is selected to secure a Web session when you use your browser to access a URL that is preceded by *https:* rather than *http:*. This form of URL directs your Web browser to a different port on the Web server, and all information transferred over the session that is established will use encryption to ensure privacy. In addition, certificates are used to establish the identity of the Web server and possibly the Web client.

When you connect to an *https://www.company.com/* form of URL, the Web server responds to this connection request by sending a certificate to the Web browser. This certificate is used to establish the identity of the Web server, so that the user of the browser can have confidence that those transactions she engages in really do go to the correct bank or other organization. This is known as *server-side authentication*. As it is possible that the Web server could be impersonated by bad guys, the use of a certificate signed by a trusted certificate issuer enables verification that the correct Web server has been reached.

Optionally, the Web server may also want to establish the identity of the user of the Web browser. Once the Web server certificate has been accepted by the browser user, the Web server may then request the user's certificate. This is known as *client-side authentication*. The browser user selects a certificate to send to the Web server and, when it has been validated, enables the Web server to have some confidence in the identity of the user accessing its services. This results in a session which has been *mutually authenticated,* where the identities of both parties have been established.

Secure Electronic Mail

Electronic mail is secured using several different mechanisms. The sender of the mail can establish his identity by digitally signing the mail. The sender creates the signature using his private key and then sending the corresponding certificate with the mail. This enables the recipient to validate the identity of the signer, and to verify that the contents of the mail have not been tampered with.

Signing the electronic mail does not provide privacy for the contents of the mail message—the details in the mail message could still be read by anyone intercepting the mail. To provide privacy, the sender must obtain the certificate of the recipient and use her public key in the process of encrypting the content. The validating recipient's certificate enables the sender to have confidence that the information is being encrypted using the correct public key, and that the recipient is the only individual who can decrypt the contents.

Virtual Private Networking

Virtual Private Networks (VPNs) enable use of the public Internet as though it were a private network. To do this, information must be encrypted as it is passed between the network users. However, as access to the network is not restricted and any network node can send to any other, the identities of the participating network nodes must be established. In the case of VPNs, you are establishing the identity of the machines that are communicating rather than the users of the machines (although this may in turn need to be established).

In the case of a VPN, the identity that is being established is that of the network node and the network address it is using. Certificates issued to end-entities in this case include the network address of the subject being identified by the certificate. VPNs have different operating modes, but in general each of the end-entities will identify themselves by presenting their certificates to others and verifying that they possess the corresponding private keys.

Why Do You Need a Public Key Infrastructure?

A PKI provides the components and services that enable practical deployment and operation of a system that uses certificates. The PKI must deal with issues such as

- Secure creation of good keys
- Validation of initial identities
- Issuance, renewal, and termination of certificates
- Certificate validation
- Distribution of certificates and associated information
- Secure archival and recovery of keys
- Generation of signatures and timestamps
- Establishing and managing trust relationships

In addition to these features, however, a PKI must be integrated with the enterprise's internal and external security to provide real value. It is essential that the PKI provide features that enable it to be integrated with and support the security services that were identified in Chapter 1.

PKI as an infrastructure is still maturing and faces many challenges. It has many powerful features, some of which we are only starting to gain experience with in environments such as e-business transactions. PKI must be useful for solving problems that are critical to the success of the businesses it supports. Essentially, it is an infrastructure that must leverage the applications that support business activities.

To be successful, PKI must ultimately become so well integrated into business applications that its users are not even aware of its presence. Critical areas that must be addressed include ease of use, transparency of the underlying infrastructure to the applications and users who rely on its services, integration with business applications, and broad interoperability between vendors of PKI components and applications. Significant progress has been made in many of these areas. Standards groups (discussed in some detail later) have helped provide the underpinnings to achieve many of these objectives.

One enterprise that recently completed a PKI pilot commented that they "bought a certificate server, but found that what they really needed was a Public Key Infrastructure." Issuing certificates is easy; providing a simple, easy-to-use infrastructure that transparently solves business problems in an interoperable fashion requires a little more effort.

User Authentication

User authentication is the process by which the identity of a user is verified. As you will see, PKI can be used as part of the authentication process for users, and can also be used to authenticate nonhuman entities such as routers or other network components.

The process of user authentication has traditionally taken many forms, but the one most familiar is the use of an identifying name or user ID, and a password or PIN. The security of a user authentication scheme is generally related to the number of pieces of proof, or factors, that are offered during the process of establishing an identity.

Factors Used for Authentication

Password-based authentication is considered a single factor scheme, as the only piece of information required is the user's demonstrated knowledge of a password. The problems with passwords are well understood.

These include poor selection of the password, improper construction using too few characters, lack of change control, cost of resetting passwords, and attacks based on social engineering or shoulder surfing. If you solve all of the policy-related issues and produce really strong, difficult-to-crack passwords, the problem becomes that with so many strong (difficult) passwords to remember, users are likely to write the password down in plain sight.

NOTE:

Social engineering *involves direct interaction with users or administrators of systems to convince them to provide passwords, believing that the attacker has a legitimate reason to know the information.* Shoulder surfing *involves the attacker using complex methods such as watching you type your password in.*

The ease of attacking password schemes is heightened by the use of a single piece of information for the authentication process. Addition of an extra factor or proof leads to *"two-factor"* authentication schemes.

NOTE:

Actual attacks on password schemes usually involve running an application that uses a dictionary of known common passwords. Successive passwords are tried until a match is found. Groups like the LOpht provide tools that enable analysis of passwords used in an organization (see their Web site at http://www.lopht.com/l0phtcrack/).

Generally, a two-factor authentication scheme requires that the user prove *possession* of some item such as the use of a token of some kind, in addition to *knowing* something like a password. In most two-factor authentication systems, you must both have something and know something.

The additional proof generally requires demonstration that the user has possession of the token when the authentication process is being run. SecurID tokens produced by RSA Security use the time at which the authentication process is run combined with a shared secret held in the token and on the authentication server to verify a user's identity.

Other examples include challenge response tokens, in which a one-time challenge is sent to the token. A symmetric key within the token is used to encrypt the challenge, enabling the challenger to ascertain that the token was present when the user authenticated. Use of a charge card in an automated teller machine is another example. The card must first be inserted into the ATM to prove that the user has it in his possession before a *personal identification number* (PIN) is entered to show that the user knows the password.

An alternate second factor might be the use of a biometric of some kind. Biometric authentication schemes rely on proving "what you are." In these schemes, some unique identifying feature of the person being identified is used. This might include a user's thumbprint, retinal pattern, voiceprint, or possibly the way in which she signs her signature. Biometrics and other authentication schemes are examined in more detail in Chapter 9.

A biometric system may sometimes be combined with a token to provide three factors of authentication. This might include high-security environments where a smart card must be used in addition to thumbprint or voice recognition.

PKI as an Authentication Scheme

PKI can be used to provide authentication to verify the identity of a client when using a protocol like SSL. Some people hold the view that PKI, when used in this fashion, enables the identity of a user to be verified. The use of public/private keys and certificates is considered by some to be equivalent to a two-factor authentication scheme.

Despite all of the effort taken to tie public/private keys to an identity, questions still remain to be answered. Are you sure the person using the private key is the same person the CA originally certified? Is the correct individual in the driver's seat making use of those keys and certificates underlying your security services? The answer to these questions is tied to the security of the key store and what authentication mechanism is used to get access to the keys.

Let's look at the way in which current implementations of PKI-based authentication typically work. In the case of a browser or other application registering for a certificate, the first time a key is generated, a key store is created. The browser user is prompted to supply a password used to construct the encrypting key to protect the key store. In many applications, there is no policy-based control over the type of password selected. Some applications enable a user to completely ignore the password request and create a key store with no password. This is perfectly reasonable choice for ease-of-use purposes, but what does it mean for authentication using PKI?

In the case where there is weak or nonexistent password protection on the key store, any user with access to the browser has access to the private keys and certificate. If the certificate is used as part of a Web-based authentication scheme, the whole process continues to work the same way, but you cannot be sure of the identity of the user driving the browser. In this scenario, how much trust can you place in the expensive identities you have created using PKI?

The fundamental issue here is reliably establishing the identity of the user who is accessing or using a private key when a cryptographic operation is performed. When performing an operation such as generating a digital signature, how can you be confident of the identity of the user accessing the private key? Requirements on the use of digital signatures in some security domains specify that users must validate themselves when the private key is used to generate the signature.

NOTE:
We could wish that all security domains specified such requirements, but we have not yet reached such an enlightened stage of deployment or specification.

So what is the relationship between authentication of a user and use of PKI in an authentication process such as generating digital signatures? The identity of a user must still be proven when a key store is accessed to perform a cryptographic operation. In this case, two-factor schemes like time base tokens or use of a smart card and PIN enable a high level of confidence to be established in the identity of the user.

Public Key Infrastructure Components

This section identifies the essential elements of a PKI. A full description of these components and the features they provide can be found in Chapter 6.

Certification Authority

The CA is responsible for establishing identities and creating the digital certificates that form the association between an identity and a public/private key pair. At a mechanical level, it comprises the set of software and hardware components and services that is used during this process. It also includes the personnel, operating procedures, environment, and policies that define how identities are established and what form of digital certificate is issued.

The CA is comprised of several distinct subcomponents or services discussed below. The most important of these include a CS, an RA, and a Certificate Repository.

A CA defines rules that enable subscribers and certificate users to satisfy themselves that the identities it certifies are suitable for their purposes and can be trusted. The rules describing how the various facets of a CA are constrained and operated are defined in a document called the Certification Practices Statement (originally conceived by the American Bar Association in its Digital Signature Guidelines).[5] *A Certification Practices Statement* (CPS) for the CA that issued the certificates should be available to the certificate user. If a CPS is not available, this should reasonably cast doubt on the veracity of the CA and reduce trust in the identities it issues.

NOTE:

Concern has been raised recently that a CPS, which was originally designed to document the operation of a CA, may in fact reveal too much information. As a result, a new type of document called a PKI Disclosure Statement *(PDS) is under discussion. It could be used to convey information necessary for operations such as certification of a CA by another CA when establishing trusted relationships.*

Registration Authority

The RA is responsible for registration and initial authentication of *subscribers*. Subscribers are the users who are issued certificates after a registration request has been approved. These interactions may also include certificate revocation and the other services that subscribers need when interacting with a PKI. An RA and its interfaces may be implemented as part of a certificate server, described in the following section, or may form a standalone component.

The duties of an RA may be carried out by a human operator. All of the identity validation process could be implemented as a set of manual procedures (in fact, direct human verification may be required for some high-security environments). Submission of a certificate request by a suitably qualified and authenticated individual is a valid completion of RA responsibilities.

The business rules controlling certificate subscriber registration and certificate generation vary widely but should be described in CPS for the CA. Aspects of the CPS should be reviewed by security administrators and legal counsel within enterprises that will use certificates issued by the CA.

Certificate Server

The certificate server is the component of a Certification Authority that many people think of when they use the term CA. It is the machine or service responsible for issuing certificates based on information provided during the registration process. The user's public key is combined with other identifying information and the resulting certificate structure is signed using the CA's private key.

The aspects of a CPS that control a certificate server include descriptions of how the keys are secured for the CA, what information will be placed in the certificate, and how frequently revocation information is generated.

Certificate Repository

The certificates and corresponding public keys need to be publicly available before they can be put to work. If a publication mechanism is provided to support dissemination of public certificates, a repository will be the usual place to publish certificates. The repositories that are usually utilized as part of a PKI are directories—occasionally X.500 directories, but more typically LDAP directories. As you will see, LDAP is actually a description of the access method and protocol used to locate information in a directory. An LDAP-compliant directory could be implemented as anything from a flat file to a relational database or even an X.500 directory, provided it complies with the LDAP requirements.

NOTE:

Certificates may also be distributed directly to specific users when the certificate owner initiates a connection to the certificate user.

Certificate Validation

Certificate users need to validate the certificates they receive. Validation of an individual certificate requires

- Verification of the certificate signer's signature
- Ensuring that the certificate is still current by checking the certificate validity period
- Checking compliance between the intended certificate use and any policy constraints specified in the certificate by the CA
- Verifying that the certificate has not been revoked (canceled) by the CA

The process of validating certificate chains is usually complex, particularly when used across enterprises. It may be performed in a client environment, usually by the application using the certificate, or may be provided as a service that the client can use to perform the same task. Certificate validation is examined in more detail in Chapter 4, and support for certificate validation protocols and services in Chapter 6.

Key Recovery Service

Public/private key pairs may be generated locally at a key store within an application like a Web browser or on a physical device like a smart card. Alternatively, the key pair may be created at a central key generation server.

In either case, there is a need to provide a mechanism that enables encryption keys to be archived and recovered if they are lost. Other cases exist such as when encryption keys are subpoenaed by law enforcement agencies. (This has been a highly controversial topic, and requirements vary with your local jurisdiction.) This allows for continued operation of decryption processes even if disaster strikes the holder of the keys. If, for example, you have encrypted some information that is important to the enterprise you work for, and you are struck by a bus and your public/private key pair is lost, the enterprise will want to use the key recovery service to recover the vital information.

NOTE:

Of course, at this point, you are in the hospital or worse and are probably less concerned about recovery of the information, which is why the IT department takes responsibility for running the key recovery service.

Time Server

Secure time, like digital signatures, is an electronic construct that allows a verifiable timestamp to be issued. It requires an accurate source of time that is monotonically increasing, where the timestamp is securely transferred so it cannot be intercepted or replaced. Finally, the timestamp is signed so that the issuer of the trusted time value can be verified.

NOTE:

Monotonically increasing simply means that time values keep increasing. It implies that the time stream cannot be reset to an earlier time value.

A number of operations benefit from the concept of secure time. These include secure audit logs, receipt acknowledgement systems, workflow systems, and electronic documents, including contracts. To provide a timestamp that can be authenticated in the future, you need a secure time source that is provided in some trusted manner, with characteristics like monotinicity (time must only move forward). In addition, you must be able to show that the document to which a time indicator is appended has not changed (which normally also requires the use of a digital signature).

If a time server is included as part of the PKI, it provides digital timestamps for use by layered services or applications. The value of an enterprise service for support of applications such as contract verification will depend on how much a third party is prepared to trust your timestamps. Use of a trusted third-party timestamp provider may be required in some cases.

Signing Server

Digital signatures may be generated by applications that manage documents or transactions to which a signature is applied. If the application does not provide such support, or if a central signing and verification service is preferred, it may be desirable to use a separate server to perform this function for user transactions. A signing server might also form the basis of a third-party service like those provided by Digital Notaries.

Key and Certificate Life Cycle Management

Key and certificate life cycle management deals with the operations necessary for management of keys and certificates from creation to retirement.

Creation of the public/private key pair is required initially to link them to the certificate used to establish the identity of an end-entity. The key pair is provided along with other identifying information as part of the process of *registering* with a CA for a certificate. The certificate is *issued* by the CA after it has *verified* the information you have provided to establish your identity.

Before certificates can be used to establish identities, they must be *distributed* in various ways to certificate users. They may be *transmitted* by the certificate owner, or they may be stored in a *repository* by the CA for later *retrieval*.

The certificate that is issued to you has a limited lifetime associated with it. When the certificate reaches the end date, it is considered to have *expired* and a certificate must be *reissued*. As part of the process of reissuing a certificate for a particular identity, some of the information in the certificate may have changed. Alternatively, as keys have a useful life expectancy based on the length of the key, either the certificate or the key must be *updated*.

A certificate for an end-entity may need to be invalidated by the CA that issued it. In this case, the certificate needs to be *revoked* and the CA needs to *publish* this revocation information.

As keys may be lost and need to be recovered to allow for decryption of previously encrypted information, there is a need to allow *key archival* and *key recovery* processes to occur.

The aspects of life cycle management are examined more fully in Chapters 4 and 5.

The Role of Authorization

The primary function of PKI is to establish identities that can be trusted. This is not the same as establishing what the holder of that identity is trusted to do. The decision about what types of access a user with a valid identity may have to information or systems is generally handled by an authorization system rather than an authentication system. Let's return to our passport analogy and recap the authentication process.

As a valid passport holder, you have a strong identity attested to by a trusted CA. When you approach the customs and immigration desk at the entry port of a different country, a procedure is used to validate your use of the passport. The immigration officer looks at your photograph and may require that your handwritten signature be signed on an entry document for comparison with the signature in your passport.

The officer then examines the holographic image, verifying that this was produced by your government, and verifies that the information encoded in the machine-readable bar code and the physical information in the passport match, ensuring that the document has not been changed. Finally, he calls up your record on the computer and checks to see if your passport has been canceled or revoked. All of this corresponds to the rules that the user of a certificate executes to verify its validity. You have just completed the authentication process to the satisfaction of the immigration official. Having completed that process, the immigration officer knows you have a good identity and allows you to enter the country—maybe.

The answer to the question, "Should entry be permitted?" lies in whether that country has a security policy requiring that you have a visa granting you access to the country. If you do not have the correct kind of visa corresponding to the type of access you want, you will be denied entry even though your identity checked out.

What is a visa? It is additional information that identifies the *access rights* that some users of your passport may wish to impose. The passport establishes your identity, but an associated document, the visa, defines what you may do.

Potentially, a visa may specify that you are allowed to enter the country but must remain in an enclave for all foreign visitors. Alternatively, it may allow you general access, but specify that you may not enter some regions of the country without an escort. It may specify that you are only permitted to study in the country but not to work, or possibly that you may work for only one employer. These additional attributes all define what your identity may give you access to.

Note that in the special cases cited previously, your identity has not changed. The issuer and the level of trust associated with it have not changed. The verification procedures for your identity have not changed. All of these are prerequisites that must be met to establish your identity. They correspond to an *authentication system*. Once authenticated, the immigration officer knows it is worth looking at your passport for a visa and this corresponds to the *authorization system*.

The reason for belaboring these points is that in many security systems the distinctions between identity, authentication, and authorization are blurred or overlooked entirely.

In some environments, this may be acceptable. For example, certificates may be issued by an enterprise purely for access to systems within that enterprise. Knowledge of your identity might be all that is required within the enterprise—it is just a general pass to allow you past the front door of your systems.

However, as PKI becomes used progressively to support interactions between different enterprises or between enterprises and their customers, the need for authorization in addition to authentication becomes more important.

Certificates and User Capabilities

The digital certificates specified in X.509 have some interesting characteristics that lead us into an area that seems to span authentication and authorization. The form of identity specified in a distinguished name creates several of these opportunities.

The X.500 naming scheme forms the basis of the distinguished name for both the subject and the issuer of a certificate. It allows inclusion of information that may allow role based identification within the certificate. For example, I can specify in my naming scheme that the issuing authority I am dealing with belongs to my company's engineering department, located in Sweden. This is what the distinguished name in this case might look like:

{Country=US, Organization=RSA Security, OrganizationalUnit=Engineering, Location=Sweden}

Alternatively, the subject of the certificate may be an individual with a name that identifies that he works in the payroll department:

{Country=US, Organization=RSA Security, OrganizationalUnit=Payroll}

By examining the names used for the trusted identity created, some conclusions could be drawn about the access rights of the owner of the certificate. I could, for instance, decide that as the certificate owner belongs to the payroll department, access to the payroll system is valid. If the certificate issuer was the CA for the Swedish engineering group, allowing the certificate owner access to the code management system used by that engineering group is supported.

So I could construct an authorization system that is divided by function and location and depends on having CAs scattered around my organization. These CAs have the attribute that they not only establish identities for that part of the organization, but also allow access to the systems owned by that organization.

Two problems arise as you try to extend such a system to a larger scale. The first is that to handle identities that need access to systems that cross functions or locations, you must either issue multiple certificates to each user or establish issuing authorities that create certificates usable in two domains. If you are the vice president of engineering needing access to engineering domains in five different locations, as well as needing to access the payroll system to verify how much to provide in the next round of salary increases, you end up with a lot of certificates or a very complex set of overlapping CAs. If you also exchange mail with other company executives and the product management group, life rapidly starts to look complex.

The distinguished name in the subject name field is not the only way to define attributes that can be used for authorization purposes. Other certificate fields allow specification of information, such as policies associated with issuing or controlling the use of certificates. Additionally, site-specific information can be encoded in proprietary extensions to the certificate.

Microsoft Windows 2000 makes use of the policy field to specify what types of access a certificate holder may have to different parts of the system. For example, you may be designated a smart card user with the right to perform signature operations using the private keys stored on the smart card. However, if you do not have the additional right to authenticate with smart cards, you cannot use the card to log on to a Windows desktop. Other policy identifiers allow control of access to Windows 2000 applications or specification of administration capabilities in different parts of the system.

The problem with this approach is that the administrator who controls access to an application may be several steps removed from the administrator authorizing registration requests for certificates. If the user needs to change the combination of applications or parts of the system that he can access, a new certificate must be issued. Particularly in an environment where the keys and certificates must be stored on a smart card that must be personalized for each use, this becomes a significant usability problem when managing a large and dynamic user space.

In general, storage of information in certificates that is used for authorization purposes is exposed to this problem: The roles or capabilities that a user possesses tend to change much faster than her identity. CAs have operational overheads that tend to make reissuing certificates to too many users expensive. As a result, the typical validity period for certificates tends to be about a year or two. The period necessary to handle changing access rights for a user may be on the order of days or hours. There is a serious mismatch between the need for a lightweight, rapidly changing access rights system and a high-assurance identity system designed for relatively infrequent changes. In addition, if you rely on an outsourced service, the cost for issuing very large numbers of certificates may become prohibitive.

Privilege Management Infrastructures

The 2000 version X.509 defines a PMI as the infrastructure that supports an authorization system. This is closely linked to the PKI that supports an authentication system.

The management of user capabilities or privileges has attracted much attention in the last few years. Many authorization systems have begun to emerge, but almost all of them have implemented proprietary schemes. The nature of the attributes managed for users, the working of the infrastructure, the trust models employed, and so on have all been developed in unique ways for each solution. Often, the separation of various aspects of the model has not been very well preserved, so it is difficult to see where identities, authentication, access rights, capabilities or roles, and authorization begin and end. Certainly, any support has been lacking for creation of user capabilities that could be shared between vendor implementations or even between different enterprises—not surprisingly, given how much time has been available for these types of systems to mature.

Recently, privilege management work that was begun in the 1997 version of X.509 and the ITU X9 standards specified for the financial industry has been refined considerably. The result of this work appears in the 2000 version of X.509. Nearly half of the current X.509 specification is given over to PMIs in support of the traditional focus of X.509, which has been PKIs.

As part of this new standardization effort, several concepts have been developed or enhanced. The fundamental unit or structure of the PMI is a new type of certificate known as the *attribute certificate* (AC), or sometimes *privilege attribute certificate* (PAC). Unlike its X.509 PKI counterpart that deals with identity certificates, PMI attribute certificates do not create an identity and link it to a public/private key pair. Instead, they encode a set of attributes associated with a user. While these attributes are not limited to access rights or privileges, that is the focus of PMI's use of these structures.

The type of architecture defined in X.509 using ACs is not the only solution, but given new work in the IETF to profile these standards, it certainly appears to be a technology worth investigating. This topic is considered in more detail in Chapter 9.

Summary

We started out by examining why the trusted identities created by Public Key Infrastructure were needed to make the cryptographic services from Chapter 2 available for useful work. The features used in a secure certificate like a passport were compared with the digital certificate equivalent. The process of proving your electronic identity and why the CA as a certificate issuer could be trusted were compared to the role of the passport office.

The components of a PKI were introduced and the roles of each were discussed.

Finally, we looked at how information other than an identity is required when someone like an immigration official is determining whether to allow you access to a country, and this led us to a discussion of authorization systems.

References

[1]DH76 Diffie, W. and M. Hellman. "New Directions in Cryptography" *IEEE Transactions on Information Theory 22* (1976): 644-654.

[2]Rivest, R.L., A. Shamir, and L.M. Adleman, "A method for obtaining digital signatures and public-key cryptosystems," *Communications of the ACM,* vol. 2, no. 21 (1978), 120-126.

[3]Zim85 Zimmerman, P. *The Official PGP User's Guide*. Cambridge, MA: MIT Press, 1995 (second printing).

[4]Draft Revised ITU-T Recommendation X.509 | ISO/IEC 9594-8: "Information Technology - Open Systems Interconnection - The Directory: Public-Key and Attribute Certificate Frameworks."

[5]Information Security Committee, Section of Science and Technology, American Bar Association, Digital Signature Guidelines (1996), Section 1.8.

CHAPTER 4

PKI Services and Implementation

In the last chapter, we examined the requirement for creating a *Public Key Infrastructure* (PKI) to supply trusted identities and introduced the components that are used to construct a PKI. We also looked at what a certificate contains and how it meets the requirements for establishing a trusted identity.

In this chapter, we will introduce the principal services used in the operation of a PKI. These are targeted at supporting the life cycle of public/private keys and certificates that was introduced in Chapter 3. The methods that may be used to implement or deploy these PKI services are then considered.

Key and Certificate Life Cycle Management

This section deals with the operations necessary for management of keys and certificates through their life cycle from creation to retirement. This includes replacement of keys and certificates when they expire, as well as revocation and validation of certificates.

Certificate Issuance

Let's return to the earlier example of a passport and look at how a request for passport issuance is processed.

The process used to establish my [Andrew's] identity required the following:

1. I filled out a registration form that provided initial details for inclusion in the passport.
   a. Where and when I was born
   b. My home address
   c. My marital status
   d. Whether I had been convicted of any crimes

2. I provided several supporting pieces of "primary" documentation.
   a. Birth certificate
   b. Marriage certificate
   c. Taxation records to prove residency

3. I provided several copies of a recent photograph.

4. A reputable person (minister, lawyer, politician, and so on—all right, I didn't make up the rules, so they are not my definitions) had to state that he had known me for at least five years and had to sign my application and photographs verifying the information was correct.

5. Wait in line for three hours . . .

6. Present myself in person when I made the application so that a trusted registrar could verify that I looked like my photograph and could verify any details with me directly.

   Oh, and of course . . .

7. I had to pay money to cover the cost of the identity verification and production of the certificate or passport.

8. Several weeks later (after various law enforcement agencies had been consulted, and other records cross checked to validate my documentation) I was issued a passport.

Phew, what an effort!

Graphically, the flow looks something like the process described in Figure 4-1.

After ten years, my original passport expired, and I needed to renew it. The reason my passport expired was ostensibly to force re-verification of the information provided to support my identity. It also gave the Aus-

Figure 4-1

Identity
validation process

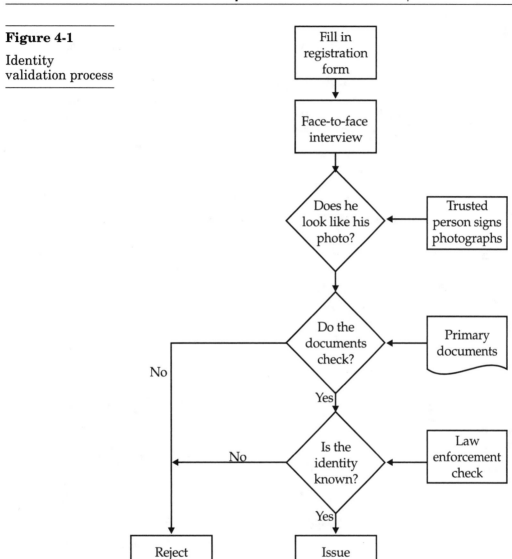

tralian government a chance to ensure my passport was actually held by
me. Actually, I think the real reason is that government departments
everywhere like to ensure that the population suffers sufficient pain on a
regular basis. Of course, if the passport office was the taxation office, they
would have this privilege annually.

Fortunately, the process to renew my passport was considerably easier and faster. This relied upon the fact that my old passport was still valid at the time of application for renewal. Because there was already a trusted identity established, it was only necessary to revalidate a minimum number of details in order to ensure that it was still me that was getting the passport. Of course, they still charged me the same amount for the application.

The amount of work and effort needed to create this identity establishes very high levels of trust in the document. As a result, most other identification processes will take presentation of a passport as a necessary and sufficient condition to issue additional identities. All of this sounds much like the process necessary to apply for a digital certificate.

The first point of user interaction with a *Certification Authority* (CA) is typically a Web interface provided with the *Registration Authority* (RA) (particularly if one of the public CA services is used). So the interface most users will use to register for their first certificate is a Web browser.

The process will look something like the following (we will use the RSA Keon Certificate Server). For this example, you'll choose a registration process that allows you to Enroll For A Personal Certificate, as shown in Figure 4-2.

Figure 4-2

Select "Enroll for a Personal Certificate"

1. You will access a URL for a Web page that provides form-based input to specify registration information (see Figure 4-3).

Figure 4-3

User enrollment data input form

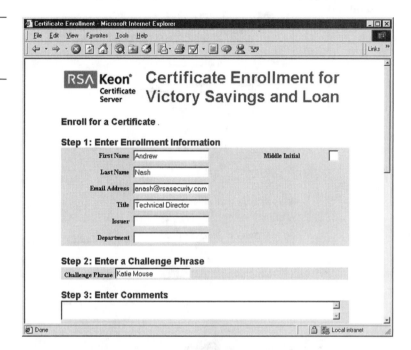

2. Somewhere on the page will be a program that is used to generate a public/private key pair. It will often appear as an input field asking you to select the size of the key. In this case, the key size is determined by the name of the cryptographic service provider selected through the browser (see Figure 4-4).

3. Submitting the form causes the browser to initiate the process of generating a key pair (see Figure 4-5). The random input necessary to initiate the construction of the prime numbers is derived from parameters on the machine or by using random keystrokes or mouse movements from user input.

4. When the key pair has been constructed, the private key is stored in a local application key store. If the key store is being constructed for the first time, you will usually be prompted for a password that is used to build a symmetric key to encrypt or decrypt the key store.

Figure 4-4

Select key strength based on the cryptographic service provider

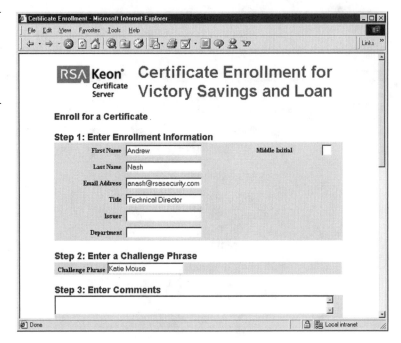

Figure 4-5

Browser key generation

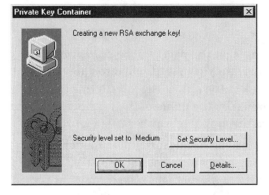

NOTE:

The choice of password used to protect the key store—and indeed whether to create a password at all—is left entirely up to the user in most browsers. This can leave the private key exposed. This is discussed further in the "Protection of Private Keys" section.

5. When key generation is complete, the public key is sent along with the information entered on the registration form to the Web server interface on the Registration Authority (see Figure 4-6). In some implementations, at this point you must prove you possess the private key. For example, if this key pair and certificate will be used for digital signatures, proof of possession of the private signing key is demonstrated by signing the registration request. The RA can verify the signature when the request is received.

Figure 4-6

Confirmation that registration submission is complete

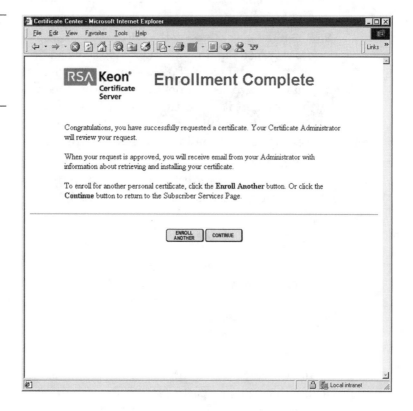

6. The registration authority examines the information and initiates some process to verify the identifying information provided by the user. The exact process will be determined by the security policy and implementation of the CA.

7. When the *Certificate Server* (CS) receives the request from the RA, it may insert additional information and set various fields in the certificate based on the issuing rules defined in the certification practices statement. For example, the type of Registration Authority and identification policy may require different classes of certificate to be issued. Based on the type of identity being issued, policy setting may vary in the certificate to constrain the way that certificate can be used.

8. The completed certificate is returned to the user. The mechanism used will again vary based on the CA implementation and CPS requirements. In this example, the user is sent a mail message containing a URL for the Web browser to use as a pickup location (see Figure 4-7).

9. When the user clicks on the URL, the certificate is downloaded to the browser (see Figure 4-8). To provide some additional security (particularly if proof of possession of the private key was not used), you may have been supplied some form of password or pickup PIN. In this example, it is identified as the "Certificate Retrieval Number." This may be supplied via a mail message or other out-of-band transmission depending on policy requirements.

10. When the browser detects the load operation for the certificate, it stores the returned certificate along with the previously generated private key in the key store (see Figure 4-9).

NOTE:

For many applications, the key stores used are specific to the application. The key store may be accessed via a standard interface such as PKCS #11 or Crypto API, which may allow it to be shared or to substitute new key stores such as a smart card. This is discussed further in the "Smart Card Key Stores" section.

In most certificate-issuing systems, renewal is generally much simpler, as it was in the passport example. By presenting the original certificate, the identity of the applicant can be determined by verifying the user's

Figure 4-7

E-mail
notification of
certificate
availability

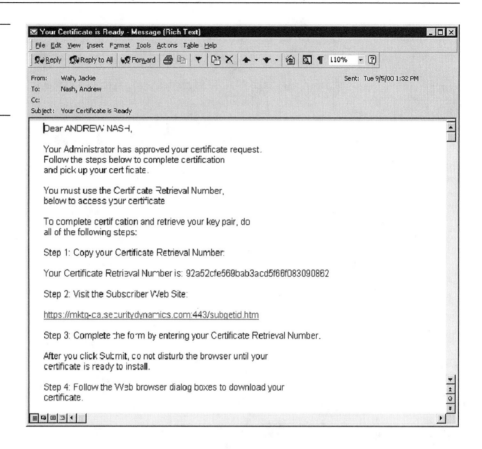

access to the private key. Provided none of the identifying information has
been changed, the certificate may be issued immediately.

How Long Will that Key Last?

Most types of cryptography are based on the use of mathematical problems that are hard to solve. The RSA algorithm[1] is based on the problem
of factoring the product of two very large prime numbers, which is difficult
and takes a long time. Cryptographic algorithms like the *Digital Signature Algorithm* (DSA) are based on other difficult mathematical problems,
such as the discreet logarithm problem.[2]

As we saw in Chapter 2, these problems are hard to solve—but not impossible. Given enough time and processing power, any cryptographic key or

Figure 4-8

Browser loading certificate to key store

algorithm is at risk. The aim is to choose problems and key sizes in which the amount of time taken to break the key, given current cryptanalytic attacks and projected processing power (discussed in Chapter 2), is far too long for practical purposes. If the information you are trying to protect is only valuable for the next ten years, and the cryptographic algorithm you choose is RSA with a 760-bit key, the currently projected time to break it is 600 months (50 years). This increases to 3 million years when the length of the key is increased to 1024 bits.[3]

Given that you can choose crypto algorithms and keys sizes that will be secure for the expected sensitive life of your information, why would you ever need to think about replacing your symmetric key or public/private key pair?

Unfortunately, mathematical attacks are not the only way to subvert a cryptographic security scheme. Keys may be discovered due to errors in poor software implementations, analysis of hardware key storage, lack of

Figure 4-9

Browser loads certificate to key store

diligence by the key owner when protecting access to the key, social engineering, or any number of other means. Occasionally, new methods of cryptanalytic attack are discovered that dramatically decrease the time taken to uncover a key, or special cases are found that expose weaknesses in a cryptographic algorithm.[4,5]

NOTE:

Depending on the hardware implementation, the sophistication of attacks may vary. It may be as simple as placing a chip analyzer on a device with exposed memory leads or may involve more sophisticated techniques, such as a setup to perform differential power analysis or the use of electron microscopes.

As a result, good security practice recommends that you periodically go through the process of re-keying or generating new keys for use in future operations. This is one reason for providing validity periods on digital certificates, since expiration of the certificate will usually be associated with generating a new key. It is also possible to use X.509 certificates to specify an independent key expiration period. This allows for special cases, allowing verification of signatures after the certificate has expired or limiting a private key used to generate a signature to a subset of the certificate's validity period.

Certificate Revocation

When you have carefully planned for expected key rollover by selecting a safe validity period for the certificate and key, are you done? Not quite.

No matter how carefully you plan, other reasons for invalidating keys still exist and are unpredictable. At some point, a social engineering attack or a software implementation problem will lead to a key compromise when it is least expected. Alternatively, the owner of the certificate may leave the company that issued the certificate. As the identity issued to the user linked him to the company, the identity must be invalidated.

To deal with events like key compromise, there must be some way of advising the CA that the user's private key has been compromised. The CA may be notified by the owner of the key or as a result of some administrative function. If issuance of certificates is linked to a user management system, deletion of the user record should result in a certificate revocation notification. The CA must then take action to revoke or invalidate the use of the certificate and advise users of the certificate that it can no longer be considered to represent a trusted identity.

NOTE:
Consistent with our definition, "users of the certificate" refers to the relying parties or certificate users. It would be valuable for the certificate owner or subscriber to be notified of the revocation as well, just in case they were not aware of the actions taken by an administrator.

The mechanism the CA uses to publish the changed certificate status in most cases is a list of revoked certificates. This *Certificate Revocation List* (CRL) contains the serial numbers of certificates that have been revoked along with the date of revocation and a status identifying the reason for the revocation. Figure 4-10 shows a graphical representation of a CRL.

Figure 4-10

Certificate revocation list block diagram

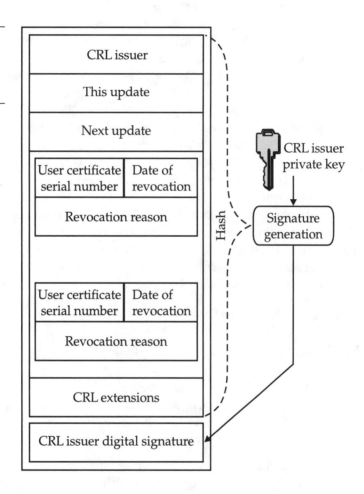

The CRL is signed by the private key of a trusted revocation service to ensure that the list can't be modified. Removal of entries that have been revoked would allow the revocation process to be circumvented, while addition of entries for certificates that have not been revoked would allow denial-of-service attacks by invalidating certificates that should still be in service. The CRL also identifies the date on which it was published and when the next later release can be expected, to ensure that the freshest CRL is used.

The CRL is generally published to a directory that can be referenced during certificate validation. The certificate user downloads the CRL from the directory as part of the process of certificate validation and searches the list for the serial number of the certificate being validated.

The period for publication of a CRL is determined by the CA. The publication interval may be on the order of a day or a week depending on the policy defined in the *Certification Practices Statement* (CPS). The frequency of CRL update has a direct bearing on the level of confidence the user of a certificate can place in it. If a CRL has just been issued and moments later a certificate is revoked, considerable delay may be experienced before the revocation status can be conveyed to the system. Note that the revocation period is determined by the CA, not by the user of the certificate and the policy she operates under.

The certificate validator may need more up-to-date information than a particular CA provides. If certificates from multiple CAs are used, the variation in CRL publication intervals may be a concern. In addition, locating the directory where the CRL is stored, loading the CRL, and then processing the contents can require considerable effort. As an alternative, an online protocol may be used to obtain more up-to-date information directly from the CA. These and other issues are examined in Chapter 5.

Certificate Validation

Certificate validation is the process of determining that the certificate can validly be used at some point in time and that it is fit for the purpose the user intends. To achieve this, it is necessary to validate multiple aspects of the certificates encountered.

- The certificate must contain a cryptographically valid signature establishing that the contents of the certificate have not changed.
- The public key of the issuer must be used to verify the signature on the certificate.
- The validity period specified by the beginning and ending dates must show that the certificate is current.
- The certificate may contain fields that are marked as critical or noncritical. All fields marked as critical must be understood by the certificate validator certificate if the certificate is to be considered valid.

NOTE:

The issuing certification authority marks fields as critical indicating that the presence and content of the fields must be understood by the certificate user before the certificate can be correctly interpreted.

- The certificate may only be used for the purpose for which it was originally created. For example, keys and certificates that are marked for use only in signing applications may not be used for encryption operations.
- Other policy constraints that specify usage conditions must be observed.
- Finally, the certificate must not have been revoked. Even with all of the information internal to the certificate indicating that the certificate is valid, you must check to see if some exceptional external event has occurred that requires the certificate to be invalidated. So revocation checking must be performed, using a certificate revocation list or some form of online verification check.

Certification Paths

In a more perfect world, a single certification authority could be established that would issue all certificates. However, the world is a very imperfect place, and as a result, many certification authorities are needed. A particular application domain may have special needs, an industry segment may require unique security provisions, or a distinct entity such as a government may need to exercise direct control over the identities issued and the mechanism used.

Often the reasons have as much to do with organizational politics or differing timeframes for deployment and functionality from one business unit to another. Within a single enterprise, there will often be separate departments with different needs or just a desire to exercise individuality. In addition, natural dynamic business processes will make even the best-planned, most centralized deployment of a PKI look like an Introduction to Chaos Theory.[6]

Mergers, acquisitions, and divestitures within business and its community will result in many different PKIs and certificate issuers being brought together within an organization; somehow they need to be integrated together.

From a deployment perspective, a single large CA may not be a reasonable option either. Managing very large user populations for all of their PKI life cycle needs may strain the administrative capacity of some CAs. The problem of establishing relationships with all prospective subscribers in a very large population makes it difficult to validate identities and issue certificates that will be acceptable to all certificate users. In fact, the more distributed a CA and the closer it is to the actual users it is identifying, the better. Further, problems of revocation processing and disaster recovery tend to lead down a path requiring you to partition the user and certificate space.

For example, some of the most sensitive public/private key pairs within a PKI are those used by a CA to sign the certificates it issues. For this reason, the private keys for the certificate server are usually kept in a secure storage location, preferably a tamper-proof hardware encryption store. If the private key used for the signature operation is compromised in some way or if the process of issuing certificates is subverted, the CA and the certificates it issued are suspect. Once this trust has been broken, it must be restored and any collateral damage associated with the abuse of the trusted identities minimized.

Minimally, this would require generating a new public/private key pair for the CA to use when issuing future certificates. In addition, all certificates issued during the period in which the CA was compromised would need to be revoked and the users run through the registration process once again. For a population of hundreds of thousands or millions of users, this is a daunting task. If the possible user and certificate space is partitioned and assigned to separate CAs, compromise of one CA will not normally affect user certificates issued by another CA. This environment is illustrated in Figure 4-11.

Finally, the general trend for most technologies is that large centralized homogeneous deployment efforts almost always fail. This has been true for networks, directories, application servers, databases, and so on. The X.500 directory standard that spawned the original X.509 specification was originally designed to allow for global networks of immense size. Today very few organizations use a full-blown X.500 solution due to its overhead and complexity. Instead, much simpler LDAP-based directories are being deployed with much more modest naming and information management goals.

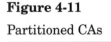

Figure 4-11

Partitioned CAs

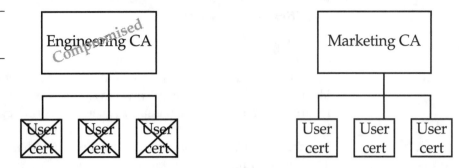

NOTE:

Of course, some X.500-like features that allowed for scaling are making their way back into LDAP.

As a result, rather than one large corporate directory, you have many smaller directories that were purchased to resolve the specific needs of various parts of the organization and applications. This is not necessarily a good thing as someone now has to manage all of this complexity and its attendant costs when interoperability becomes an issue, but that gives the next generation of technology a chance to solve some of the problems.

It is reasonable to expect that PKI will develop along similar lines. Although some companies and organizations may be successful in deploying a homogeneous CA, the vast majority will not. A model that allows for multiple CAs to be deployed at different times is required. The challenge is to plan for a flexible deployment structure, yet allow convergence and integration into a common infrastructure.

The problem that emerges when multiple CAs issue certificates is that each CA must somehow be trusted by the certificate users. This becomes a problem when an e-mail user needs to verify signatures from many different enterprises, each of which issues its own certificates. In order to ease the burden on the certificate users from having to retain knowledge of trust of a large number of disparate CAs, there needs to be some way to build trusted relationships between CAs. Chapter 8 examines this question of building trust models in more detail, but for the moment, let's consider one way you can deal with this problem.

Certificate Hierarchies

Not only can CAs certify entities such as users and network routers, they can also certify the identity of another CA.

In this model, a CA you trust will attest to the validity of another CAs identity. This is much the same process that is used when a highly trusted identity mechanism like a passport is used as a primary identity to establish other identities like drivers' licenses or credit cards. As a result, some identities and CAs are considered subordinate to other identities and CAs. The resultant hierarchy is shown in Figure 4-12. In a large-scale environment, it is likely that some CAs will have the sole task of identifying other CAs.

Figure 4-12

CA hierarchy

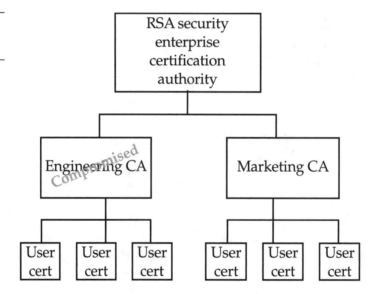

What does this model look like when it comes time for an application to validate a certificate?

In the example provided in Figure 4-13, you have been issued a certificate by the Engineering CA. The name of the CA is specified in the issuer name field of the user certificate, and the signature is generated using the private key of the Engineering CA. However, before an application can validate the CA signature, you need to obtain the public key of the Engineering CA. This public key is used to verify the signature on your certificate.

Figure 4-13

Certificate chain

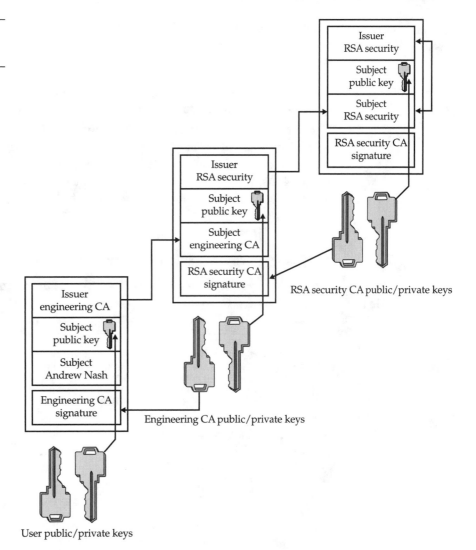

RSA security CA public/private keys

Engineering CA public/private keys

User public/private keys

The Engineering CA that issued your certificate is in turn certified by a higher-level Corporate CA. When you look in the issuer field of the Engineering CA certificate, you find the issuer name is the Corporate CA. Continuing in the same process, you locate the Corporate CAs certificate. The Corporate CA provides the public key you need to validate the signature on the Engineering CAs certificate.

How is this processing terminated? In the last case, when you examine the name of the issuer for the Corporate CA certificate, you find it is the same as the subject name of the CA. This is known as a self-signed or root certificate.

The series of certificates you have followed is a certificate chain or certification path. Most PKI users today are familiar with this trust model. The set of root certificates that are already trusted are stored in a list within an application such as a Web browser. An example of the list of trusted root certificates from Microsoft Internet Explorer is shown in Figure 4-14. As we will see later, the hierarchical model you have just seen is a special case of more general trust models.

Figure 4-14

Web browser
trusted root list

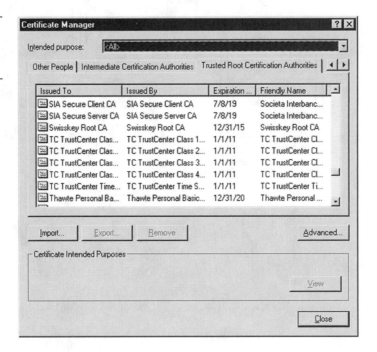

Note that all of the validation logic we discussed earlier, including date processing, revocation checking, and signature validation, still has to be executed for each of the certificates in the chain.

Types of Keys

The application and suitability of a public/private key pair to a particular cryptographic technique will depend on several attributes associated with a particular key.

The first is the type of cryptographic algorithm the keys were constructed to support. For example, the RSA algorithm can be used for both signing and encryption operations, while DSA[2] is limited to generating signatures.

The lifetime of the data that needs to be protected will determine the size of the key. In general, the longer the key, the more secure it is, and the longer the encrypted data can be considered safe. This topic was considered in Chapter 2 when we considered the impact of key length on encryption strength.

The need to have a third party recover or access a key (or not) will determine the processes used to generate and archive the key.

The time period for which a key pair and/or certificate are considered valid will depend on the type of key and the operations that will be performed. Some operations may be performed using different parts of a key pair after expiration of the certificate.

The sensitivity of the information protected or other legal or procedural requirements will determine how secure the storage of the private key must be. All of these factors will be determined by the intended use of the key. These constraints on how keys and certificates are used are defined by various certificate extensions.

In order to provide a consistent way for all users of the key, and the PKI itself, to know what services or procedures are valid to use during the life cycle of the key, the certificate contains an attribute known as *KeyUsage* that defines how the key is intended to be used. We will look at this field and its meaning in more detail later, but for the moment there are two major types of key usage that are worth considering.

NOTE:

Additional attributes describing the treatment of some types of keys include the extended key usage *and the* private key usage *period.*

Encryption Keys

X.509 refers to these as *encypherment keys* and explicitly calls out a distinction between *key encypherment* for key transport or key exchange, and *data encypherment* for encryption of general user data.

NOTE:

As we saw in Chapter 2, bulk data encryption is generally performed using a symmetric key that is wrapped using a public encypherment key.

To recap the use of public/private keys for encryption purposes, the public key of the recipient or holder of the information is used to encrypt the data. The private key is used for decryption purposes.

When encrypting data there may be a need to provide an emergency exit so that data can be recovered if the decryption key is lost or destroyed. Within an organization, if the holder of the keys leaves, dies, or is otherwise unavailable and authorized users need to get access to the protected information, some form of data recovery process needs to be implemented.

This is a highly controversial area, as the existence of an emergency exit conflicts with the need to ensure continued privacy for the information. If there is a back door, emergency exit, or recovery process, how is it protected? Who has access to it? Under what conditions will it be activated, and what guarantees do the users have that guidelines established in this area will be followed?

NOTE:

The U.S. government requirements for a key escrow system that would require a third party to hold the keys definitely helped fuel the furor associated with this area and has raised the general sensitivity of PKI implementors for the support of key escrow features. The U.S. government has since dropped this requirement, much to the relief of everyone.

Particularly when it comes to privacy of personal information, people have legitimate reason to be sensitive and concerned. However, for protection of information owned by an enterprise, good business practice requires provision of a data recovery service. This is discussed further in Chapter 5 when we look at key archival and recovery.

What operations can you perform with a public/private key pair when the corresponding certificate has expired?

In this situation, the public key should not be used for encryption. In this case, the certificate expiration period limits the useful encryption life of the public key. However, for decryption operations, the private key is required. The private key is held directly by the key pair owner, and its use is not constrained by the certificate or validity period. The private key holder can continue to decrypt information long after the certificate has expired.

Digital Signature Keys

X.509 identifies several different types of signatures that may be generated. The one we will consider here is the use of signatures by users to protect the contents of their own documents.

To recap the process of generating a digital signature:

1. A cryptographic hash is first created over the information that is to be protected by the signature.
2. The private key owned by the individual or entity that is performing the signing operation is used to encrypt the hash value.

When signature verification is being performed:

1. The cryptographic hash is recalculated.
2. The public key is used to decrypt the signed hash and the two hash values are compared.

Digital signatures are used in many situations with different needs and goals. However, if you are striving for some form of non-repudiation (this may be technical rather than legal non-repudiation), you must have confidence that the owner of the certificate is the only one who can access the private key used to generate the signature.

Almost all PKI usage models proscribe the use of any form of key archival or recovery scheme for digital signature keys. If multiple copies of the signing key exist, it is not possible to support the requirements for non-repudiation of signed documents we discussed in Chapter 1.

What happens, then, if the private key used for signing is lost?

Obviously, digital signatures can no longer be created with that key pair. Provided the certificate and the public key it includes are still available, signature verification can continue. A new signing key pair and certificate can be issued and used for signature generation and verification from that point on.

NOTE:

This does raise policy issues for the PKI about when the certificate may be deleted from public repositories. Expiration of the certificate may not reasonably exclude the use of the public key to verify the signature some time later.

Validation of signatures and the life cycle for corresponding certificates have some special considerations. These are supported by additional extensions within the certificate.

The valid life of a document containing a digital signature may be much longer than the validity period of a certificate. As a result, there may be a need to use an expired certificate to verify a signature on a document. In this case, the check on the validity period for the certificate should take into account the time when the signature was created.

Alternatively, a certificate may specify a private key usage extension that limits the period for which signatures may be generated to a much smaller interval than the validity period for the certificate. Potentially, you may have a certificate with a very long lifetime to ensure it is still valid while signature verification is required, but which will limit the time a signature can be generated, based on the private key lifetime.

Certificate Distribution

Security services involving the use of the public key cryptography require access to the certificate that links the public/private key pair to the user's identity.

In the case of certificate use by e-mail, a public key is used to verify the signature of the sender or to encrypt e-mail being sent to another user. For signature verification, the receiver of the e-mail must have access to the sender's certificate. Encrypting e-mail also requires that sender to have access to the receiver's certificate. The solution to the problem of how to obtain that certificate differs between security services.

Certificate Distributed Within the Protocol

A certificate may be provided as part of the protocol exchange used to implement a cryptographic service.

Electronic Mail   When signing e-mail implemented using the S/MIME protocol, the certificate and public key corresponding to the signer's private key are sent with the e-mail message. In addition, the rest of the certificates in the certification path may also be sent. In this case, all of the components necessary to validate the certificates in the chain (other than revocation checking) are present.

Client-Side SSL Authentication   Client-side authentication in the *Secure Socket Layer* (SSL) protocol is a similar case. (A more detailed description of the various aspects of SSL may be found in Chapter 7.) The client certificate is sent by a browser or other client application through the protocol when prompted by the SSL server. The SSL implementation requires that the server have access to any intermediate certificates in the chain, up to and including the root, to allow the client certificate to be validated. The server must obtain the CA certificates in some other fashion in this case.

Certificate Distribution Using a Repository

Access to very large sets of certificates, as when communicating with a collection of users or authenticating a single user out of a potentially large database of user accounts, requires a more scaleable solution than "in-band" transmission of certificates.

Electronic Mail   In order to encrypt a mail message to be sent to one or more recipients, the certificates containing the public keys of each recipient must first be obtained. The public keys are required in order to encrypt the message, and the certificate provides the identity of the owner of the keys.

You need to verify that the public key used for the recipient has been correctly attested to. This ensures that you are encrypting the message for the expected individual. If you cannot be confident of the identity of the recipient (the public key may belong to an attacker), you do not know if you are ensuring the privacy of the transmission.

In the case where the mail is sent to a distribution list, each of the recipients will possess a different public/private key pair and a unique certificate. If you are sending the message to one or two well-known recipients with whom you deal regularly, the certificate for each user is probably found in the local address list of the e-mail client.

How did you obtain those certificates? The original certificates may have been sent to you in the body of an e-mail message explicitly used to distribute them. More likely, the certificates were sent to you as part of a digital signature process when those individuals sent you a signed e-mail message, as described previously.

NOTE:

This process may not work correctly in a dual key system where a separate signing and encryption public/private key pair is created. In this case, the key usage indicator in the certificate will normally dictate that the keys used for signing are not available for encryption purposes. Implementations that store a public key and certificate marked for signing only and then use them for encryption purposes are incorrect. At least one popular e-mail client was incorrectly coded—it allowed for simple deployment of a set of certificates, but did not comply with the rules for certificate usage.

Each certificate is stored in the address book in an entry corresponding to the certificate owner. Over time, a set of certificates for the users you regularly correspond with is established.

What happens when you need to communicate with a very large set of recipients, or you need to encrypt e-mail for someone with whom you have not previously communicated?

A more general solution involves the use of a shared repository or directory where certificates associated with an e-mail recipient can be found. This is usually an LDAP directory, tied back to the address book for an e-mail client. Each user entry in the address book is linked back to the LDAP directory entry corresponding to the user. At the time of writing, this process turns out to be much more difficult in most e-mail clients than should be expected. The steps taken to configure most e-mail applications to provide this support are torturous and bewildering.

Server-Side SSL Authentication   Let's consider SSL as an example again. When validating the certificate presented by a Web server during server-side SSL authentication, the CA certificates needed to complete validation of the certificate chain could be found in a certificate repository. The browser could use a directory to look up the CA certificates. However, this is a special case, as individual users may trust different sets of root certificates.

Two different solutions are commonly employed to solve this problem. The browser can contain a local list of trusted CA. This list of trusted CA certificates, particularly the root certificates, must be protected; otherwise, the trust model could be invalidated by surreptitiously substituting an untrusted root certificate. The browsers prompt the user to verify that any root certificate that is added can be trusted. For an individual user, this model works well. However, for an enterprise, leaving decisions that extend the trust model for the enterprise up to individual users is not a satisfactory solution.

A better solution in an enterprise context is to provide a centrally managed list of trusted issuers. This list must be authenticated, possibly by having it signed by a secure server designated for this task. The list itself must be dynamic, so that it is possible to remove trusted issuers in a timely fashion. Access to the list may be provided by pushing it down to the client application. Alternatively, the trusted issuer list may be placed in a directory and accessed directly by the application. This is one of the solutions provided as part of the Windows 2000 desktop in conjunction with Active Directory. The signer in this case is Microsoft itself.

Fundamental Requirements

The foundation of PKI rests on two concepts. The first is that there is some trusted entity that can create an identity that is verifiable and linked to a publicly shareable key. We have spent time in this chapter introducing this first concept. The second concept is that there exists some private key that can be confidently assumed to be in the possession of *only* the user whose identity is being asserted by the digital certificate. This concept of no more than one copy of a private key is referred to as the *singularity* of the key.

The reason that privacy of the private key is so important is that users of a certificate must be able to prove that you are the correct holder of the identity. The certificate is a public structure, potentially freely and widely available in public directories, and anyone could pick it up and present it. Proving possession of a private key becomes a critical part of establishing the identity with a certificate.

At the time the certificate is used, the presenter is challenged to show that she has the private key corresponding to the certificate. The verifier encrypts a random piece of information, called a *challenge*, with the public key and passes the encrypted challenge to the certificate owner. The presenter of the certificate decrypts the challenge and returns it to prove she has the private key.

NOTE:

This process is more difficult to implement in practice than it looks. Practical implementations have to take into account attacks like "man in the middle." See the description of SSL in Chapter 7 for an example of implementation.

Guaranteeing the security and singularity of the private key requires considerable effort. If it is possible that more than one user has a copy of the private key, the validity of the system is called into question. If the key is shared by design or accident (due to poor software implementation or procedures), the value of a security service such as authentication or a digital signature becomes suspect.

For example, if the signer of a document can reasonably claim that another person had access to the private key, she may be able to deny (or *repudiate*) having signed the contract. In another example, you may be using unique identities to control access to a Web site that uses a business model based on subscription or pay-per-view access to information or services. If your customers can replicate their identities and share them with their friends, it becomes much more difficult to control your service.

To provide acceptable guarantees of the uniqueness of the private key, all phases of the life cycle of the private key and its handling are important; some of these, such as key recovery, have already been introduced. Aspects of private key usage that are critical are the *storage location* and *protection* of the private keys, and the way in which a user *validates* his identity in order to get access to the key store.

Protection of Private Keys

In current implementations of PKI, most users' experiences are determined by the applications they use. The first time most users will encounter public keys and certificates is when they use their favorite Web browser to contact a Web site protected using SSL and a server-side certificate.

In fact, much of the experience that end users have with PKI is determined by the effectiveness with which Web and e-mail applications have integrated with PKI. The acceptance of PKI as a solution will largely be determined by the degree to which these applications allow PKI to be transparent to their users.

Application Key Stores

For most users, the next step in the use of PKI-enabled features will be using personal certificates to sign e-mail or to identify themselves during client-side authentication when connecting to a Web site. In either case, the registration process to obtain these personal certificates will often involve the use of a Web browser to interact with a Web-based interface to the RA. We looked at an example of this kind of interface in the "Certificate Issuance" section earlier in the chapter.

In the example, the Web browser generated the key pair and then stored the keys and the corresponding certificate in the browsers' application key store. Key stores may occasionally be shared between applications, at least in the case where the applications come from the same vendor. Netscape browsers and e-mail clients share the same key store. Microsoft applications share key stores that are located in the user profile in the Windows Registry.

This raises a problem. If some of your applications have different key stores, but you want to use a digital signature in each of them, you would like to be identified as the same user in each case.

NOTE:

This would be true where you want to sign your e-mail messages as well as provide a signature to authorize an activity controlled by a workflow application or sign a document controlled by a content management system.

This means that the same identity needs to be used by each application. Generally, the same certificate issued by the same CA needs to be used to establish your identity. (Other solutions would allow an identity to be mapped between issuers. We will consider some of the trust models that would allow for that in Chapter 8.) In order to have the same identity, you must also be able to use the same private key to generate signatures.

NOTE:

This is self-evident given that the certificate issued to you contains not only an identifying name but also your public key. If your certificate has been obtained from a public repository or has been cached from earlier usage, the corresponding private key must be used.

An alternate example is using two different Web browsers to perform client-side authentication when accessing a protected Web site. Both browsers must be able to access the same key and certificate. If you want to use different e-mail applications to decrypt e-mail sent to you, you are faced with the same problem.

This problem becomes much more complex if you switch between different computers at work as you move between facilities or when you work from home. Many of us have three different systems we use regularly: the one at work, the laptop used while traveling, and the system at home. You need to have the same identity at different locations, using the same application or a different application. Many of the key stores currently implemented are not only inaccessible to different applications on the same machine, but cannot be accessed by the same application used on multiple systems.

NOTE:

Use of facilities like Internet kiosks at airports present another interesting challenge, as you certainly want your keys and certificates accessible to work with private information, but you do not want them to remain at the workstation when you leave, as this may expose your private key.

Key and Certificate Interchange

The solution usually implemented is to allow an export and import of a user's private key and corresponding certificate. In order to protect the keys while they are transported, a secure mechanism must be used that is understood and accepted by most PKI applications.

The secure interchange format normally used is defined in a standard issued by RSA Labs known as PKCS #12[7]. This interchange format is generally accepted by most PKI applications. Your private key and certificate are extracted into a software container that is usually protected by a symmetric encrypting key derived from a user password.[8]

The PKCS #12 package is usually transported as a file. So now you can take advantage of this mechanism to import your private key and certificate into different applications and share them between computers you use.

PKCS #12 certainly provides an opportunity to manually synchronize keys, but practically it has a few problems. There is no way to ensure that the keys are updated in all of the locations in which they were stored when a certificate replacement event occurs, which happens at least once every year in most PKI deployments. You run the real risk that some of your certificates will not be the same, and your identity will not be consistent. In this case, the warning you will receive is a usually cryptic message indicating you have no access to a Web site or can't decrypt e-mail. The whole process of doing an export and import is somewhat clunky.

The other problems are actually much more fundamental and, depending on your environment, potentially debilitating. The ease-of-use features that allow keys to be copied between applications also open up the possibility that a user could replicate as many copies of the key as she wants and hand them out to her friends. This devalues the use of PKI as an authentication scheme as now multiple people share the private key, and you can no longer count on singularity as a way to ensure an identity.

Even if a user is not sharing her largesse by allowing her friends to access your subscription service, there is another risk. The passwords used to protect the PKCS #12 packet are not controlled by any central policy in many of the implementations. As a result, poor selection of user passwords means that the keys within the PKCS #12 file may be at risk. This becomes more important if PKCS #12 files are not automatically cleaned up after use. Potentially, every system she moves to will end up with a set of user keys that could be targeted by an attacker.

These risks to the security of the private key and its singularity mean that the non-repudiation aspects of operations based on a PKI may be completely annulled.

In many applications, the key stores are accessed via a standard interface that allows the key store to be replaced. For Microsoft applications, this will normally be Crypto API (see Figure 4-15). For other applications, such as Netscape, this will normally be PKCS #11.

The reason for allowing key stores to be replaced is to allow a key store with different capabilities to be selected. Key store capabilities that might be selected include roaming user support or stronger key protection. A typical need for a stronger key store is a requirement for high levels of non-repudiation or protection of the user's private key. As an example, users of the *Identrus Certification Authority* (ICA) service in the financial industry are required to store their private key on a cryptographic storage device such as a smart card. The smart card affords significant tamper-resistant features that meet requirements for strong key protection.

Figure 4-15

Standard credential store APIs

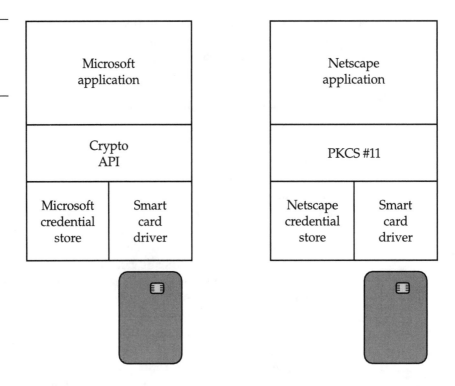

NOTE:

Smart cards have had a number of deployment problems, including cost and standardization, that have inhibited their deployment until recently. Many of these problems have been solved. However, cost of deployment may still be an issue, especially if the value of information being pro- tected does not warrant the investment in a high-end smart card. A num- ber of vendors have implemented software analogs of smart cards, which have similar characteristics but do not have the same level of tamper resistance. A new working group has recently been formed in the IETF looking at standardizing software smart cards.

Smart Card Key Stores

A cryptographic smart card such as an RSA card has a separate crypto- graphic processor with its own on-card secure memory. Cryptographic operations such as key generation or digital signatures are performed directly on the smart card. The private key is used directly on the card by the cryptographic processor on the smart card. The private key cannot be copied from the card, so it is not exposed on a user's computer nor can it be copied to another system. The card is transportable, so it supports the needs of users to carry their credentials or keys and certificates securely with them to different computers.

Provided all applications can share access to the card, only a single copy of the smart card is required. This eliminates the need to copy keys, as well as the problem of providing consistent updates, as there is only one copy to update when a certificate expires. Tamper-resistant features on the cards prevent an attacker from reading or modifying the contents of the card. (This topic is discussed in more detail in Chapter 9.)

Other reasons exist for the use of smart cards. Generation of the public/private key pair has been a problem in a number of applications due to issues related to the procedures used to generate keys. In many cases, these problems have been caused by the way in which a pseudo random number generator was implemented. Smart cards are often delivered complete with pre-generated keys and certificates and as a result are not subject to the vagaries of different application implementations. Alternatively, smart cards may provide facilities to allow creation of the keys onboard the card when a certificate registration request is made. In the latter case, the public key is then delivered up from the card to be sent to the RA, while the private key remains in secure storage.

This may have implications for a key recovery system. If the private key cannot be retrieved from the card, it must be archived before it is written onto the card. This means that onboard key generation may only be suitable for signature keys where key recovery is not required.

NOTE:

Pseudo random number generators are not true generators of random numbers. They are usually implemented in software, and will generate the same "random numbers" if the same original conditions are used each time. However, provided the set of inputs to the algorithm are varied sufficiently, the output approximates truly random numbers.

Virtual Smart Cards

Due to problems with the cost of smart cards or the overhead of installing smart card reader hardware on a large number of desktops, some vendors have implemented a software or virtual smart card solution. A virtual smart card emulates the operation of a physical smart card by supporting standard credential store interfaces used by applications. It may be used to share access to keys between applications. Some implementations support roaming users by allowing the virtual smart card to be downloaded over a secure channel from a secure server to a desktop computer.

The keys and certificates used within a virtual smart card are generally stored in an encrypted software container. This container will be accessed on the user's desktop by PKI-enabled applications using standard interfaces. The container itself may be permanently stored on the desktop, or if it provides support for roaming access, may be downloaded from a server.

Smart cards' high-security features such as tamper resistance and on-card execution of cryptographic algorithms are lost using this solution. However, provided sufficient attention is paid to such requirements as protecting the encrypting keys within the store and ensuring that the store is not left exposed to attack, a virtual smart card may provide a solution that meets security requirements for protection of less sensitive information.

This solution is certainly much cheaper and simpler to deploy than physical smart cards. Provided the safeguards provided are sufficient for the value of the information being protected, virtual smart cards may be a reasonable solution.

Deploying PKI Services

A number of different solutions exist for deployment of a public key infrastructure. These include

- Public CA services
- In-house enterprise CAs
- Outsourced enterprise CAs

Each of these solutions has advantages and fits different requirements. The cost of management of these solutions vary considerably; Chapter 11 examines the issues of cost of ownership.

Public Certification Authority Services

A public issuing service is a Certification Authority that is used to issue certificates to the general population independent of enterprise or other organizational boundaries. The certificates are targeted at supplying identities in a public environment. This is analogous to using a public power-generating utility shared by the population at large rather than building your own power-generating plant as part of your organization's infrastructure.

CAs have been created by private enterprises or government agencies to supply certificates to the population at large, for identities that can be used when transacting business across the Internet or when interacting with government agencies.

Certificate Classes

In many ways, the provision of identification to the great unwashed mass of Internet users is the most difficult identification problem. When establishing an identity within an organization, local proofs such as knowledge of a user by her manager are much easier to rely on. The effort invested in verifying the identity of a user is a sliding scale that is directly proportional to the confidence that users will be able to place in the certificates issued.

For example, some user certificates are issued for use in conjunction with e-mail applications. The information that is required by most public CAs to validate the user's identity before issuing this certificate is the e-mail address of the user. The certificate is returned via e-mail to the address specified in the request. Provided the holder of the private key receives the mail containing the certificate, the identification loop is closed and the identity is considered verified. This is the absolute minimum form of proof of identity. As a result, this certificate will also provide the absolute minimum level of confidence in the identity.

If you receive a signed e-mail message guaranteeing a multimillion dollar order, how willing will you be to accept this e-mail as proof? How much effort went into verifying the user's identity as defined in the certificate used to verify the digital signature? Did the user only have to supply an e-mail address, or was there some more significant form of identity verification procedure?

This leads to the concept of defining specific classes of certificates for use by particular applications or under specific business rules. The policy document that describes the class of certificate that may be used and when it may be used is specified for the certificate user in the *Certificate Policy* (CP).

The CP is owned by those responsible for security decisions made within applications that *use* certificates. This differentiates it from the CPS, which is owned by those responsible for the security and operation of the CA (the place that *generates* the certificates).

The requirements for identity verification for a specific class of certificate are specified in the CPS for the CA. If you need to know whether a particular CA and the class of certificates it issues comply with the user's CP, you can check the relevant CPS. If a CPS does not exist for the CA you are dealing with, this may be a reason to limit your trust in the identities it issues.

X.509[9] and the IETF[10] specifications dealing with PKI both include support for policy identifiers in the certificate that allows some basic mechanical policy verification when the certificate is used.

There is no global standard defining certificate classes. However, there are many usage domains such as the United States or Canadian governments or vertical markets such as financial institutions that specify their own certificate classes and policies. This is examined in more detail in Chapter 8 when we examine trust models.

Value Provided

A benefit provided by public CAs is that the root certificate they use has been published in widely used PKI applications, including popular Web browsers and e-mail clients. This is not strictly an artifact of using a public certification authority. The browser vendors were convinced that shipping the root certificates with the browser was a good start on interoperability and sharing trust. Mechanisms do exist to allow an enterprise to include its own root certificate in browsers such as those supplied by Microsoft.

E-Mail Certificates

E-mail certificates have already been discussed earlier. They include the user's e-mail address and are used to verify that the signer of the e-mail has a certificate that corresponds to the sender's e-mail address.

Server-Side SSL Certificates

The most widely deployed form of certificate is the SSL server certificate, used to identify a Web server when a browser user connects to it. The server certificate can be used for any server that allows an SSL connection. The mechanisms for SSL are discussed further in Chapter 7. The browser will receive the server certificate and validate the certificate chain. If the root certificate in the chain has been provided by a public CA and it is stored in the browser's trusted signer list, the certificate chain can be successfully validated. The user has a reasonable level of assurance, based on the trust associated with the public issuer, that they are talking to the Web server representing the enterprise with which they intended to do business.

This form of certificate normally requires that additional information be supplied to the Certification Authority in order to establish trust in the association between a server certificate and the firm that owns it. This information might include supporting documentation on company letterhead, verification of the existence of the firm, and confirmation that the request originated with duly authorized officials within the firm.

The fundamental value derived from the use of these certificates is to allow the browser user to have confidence in the identity of the Web server.

Client-Side SSL Certificates

Most use of SSL has left authentication of the user to some password-based scheme such as a bank account number and PIN. To avoid problems associated with password-based systems, two-factor authentication devices like the RSA Security SecurID tokens have been used to establish user identities with greater confidence for higher value transactions.

The use of certificates to establish the identity of a user in an SSL session has been implemented much more slowly than server-side SSL. Client-side certificates provided by a public CA have the potential advantage of allowing a user to obtain a single identity that could be used across multiple enterprise Web servers for e-business transactions. Provided a large enough set of enterprises accepts a user identity of this type, this could become a significant method for identifying users.

Code Signing Certificates

In addition to establishing the identity of users and servers, there is a growing need to establish trust in the application code that is being run. As more applications are downloaded in the form of Java applets, browser plug-ins, ActiveX controls, and so on, there is a greater requirement to ensure that the code came from a trusted application provider. Using PKI, this can be achieved by signing the application code container and shipping it with a certificate that attests to the authenticity and source of the code.

CA Certificates

As you will see in the next section, a disadvantage of in-house enterprise CAs is that the certificate chains they issue are not signed by a root CA that is automatically recognized by PKI-aware applications. One solution to this problem is for a public CA to include the in-house CAs within an enterprise under its own certificate hierarchy. To achieve this, the highest-level CA in the organization is issued a certificate by the public CA.

This has ramifications about the type of trust that a public CA is perceived to impute to an organizational CA. Although a few of these services have been offered, most public CAs are unwilling to actually perform this service. Apart from issues of trust and management, a public CA can usually obtain a higher revenue stream by selling certificates directly.

In-House Enterprise Certification Authorities

An in-house certification authority is created to provide certificates for use by an organization. An organization's users may include members or employees and may be extended to partners, suppliers, or customers. All the operational procedures, security, and life cycle management are fully maintained by the organization.

Value Provided

As PKI is concerned foremost with creating identities that are used as the basis of other layered security services, many enterprises want to keep direct control of all aspects of issuing these identities. Greater flexibility is available to tailor certificate types and to issue policies that meet specific organizational needs, including use of certificate fields that have specific meaning to the systems used within the organization. The cost of running an in-house CA may prove to be lower than a corresponding service offering, especially over longer periods.

In-house CAs also allow tighter integration with the other systems that are deployed within an organization. This allows processes such as user registration to be hidden from the user and integrated with HR systems, or certificate renewal to be integrated with desktop applications.

Issues

The work to establish a general purpose CA for the whole organization requires significant planning, staffing, and deployment. Issues such as the structure of the trust model (single CA, chained departmental CAs), the policies used to issue various classes of certificates, the security of the environment in which the CA runs, and support for life cycle management are considered more fully in Chapter 10 on CA deployment.

Outsourced Enterprise CAs

Parts of the PKI may be outsourced, such as the RA, the CS, or the *Key Recovery Server* (KRS). Unlike the public CA, the outsourced enterprise CA is dedicated to the delivery of certificates for that enterprise. Depending on the supplier of the service, different combinations of outsourced or resident components may be used. The service provider will take responsibility for certain parts of the certificate life cycle process.

Depending on the options offered by the provider, you might establish an independent certificate hierarchy or become a part of the service provider's certificate hierarchy. Different certificate hierarchies may have different implications for the trust they provide or requirements that will be placed on the enterprise.

Components Outsourced

A typical managed certificate service will maintain the server used to issue the certificates at its own facility. This provides security controls for access to the CA, tamper-resistant hardware storage for certificate signing keys, and secure backup facilities. No direct access to the certificate server is provided to the enterprise or required for operation. The RA provides a controlled entry point for submitting requests to the CA.

The RA may also be located at the service provider site, but will usually be physically located at the enterprise—in either case, the operation of the RA will be left to the enterprise. The interface to the RA in this model is usually a Web-based administration tool used to examine certificate request queues and authorize certificate issuance by the CA. In this model, the staff required to operate the RA, the procedures defined to identify users and the policies that constrain the operation of the RA (CPS) are all owned by the enterprise.

Additional outsource services provided may include key archival and recovery. The storage of user private encryption keys will usually be performed at the secure facility operated by the service. However, most enterprises will not feel comfortable allowing the service to have open access to those keys, so some protection scheme may be implemented to prevent access to the private keys without authorization from the enterprise. The degree to which an enterprise can be assured of the effectiveness of these protection schemes will vary depending on the security policies and techniques employed.

Value Provided

Knowledgeable and experienced staff to operate a CA are not widely available at this point. Rather than build this expertise, some organizations choose to allow other professionals within the outsourcing organization to provide parts of the service. For some enterprises, use of the outsourced service may be considered a learning experience. When sufficient expertise has been developed internally, the CA functions may be moved in-house, as many enterprises will be unwilling to allow management of their users' identities to be controlled by any external service provider.

The actual benefits derived from different service providers need to be examined carefully. In some cases, the actual operational work and ownership of risk is fully assumed by the enterprise, while the service provider offers little more than a secure offsite facility where the certificates are generated. Other services will take total control of all aspects of certificate life cycle, including issuance, management, and renewal, and will require only that you provide a list of qualified users.

How Do You Decide?

So how do you decide what form of CA deployment you want to use for your organization? In some cases, a vertical market segment may develop its own CA structure for use by members of an association (lawyers using certificates issued by the Bar Association is a hypothetical example). In other cases, each enterprise may be expected to run its own CA, but the shared root may be established for participating enterprises in a trust model like Identrus or Global Trust Authority. Trust models will be discussed further in Chapter 8. If the organization's need is only for server certificates, a well-known public CA may be sufficient.

Departmental or Global Decisions?

Many enterprises embark on deployment of an infrastructure like PKI by determining a set of policies that will be used by all PKI users and all departments that will deploy PKIs. This worthwhile endeavor will allow many interoperability issues to be resolved before they become entrenched. Issues such as common naming schemes, certificate policies, and certification policies should be dealt with in a uniform fashion across the enterprise.

Most large-scale deployments of any infrastructure grow without the control of a central IT group, even if they were carefully planned initially. This is true for networks and directories as much as public key infrastructures.

Many factors contribute to this. Business units have their own priorities, and often they can't afford to wait for corporate policies to be complete before they launch a new application. Politics within the organization may establish fiefdoms that will not communicate or cede sufficient authority for a centralized deployment to work. Engineering groups often believe they understand the technology much better than IT administrators and determine that they should just do it their way, expecting that the rest of the organization will eventually come around to their way of thinking.

When all the human and organizational factors have taken their toll, you will almost certainly end up with a heterogeneous environment with different technologies, different vendors, and probably multiple CAs. It will usually be beneficial to assume the worst and plan for the greatest interoperability possible.

Mergers and Acquisitions

Even if all of your careful planning is fully adopted by all of the organization and executed correctly, there are still traps waiting for you. What will happen when you acquire a new company and it has a different CA and issuing policy from those you have adopted? Can you afford to dump several tens of thousands of certificates and reissue them, or will you need to find some way to use the new CA for a short or extended period?

What happens if instead the organization needs to divest a division? Did it have its own CA or were the certificates issued by your central CA? How do you invalidate the certificates in a controlled fashion? Will you even know that the divestiture has occurred?

NOTE:

One very large organization divested itself of a large division a number of years ago. It was not until after five firewalls had been upgraded to deal with Y2K issues that it became clear that the firewalls were actually now owned by the company that had picked up the division. No one had bothered to notify the IT department.

Planning for a PKI should provide features that deal with interoperability and highly heterogeneous environments; for most of us, they will become reality. The areas related to interoperability and features that allow you to deal with these issues are described in Chapter 10.

Summary

We have covered a lot of territory in the last two chapters introducing PKI. If you made it this far, you are doing well.

In this chapter, we examined the aspects of key and certificate life cycles and how they are managed. We started out by continuing our passport example, but looking at the processes associated with establishing an applicant's identity and then issuing the certificate.

Creation of keys and issuing certificates after verifying the identity is just the beginning. The certificates have to be distributed to users in different ways depending on the application being used. Expiration and reissuance of certificates has to be handled, as do exceptional conditions that require revocation of certificates and notification of certificate users.

Finally, archival and recovery of keys (where it is allowed) is necessary to ensure access to encrypted information when the encryption keys have been lost or destroyed.

The various implementations or deployment schemes for CA were considered. Public CAs, Enterprise CAs, and CA services are all valid deployment models, but each presents its own set of challenges and opportunities.

So, we have pretty much beaten the passport example to death. It may be referred to from time to time, but you will be relieved to hear its job is finally done.

References

[1]Rivest, R.L., A. Shamir, and L.M. Adleman, "A method for obtaining digital signatures and public-key cryptosystems," *Communications of the ACM* (2) 21 (1978), 120–126.

[2]National Institute of Standards and Technology (NIST), FIPS Publication 186: *Digital Signature Standard (DSS)*, 1994.

[3]Silverman, R.D., "A Cost-based Security Analysis of Symmetric and Asymmetric Key Lengths," RSA Laboratories, bulletin number 13, April 2000 ftp://ftp.rsasecurity.com/pub/pdfs/bulletn13.pdf.

[4]National Institute of Standards and Technology (NIST), "The Digital Signature Standard, proposal and discussion," *Communications of the ACM* (7) 35 (1992), 36-54.

[5]Smid, M.E., and D.K. Branstad, "Response to comments on the NIST proposed Digital Signature Standard, Advances in Cryptography," Crypto '92, Springer-Verlag (1993), 76-87.

[6]Gleick, James, "Chaos—The Amazing Science of the Unpredictable."

[7]PKCS #12 v1.0: Personal Information Exchange Syntax, RSA Laboratories: ftp://ftp.rsasecurity.com/pub/pkcs/pkcs-12/pkcs-12v1.pdf.

[8]PKCS #5 v2.0: Password-Based Cryptography Standard, RSA Laboratories: ftp://ftp.rsasecurity.com/pub/pkcs/pkcs-5v2/pkcs5v2-0.pdf.

[9]Draft Revised ITU-T Recommendation X.509 | ISO/IEC 9594-8: "Information Technology - Open Systems Interconnection - The Directory: Public-Key and Attribute Certificate Frameworks."

[10]RFC 2459 R. Housley, W. Ford, W. Polk, D. Solo, Internet X.509 Public Key Infrastructure Certificate and CRL Profile http://www.ietf.org/rfc/rfc2459.txt.

CHAPTER 5

Key and Certificate Life Cycles

In Chapter 4, we introduced the services used within a *Public Key Infrastructure* (PKI). In this chapter, we will expand on those concepts by looking at the details associated with the life cycle of keys and certificates.

Non-Repudiation and Key Management

Before we look at the issues and management of key and certificate life cycles, we should take a few moments to discuss non-repudiation. In Chapter 1, we defined non-repudiation as a security service that provided a property that prevented certificate owners from repudiating or denying that they had done something.

For a moment, let's forget the world of electronic commerce and think about a simpler time when signatures had to be written by hand. The most common use of the term "repudiation" is in the context of a signed document, where the supposed signer may deny that she signed the document based on:

- The signature being a forgery
- Where the signature is not a forgery, but where it was obtained by one of the following:
  - Fraudulent conduct by a party to the contract ("Just sign this last piece of paper, please . . .")
  - Fraud instigated by a third party
  - Undue influence exerted by a third party

The way that repudiation is dealt with in the legal world is to have a witness to the signing. Attaching the signature of the witness to the document validates that the document was intact or correct at the time of signing, and that it really was signed on the date specified.

Okay—that's enough—back to the brave new world. What does this mean for digital signatures? In order to have some confidence that a digital signature can be ascribed to the correct individual, we need to have confidence that the private keys belonging to the user were not accessible by anyone else.

This has some implications for the management of digital signature keys. Some of the issues we are concerned about include:

- No copies of the signing key can exist.
- The key must be stored in a suitably secure location.
- Access to the key must be authenticated before the key is used for a signature operation.

The requirement for a singular signing key means that the private key must be strongly protected at each stage of its life cycle. Preferably, the key should be generated locally within a strong storage location using a device like a smart card. The signing key should not be archived as this exposes it within the archival system to possibly unethical operators, insecure transports, and other poor implementation security holes. An authentication scheme should be enforced so that access to the private key for a signing operation requires validation of the correct user.

The exact requirements imposed on any solution protecting the digital signing key will vary with the environment and the needs of the system. For example, the needs of technical non-repudiation may require a sufficiently secure environment to meet the demands of auditors for correct operation. These requirements may become much more onerous if it is necessary to prove non-repudiation to the satisfaction of the legal system.

Key Management

Key management deals with the processes of:

- Creating keys
- Distributing keys
- Protecting keys
- Archiving keys
- Recovering keys

The key management discussed here is focused on public/private keys rather than symmetric keys. As we saw in Chapter 2, public/private key systems may in turn be used for distribution of symmetric keys.

NOTE:

Public / private key management is a complex problem, but nowhere near as difficult as management of a pure symmetric key system. This can be seen in most households as you search for the symmetric key used to start your car in the morning.

Key Generation

In Chapter 2, we introduced some cryptographic concepts, including a discussion on how public/private RSA keys are used and created. A number of aspects of key generation are interesting and worth some additional consideration. The size of the keys generated for a particular encryption algorithm directly determines how difficult it will be to crack a specific key. In general, the amount of processing power and time required grow very quickly as the number of bits in the key increases.

Due to constraints imposed by the U.S. government, the sizes of keys that could be generated and used were historically restricted to relatively small key lengths. Recently, the export restrictions applicable to key generation have been changed, allowing unrestricted key lengths. However, the overhead associated with generating long keys may be too great for many applications. The general recommendation (in 2001) for RSA key lengths currently is around 1024 bits for personal use, and 2048 bits for more sensitive keys like those used by CAs for signing end-entity certificates.

NOTE:

As we saw in Chapter 2, the estimated time to crack a single 1024-bit RSA key is on the order of 3 million years, given 10 million dollars to spend. The time to crack a 2048-bit key is too big a number to contemplate.

In the case of the RSA algorithm, random numbers are used to generate the prime numbers that form the public and private key components. To ensure that the keys are sufficiently strong, the two prime numbers generated should be about the same length, but not too close together. In addition, the pseudo-random numbers that are used to generate keys in software must be sufficiently random. For pseudo-random number generators this generally means that the initial inputs to generator must be selected from sufficiently random data sources. In addition, the algorithms used to generate the prime numbers must be carefully designed to ensure that real prime numbers are created (a more difficult problem than you might imagine). For more detail on random number generators, refer to Chapter 2.

Then there are software implementation issues that may impact the security of the keys. For example, are the memory blocks used to create the keys securely deleted so they cannot be found by someone trying to steal the keys? Is the key storage area encrypted with a sufficiently strong pass phrase? Can security policies be applied to prevent users creating unprotected key stores? Are the pseudo-random number generators correctly initialized and used so that their output is sufficiently random? Are the prime numbers selected really prime?

NOTE:

A prime number is one that can only be evenly divided by itself and the number 1. If you are dealing with very large random numbers, the time taken to determine if the number is prime is tedious and time consuming, so probabilistic methods are used to determine the "primeness" of the number. If these methods are not well designed, you may find that the numbers are not in fact prime.

So why do you care?

Well, when it comes to deploying a key generation system, it may be very important to you. These and other considerations may influence your choice of centralized or distributed key generation systems. For example, the availability of high power central processing units with support for hardware random number generators, and a single validated implementation of key generation may lead you to choose a central key generation service. Conversely, central key generation schemes present problems like secure transport of the keys to the end-user, and ensuring that you have sufficiently secure procedures to prevent your operations staff from subverting the output of your key generator. In addition, some client applications may have no provision to accept externally generated keys, even if you can securely produce and manage them.

Although central generation of public/private keys used for purposes of encryption may be acceptable, most PKI implementations stipulate client-side generation of digital signature keys. The reason for this is to support conditions necessary for non-repudiation, either legal or technical.

Just to complicate matters, there are additional pros and cons for central key generation models.

Central key generation simplifies services such as key archival and recovery, as only a small number of infrastructure components have to interface to the archival system. This works well in most cases, as encryption keys are the most likely type of keys that will need to be stored in an archival system. Digital signature keys, which are generated locally, are almost never archived.

The negative aspect of deploying a centralized key generation and distribution system is that it becomes a very sensitive security component. It forms an obvious place for an attack by someone trying to subvert your PKI. The important nature of the system and the number of keys that it generates means that it must be highly reliable, available, and secure. Finally, the staff that has access to the system and operating procedures that are used must be carefully monitored to ensure that keys (and by association the data they protect) are not exposed during the life of the key.

Applications that use keys for digital signatures may impose additional constraints on the PKI implementation. For example, smart cards may be required as secure storage containers for the private keys. If this is the case, the same implementations will generally require that the keys be generated on the smart card directly. For digital signature keys where archival is not desirable this works fine, but if encrypting keys are generated on the card, there is no way to copy them to a key archive.

As a result, many PKI implementations will use a split model that generates encryption keys centrally, but generates digital signature keys at an application client or smart card.

Key Stores

Public/private keys and the corresponding certificates are often kept in an application-specific key store. In some cases, these key stores may provide a standard API so that other applications using the API can share access to the same key materials. In the case of Netscape and many products that support UNIX platforms, this interface will be PKCS #11; for applications that support Microsoft platforms, the interface will be the Microsoft *Cryptographic API* (CAPI). PKCS #11 was originally designed to act as an interface to cryptographic devices such as smart cards, although it is equally as suitable for software key stores. Microsoft's CAPI provides similar capabilities. However, for many applications, software key stores will be accessible only through interfaces that are private to the application—in this case, shared use of keys will generally be impossible.

NOTE:

PKCS #11 implementations also exist for Microsoft platforms, but they do not have the same level of operating system support as CAPI. More importantly, it is not the Microsoft-anointed API, so it will not be the first choice for implementers working in a Windows-only environment.

Sharing keys and certificates between applications is a highly desirable feature of a PKI implementation. Shared access to keys and certificates allows a user to minimize the number of keys and certificates used to identify them. For example, if you use more than one e-mail or Web browser application, it is desirable to have messages signed or encrypted by either application using the same keys. The aim is to have the messages appear to originate from the same user. The simplest way to do this is to share the same identity, but this means using the same keys (and probably certificates) within all applications.

For the purposes of sharing keys, applications that use private key stores are a significant problem. However, the existence of two competing API standards that an application developer may use to access a key store —PKCS #11 and CAPI—is just as big a problem. The usual problems exist for application developers trying to select one API over the other. The functionality is not identical for both APIs, and each makes different working assumptions about the application context. CAPI is available only on Microsoft platforms and not UNIX platforms. Although PKCS #11 is available on both Microsoft and UNIX platforms, it is not the Microsoft-sanctioned API. The result is that applications must choose to implement both, or select one and be incompatible with other application key stores that the user may have stored keys in.

The quality of application key stores varies significantly. For example, many of the current implementations do not provide strong authentication schemes to verify the user who is accessing the key store. Password-based authentication schemes are often weak and provide little or no policy control for an administrator to exercise over application users. It is entirely possible for a user to choose to omit a password when creating a new key store. As a result, anyone who has access to the user's desktop has open access to the keys and certificates and can fraudulently sign messages. The outcome is that the use of weakly protected key stores may seriously reduce the effectiveness of the PKI when supporting authentication or digital signatures.

Smart cards provide a form of strongly protected key stores that also incorporates 2-factor authentication. For many PKI implementers, smart cards form an essential basis for the protection scheme for user keys.

Key Transport

As a single common API does not exist for access to key stores, the alternative approach to sharing keys is to provide import/export mechanisms that allow keys to be transferred between key stores. The PKCS #12 standard defines an encrypted storage container that can be used as an interchange format for transferring keys securely between key stores. Netscape, Microsoft, and many other application developers have implemented PKCS #12 for this purpose.

So it seems that the problems we described earlier with shared application access to keys can now be resolved. We can share keys by using PKCS #12 containers to move keys from one application to another. PKCS #12 containers may be transported in mail messages, files, or in general network protocols like HTTP. Phew, what a relief, we have a solution to sharing keys—however, it turns out that we have now introduced a whole raft of other issues we need to contend with.

First, there is a usability problem. The process of exporting keys through PKCS #12 implementations in most applications is way too hard for my [Andrew's] grandmother to use. (Some people might consider that this is because my grandmother passed away many years ago. However true this may be, I still contend she would not have been able to use most of the current implementations.)

Next, there is a consistency problem. Even if your users work out how to correctly export keys from one application and then import them into another, will they do so correctly in all of their applications? Assuming your users are particularly smart and successfully manage to initially export their keys to all dependant applications, what happens when a key rollover event occurs and you need to replace the users' keys and certificates? How many of your users will remember all of the places where the keys were transferred to, and manage to transfer the updated keys this time?

Then there is a potential security problem. PKCS #12 containers are often transferred within files. There is no automatic purge process that will clean up these files when you are done with them, so it is entirely likely that PKCS #12 files will float around on users' disks for a long time. The container within the file is protected using a password that the user selects when the keys are exported. If the password chosen by the user is weak and easily cracked, old PKCS #12 files may become a rich opportunity for hackers to discover keys and the corresponding certificates.

Finally, there is a significant security problem with this whole concept of copying keys at all. Imagine a system where each user is allocated a key and certificate for authentication to a subscription service. What is to prevent a user from copying the keys and certificates and providing them to all of her friends? The ability to replicate identities without control has led some PKI implementers to discount the value of PKI as an authentication scheme. Fortunately, more robust PKI solutions that do not permit propagation of keys reduce these concerns.

One of the advantages of smart cards as a secure key store is that they prevent export of the key material. In addition, smart cards allow keys and certificate to be securely transported between applications and different computing environments, allowing user mobility. Some software smart card solutions available today have similar properties.

PKCS #12 transport containers provide a very valuable mechanism for occasional use, where keys need to be transferred between key stores. It is not a desirable long-term solution for supporting key mobility and shared access to keys.

Key Archival

As any IT manager will tell you, life would be much easier without pesky users. Users persist in nuisance activities such as forgetting their passwords and calling the helpdesk to get a new password to access their account. Among the other problems they can cause in a PKI is losing their data encryption keys. Alternatively, they may prove to be ingrates and decide to leave your employ, or possibly, they may inconvenience you by being struck by a bus. As part of the requirement to provide a robust system, most organizations will add the use of a key archive and recovery system to allow users to regain lost keys, or provide the organization with the ability to access its corporate data that has been encrypted if the user is rendered inoperable.

From time to time, various governments have also expressed interest in obtaining encryption keys to access private or corporate data (usually in the interests of law enforcement). Not surprisingly, these moves have been vigorously opposed by individuals, corporations, and privacy groups. The stated need for government agencies to have access to encryption keys (to battle drug cartels or child pornographers who encrypt their illicit transactions) continues to arise periodically.

Various forms of control have been tried to date. The U.K. government recently entertained legislation that required any employee of a company to provide access to encryption keys upon request from a government agency. Other schemes tried by the U.S. government required that a company deposit copies of encryption keys with a third party known as an escrow agent. This form of key recovery system is generally known as a *key escrow* system.

To distinguish legitimate control of access by a company to its own data, we will distinguish the systems discussed here from key escrow systems by referring to them as *key archival* or *key recovery* systems. Not unreasonably, the privacy and security policies of an organization should be updated to allow for secure and controlled access to key archival systems.

A key archival system is principally concerned with secure storage of keys in a key backup repository or archive. A key recovery system is primarily concerned with the operation of restoring keys. The two systems and their corresponding mechanisms are of course tightly linked, but depending on organizational security policies and design constraints, they may be kept as distinct systems.

Access to the key archive needs to be tightly controlled. The security needs of this system are at least as sensitive as a central key generation system. Whereas the key generation system may be attacked to copy keys as they are created, the key archive contains all keys that have already been certified by the CAs registration process. Keys may need to be secured in a tamper-resistant secure hardware module. Access to the system may require several administrators to be present at once to reduce potential fraud or theft of stored keys.

NOTE:

This form of system is sometime referred to as an m of n authentication scheme. Of a set of n administrators who are permitted access to the system, m (where m is a number smaller than n) of them must be authenticated (and possibly physically present) at the same time. As an example, if five administrators are allowed access to the system, the lower threshold value for m might be set at three. Under these conditions, any three administrators must be authenticated to the system before it can be enabled or keys accessed.

Strong physical security may be required for the key archive, and operational procedures to control access will be needed.

The key archive will need to interface to several different types of systems depending on the security policies and PKI implementation. The cases described next are illustrated in Figure 5-1.

If a central key generation system is implemented, as it generates keys for delivery to users, it must also replicate the key and transmit it to the key archive. Some systems may integrate hardware support that performs the key generation and archival within the same secure environment. The form of hardware supported for the archival process will directly impact the way the recovery process must be run to restore the key held in the archive. If the key recovery process that runs needs not only a key recovered, but also the corresponding certificate, it may be necessary to store the corresponding certificate along with the key pairs. Alternatively, the certificate corresponding to the key may need to be located within the repository and transmitted to the user as part of the key recovery process.

Client-side key generation requires that any application that generates keys for a key store must interface to the key archival system to support saving the keys. Standard protocols such as CMP (described in Chapter 6) are emerging that facilitate secure transport of keys from clients to

Figure 5-1

Key archival
system linkages

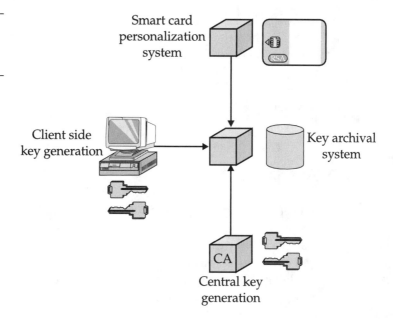

archival systems. Currently, systems that allow clients to generate keys use secure transports such as SSL/TLS or PKCS #12 containers to transport the keys between the client and the key archival system.

Smart cards present a special case for key recovery systems. If on-card key generation is implemented, those keys cannot be replicated to send to the key archive. One way to deal with this problem is to use a central key generation system that writes keys to the smart cards when the cards are being personalized (see Chapter 9). This allows the central key generation system to transmit the keys to a key archival system, as in the first case we looked at.

NOTE:

Private keys may be generated onboard a smart card (assuming it is a true cryptographic card, rather than a memory-only card) by the secure processor and then stored in its internal secure memory. Alternatively, the key may be generated external to the card and then imported or written to a secure memory location. In either case, the key cannot be directly accessed except by the cryptographic processor on the card. As a result, it cannot be read or copied outside of the card.

As we said, keys must be transmitted to the archive server securely. However, when they arrive at the archive, they will normally need to be rewrapped under a data storage key owned by the recovery server. Operations using this key will usually require the use of an m of n authentication scheme by the appropriate administrators before keys can be decrypted.

Key Recovery

For the purposes of this discussion, we will deal with recovery of keys that are used for encryption, not digital signatures. Providing a key recovery system for signing keys has such a dramatic impact on the non-repudiation characteristics of digital signatures that any form of signing key recovery is proscribed by most implementation profiles.

Although all keys of a specific type may be created equal, for key recovery purposes the same key can have different requirements at different times.

From the perspective of key recovery, we will identify three categories of keys:

- Current or active key
- Previous key
- Older keys

The Current Key

The current key is a key that has not expired and is currently in use.

Why would you want to recover such a key? This is the case where a key has been lost or otherwise destroyed (remember from Chapter 3, the smart card that was in your wallet when you were run over by the bus), and you want to restore it so it can continue to be used. The certificate corresponding to the key will usually be required if you intend to continue use of the key after it has been recovered. The other case that may be applicable here is if a new smart card-like device (this could be a real smart card or something like a USB dongle) needs to be initialized with an existing encryption key when it is personalized. A special version of this may exist if you are moving keys from a virtual or software smart card as part of a move toward support of physical smart card devices. (One of my reviewers objected that the bus example was not useful because you were run over by the bus as well, and no longer cared . . . sigh!)

A more realistic example of the need to recover the current key is where public/private keys are used as an authentication and security mechanism by employees of an organization. The keys may have been stored on a smart card, which the employee has inadvertently left home for the day. To keep your valuable (but annoying) employee productively employed, the security policy may allow a temporary physical smart card (or software smart card) to be issued to allow him access to your systems. If this employee needs to encrypt e-mail messages, you need to ensure that the same key that was in the original smart card is available for use. When the smart card is created (physical or software), you would like to populate it with the user's current key and certificate.

Rather than recover the current key, the local policy may be to generate a new key and register for a new certificate for the user. In this case, the "current" key will become the "previous" key and this becomes the case covered in the next section. An example of this policy is where an organization may directly issue a new smart card to the user and invalidate the old card, usually revoking the certificate associated with the key.

Of all keys, the impact of losing the current key is the most significant. Every sensitive encrypted document that a user is working on and all incoming mail encrypted for him by other users (based on his published certificate) need to be accessible. If the user really has been struck by a bus, the enterprise must also be able to pick up the current work he is engaged in and hand it off to another employee.

Temporary loss due to misplacing or forgetting a smart card or other authentication device carrying the user's keys is one of the most significant cases where recovery of the current key is required. Given normal user patterns for loss of authentication devices, recovery of the current key should be as transparent and easy as possible; otherwise, your helpdesk load will be astronomical.

Previous Key

In order of importance, the previous key comes in a very close second to the current key for key recovery purposes. Why? Well, every current key will one day become the previous key (this is a "circle of life" kind of thing). In many PKI implementations, this will probably happen overnight, under the covers without the user even knowing about it, when a key rollover event occurs. One morning she will come into work and find that the previous evening the old keys were replaced with freshly generated keys and new certificates were issued. This is wonderful, until she tries to read the encrypted mail that arrived yesterday and finds that the current key will not allow it to be decrypted.

NOTE:

Of course, in many existing systems, the key rollover event is announced to the user and she must take direct and explicit action to allow it. This merely makes the rollover event a painful process, and does little to ease the issues associated with recovering the key. If we work really hard and develop supportive application and user environments, transparent key rollover can become the normal case—otherwise, key rollover may disrupt PKI deployments.

At this point, the previous key needs to be used to decrypt yesterday's mail. In fact, if this is an e-mail system, the mail that arrived encrypted over the previous twelve months (assuming a key and certificate validity period of twelve months in most organizations) all requires the previous key in order to decrypt it.

Now comes the next challenge. In most applications such as e-mail, the user may not know how to access the previous key. The first warning that a problem exists is often an error message stating that the e-mail that was accessible yesterday can no longer be decrypted. The application will not generally be sophisticated enough to try multiple keys even if they are available. The result will be a cryptic call (no pun intended) to the helpdesk by your user indicating that she cannot access her e-mail. Even if the previous key is saved by the application, the user must know enough about key stores to allow them to select an appropriate alternative key (assuming they have worked out what the problem is in the first place).

If the previous key were not kept on hand after a key rollover event, access to the key would require a call to the helpdesk to initiate a key recovery event from the key archive. Given the frequency of this event (it will happen to everyone during the span of a certificate validity period), reliance on a helpdesk as the primary recovery mechanism to cover this event is unworkable. Not only will your helpdesk be swamped, but the cost of dealing with these events may be enough to seriously impact the viability of your PKI deployment.

For all practical purposes, the previous key needs to be kept on hand and as accessible as the current key. The length of time this is required will vary by implementation and individual, but should probably be on the order of the validity period of the new current key and certificate (at least twelve months).

Some applications keep all old keys and certificates in the user's key store. Unfortunately, the user is provided no real assistance in selecting the relevant key. In addition, this mechanism does not support roaming users, users with smart cards, or users whose machine crashes, destroying the local copy of the key store. A central key archive and recovery service must be integrated with these applications to overcome these problems.

Older Keys

The last category of keys we will consider for this discussion is keys that are a generation older than the previous key. It seems that many of these keys will not need to be as readily accessible as the current key or the previous key. For example, transparent (or at least easy) access to the current and previous keys would allow you to decrypt between a year and two years' e-mail archive in most PKI implementations. In many organizations, e-mail more than a year old cannot be accessed without having to resort to an offline storage archive.

This does not decrease the value of older keys, but does decrease the relative frequency that access to these keys is likely to be necessary. Under these conditions, a more onerous mechanism such as invoking a key recovery operation to access an older key within a key archive is probably acceptable. Why would we bother to make the distinction? Those pesky smart cards are a major reason. Although we could probably manage to store one previous key (and possibly a certificate) on the card to deal with the previous key, there is just not enough memory currently to store several generations of older keys. Even as smart card memory continues to increase over time, there is still a limit on how much of this memory will be available for storage of old keys (there are many contenders for smart card real estate). Besides, at some point that smart card will wear out, be misplaced, or get hit by a bus, and then you will need access to all of the keys stored in the archive.

Access to Archived Keys

Assuming you have a key archive with all three categories of keys securely squirreled away, how are you going to control access to the keys?

The first answer will usually be that you want to constrain access to only highly trusted archive administrators, and then only when there are several of them all together in one room to prevent collusion. In the kind of high-security environment where you could afford such protection, the keys are probably archived in a secure tamper-resistant hardware storage device. To access some of these devices, each of the administrators may actually have a physical key that needs to be used in conjunction with keys inserted by other administrators.

Alternatively, access in a software-only (meaning absent special purpose hardware security storage) key archive may just require each administrator to authenticate herself (using passwords, or preferably some other form of 2-factor authentication like tokens or smart cards).

The issue with either of the solutions just described is that it involves a heavy investment in highly trained and trusted people to make this system work. Many organizations will not be willing to make this investment. In addition, any process that explicitly requires an administrator to participate will involve overhead that will be painful for the user. If the administrator is not available outside of normal business hours, or if he is only available for key recovery on a part-time basis, recovery of keys may involve considerable delay. The impact of these delays will vary depending on the category of recovery key you are considering. The impact may be intolerable for recovery of the current or previous key, but possibly acceptable for older keys.

For the current or previous key, it is most desirable that recourse to a central archival system is not required at all. This could be handled by utilizing local storage (possibly in a smart card if it is available) to hold the previous key and storage triggered by a key rollover event. If a real key recovery operation is required, it seems desirable from the perspective of convenience and minimizing overhead that the recovery of the keys be driven directly by a user. This naturally raises issues about the security and privacy of the keys, but for many implementations, use of a suitable authentication scheme for users may make this possible. Of course, policy constraints—such as the time of day when the system can be accessed remotely and the need for administrators to enable hardware security storage—could be applied to increase the security of such a solution.

NOTE:
Any local storage should be secured before writing the previous key to it. Use of a smart card, either physical or virtual, may be an option here.

One consideration that is important here is how applicable user-accessible key recovery schemes may be for recovery of the current key. As the key itself is being recovered, it cannot be used as the basis of authentication to the recovery server. Unless some form of authentication that is equivalent in strength to the key being recovered can be used, this may not be a sufficiently secure solution. This is definitely a good reason for retaining the use of administrator control over recovery of the current key.

There remains a very good reason in the short term for key recovery systems that use operators or administrators. Given the amount of information that is currently provided by most applications to identify the required key, the helpdesk will almost certainly have to assist the user to determine the appropriate key that needs to be recovered. As a source of additional information, the certificate should probably also be stored with the archived key. So, for example, if a user can identify that an e-mail message received on a particular date could not be decrypted, the set of certificates that were valid for that time could be used as the selection criteria. This information could also be stored independently along with the key, but as you will probably need to restore the certificate as well as the key in most cases, it seems like a reasonable combination to keep.

NOTE:

Although it is possible that users may be able to select a key from a set of menu choices based on the date of the message to be decrypted, it is not clear how usable such a system will be. This is definitely a case where tight integration of the application with the PKI and especially the key recovery system is required if a suitably transparent key recovery solution is to be produced.

Irrespective of the access method implemented, the key recovery system will need to keep strict audit logs of who accessed what keys, under what circumstances and using what form of authentication.

Certificate Management

Certificate management deals with the set of operations that apply to certificates throughout their entire useful life. The CA is responsible for the certificate well after the registration process has been completed. Certificate management includes the processes of:

- Registration
- Certificate renewal
- Certificate revocation

Certificate Registration

We introduced the certificate registration process in Chapter 4. In this section, we will examine the issues and requirements for the registration process.

Initialization

Before an end-entity can make use of the PKI, there are several pieces of information that must be established during some form of initialization phase. The operation of this phase is omitted from most standards—the requirements are given, and then it is assumed that some out-of-bound or a priori mechanism is utilized. In practice this means that someone entered the initial information when the system was configured, or used sneakernet to transfer the require information (or mental telepathy, as appropriate). Figure 5-2 shows some of the information required for initialization.

The end-entity must be advised what services are offered by the various PKI components and where it should connect to in order to obtain those services. For example, the network names or addresses of the RA or CA used for registration (and any other services) may need to be configured, or the URL corresponding to the appropriate service may be located on a corporate Web server.

If the services in the PKI need to be authenticated before any transactions can take place, some suitable form of shared secret must be installed in the end-entity. This could be a pass phrase of some kind or it could be the public key used to verify a certificate for a PKI service. One proposed solution to this initial trust problem is to hash the server certificate passed to the end-entity and call the operator of the CA or RA and confirm that the hash value matches one they would send (of course, this would only be necessary while the system is being bootstrapped).

Figure 5-2

Initialization
requirements

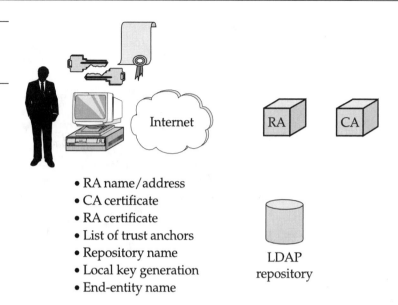

- RA name/address
- CA certificate
- RA certificate
- List of trust anchors
- Repository name
- Local key generation
- End-entity name

It is generally appropriate to distribute the trust anchors to end-entities during the initialization phase. Most of the management protocols allow intermediate CA certificates to be transferred within the protocol itself (for example, when a certificate is delivered to an end-entity in response to a registration request). However, due to the problems of ensuring that a self-signed CA certificate or other trust anchor identification can really be trusted, this step is left squarely in the lap of the PKI implementer to devise. One mechanism that many deployments have accepted with little question to date has been to trust the set of root CAs published in their friendly Web browser (as we will see in Chapter 8, leaving these decisions to application providers is not highly desirable).

The end-entity may generate a public/private key pair that it will use for the registration request. This may be generated by an application such as a Web browser, client-side PKI software, within the Windows desktop environment, or by the smart card used by the end-entity. Alternatively, the end-entity may use a central key generation service. The keys may be generated at a smart card initialization service, or may be generated in software and securely transported to the end-entity (possibly as part of the registration process).

The name of the end-entity to be used within the registration request must be configured or known in some fashion, and other information needed to establish the identity of end-entity or configure the attributes of the certificate may be required.

For operations such as a Web browser-based registration process, much of this information may be supplied by the good offices of the user who fills in the Web form used to initiate registration. This is certainly the simplest mechanism, but it exposes one of the major obstacles to wide-scale PKI deployment to date. Manual registration using Web browser interfaces is error-prone and exposes vast amounts of the complexity of PKI to users. We will examine some approaches to reducing this complexity level and dealing with the transparency of the registration process in the next two sections.

Initial Trust

Once we have initialized an end-entity with the information necessary for it to interact with the PKI, we move to the next problem in the registration process. How do you verify the identity of the end-entity that you are going to certify?

One mechanism is to use a completely manual process that mirrors the passport application process we discussed in Chapter 4. You could require that all subscribers present themselves in person to a registration officer and provide all of the physical evidence of their identity based on primary documentation such as birth certificates, passports, driver's license, and so on. The registration officer would then examine the proofs they provide, verify their photograph matches the person in question, and when satisfied he would do the data entry to initiate a registration request. As part of the process, he could authenticate himself to the Registration Authority system to prove he was duly authorized to submit requests, or he could digitally sign the request to achieve the same end. When the RA and CA receive the request, they would see that it was in fact "pre-vetted" by the registration officer and that no further evidence was required to establish the identity of the subscriber. With minimal additional checking, the certificate could be issued.

The advantage of this type of system (the U.S. *Department of Defense (DOD)* registration system is just such a system) is that you place no requirements about the knowledge of the system on the subscribers. Most of the identity verification can be performed up front. With some thought, the certificate could be delivered in a convenient package such as a smart card, which would make the whole process look much like getting a sophisticated credit card or corporate badge. On the whole, a system like this works well for the DOD as they have stringent requirements about face-to-face processing of personnel that tie in well to this form of registration. For most enterprises, the expense, the manpower requirements, and the overhead of such a system are prohibitive.

An alternative for less security sensitive organizations than the DOD might be to assign a user ID and a one-time password to new subscribers. This may be provided in an out-of-band mechanism like e-mail, over the telephone, or through the post office, depending on the security policies applied by your organization. When the user registers, presentation of the user ID and password allows verification of the subscriber's identity. This does not necessarily deal with the data entry and transparency problems that we identified. However, if we link access to the personnel database in to the RA or CA, we could potentially reduce the amount of information that the user would need to provide. In practice, most large organizations find that the hardest part of this problem is coming up with a unique user identifier that works for their whole organization and then mapping sufficient information in the personnel database to the registration requirements of the CA—but access to this data provides a good start.

The fundamental problem we are looking at here is initial authentication. If you already have an authentication system in place, it may be possible to leverage the information that it has already built in to simplify the registration process. Two-factor authentication schemes like SecurID tokens or smart card systems provide high levels of assurance about the identity of the subscriber when they authenticate. In addition, the information that is established for systems like these match many of the requirements for registration. If an automated process and set of policies can be established at the back-end of the CA to complete registration processing, the user may need to do as little as authenticate themselves on a registration page and have the certificate automatically loaded into an application such as a browser.

Initial registration processing could also be handled using a model similar to those implemented for credit card provisioning. A central site could establish a smart card personalization system that takes lists of users, looks up relevant information in personnel or other databases, and uses this to generate the requests that are sent to a CA. In this case, the smart card personalization system is a trusted registration request system and may be considered to act as the RA in this model. Validation of the user identity might be defined by a two-part process where the card is sent to a known address and the pin number to access the card is sent via a separate mail message or transmitted by telephone.

Many other methods for registration processing and identity verification exist. Some systems determine your identity by asking specific questions that only you should possess and compare them to information already known about you. For example, with sufficient access to financial records, the registration system could ask very specific questions such as, "What date did you make your last mortgage payment?" Or, "How many times have you refinanced your mortgage?" Or, "How much did you pay in late fees on your credit card in December last year?" By asking a sufficient number of these questions, these registration models believe they can conclude to their satisfaction whether you are who you claim to be. In this sense, it is much like tapping into a collection of privately held information that effectively forms a shared secret. There are certainly objections to the effectiveness of such an approach for establishing identities, but for some classes of identity validation, particularly if it is for use by the financial institutions performing the validation, it seems to be acceptable.

NOTE:

It seems unlikely that such a scheme would work in geographies like Europe where the privacy of this type of information is much more tightly protected by law.

There is a trade-off between the amount of information required to validate a subscriber's identity and the overhead and complexity of providing it. The time taken to process a registration request is directly affected by the amount of information that must be presented and processed. Schemes that use previously established authentication are able to effectively leverage an existing body of information and require very little data input to initiate this process (just the user ID and pass phrase used for authentication). What do we do about registration of very large populations (in the multiple millions) where a single authentication scheme cannot be expected to cover such an enormous user population?

The questioning scheme described previously (or some variation on it) could be used to cheaply create very large certificate populations. Providing a sufficiently large information base that allows users to be identified in this way is the challenge. One intriguing system relies upon the fact that a subscriber can be identified by their proximity to well-known addresses. This system requires that a phone number associated with the user can be accessed at some point in time. During the process of registration, the Registration Authority will place a call to a particular phone number and require that the user enter a shared secret through the phone that has been provided as part of the initial registration process.

Registration Requirements

Information utilized during the registration process should not necessarily be published as part of the certificate that is eventually issued by a CA. Content such as personal phone numbers or addresses are obvious issues and have direct privacy implications when publishing a certificate for general distribution. However, many other fields within a certificate have the potential for exposing different levels of sensitive information. For example, the distinguished name of the subscriber may reveal information about the structure of your organization that you do not wish made public. Would it be possible to identify all of the salespeople in your organization because the certificates issued used an organizational unit name of "Sales"? If someone were prospecting for salespeople to hire, this might be a very valuable information source.

In situations where a CA uses back-end databases to source information about users to reduce the amount of data entry required, there may be a valid concern that the final information included in the certificate reveals more than the subscriber is happy with. As a result, some models for certificate issuance require the user to provide positive acknowledgement about the content of a certificate before it is published to a public repository. This allows the user to verify any information that may have been added or modified by the CA during the issuance process.

Proof of Possession

A concept that has gained significant recognition as a requirement for registration requests is verification that the subscriber actually holds the private key corresponding to the public key that is being registered. A public key could be obtained from many sources as, by definition, the public key requires no secure storage and is intended to be shared. The private key, however, is assumed to be stored in a secure storage device or protected location. PKIX makes very strong assertions about the need to prove that the subscriber is the holder of the private key before a certificate is issued. Although this proof could be established when the public key is presented, the concern is that there are protocols in use that do not perform this verification. As a result, the linkage between the identity and the private key should be established at registration time.

NOTE:

PKIX does not require that proof be established via technical means. It does require proof of possession, but may allow the subject's assertion that they have the key as sufficient (RFC 2459, Section 3.1). However, the requirement in CMP specification (RFC 2510, Section 2.3), discussed in the next chapter, provides much stronger wording about proving ownership even if it is done in some out-of-band scheme.

The name of this key ownership verification step is *proof of possession* (POP). There are numerous methods that can be used to show proof of possession. The method used will normally be determined by the intended use of the key (as recorded in the certificate Key Usage field).

If the key is to be used for digital signatures, the key is generally used to sign the registration request. The signature can then be checked by the RA using the public key submitted in the request. This allows the signature private key to remain in the secure storage container for the end-entity without being shipped to the RA. Non-repudiation requirements on digital signatures would be damaged if the key was to leave the end-entity storage.

For encryption keys, the problem is a little more difficult. The private key itself could be transmitted, as there are not generally non-repudiation issues to consider. If a centralized key archival system is required, this could be a useful collection point—as the keys are generated, they can be saved off to the key archival system. However, if key archival is not considered desirable for security or privacy reasons, transmitting the private key may not be acceptable. If the private encryption key is stored on a device like a smart card, the key cannot be read from the device.

The alternative for POP on encryption keys is for the RA to generate a random challenge and encrypt it using the public key submitted with the registration request. If the subscriber can decrypt the challenge, this verifies that she holds the private key.

A third method may also be used for encryption keys. The certificate issued by the CA can be encrypted using the public key. Only the holder of the private key will be able to decrypt the certificate to use it. This method does place restrictions on publishing the certificate in a public repository—when should a clear-text version of the certificate be published? This may be acceptable where the PKI does not rely on publication to a directory for certificate dissemination.

If the keys that are being registered are used for a key agreement scheme such as Diffie-Hellman, the problem is more difficult still. The only way to verify the subscriber has the corresponding key is to actually engage in the process of key agreement.

If a key can be used for multiple purposes (RSA keys can be used for signing, encrypting and others, while DSA keys can only be used for signing), including digital signatures, it is reasonable to rely on the mechanism for signing the request as sufficient proof of the existence of the key.

End-Entity Certificate Renewal

Certificate renewal assumes that you have already been through the process of establishing your identity and all of the other constraints we discussed earlier. Provided the key has not been compromised in some fashion, this should prove a base for us to use when renewing your certificate.

There are several reasons for issuing a new certificate. The key associated with the certificate may have reached the end of its useful life. The certificate may have expired—note that this is not the same as key lifetime in X.509, although many certificate profiles do not allow a distinction. Some of the attributes that have been certified in the certificate may have changed and the new values for those attributes must be recertified.

Fortunately, as long as the certificate has not been revoked, the previous keys and certificates can be used to complete the authentication process. For example, when the user registers for a new key, signing the request with the old key and certificate will be sufficient for most authentication purposes. Your security policy may require face-to-face identity validation with a human operator every third certificate to act as a consistency check.

CA Certificate Renewal

The update of a CA key pair is conceptually similar to update of an end-entity's key pair. However, due to the number of parties that rely upon root CAs in particular, some steps can be taken to smooth transition to the new keys and corresponding CA certificate. PKIX identifies a model for doing this with root CAs in the CMP specification (see Chapter 6). This procedure works for root CAs as they can issue self-signed certificates.

The procedure relies on the CA using its previous keys to sign the new certificate, and the new keys to sign the old certificate. The result is that four certificates are created for a root CA undergoing a key update. These certificates are referred to as:

- **OldWithOld**   The original self-signed certificate where the previous CA private key was used to sign the previous public key within the CA certificate

- **OldWithNew**   The original public key in a CA certificate signed using the new CA private key

- **NewWithOld**   The new public key in a CA certificate signed with the previous CA private key

- **NewWithNew**   The new public key in a CA certificate signed with the new CA private key (this is the self-signed CA certificate all relying parties that use this CA as a trust anchor will migrate to)

The previous CA certificate (OldWithOld) is held by all relying parties at the time the key update event occurs. The NewWithOld certificate allows the newly generated CA public key to be attested to by the previous and already trusted key. Once the new key is trusted, relying parties picking up the new CA certificate (NewWithNew) will be able to trust it, at which time the OldWithOld and NewWithOld certificates are no longer necessary to the relying party. The validity period for the NewWithOld certificate starts with the key generation time of the new CA keys, and ends with an appropriate date that allows (forces?) all relying parties to move to recognition of the new keys. The latest possible time for this expiration will be the expiration period of the previous keys.

So why do we need the OldWithNew certificate? To allow for a smooth transition to the new key pair, most implementations will use a certificate overlap period during which both the old CA certificate and the new CA certificate will be in use. It is still possible during the overlap time to receive a certificate from an end-entity where the certificate chain is terminated with the old CA certificate. The OldWithNew allows relying parties that have already switched to the new key to continue to trust or validate the old CA certificate. The validity period for the OldWithNew certificate starts with the date of the previous key pair generated, and ends with the expiration date of the OldWithOld certificate.

Certificate Revocation

Certificates are revoked when conditions require termination of the validity of the certificate prior to the end date in the certificate, or disassociation of the user's identity from the private key. These conditions could include a change in status of the subscriber, such as when employment is terminated for an employee. The information included within the certificate may have been modified—for example, the subscriber's name or whom they report to within the organization may have changed. Finally, the private key associated with the user identity may have been compromised is some way—doubt about the unique access to a signing key may impact the non-repudiation status of contracts or other communications signed by the subscriber.

If you conclude that a certificate must be revoked, it must be possible for certificate users to be notified of the date at which the certificate is considered invalid. As the CA is the ultimate owner of certificate status, the CA must be notified of the requirement to revoke the certificate. The CA in turn is responsible for changing the status of the certificate and then publishing or announcing to the certificate user community that the certificate has been revoked.

At least two dates are important when considering certificate revocation. For conditions such as change in user status or certificate contents, the date at which the revocation request was made must be known. This clearly states that the certificate contents and the identity association it represents can no longer be trusted from that date. In the case of key compromise, however, the date of the actual key compromise may not be accurately known. The second date identifies the latest date that operations such as signing can be considered to still be valid.

This suspected compromise date creates some interesting problems. Potentially, the subject of a certificate could seek to invalidate a contract that she signed by reporting a suspected key compromise date that predated the digital signing operation. As a result, it may be necessary to use a notary service that witnesses the correct signing of a document at a particular date.

A revocation request may be initiated by the certificate subject when they become aware of a key compromise event. Alternatively, the request may be made by some other authorized individual such as a security officer. A revocation request may involve reporting the event to a CA operator who will then revoke the certificate and schedule notification of the revocation.

This process has the potential to overwhelm a helpdesk in a large certificate population, so it may be preferable to allow the certificate owner to directly schedule a revocation request via a CA or RA interface. As an example, the user could be provided with a Web page that allows certificate revocation to be requested. PKI management protocols may also allow revocation requests to be made from an end-entity application.

In all of these cases, however, there is a requirement for the individual requesting the revocation to be authenticated. If a key compromise event is being reported by the owner, the key associated with the certificate may not be appropriate to authenticate the revocation request. Instead, some other form of shared secret is usually established (normally during the registration process) that allows the certificate owner to authenticate herself.

NOTE:

There may be a special case for allowing authentication only when handling the revocation request. This is on the grounds that someone who has gone to the trouble of compromising the key would not apply to have the certificate revoked.

Finally, the revocation mechanism may be used to suspend a certificate. The concept of suspended certificates is a little slippery, but is intended to place a certificate on hold temporarily. This could be because the certificate owner knows that she will not be actively using a certificate for some time (she may be going on sabbatical) and wants to ensure that the certificate is not used during that time. Alternatively, the status of the certificate may be ambiguous for some reason (possibly the certificate owner has been officially listed as "missing, presumed dead").

In any case, the certificate can be placed in a suspended state—using a revocation reason of *Certificate Hold*. The action taken on receipt of a suspended certificate may be defined in the optional *Hold Instruction Code* CRL entry extension. X.509 does not list any hold instruction codes at this time. The certificate may later be revoked with a corresponding reason, or it may be released, in which case it will be removed from the next published CRLs and may be used as a valid certificate again.

NOTE:

The PKIX specification, which is discussed in the next chapter, defines hold instruction codes.

X.509 identifies a specific form of revocation list that is used to publish revocation notices for CAs whose keys have been compromised. This is known as an *authority revocation list* (ARL). The same principals apply to ARLs as CRLs, but conceptually to the serious nature of such an event, a separate list may need to be maintained. PKIX does not support this concept, although it has been recognized by some other PKI profiles. PKIX does provide equivalent support through CRL distribution points that may be limited to providing CRLs associated with events like CA compromise. CRL distribution points are discussed a little later in this chapter.

Revocation Announcement or Publication

The CA as the owner of the certificate life cycle is responsible for certificate revocation and then the announcement or publication of the revocation notice. The CA may delegate access to the published information to a repository such as a directory—this is usually the case when a revocation list is used as the revocation notice. Alternatively, the CA may delegate responsibility for responding to queries for revocation status to a different service or responder if an online revocation service is being used.

In either case, revocation announcements that are provided have some characteristics that are important to the certificate users relying on the notices that are provided by the CA. The timeliness of the notice provided by the CA will determine the confidence level that a certificate user can place in the revocation scheme. The intervals used by a CA to publish notices may not correspond to the requirements of the certificate user. The CA policy may prescribe publication of revocation notices once a week, but if the certificate user is processing high-value financial transactions, she will probably want notices that are published on an hourly or better basis.

The ease with which a certificate user can access revocation information is also important. The directory or other repository used to store revocation information must be accessible by all certificate users, including those outside the organization that owns the directory.

The revocation scheme provided by the CA needs to account for several factors. If the number of certificates you expect to revoke is large, this will have an impact on the size of a revocation list. If you have a client with constrained processing capabilities, memory limitations, or network bandwidth constraints, transferring a large list to a client application for processing will become a problem. If the certificate user needs very timely information or quick response times, a certificate status service may be required. The certificate user must be able to trust the source of revocation information, so the list produced by the CA must be signed or the response from a service provider must be authenticated in some form.

CRLs

Certificate revocation lists (CRLs) are required by X.509 as a revocation notification scheme. The simplest form of CRL is a list published on a regular basis by the CA identifying all of the certificates that have been revoked through the life of the CA. This is limited by the certificate validity period. When a certificate has expired, it may be removed from the list.

NOTE:

X.509 allows that other forms of revocation schemes may be provided, but requires that CRLs be supported as a minimum requirement.

The CRL is a signed structure so the certificate user has confidence that the information has not been changed since it was issued by the CA. As the CA needed to be trusted for certificate validation purposes, the certificate user probably has the CA certificate to allow the CA signature on the CRL to be verified. As the CRL is in a sense self-protecting, there is no need for particularly secure storage, since the certificate user can detect substitution of a CRL or modification of the revocation notices in the CRL. Protecting the repository to prevent deletion of CRLs is worthwhile to ensure that the certificate user is not denied access to the CRL.

NOTE:

The CRL is the published form of the revocation status of the certificate. The actual state of the certificate is maintained within the database of the issuing CA.

The CRL is usually issued by a single CA for the certificates it manages. However, it is possible for a CRL to be used to provide information for multiple CAs if it is defined as an indirect CRL. This information is carried in the *CRL Scope* extension. The CRL may identify that it contains revocation notices from multiple CAs or that it contains update notices from multiple CAs (see "Delta CRLs" following). If the CRL is indirect, the entries in the CRL must be qualified with the *Certificate Issuer* extension that identifies which CA issued the revocation notice.

Configuration changes in the PKI may mean that sources of revocation information may change over time. This is particularly true if explicit CRL distribution points are used (see the later "Distribution Points CRLs" section for more information). To allow for these changes, the CRL may contain a *Status Referral* extension. Use of this extension means that the CRL contains only references to other CRLs; it does not contain revocation notices.

The Status Referral extension may list a set of CRLs and provide information about them (such as the time of last update). Alternatively, the referral extension may be used as a redirection mechanism to identify what source should be referenced to find actual revocation information. The status referral could be extended in the future to reference sources for revocation notices other than CRLs. This could allow for sufficiently aware client applications to be switched to online certificate validation sources.

Appendix C describes the extensions and contents of a CRL. As with certificates, PKIX defines a profile that describes the form and content of a CRL.

Simple CRLs

The simple form of CRL is a container holding a list of revoked certificates identified by the certificate serial number. The container itself contains information such as the time the CRL was published, when the next CRL will be published, and the CA that issued the CRL.

The CRL is just a sequential file that grows over time to include all certificates that have not expired, but have been revoked. Each entry contains such information as the reason why the certificate was revoked. This includes key compromise, compromise of the issuing CA, withdrawal of privileges identified in the certificate, or change of other certificate information (referred to as changed affiliation). The date when the certificate is believed to have been invalidated due to key compromise may also be included.

The actual size of a CRL is minimized as a certificate identifier is used to identify revoked certificates rather than a copy of the certificate, but even so the list can grow substantially. A certificate revocation rate of around 10 percent per year is probably reasonable. If you have a certificate validity period of two years, and a stable certificate population of 100,000 certificates, your average CRL size will be 20,000 entries. This is a pretty big list to send to a lightweight PKI client application like a cell phone, especially as the application has to process the list sequentially to verify if the certificate being validated is present.

NOTE:

The revocation rate for certificates will be directly tied to the amount of additional information stored within a certificate. For example, if phone numbers or role information such as the subject's job title were included, the number of revocations required due to changes in this information may mean a much higher rate than 10 percent.

Several different alternatives have been proposed to make CRLs more usable. Most of them are focused on providing the most relevant subset of revocation information to the certificate user. Two of these schemes are described in the next sections.

Delta CRLs   Delta CRLs are designed to reduce the size of the CRL that is transmitted to an end-entity. Initially, and then on a planned periodic basis, a full CRL containing all known revocation notices is published—this is known as the *base CRL*. The base CRL allows end-entities to establish a known correct list of all certificates revoked by a CA at a particular date. From that point, a series of updates are provided that show the changes or *deltas* that have been made to the list of revoked certificates by that CA since the issuance of the last base or delta CRL. Each update is distributed as a CRL, and is issued and signed by the CA in the same fashion as a normal CRL.

However, delta CRLs are identified using a critical extension called the *Delta CRL Indicator*. The extension is marked critical, as the end-entity must be aware that the CRL is not a complete list of revocation information. Instead, it must be combined with previously received revocation notices to construct the full list of revoked certificates. The delta CRL identifies the starting date (in the *Base Update* extension) for revocation notices carried in the update. Each CRL also carries a sequence number that allows an end-entity to be aware if CRLs have been missed.

A base CRL may also carry an indicator (*Delta Information*) that tells an end-entity that delta CRLs will also be available corresponding to the full CRL they are processing. The location of the delta CRLs and optionally the time at which the next update will be issued are also provided.

One special case that arises for delta CRLs is how to remove a certificate from the revocation list. This could be achieved by sending a new base CRL where an expired certificate or one released from the hold state has been removed from the list. However, timely removal of certificates is important to keeping the set of revocation information small. In addition, a newly released certificate needs the change in state to be propagated as quickly as possible. To support removal of certificates, delta CRLs provide a special reason code for the certificate named *Remove From CRL* whose job it is to advise the certificate user to remove the certificate from the revocation set they are maintaining.

Delta CRLs provide a useful mechanism for limiting the size of CRLs that are transmitted on a regular basis. This may be applicable where constraints like network bandwidth make shorter CRL updates useful. However, a certificate user is still required to hold all of the CRL information, which implies that a significant amount of storage may still be required. Delta CRLs do not reduce the overhead of searching for a particular CRL entry or limiting the information that a client implementation needs to hold or process.

Distribution Point CRLs   Distribution point CRLs are designed to focus the set of CRLs that need to be searched to a subset of available revocation information. The concept behind a CRL distribution point is that certificate revocation notices may be categorized by the type of certificate being processed, the type of CRL published, or the type of revocation notice being issued.

The type of certificate includes user certificates or CA certificates. The type of CRL includes indirect CRLs. The type of revocation includes *Certificate Hold*, *Key Compromise*, *CA Key Compromise*, *Affiliation Changed*, and so on. CRL distribution points may support only a subset of certificate and CRL types or revocation reasons. As a result, the set of revocation notices that are returned should be much smaller.

When the end-entity certificate is issued, it may contain an extension named *CRLDistributionPoints*. This contains a list of *CRLDistributionPointNames* that allow a certificate user to identify what CRL distribution points are valid for this certificate. The distribution points identify for the certificate user where she can obtain status information for the certificate being validated. The extension may be marked critical, in which case revocation information must be sourced from one of the listed distribution points. If it is not marked critical, the information is for advisory purposes only.

The CRL may contain an extension named *IssuingDistributionPoint* that identifies the distribution point that provided the CRL. This also supplies information about what type of revocation information (including those described previously) and what kinds of certificates (user or CA) are carried in the CRL. The last piece of information this extension may carry is an *IndirectCRL* indicator. If IndirectCRL is set, this indicates that the CRL may carry information from multiple CAs in addition to the issuer of the CRL. The complication this adds is that now each revocation notice in the CRL must identify which CA issued it (to overcome issues where serial numbers may collide between different CAs). This set of relationships is shown in Figure 5-3.

As we identified earlier, references to explicit distribution points in a certificate may become stale over time as the configuration of the PKI changes. If distribution point sources are changed, some form of redirection capability is required—particularly if the distribution point extension in the certificate was marked critical. The Status Referral extension discussed earlier provides such a redirection function (assuming the application client can interpret it). An example of this environment is shown in Figure 5-4.

Distribution points for CRLs are a useful way to restrict the amount of information that a client application needs to process for revocation checking. If the information presented at each source becomes too large and the revocation information needs to be repartitioned, the referral mechanism allows you some flexibility in reconfiguring the PKI. However, the client application will still be delivered a set of status information it must process, where the majority of the time there will not be any information relevant to it—after all, finding a revoked certificate should be an exception condition. To move to a more targeted and less wasteful solution, we need to look at online certificate validation or revocation checking services, but as we will see, these are not without their own problems.

Figure 5-3

Distribution
point CRL
relationships

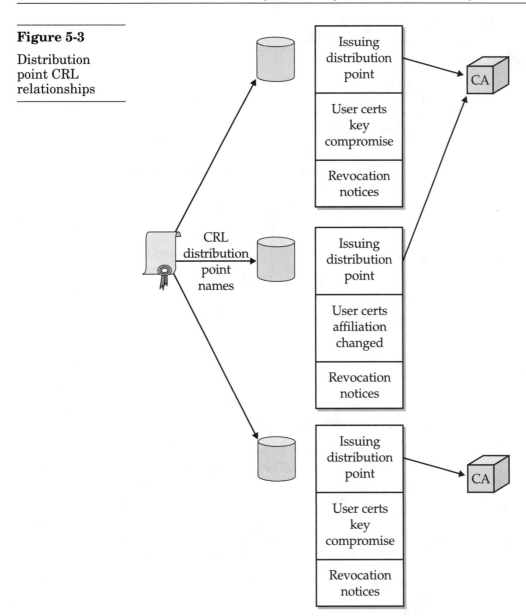

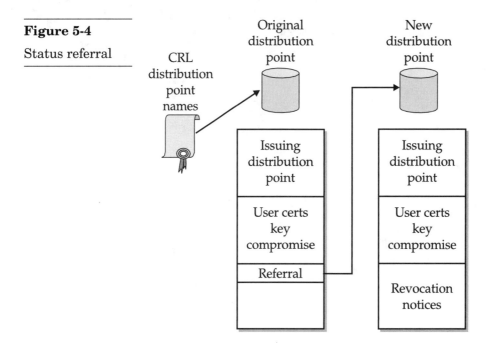

Figure 5-4

Status referral

Online Certificate Validation

Online schemes for checking the revocation status of a certificate or possibly performing other certificate validation checks have been proposed. In Chapter 6, we examine the OCSP, SCVP, and OCSP extended protocols currently standardized or under consideration within the PKIX model. In this section, we will consider the implications of online services of this type, and leave the PKIX protocols for the next chapter.

The motivation for using an online service includes the following:

▪ Freshness/timeliness of responses

▪ Fast response time

▪ Minimal use of available network bandwidth

▪ Low client processing overhead

▪ Central policy evaluation of certificate validity

Let's consider a few of these in the light of some of the implementations we know about today.

For applications that are very sensitive to certificate revocation, the timeliness or the freshness of the responses that are provided may become critical. If you consider an online service supplying high-value monetary transactions, the need to validate the revocation status of a certificate associated with a particular trade may require near real-time revocation notices. Theoretically, an online service would provide this kind of characteristic.

However, just because the query and a response interaction with a status—checking service such as an OCSP responder are returned quickly over the network, this does not necessarily indicate how fresh the data may be. The implementation may send the query to the CA or its nominated server that will directly verify the specific certificate in the CA database and return the response. However, it is just as likely that the CA is still generating CRLs on a regular basis and sending them to the query responder. If the CA is not providing better updates for the CRL weekly (although most are at least configured to update them daily), it does not matter how fast the response is from the responder, the status information may still be stale.

Protocols such as OCSP do not leave their clients in the dark about these issues. Information about when the status information was generated is provided so that the client can make sensible decisions about the usefulness of the data. It certainly pays to check, as there may not be any guarantees about the freshness of the data returned by the service.

The speed of responses will generally be determined by the network bandwidth and topology (how many servers are available, how close they are to you, how powerful they are). However, just as the freshness of data is not necessarily a given, neither is the speed of response. If the responder implementation is not directly accessing a certificate database, it may be using a CRL stored within a directory. In addition to the overhead of the directory query to obtain the relevant CRL (CRL distribution points may be in use), the responder must still sequentially process the CRL looking for the certificate that is the subject of the status query. If referrals are being used to provide redirection, this will all add to the overhead associated with responding to a given query.

Network bandwidth is generally well optimized with an online service, as the query and the response are relatively small—particularly when compared to sending a large CRL across the network. The aggregate impact on the network may not be so obvious, however. If the client performs a very large amount of certificate status checking, in some cases transferring a distribution point CRL may have less impact, particularly if it is accessed outside of peak usage periods for the network.

The processing overhead required from the client can reasonably be expected to be small—after all, the client does not have to stomp through all of those CRL entries. In addition, it does not need large amounts of memory or offline storage to maintain and process CRLs. For some online protocols, such as OCSP, which is limited to revocation status checking, the client still has to do a huge amount of work. For example, before a request can be made to check the status of a certificate, the client must locate the CA certificate for the issuer and create a hash from that CA certificate (this is a fingerprint to uniquely identify the CA). To validate a certificate chain, the client must do this for every certificate in the chain and make a separate revocation status check for each. Fortunately, CA revocation occurs infrequently, so if CRL distribution points or separate authority revocation lists are used, the processing overhead for the service response should be small.

The overhead associated with the rest of the actions required for certificate validation, plus the need for multiple round trips before a certificate chain can be checked for revocation status at each level, has led to more sophisticated protocols such as SCVP and OCSPX (OSCP extended). These protocols allow a full certificate to be sent to a server and utilize a much broader set of validation processing, including validation of a full certificate chain. A particularly nice aspect of this is that centralized evaluation of security policies are possible when the certificate chain is being validated. At first sight, this appears to be a wonderful opportunity to offload processing from a client application. However, when you consider the amount of information that must be transferred to the validation service (trusted roots and intermediate certificates to use, policies that should be complied with, partial results that may be returned, and so on), it becomes clear that this is no longer a simple problem to resolve.

Online services do have a major limitation—what if you need to check revocation status and you are not online? CRLs may be loaded from the repository where they are published as needed and then the client may use the stored information for its checks. This means that applications that have a high requirement may need to keep a local cache for revocation information or handle limited revocation capabilities when offline.

Additional security issues are raised when using online services. Unlike the CRL that is signed by the CA, the online responders may be a completely different service (see Figure 5-5). This may require distribution of certificates and the associated trust that allows online service providers to be authenticated by their clients. In addition, the responses that are provided need to be signed by the responder or transferred over a secure network session that prevents modification of the responses.

Figure 5-5

Online validation
service

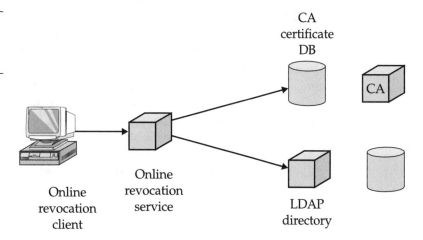

On balance, it seems that online services are solutions that are required for useful PKI solutions in the future, particularly as we add low-end clients like cell phones and PDAs. However, the technology certainly needs refinement, and there are likely to be issues such as the ones described above that clients will need to be aware of for some time to come.

Hash-Based Schemes

To finish this discussion of revocation, it is worth mentioning that variations on standard CRLs have been implemented possessing many of the same benefits of CRLs but with better operational characteristics. Generally, the more interesting and well-developed technologies in this area fall into the category of hash-based schemes.

In the case of revocation hash schemes, the aim is to reduce the set of information about revoked certificates down to a very small representation of all the revocation notices. This information set is generally signed, so it has the same protection characteristics as a CRL and does not require the use of a secure server or transport.

The best-known commercial version of this class of systems is that provided by ValiCert. In the ValiCert case, a special hash tree is created known as a Certificate Revocation Tree (CRT). The leaf nodes of the tree represents a range of certificates where the lowest certificate serial number is revoked, but all higher certificates are still valid. By comparing a specific certificate to two adjacent leaf nodes, it is possible to determine if the certificate falls into the valid range.

CRTs may be built from any number of revocation sources like CRLs. The advantage is that the representation and size of the CRT is very light compared to a CRL. In addition, the process of checking for a certificate status has low overhead compared to walking through a linear CRL. In addition, if the certificates in a certificate chain all fall within the same CA tree, it is possible to verify the entire chain with a single validation operation. The disadvantage is that a very large amount of CRT recomputation may be caused by the addition of a revoked certificate.

Summary

In this chapter, we have examined a range of issues related to life cycle management of keys and certificates. The areas that we considered related to keys included how and where keys are generated, as well as the size and quality aspects of the keys produced. We looked at key stores and their security aspects, PKCS #12 containers as a secure key transport mechanism, and key archival and recovery.

Certificate life cycle starts with registration processing, which includes initialization of end-entities, distribution of initial trust, the requirements for registration, and proof of possession of the private key corresponding to the public key being registered. The certificate will need to be renewed at the expiration of its validity period. Once the certificate has been issued, the CA is responsible for maintaining state about the certificate, including the revocation status. We examined the various types of CRLs, including simple CRLs, delta CRLs, and distribution point CRLs. To round everything out, we considered online validation protocols.

CHAPTER 6

A PKI Architecture—
The PKIX Model

Public Key Infrastructure Architecture

In Chapter 3, we introduced the components of a Public Key Infrastructure, identified their roles, and briefly discussed their functions. Chapter 4 expanded on some of those concepts, looking specifically at areas including the processes associated with managing keys and certificates. Chapter 5 discussed the issues associated with key and certificate life cycles. In this chapter, we will examine how the various PKI components and services may be tied together and look at an architecture that defines interactions between PKI components.

The PKIX Model

The X.509 standard defined certificate formats and fields, and procedures for distribution of public keys. As a broad standard that needs to encompass many fields of use, it allows many variations on certificate content and supports many potential operational models. Subsets of the range of X.509 capabilities may be defined for particular communities or fields of use. The value of a subset is that the tighter constraints that are applied allow more interoperable versions as each implementation does not need to support all possible options.

The *Public Key Infrastructure X.509* (PKIX) working group was formed by the *Internet Engineering Task Force* (IETF) to define a set of certificate profiles and an operational model that was suitable for deployment of X.509 public key certificates in the Internet. Other PKI models have been created for different application domains, such as the standards developed by ANSI ASC X9F for financial institutions. Each model selects attributes of the X.509 standard as required and may add certificate extensions or concepts to support the needs of the application domain.

The Internet is used by a broad cross-section of the general population, so it seems a suitable candidate to examine as an X.509 application domain. In this chapter, we will examine the PKIX model. PKIX does not support all features of X.509, and in many cases defines usage models that restrict the features that are supported.

NOTE:
PKIX has been expanded recently to include support for Privilege Management Infrastructure—this is described in Appendix C.

PKIX identifies the major functions of a Public Key Infrastructure as:

- Registration
- Initialization
- Certification
- Key pair recovery
- Key generation
- Key update
- Cross-certification
- Revocation
- Certificate and revocation notice distribution/publication

We have already seen the description of these services in Chapter 5.

PKIX has developed documents describing five major areas in support of its architectural model. These areas include

- X.509 V3 certificate and V2 certificate revocation list profiles
- Operational protocols
- Management protocols
- Policy outlines
- Timestamp and data certification services

These divisions allow refinement of the basic X.509 description in several ways. The profiles allow subsetting of X.509 to include those extensions that are perceived to be useful to the Internet community (in fact, one extension has been added so far). In addition, the extensions may be identified as critical or optional to Internet operations in different contexts.

The operational and management protocols describe the messages that must be supported for PKIX-compliant components to interoperate with each other. You will notice that significantly more attention has been expended on management protocols as opposed to the operational protocols. This is primarily because the operational protocols make use of services provided by existing Internet protocols such as FTP or HTTP, and only minor specifications are required in most cases to identify how those protocols should be used to support the PKIX model.

The policy outlines describe how certificates should be used or how a PKI component should be operated. In most cases, the outlines are indications or guides to PKI implementers about the sort of documentation that should be provided to control operation of the PKI.

The last area is a slightly different case. It includes documents that describe layered or ancillary services that will probably be required by PKI implementers when creating a security service.

PKIX Architecture

The major components within the PKIX architecture include

- Clients
  - The user of a PKI certificate, otherwise identified as end-entities
  - The end-user or system that is the subject of a PKI certificate

- Certification Authority (CA)
  - Issues and revokes PKI certificates

- *Registration Authority* (RA)
  - Vouches for the binding between public keys and the identity of certificate holders

- Repository
  - A system (possibly distributed) that stores certificates and CRLs
  - Provides a distribution mechanism for certificates and CRLs to end-entities

The PKI components and the major relationships between them are shown in Figure 6-1.

Figure 6-1

PKI components

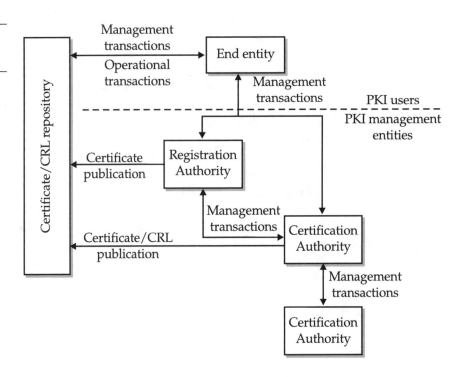

The flows between PKIX components in Figure 6-1 include

- Operational transactions
- Management transactions
- Certificate and CRL publication

Operational transactions are the message exchanges that are included in the operational protocol documents and provide the underlying transport for certificates, CRLs, and other management and status information. Management transactions, of course, are the message exchanges described in the management protocol documents that provide the messaging services to support management transactions or operations within the PKI. Publication is used to distribute certificates and CRLs to public repositories.

PKIX Functions

We have already examined many of the functions or services identified by PKIX earlier, but for completeness, here is the PKIX view of PKI functions.

Registration

Registration is the process whereby an end-entity that will be the subject of a certificate makes itself known to a CA. This may be done via an RA or directly to a CA, assuming that the CA implements RA functions. The name and other attributes used to identify the subject must be validated according to the certification practices statement under which the CA operates.

Initialization

Bootstrapping problems exist when an end-entity needs to begin communicating with a PKI. How does the end-entity determine which PKI components they need to communicate with? How are the public key and certificate of the CA provided to the end-entity? How does the end-entity establish a secure communications channel with the RA or CA? How are the end-entity public/private keys generated for use during the registration process? These are all questions that information provided during initialization should answer.

The initial values that need to be created or conveyed between the parties before communication can begin are part of the initialization function within the PKIX model.

Certification

The CA issues a certificate for a subject public key and returns that certificate to the end-entity or publishes it in a repository.

Key Pair Recovery

Keys used for encryption of data or other keys (for purposes of key transport or exchange) may need to be archived in order to meet local policy requirements. This allows recovery of keys when a key is lost and previously encrypted information needs to be accessed. Archival and recovery operations may be performed by a CA or separate key recovery system.

Key Generation

PKIX allows the public/private key pair for the subject of a certificate to be generated in the end-entities' local environment and then conveyed to the RA/CA in a registration request. Alternatively, the key pair may be generated by the RA or CA, provided the private key material can be distributed to the end-entity in some secure fashion.

Key Update

PKIX expects a key pair to be replaced on a regular basis, when the key expires, or when it is compromised. If the key update occurs in response to normal key expiration, the transition to the new key should occur gracefully, and this requires support of suitable notification mechanisms and periods. In the case of a key compromise, certificates must be declared invalid, and the new certificate validity and availability must be announced. Given the unplanned nature of this event, it will be anything but graceful.

Support for CA key and certificate update is also required—in fact, handling this transparently will be essential to the smooth operation of the PKI over time. Update of CA keys and certificates may be supported by the same protocols and procedures for normal key expiration, but may need support for out-of-band notification when a CA key compromise event occurs. CA key compromise is a catastrophic event, leading to the revocation of the CA certificate and all certificates issued by the compromised CA and those subordinate to it.

NOTE:
Timestamping of the CA certificates issued to subordinate CAs is one method that could be applied to limit the impact of a superior CA key compromise event.

Cross-Certification

PKIX identifies a cross-certificate as a certificate issued by one CA to another CA to certify the public/private key pair used by the CA for signing certificates. Cross-certificates may be issued within the same administrative domain or across administrative domains. Cross-certificates may be issued in one direction between CAs or in both directions. This topic is considered in more detail in Chapter 8 when we consider trust models.

Revocation

PKIX CAs are responsible for maintaining information about the state of a certificate. This includes support for revocation of certificates that have become invalid prior to the certificate expiration period. X.509 V2 CRLs may be used as a mechanism for conveying information about the revocation status of the certificate. Entries are added to the next published CRL after the certificate has been revoked.

Alternatively, CAs may use an online revocation notification mechanism such as the *Online Certificate Status Protocol* (OCSP)[1] to reduce latency between revocation of the certificate by the CA and notification to end-entities. Unlike CRL publication mechanisms, end-entities using online methods for certificate validation must be able to establish the identity of the online service provider. In the case of OCSP, this requires that the responders signature be validated on responses provided to the client.

Certificate and Revocation Notice Distribution and Publication

The PKI is responsible for distributing certificates and notices of certificate revocation. Certificates may be distributed by transferring them to the owner on completion of registration processing and/or when they are requested by certificate owners or users. As an alternative, the services of a repository such as an LDAP directory may be used as a publication mechanism.

Revocation information or notices may be distributed by publishing a list of revoked certificates in the form of CRL to a repository such as an LDAP directory, producing announcements that are forwarded to end-entities or providing access to online services (or responders) that are queried by end-entities. CRLs may be published on a regular timed basis or aperiodically.

PKIX Specifications

The PKIX specifications broadly fall into the categories of

- X.509 profiles
- Operational protocols
- Management protocols
- Policy outlines
- Timestamp and data certification services

X.509 Profiles

As you can see from the full X.509 certificate description provided in Appendix A, many of the certificate fields and extensions support different options. This flexibility allows X.509 certificates to be used in many application contexts, but means that it is difficult to guarantee interoperable implementations. PKIX defines a profile that restricts the set of options used to a set that are useful to Internet users. The restrictions have the added advantage of making interoperability between implementations more likely.

The X.509 Internet Profile defined by PKIX is described in RFC2459[2]. It describes each X.509 V3 certificate and V2 CRL extension and defines for each whether it

- Must be supported
- May optionally be supported
- May not be supported

Appropriate ranges for the values used in each extension are also provided.

An example of an addition provided in PKIX over X.509 is the inclusion of hold instruction codes for use when a certificate is suspended. X.509 does not explicitly list hold instruction codes, but PKIX does. PKIX also adds an Internet-specific certificate extension named AuthorityInfoAccess that identifies the format and location of additional information about the issuing CA. It is expected that this extension will allow an online validation service to be identified for the CA.

Operational Protocols

Operational protocols provide the underlying transport that is used to deliver certificates, CRLs, and other management and status information to the different components within the PKI. Each transport has its own set of requirements for interaction, so specific procedures are called out for use of LDAP[3], HTTP, FTP[4], and X.500 as transport mechanisms.

Management Protocols

Management protocols support transfer of management requests and information between PKI end-entities and PKI management entities and for communication between PKI management entities. The protocols may, for example, carry registration requests, revocation status, or cross-certification requests and the corresponding responses.

The management protocols define the format of messages that are sent and what information may be requested. In addition, they define the ways in which messages may be exchanged between pairs of communicating entities.

Policy Outlines

PKIX has created outlines for *certificate policies* (CP) and *certification practices statements* (CPS) in RFC 2527[5]. These provide guidance to PKI implementers about what should be considered in the creation of a document such as a CP that determines the applicability of a certificate to an application domain, or a CPS that controls the operation of a Certification Authority.

Timestamp and Data Certification Services

Timestamping and data certification services provide layered security services built on top of the PKI. The timestamp service[6] is provided by a trusted third party known as a Time Stamp Authority that signs a message indicating that it existed prior to a specific time. This provides support for non-repudiation, as it can be shown that a document had been signed prior to the compromise of a private key.

The *Data Certification Service*[7] (DCS) is a trusted third party that verifies the correctness of data submitted to it. The concept here is that you can use the notary-like services of a of a Data Certification Service to establish that a document contained validated and verifiable information at some point in time. An example might be where you wanted to validate registration of a piece of property. To avoid later arguments, the DCS could be used to document that boundary coordinates were recorded correctly when the registration took place.

The DCS certifies possession of data or verifies another entity's signature by generating a data validation token or certificate when it has completed its validation. This token provides documented evidence that a signature and public key certificate were valid at a specific time. The token can be used even after the certificate corresponding to the original signature has expired or the revocation information corresponding to the certificate is no longer available.

PKI Entities

In this section, we will examine the entities that are defined as part of the PKIX view of a PKI.

Registration Authority

A *Registration Authority* (RA) is an optional entity within a PKI that has responsibility for the administrative tasks associated with registering the end-entity that is the subject of the certificate issued by the CA. If an RA is not present in the PKI, the CA is assumed to have the same set of capabilities as are defined for a Registration Authority.

The functions that a particular Registration Authority implements will vary based on the needs of the PKI deployment, but must support the principle of establishing or verifying the identity of the subscriber. These functions are likely to include

- Personal authentication of the subject registering for a certificate
- Verification of the validity of information supplied by the subject
- Validating the right of the subject to requested certificate attributes
- Verifying that the subject actually possesses the private key being registered—this is generally referred to as proof of possession (POP)
- Reporting key compromise or termination cases where revocation is required
- Assignment of names for identification purposes
- Generation of shared secrets for use during the initialization and certificate pickup phases of registration
- Public/private key pair generation
- Initiation of the registration process with the Certification Authority on behalf of the subject end-entity
- Private key archival
- Initiation of key recovery processing
- Distribution of physical tokens (such as smart cards) containing the private keys

In general, the Registration Authority handles exchanges (often involving user interactions) between the subject end-entity and the PKI for registration, certificate delivery, and other key and certificate life cycle management processes. However, under no circumstances does the RA actually originate trusted statements about the subject (other than vouching for them as part of the identity process to the CA). As a result, only a Certification Authority may issue a certificate or originate certificate revocation status information like a CRL.

The deployment of a separate Registration Authority is a matter of the business processes associated with the operation of the PKI. For example, in a managed PKI service, the operation of an RA may be performed at a customer site, while the CA and its operation may be outsourced. Alternatively, the issuance of certificates may be maintained within an organization, while the registration processing may be distributed to your business partners or operated as a franchise. The latter case might include the use of an organization like the Post Office as a provider of registration services to supply your certificates.

In some cases, network topology may require access to a Registration Authority server by end-entities outside of the administrative domain of the Certification Authority. An example, shown in Figure 6-2, is the registration of end-entities within your partners' organizations in an extranet environment when using certificates for authentication into your business systems. In this case, the RA may be placed in the network DMZ while the CA is maintained behind a network firewall to protect it.

Figure 6-2

Access to
Registration
Authority in a
network DMZ

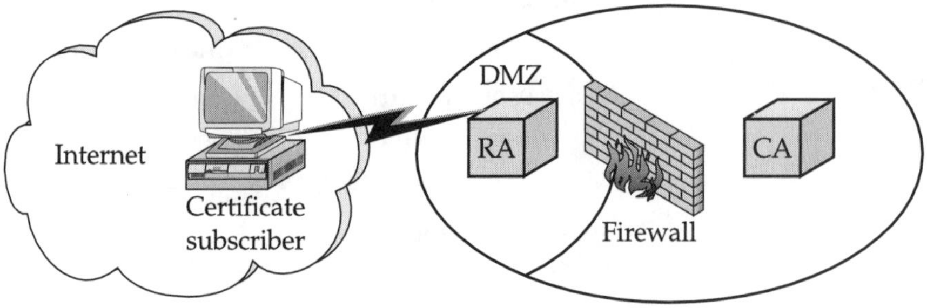

Certification Authority

The Certification Authority is responsible for creating and issuing end-entity certificates. End-entity certificates associate the identity of the subject end-entity as expressed through the subject name being registered with the public key corresponding to the private key held by the subject. In addition, the CA is responsible for management of all aspects of the life cycle of the certificate after its issuance. This includes tracking the status of a certificate and issuing revocation notices if the certificate needs to be invalidated. Even when revocation notice has been served, the CA will normally still have requirements placed on it to maintain a certificate archive and audit trail associated with the certificate for later verification purposes.

In PKIX terms, there are a number of specific terms associated with particular types of CA. A "root CA" is a CA that is directly trusted by a certificate user. However, this terminology is not used consistently throughout PKIX, and in this book we have used the term "trust anchor" to refer to the CA trusted by a certificate user.

Repository

The repository is used for public storage of certificates and CRLs. Originally, the repository was an X.500 directory. For support of PKIX, the repository will usually be an LDAP directory. LDAP is listed as one of the operational protocols specifically supported in PKIX. Although operations within a management protocol like CMP may provide query support to obtain certain certificates or CRLs, LDAP may be used directly as a lookup protocol for the same information.

In addition to certificate and CRL storage, other entries in the directory such as the CA directory objects may be used to store additional information. This includes identifying relationships such as cross-certification between CAs.

PKIX Management Protocols

Currently the management protocols are defined in three documents. Certificate Management Protocols (CMP), RFC 2510[8], and Certificate Management Messages Over CMS (CMC), RFC 2797[9], describe two management message interchange protocols. *Certificate Request Message Format* (CRMF), RFC 2511[10], describes the message formats for management requests and responses.

The use of CMP over HTTP[11] and TCP[12] as transport protocols is described in two separate draft documents.

The management protocols defined by the PKIX working group have had a checkered development process. CMP was developed by PKIX as a messaging protocol for communication between PKI entities. Around the same time, the *secure e-mail* (S/MIME) working group was working on a PKCS #10 based messaging scheme. PKCS #10 had previously been used as a certificate request structure within the secure e-mail community.

The PKIX group defined a set of certificate enrollment messages known as the CRMF, which was intended to replace both CMP and CRS for certificate requests, but unfortunately it did not include support for PKCS #10 formatted messages. Support for a wider set of management messages was provided with the creation of the *Certificate Management Message Formats* (CMMF). CMMF supported PKCS #10, and in combination with CMS (Cryptographic Message Syntax, part of S/MIME from the e-mail protocol world) allowed the use of e-mail as a transport protocol. The result was a protocol specification called CMC (CMMF over CMS). At this point, the specification work on CRS was dropped.

To make life interesting, content from the CMMF specification has now been moved into both the CMP and CMC specifications, and as a result, the CMMF specification has been dropped.

So where does this leave us? A single separate document still exists that defines the message formats for certificate requests: CRMF. However, we now have two competing specifications for the messaging protocol: CMP and CMC. Most of the functionality between each protocol is very similar. Both have now been accepted as standard documents within PKIX. For PKI implementers, the problem is which to select. Interoperability is hard enough to achieve when you have an agreed-upon specification. Now that there are two specifications being implemented by different vendors, interoperability becomes much more difficult.

At the time of writing, CMP is a little ahead of CMC. A second round of the CMP specification[13] has been developed based on development experience and interoperability testing from a number of PKI vendors. Interoperability testing has not been started on CMC yet, but is expected to commence soon.

There appears to be no way to rationalize the two management protocols to produce a single PKIX management protocol—after significant effort we still have two standards. The result for implementers is that it is necessary to be aware of which protocol is provided by a PKI vendor, to ensure maximum interoperability. Over time (short of one protocol gaining acceptance over the other), it is likely that PKI management entities will support both, and end-entities will implement one or the other. At the risk of additional overhead and complexity, that will allow us interoperability between all components.

CMP

Figure 6-3 shows the PKIX architectural model overlaid with the CMP management operations.

Figure 6-3

MP management
operations

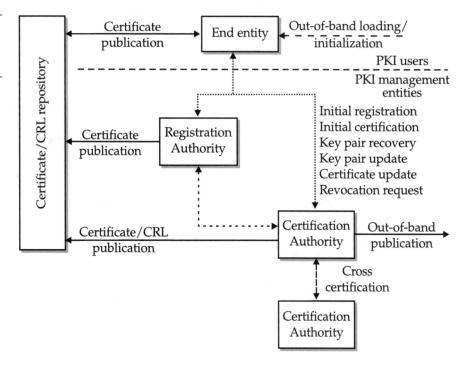

CMP Operational Groups

CMP defines the following operational groups for management messages:

- CA establishment
- End-entity initialization
- Certification
- Certificate and CRL discovery
- Recovery operations
- Revocation operations

The next sections look at the type of information stored in these messages.

CA Establishment　This deals with issues related to creation of a new CA, including production of initial CRLs and distribution of the CA's public signing key.

End-Entity Initialization   These operations support the steps necessary to initialize an end-entity. The end-entity will minimally require the CA's public signing key and may need to know where PKI management entities are located and what services and options they provide.

Certification   Operations in this group result in the creation of new certificates.

Initial certification deals with the first time that an end-entity registers for a certificate with a CA or RA. A new certificate is issued by the CA and returned to the end-entity or published to a public directory. As part of this process, the end-entity's own keys are created and stored.

Key pair update allows for keys that are reaching the end of their life to be replaced and a new certificate issued.

Certificate update allows for a certificate that has expired to be replaced by a new certificate containing the same information.

CA key pair update deals with the special case of a Certification Authority key expiration. The new keys need to be securely distributed to relying parties. Relying parties and end-entities need to handle special cases such as receiving certificates signed by either the old or the new signing key during the changeover period.

Cross-certification request provides for a CA to request that another CA certify its signing keys. The process of cross-certification is discussed in detail in Chapter 8 on trust models.

Cross-certificate update allows certificates to be updated where the original certificate was issued in response to a cross-certification request.

Certificate and CRL Discovery   This group includes the set of management operations and messages that cause certificates or CRLs to be published.

Certificate publication may be handled by using the CMP announcement messages *CA Key Update Announcement* or *Certificate Announcement*, or may directly use an operational protocol such as LDAP.

CRL publication may be handled by using the CMP announcement messages *CRL Announcement* or *Revocation Announcement*, or may directly use an operational protocol such as LDAP.

NOTE:

It is not always clear how an announcement message of this type can be used, or if the CA will know all of the parties that need to be sent announcement messages. Nor is it entirely clear how to handle cases where end-entities may be offline (permanently or temporarily).

Recovery Operations Recovery operations are used for restoring lost key and certificate stores, referred to as a *Personal Storage Environment* (PSE) in PKIX. Key pair recovery operations are used to recover or restore private keys or other materials that have been lost, where a backup version is available in a key archive. Chapter 5 discussed the various types and classes of keys that may need to be recovered.

Revocation Operations This covers operations that cause the creation of a new CRL or CRL entries. Currently, the only operation is a revocation request used by an authorized person to indicate to a CA that a certificate needs to be revoked.

Initial Registration/Certification

CMP is designed to support a wide range of operational and business models. Some of the considerations necessary to support these models are described here.

Messages that originate with an end-entity may or may not be authenticated. If they require authentication, the keying material necessary for this authentication is provided by the CA or RA in some out-of-band mechanism (such as men swapping black briefcases, or your administrator calling you to provide a password used to generate a key). PKIX does require that conforming PKI implementations support end-entity originated message authentication. All messages that originate with the PKI management entities are required to be authenticated.

Key generation from the CMP protocol perspective is defined as the first place that either the public or the private component of a key pair appears in a CMP message. Both central and local key generation are allowed for, as CMP does not cover the process of key creation and transport. No key transport protocol is defined.

Proof of Possession (POP)

PKIX requires that end-entities prove that they hold the private key corresponding to the public key sent in a certificate registration request. This proof of possession can be verified using out-of-band (non-CMP) mechanisms, but all conforming CAs must verify the possession of the private key by the certificate requestor in some way. The proof of possession is achieved in different ways for different key types (if the same key can be used for different purposes—signing and encryption in the case of RSA—any one method can be used). Signature keys are verified simply by signing the registration request and verifying the signature with the corresponding public key sent in the request message.

NOTE:

The actual letter of law in RFC 2459 (PKIX Certificate and CRL Profile) is actually a little less assertive here than is desirable. In section 3.1, it states that the "CA may base this assertion upon technical means (a.k.a., proof of possession through a challenge-response protocol), presentation of the private key, or on an assertion by the subject."

Encryption key possession can be verified by sending the key to the RA or CA as part of the registration request (this method works well if key archival is a requirement). Two other alternatives exist for proof of possession of the private encryption key.

A challenge may be encrypted with the public key submitted as part of the registration request, and the end-entity is required to show that it can decrypt it. The challenge may be sent directly to the end-entity where a response can be returned by the end-entity. Alternatively, it may be sufficient to encrypt the certificate that is issued to the end-entity with the public key. The result is that only the intended party holding the private key can make use of the certificate.

If the key is to be used for a key agreement protocol (such as Diffie-Hellman, discussed in Chapter 10), the end-entity and the RA or CA must actually run through the process of establishing a shared secret in order to verify possession of the private key.

CMP Message Capabilities

Protection of CMP messages may be achieved by the use of a MAC or signature to provide integrity checking of the message contents. CMP allows for external protection mechanisms such as the use of PKCS #7, S/MIME, or potentially other secure protocols such as SSL or TLS. Multiple levels of integrity checking may be applied, such as the case where an end-entity request is sent to an RA, which in turn signs the request and forwards it to a CA. Specific fields within a message, such as the private key or certificate, may be encrypted by the originator of the message to ensure privacy of sensitive information.

CMP messages support the transfer of extra certificates in addition to the certificate that is being issued. In general, the description of this capability is to support the transfer of certificates that "may be useful" to the message recipient. An example of this may be where intermediate CA certificates are needed to verify the subjects certificate. The use of this support is not restricted to the transfer of certification paths—for example, other certificates that assert the identity of service providers within the PKI may be sent; however, the user may need to explicitly decide to trust these certificates.

CMP supports a transaction context field that allows multiple messages to be sent as part of a transaction necessary to complete an operation. Most transactions are simple request and response pairs that do not need to use this field.

CMC

CMC is designed to use many of the features of previously defined standards, such as CMS, PKCS #10, and the CRMF specifications. Much of the motivation came from the need to support S/MIME requirements for PKI. As a result, explicit requirements include the need to support existing enrollment protocols and to cover all encryption algorithms used by S/MIME.

The prior practice of using PKCS #10 for requests and PKCS #7 responses is supported to maximize the use of existing implementations. The aim for all CMC operations is to complete the operation with a single round-trip transaction using a simple request and a response (we cannot quite achieve this in all cases, but it is a good working principle).

Unlike CMP, CMC does not create special cases for operations like certificate renewal, rekeying, or cross-certification. Operations like renewal and rekeying are considered to have the same requirements as the original enrollment request, except that the validation of the identity can be determined by using a certificate previously issued by the CA.

In addition to certificate registration, CMC supports messages for retrieval of previously issued certificates. The repository holding the certificates may be implemented within a CA, an RA, or some separate service. The intention is to support clients that are resource constrained and cannot maintain some set of certificates (possibly including their own) in memory.

CRL retrieval is supported in the same way that certificate retrieval is provided, but using a CRL retrieval message. The CRL may be stored in a repository access by a CA, RA, or other service.

Revocation messages allow a client to request revocation of a previously issued certificate. As authentication using the signing private key may not be possible if the signing key itself has been compromised, CMC supports the use of a previously constructed shared secret. Signing revocation requests is the preferred method and must be supported by CMC clients, but the use of shared secrets is an option that may be implemented at the discretion of the PKI implementer.

CMC Message Types

CMC messages are designed to allow maximum interoperability with older protocol interactions like PKCS #10 requests. The alternative scheme that is defined uses CRMF message formats. The result is that both message formats are defined for each of the operations. In general, some of the more powerful or flexible aspects of the protocol may not be available unless the newer CRMF formatted messages are used. The CMC specification details the combinations of message types that may or must be sent or received by management entities and end-entities. In general, the management entities must be able to process CRMF formatted messages, while end-entities are permitted to send them.

There is a certain level of redundancy or overlap between the attributes that are defined specifically within CRMF and those defined in CMC. Remember that CRMF is a shared base-level format used by both CMC and CMP. In some cases, certain features that are exploited by CMP, including a method for performing indirect proof of possession of a private key, are explicitly prohibited. In other cases where there may be an overlap, CMC message attributes are considered to take precedence over the CRMF attributes. This allows CMC to maintain maximum flexibility and power while still allowing use of the PKCS #10 message format.

CMC supports the notion of separate Registration Authorities by allowing an RA to take a registration request and wrap it in a second layer of a request message, including identification of new attributes, before passing it to a CA. This may occur multiple times if there is a requirement to support a layered set of RAs between the end-entity and the CA.

All of the messages in CMC are considered signed objects. In fact, in the case where a key agreement scheme such as Diffie-Hellman is being used, a null signature must be provided (see the discussion in the next section on POP for Diffie-Hellman keys).

Where privacy of the data is concerned, a separate data envelope is provided by CMS that is used to wrap the original signed message as an encrypted structure. Currently, the entire request is wrapped if privacy is required (it is an option). CMS indicates that the same enveloping technique should be used for wrapping private keys that are being transported for key archival purposes. As an alternative to wrapping the message, a secure, authenticated transport such as SSL or TLS may be used.

Certification Requests

Clients may request any set of valid X.509 certificate attributes in a certification request, and the CAs and RAs must be able to process them. However, CMC supports the notion that the CA or RA may modify any of the requested extensions, provided it does not change the original intention behind the request. For example, if the client had requested a certificate with a key usage field indicating that the key should be used for encryption only, the usage could not be changed to signing. Instead, the CA should reject the original request if such a change is required, as it would substantially alter the original intent of the subject registering the key. Alternatively, the CA could potentially modify information such as the subject name, or add additional identifying information to the certificate.

Proof of possession of private keys is supported in CMC, but if it is required, must support a direct method such as signing the certification request when a signing key is used. Proving possession of an encryption-only key is more difficult (if the key usage supports signing and encryption, the POP method for signature keys may be used). This is an area where CMC must relax its requirement for a single round-trip pair of messages. The algorithm defined for POP of encryption-only keys requires two round trips for request and response messages using a challenge encrypted by the CA based on the public key provided in the certification request. To support Diffie-Hellman keys for key agreement, a separate process is used to verify the existence of the key for POP purposes.

The response to a certification request may contain a set of certificates satisfying the original request. CMC refers to this as a *certificate bag*. This may include support for certification request for multiple keys. In addition, intermediate certificates necessary to form a certification chain to a self-signed certificate may be included. The self-signed certificate itself may also be returned in the certificate bag, but an end-entity is advised against implicitly trusting it without some form of external validation.

Finally, CMC supports a certificate registration model where there may be some delay in the return of a certificate while the approval process is being conducted by the RA or CA. A query message may be sent identifying a particular certification request to obtain the status of the certification request.

Non-PKIX Management Protocols

To diverge slightly from the topic of this chapter, one management protocol is worth considering that is not currently, nor is it intended to become, an RFC. Cisco Systems produced a registration protocol known as SCEP that is widely deployed by most CA vendors and many network device vendors. SCEP was produced prior to completion of either CMC or CMP. The breadth of its support makes it worth considering for pragmatic reasons, although limitations in its functionality and scope seem to indicate that it will be replaced by CMP and CMC.

SCEP

Cisco Systems has submitted a draft of a certificate registration protocol named the *Simple Certificate Enrollment Protocol* (SCEP), which is used particularly within the IPsec *virtual private network* (VPN) community. The draft is submitted for informational purposes, which means that Cisco is advising the Internet community of the way their protocol works, but does not currently expect it to become an IETF standard.

The goal of SCEP is to support certificate issuance to network devices. As an enrollment protocol, it has goals similar to CMP and CMC, but without the same scope or architectural framework as PKIX. SCEP uses PKCS #10 requests and PKCS #7 formatted responses as the basis of the protocol messages. HTTP is used as the transport protocol.

SCEP supports the following operations:

- Public key distribution for RAs and CAs
- Certificate enrollment
- Certificate revocation
- Certificate query
- CRL query

End-entities in SCEP have a restricted naming scheme supporting the following forms for subject names:

- Fully qualified domain names such as router.cisco.com
- IP address
- Serial number

Key generation in SCEP is supported only in end-entities, and for a given subject name and key usage, only a single key pair is expected. This creates some interesting issues when dealing with key update or certificate renewal. The single key pair constraint does not allow for overlapping certificates, which makes the process of updating keys and certificates more difficult. Note also that only RSA keys are supported in SCEP currently.

Authentication of enrollment requests may be supported by out-of-band manual authentication at the CA or RA. Alternatively, preshared secrets may be used to authenticate the end-entity. If preshared secrets are used, requests can be processed automatically and the response returned synchronously to the end-entity. If manual authentication is required, the end-entity must wait for some time to expire. To handle this, SCEP provides a message that can be used to poll the CA to pick up the approved certificate.

A unique aspect of the protocol is that PKCS #7 is used to secure the messages transmitted from the end-entity to the CA. PKCS #7 requires that both the end-entity and the CA have each other's certificates. This is something of a problem for certificate enrollment, as the end-entity does not yet have a certificate. SCEP solves this by having the end-entity generate a self-signed certificate for the key pair it is registering.

An SCEP client is sent a root CA certificate in an unencrypted HTTP message. When the certificate is received, the client is required to calculate a hash across the entire CA certificate and then contact the CA operator to verify that the received certificate is in fact valid. SCEP assumes that any RA certificates are signed by the root CA.

Certificate and CRL queries are designed to allow resource-constrained devices to look up certificates (including its own) and CRLs, as they are needed. If LDAP is to be used as a CRL query protocol, the certificates must support CRL distribution points (more information can be found in Chapter 5 and Appendix A).

PKIX Certificate Validation Protocols

In addition to the PKIX management protocols, there is a set of protocols that can be loosely clumped together under the heading of certificate validation protocols. These are part of the PKIX protocol set, but are being separately distinguished as they are more focused than the general management protocols. These protocols deal with problems associated with certificate revocation and validation.

CMP as a management protocol supports the following revocation-related operations:

- Revocation request
- Revocation response
- Revocation announcement
- CRL request

CMC provides similar operations, including:

- Revocation request
- Revocation response
- CRL request

In both of these cases, however, the end-entity or relying party has to process a certificate revocation list. To be sure, there are many varieties of CRL that allow information to be partitioned in various ways—by time, by certificate type, by issuing distribution point, and so on. However, all CRLs at some point form a list that must be downloaded and processed by the relying party. Furthermore, the relying party must access multiple CRLs corresponding to the different CAs in a certification path.

The alternative is to provide an online service that allows the status of a certificate to be checked. This could be done by allowing individual certificates to be checked (as is the case for OCSP), or by handing off the whole problem of validating a certificate chain to a validation service (this is the case for SCVP described in the next section). In addition to eliminating the need to send lists of certificates to relying parties, online protocols provide the opportunity to obtain more timely information than is available using CRLs (after all, the CA produces CRLs when it wants to, not when the relying party wants them). You might assume that an online service that queries a CA or a related service should be able to provide much more up-to-date information on the revocation status of a certificate. As it turns out, some implementations of an online service may still rely on publication of a CRL by the CA, so this expected benefit may not accrue in all cases.

The downside of using an online validation service is that the service provider must authenticate itself to the relying parties. This is not a problem for CRL mechanisms, as a CRL (like a certificate) is a signed structure that is self-protecting. Although it may be necessary to protect the repository a CRL is stored in to prevent its deletion, it cannot be modified without detection. In addition to authentication requirements, the online service must ensure that status responses are securely transferred to the relying party. This may be achieved by authenticating the service as part of establishing a session with the service provider, or by signing each of the response messages. In either case, the provider is generally a separate server that requires its own certificate and keys to be authenticated by the client of the validation service.

NOTE:

The service provider is normally separate from the CA for scaling reasons, and to restrict the keys that the CA uses to only signing issued certificates or CRLs. As a separate key and certificate are used for the validation service, distribution of the certificate and establishing trust become an additional issue for end-entity initialization.

There has been significant disagreement within the PKIX community over how much functionality should be provided by an online service. As a result, there are several alternative revocation checking protocols.

OCSP

The *Online Certificate Status Protocol* (OCSP) is defined in RFC 2560. The motivation for OCSP is to overcome limitations in CRL-based revocation schemes (see Chapter 5), and provide immediate, up-to-date response to certificate status queries. Specific certificate revocation information is returned rather than a large linear search list in the form of a CRL.

OCSP Operation

OCSP is a simple request/response protocol that may be transmitted over multiple transport protocols, but the one used most frequently is HTTP.

OCSP identifies the certificate that is the target of a query by using the serial number of the certificate combined with a hash value for the name and public key of the issuing CA. The certificate status is returned by a service known as an OCSP "responder." The response indicates the status of the certificate returning the values "good," "revoked," and "unknown" (when the certificate could not be identified).

In addition, a number of "liveness" indicators are returned that show the timeliness of the information returned in the response:

- **thisUpdate**   The time at which the status was known to be correct
- **nextUpdate**   The time when newer status information will be available
- **producedAt**   The time the OCSP responder signed the request

There are a number of limitations inherent in the way that OCSP works.

Information is returned only on a single certificate. The validity of the chain associated with the certificate is not verified. The relying party software must perform the rest of the work required for certificate chain or path processing. For example, the relying party must locate the certificate for the CA that issued the end-entity certificate before the end-entity certificate can be validated. The public key of the issuer is required in order to compute a hash value required for the request for status on the end-entity certificate.

The OCSP responder provides no certificate path construction. Location of the relevant certificates to construct a path is left to the relying party.

The OCSP responder is not sent the full certificate. Instead, information such as the certificate serial number is sent to the OCSP responder for validation, so it is not possible to verify the signature on a certificate.

Other validation information such as the certificate validity period, key usage compliance, and other constraints must be checked by the client. OCSP is only concerned with the revocation status of a certificate.

Functional Options

An OCSP responder can be configured to directly access a certificate database to check the current validity of a set of certificates, or may make use of existing CRLs published by the CA. The "liveness" indicators provide qualitative information that a client can use when performing certificate validity checks against policy requirements. In some cases, the latency associated with using CRLs to support an OCSP implementation may be less important than the convenience of not having to locate a directory, download a whole CRL, and process it.

Applications such as a subscription service, where the time taken to instantiate or terminate a user may be on the order of a day or more, may not be sensitive to CRL publication intervals. In this case, the convenience of an online service with a simple message interface makes OCSP a desirable solution. The fact that normal CRL updates to the OCSP responder database are occurring in the background are not relevant in this case.

For optimization purposes, it is valid for implementations to preproduce certificate validation responses. This would allow responses to be signed in the background and stored where an implementation response time is constrained by the rate of signing operations it can perform.

OCSP allows for delegation of certificate validation so that the OCSP responder does not have to be implemented on the certificate server. This allows for more scalable implementations, as well as keeping the CA signing keys separate from the certificate verification system.

SCVP

The *Simple Certificate Validation Protocol* (SCVP)[14] was designed to overcome perceived shortcomings in OCSP.

NOTE:

At the time of this writing, SCVP is an IETF Internet Draft. Its status is currently unclear as debate continues over the future of SCVP as an extended validation protocol.

SCVP maintains a view of both untrusted and trusted servers. Untrusted servers may, for example, provide intermediate certificates necessary for path construction, as the normal process of client-based certificate path validation is sufficient security in this case. Trusted servers may perform full validation services for the relying party. The goal of a trusted server is to eliminate the overhead of path validation from client software and to allow central validation policies to be executed.

SCVP uses a simple request response protocol, designed to run over HTTP or e-mail. All SCVP responses are signed. The requests may also be signed if authentication of the client is required or if the request is to be logged as part of an audit trail for non-repudiation purposes.

The SCVP client sends a collection of certificates in the enquiry to be validated. This is a major distinction from OCSP where an identifier for the certificate is sent. The result is that far more validation steps can be performed for the certificate. The client may send a collection of intermediate certificates that the SCVP server may consider as part of the validation processing. The client may also send a set of trusted root certificates, identifying which roots are trusted by the client. These certificates must be used by the SCVP server during validation processing.

Other constraints that the client may specify with the request include the type of checks to be performed, the type of revocation information to be considered, and the policies that must be used for certificate validation. The checks can specify that only revocation status should be checked, or that full path validation processing should be performed. The type of revocation information allows the client to specify that CRL or OCSP services should be used to get revocation status for the certificates.

The client may identify what type of information is to be returned by the server. It can request that proof of the revocation status be returned, or that a certificate chain used to validate the certificate be returned for further processing by the client. This is separate from the status returned about the validity of the certificate.

The SCVP client may also request that a certificate be validated at a particular point in time. This could be used when validating a signature, for example, to prove if the signature is considered valid at the time it was generated based on the certificate status at that time.

Overall, it appears that SCVP is perhaps not as simple as the name might suggest. It certainly allows considerable flexibility in certificate validation and allows a central server to offload a significant amount of processing overhead from an end-entity. However, a considerable amount of information must be conveyed to the server to determine whether the certificate status is meaningful.

SCVP has not yet been approved as an RFC by the IETF, and the number of implementations is very small to date.

OCSP-X

Given the reliance of SCVP on existing mechanisms such as CRLs or OCSP, and how closely aligned its processing is with certificate status checking, some people were led to believe that extending OCSP might be a more suitable solution. As a result, OCSP Extensions[15] has been proposed as part of the IETF standards process.

NOTE:

At the time of this writing, OCSP-X is an IETF Internet Draft. Its status is currently unclear as debate continues over the future of SCVP and OCSP-X as extended validation protocols.

The goals for OCSP-X are similar to those of SCVP, but more effectively stated in the RFC. The additional functionality supported includes validation of attribute certificates used within a privilege management infrastructure for authorization purposes.

An OCSP principle is that if you delegate responsibility for making a trust decision about a certificate to a server, the client should not have to duplicate the trust processing. As a result, information such as the certificate chain actually validated or relevant CRLs used in the process are not returned to the client.

Extension fields that have been added to OCSP requests include

- Specify trusted root
- Specify processing rules
- Evaluate trust path
- Register trust path

Specify trusted root allows the client to query the validity of the certificate using the specified root CA certificate as the trust anchor. If the server cannot build a trust path from the end-entity certificate to the root, an error is returned. OCSP-X does not identify how information necessary to build the path is obtained—that is an implementation issue.

Specify processing rules allows the client to identify processing rules that should be used during the certificate path validation.

Evaluate trust path asks the OCSP_X server to construct a path originating from a trust root, and optionally return part or all of the data used to construct or validate the certificate chain.

Register trust path allows the client to indicate to the server that the trust path that was specified will be useful for some specified period of time. This allows the server to cache the information associated with the trust path for optimization purposes.

Summary

The set of standards and draft standards that comprise the IETF PKIX architecture is a concrete example of an application domain that has chosen to use X.509 as a Public Key Infrastructure. In the case of PKIX, the application domain is that of Internet users.

In previous chapters, we examined the principles, techniques, and certificate fields that can be used to support the features of a PKI. PKIX extends this set by defining profiles that identify a working subset of X.509 extensions and define their use. In addition, PKIX defines protocols that are used for communication of management and other information that is necessary to construct a working PKI.

We examined the management protocols in particular, identifying the two major (and competing) standards in this area: CMP and CMC. In addition, we briefly discussed a non-PKIX protocol submitted to the IETF for informational purposes by CISCO Systems that is in widespread use today. We also considered the special class of protocols dealing with certificate validation and discussed OCSP, SCVP, and OSCP-X.

The standardization of these PKIX protocols and specifications allows vendors to develop products that interoperate and use a common underlying architectural model. This has the benefit of allowing (hopefully) PKI implementers in the future to select products from different vendors that can interoperate when designing and building a Public Key Infrastructure.

References

[1]Myers, M., et al, RFC 2560, "X.509 Internet Public Key Infrastructure Online Certificate Status Protocol—OCSP"
http://www.ietf.org/rfc/rfc2560.txt

[2]Housley, R., et al, RFC 2459, "Internet X.509 Public Key Infrastructure Certificate and CRL Profile"
http://www.ietf.org/rfc/rfc2459.txt

[3]Boeyen, S., T. Howes, and P. Richard, RFC 2559, "Internet X.509 Public Key Infrastructure Operational Protocols—LDAPv2"
http://www.ietf.org/rfc/rfc2559.txt

[4]Housley, R., and P. Hoffman, RFC 2585, "Internet X.509 Public Key Infrastructure Operational Protocols: FTP and HTTP"
http://www.ietf.org/rfc/rfc2585.txt

[5]Chokhani, S., and W. Ford, RFC 2527, "Internet X.509 Public Key Infrastructure Certificate Policy and Certification Practices Framework"
http://www.ietf.org/rfc/rfc2527.txt

[6]Adams, C., et al, "Internet X.509 Public Key Infrastructure Time Stamp Protocols," work in progress, IETF PKIX WG
http://www.ietf.org/ids.by.wg/pkix.html

[7]Adams, C., et al, "Internet X.509 Public Key Infrastructure Data Certification Server Protocols," work in progress, IETF PKIX WG
http://www.ietf.org/ids.by.wg/pkix.html

[8]Adams, C., and S. Farrell, RFC 2510, "Internet X.509 Public Key Infrastructure Certificate Management Protocols"
http://www.ietf.org/rfc/rfc2510.txt

[9]Myers, M., et al, RFC 2797, "Certificate Management Messages over CMS"
http://www.ietf.org/rfc/rfc2797.txt

[10]Myers, M., et al, RFC 2511, "Internet X.509 Certificate Request Message Format"
http://www.ietf.org/rfc/rfc2511.txt

[11]Tschalar, R., A. Kapoor, and C. Adams, "Using HTTP as a Transport Protocol for CMP," work in progress, IETF PKIX WG
http://www.ietf.org/ids.by.wg/pkix.html

[12]Tschalar, R., A. Kapoor, and C. Adams, "Using TCP as a Transport Protocol for CMP," work in progress, IETF PKIX WG
http://www.ietf.org/ids.by.wg/pkix.html

[13]Adams, C., and S. Farrell, "Internet X.509 Public Key Infrastructure Certificate Management Protocols," work in progress, IETF PKIX WG
http://www.ietf.org/ids.by.wg/pkix.html

[14]Malpani, A., and P. Hoffman, "Simple Certificate Validation Protocol (SCVP)," work in progress, IETF PKIX WG
http://www.ietf.org/ids.by.wg/pkix.html

[15]Myers, M., et al, "OCSP Extensions," work in progress, IETF PKIX WG
http://www.ietf.org/ids.by.wg/pkix.html

CHAPTER 7

Application Use of PKI

Applications can incorporate PKI in a number of ways, where the most difficult is to rebuild the application from scratch and use low-level cryptographic functions to implement PKI. Fortunately, PKI implementation doesn't have to be that hard. This chapter explores services, protocols, formatting standards, and APIs that can be used to build PKI applications.

PKI-Based Services

PKI-based services are reusable functions that provide commonly needed PKI functions. The services covered here include digital signature, authentication, secure timestamps, a secure notary service, and a non-repudiation service.

Digital Signature

Signatures are commonplace—you routinely sign checks, credit card transactions, and letters. A digital signature is the electronic analogue to a written signature; it identifies the signer and states a relationship between the signer and the signed data. As discussed earlier, a digital signature is the output of a mathematical computation that has particular characteristics. Its security is based on asymmetric encryption, where the encryption and decryption processes use separate keys. Recall that a digital signature computation starts with the calculation of a hash of the data to be signed; the hash is then encrypted with the signer's private key. The hash provides a way to detect if the data is changed, and the digital signature prevents the hash from being altered. A digital signature thus provides strong proof that the data is the same data as when the signature was calculated.

Since a single, unique private key creates the signature, the data can also be tied to the identity that is associated with the private key. This association is done through verifying the signature with the entity's public key. If the signature calculation verifies and the public key is known to be associated with the entity, such as through a public key certificate signed by a trusted signer, the digital signature can be used as proof that the signed data came from the entity identified in the certificate.

A PKI digital signature service therefore will have two parts: a signature generation service and a signature validation service. The signature generation service requires access to the signer's private key. Since this key identifies the signer, it is sensitive and must be protected. If stolen, others could sign with the key and pretend to be the signer. A signing service is thus usually part of a secure application that has protected access to the signing key. In contrast, a verification service can be more open. Public keys, once signed by a trusted signer, are generally considered public knowledge. The verification service receives the signed data, the signature, and the public key or public key certificate, and then checks if the signature validates with the supplied data. It returns an indication of verification success or failure.

Authentication

A PKI authentication service uses digital signatures to establish identity. In most PKI authentication services, the basic process is to present the entity to be authenticated with a piece of random challenge data. The entity must either sign or encrypt the challenge with their private key, depending on their key's usage type(s). If the challenger can either verify the signature or decrypt the data with the public key in the entity's certificate, the entity is authenticated. Note that the challenger should also validate the entity's certificate chain, plus check that each certificate is within its validity period and that its key is appropriate for the way it's being used. In some services, the entity being authenticated sends their certificate (and certificate chain) with the authentication response. In others, the authentication service retrieves the certificate from a certificate directory.

Timestamp

A secure timestamp service provides proof that a set of data existed at a specific time. Secure timestamps can be used to establish when an electronic action occurred, such as a transaction or a document signature. This is particularly useful if the action has legal or financial consequences. Examples could be a proposal that must be submitted before a deadline or a contested will that must be proven to have been signed by the deceased.

In general, a timestamp service follows a basic request and response model. The entity that wants a secure timestamp sends a timestamp request to the timestamp service. The request contains a hash of the data to be timestamped. The timestamp service then obtains a time reading from its time source and signs the concatenation of the data hash and the time with the time service's private key. For the service to have any value, the time service's time source must be highly accurate, such as an atomic clock. Since the timestamp service only requires a hash of the data and not the data itself, this service can be totally anonymous.

As further added security, the timestamp service can publish the hashes of the documents that it has timestamped in a public place, such as in a newspaper. If the timestamp is contested—that is, a challenger seeks to prove that the timestamp was backdated—the challenge can be resolved by finding the published hash in the newspaper and verifying the newspaper's publication date.

Secure Notary Service

A secure notary service is modeled after a physical notary, where a notary's signature provides a statement that an impartial witness observed the act of a document being signed. By training, a human notary provides three main functions: positive identification of the signer, determination of the signer's willingness to sign (that is, he isn't being forced), and an assessment of the signer's awareness of the consequences of signing. Historically, this has required that persons requiring notarization must physically present themselves and their document to the notary. Some digital signature legislation is changing this requirement. In parts of the United States, for example, digital signatures can be used as the equivalent of a physical notary signature. Furthermore, the legislation does not require that the signer physically present himself to the person or entity taking the acknowledgement (see, for example, Nevada Administration Code Chapter 720.770). Some notary organizations are concerned that this weakens the notary function. A remote digital notary service obviously cannot determine the signer's willingness, although it can prompt users to acknowledge their awareness of the impact of their signature. The regulations for digital notary services are likely to evolve as more digital notaries are used.

In practice, electronic notaries are being interpreted in different ways. One way is very similar to a secure time service, except that the notary maintains a record of the timestamped action, including the submitted hash, the resulting secure timestamp, and information about the requester. Another way is closer to the physical notary: the user submits a document signed with her private key to the notary. This submission could be via e-mail, a Web form, or another means of electronic submission. The notary thus "witnesses" the document and the signature. The notary service then signs a hash of the original document plus the original signature. The notary service must maintain a record of the documents it has signed, including the hash of the document plus the original signature, the time the notary "witnessed" the signature, and the notary's signature.

Non-Repudiation

A non-repudiation service provides undeniable evidence of an interaction between two parties. As opposed to authentication, non-repudiation's focus is on an action and verifying that two parties intended to and did in fact participate in the action. An Internet banking user, for example, would like to have a non-repudiation service when transferring funds from her checking account into a merchant's account for bill payment. The user would like to ensure that the bank cannot deny the transfer occurred in case the merchant later claims the payment was not made. Similarly, the Internet bank would like to ensure that the user cannot deny having made the transfer. Non-repudiation is a term that is frequently bandied about in the PKI world, unfortunately usually without much understanding of its full implications. For example, a digital signature alone usually does not provide enough evidence to support non-repudiation.

The main standards addressing non-repudiation are from the *International Organization for Standardization* (ISO). ISO standards covering non-repudiation include the Open Distributed Processing Reference Model, the X.400 series, and the X.800 series. According to the Open Distributed Processing Reference Model, "The non-repudiation function prevents the denial by one object involved in an interaction of having participated in all or part of the interaction." ISO/IEC 13888 states that, "Non-repudiation can only be provided within the context of a clearly defined security policy for a particular application and its legal environment," and "The goal of the non-repudiation service is to collect, maintain, make available, and validate irrefutable evidence."

The ISO standards define a comprehensive set of non-repudiation roles that include the following:

- **Data originator**   The original source of the data in the interaction.
- **Data recipient**   The original recipient of the data.
- **Evidence generator**   An entity that generates non-repudiation evidence.
- **Evidence user**   An entity that uses the non-repudiation evidence in an interaction.
- **Evidence verifier**   An entity that verifies that the non-repudiation evidence is valid.
- **Notary**   An entity that provides functions that may be required by the originator and/or recipient. These may include notarization, timestamping, monitoring, certification, certificate generation, signature generation, signature verification, and delivery.
- **Adjudicator**   An entity that collects information and evidence from disputing parties (and optionally from notaries) and applies a resolution function.

In the X.400 standards, ISO defines non-repudiation services that include non-repudiation of origin (the originator cannot dispute that they started an action), non-repudiation of delivery (the recipient cannot deny that they received something), non-repudiation of submission (intermediate proof that the originator submitted the data for transport), and non-repudiation of transport (intermediate proof that the data was carried over a communications medium).

Getting back to the Internet banking user, what would a non-repudiation service need to do to provide irrefutable evidence? Part of the answer depends on what constitutes "evidence" for the user and for the bank. This will depend on the laws governing the Internet bank (lawyers love non-repudiation!). In most jurisdictions, the evidence must constitute proof that the transaction took place as well as proof that the user was aware of the consequences of her actions. Digital signatures can help provide the proof of the transaction. For example, the user can sign data pertaining to the transaction amount and the accounts involved. The user can then have the transaction data securely timestamped, and then submit the signed and timestamped request to the Internet bank. When the bank receives the user's transaction, the bank can sign the user's transaction request as proof of receipt and have the receipt securely timestamped.

Proving user awareness and coupling that proof together with the transaction proof can be harder since the bank must prove that the user was aware of the consequences of signing that particular transaction at that particular point in time. The Internet bank could state the consequences of signing transactions in its user agreement and use that agreement as a binding document for any disputes. Or, for a more constant reminder, the banking application could pop up a window that states the consequences of signing whenever the user clicks the "submit transaction" button.

This discussion provides an overview of some of the issues surrounding non-repudiation. Fully understanding this topic and its consequences for a particular application will require understanding the laws governing the application and its users.

PKI-Based Protocols

The Secure Sockets Layer is by far the most widely known and adopted protocol based on PKI. Before there was SSL, however, there was Diffie-Hellman. Gaining in popularity more recently are the IPsec and S/MIME protocols. We begin with Diffie-Hellman since it provides the fundamental underpinnings for most PKI protocols.

Diffie-Hellman Key Exchange

Diffie-Hellman, the first public key algorithm, was first published in 1976 by Whitfield Diffie and Martin Hellman. The Diffie-Hellman algorithm enables two parties to compute a shared secret. It is very widely used due to its main selling point: the algorithm doesn't require encryption, making its implementation overhead low. One of the most common uses of a Diffie-Hellman shared secret is as the basis for additional encryption keys that the two parties will use to protect information they exchange.

The fundamental concept underlying the Diffie-Hellman algorithm is the mathematical difficulty of calculating discrete logarithms in a finite field. The algorithm starts with two values, p and g, that are not secret, but that do have particular attributes. Parameter p must be a prime number. Parameter g (called a generator) must be an integer. Parameters p and g must also have the following property: for every number, n, between 1 and p-1 inclusive, there is a value g^k such that $n = g^k \bmod p$. Here's how the algorithm works (see Figure 7-1):

1. Two parties pick the parameters p and g that they will use. We'll call these two parties side 1 and side 2.

2. Each side generates a random value, say *rand1* and *rand2*. Both random numbers are less than p-2. Each side keeps its random value private.

Figure 7-1

Diffie-Hellman algorithm

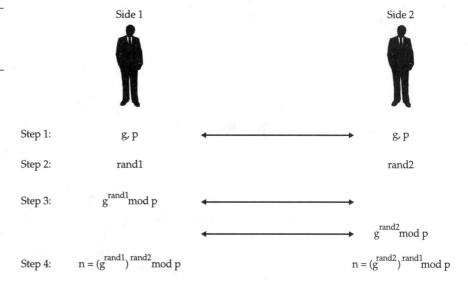

	Side 1		Side 2
Step 1:	g, p	⟷	g, p
Step 2:	rand1		rand2
Step 3:	$g^{\text{rand1}} \bmod p$	⟶	
		⟵	$g^{\text{rand2}} \bmod p$
Step 4:	$n = (g^{\text{rand1}})^{\text{rand2}} \bmod p$		$n = (g^{\text{rand2}})^{\text{rand1}} \bmod p$

3. Both sides calculate public values based on g, p, and their respective private values; g^{rand1} mod p for side 1, and g^{rand2} mod p for side 2.

4. Each side sends the other its public value.

5. Side 1 computes $n = (g^{rand1})^{rand2}$ mod p. Side 2 computes $n = (g^{rand2})^{rand1}$ mod p. Due to the basic properties of g, they now have a shared value, n.

One flaw in the Diffie-Hellman algorithm is that it is vulnerable to man-in-the-middle attacks because it does not authenticate the two sides in the exchange. This means that a third party could intercept the communication and manipulate the exchanges so that the original participants still think they are directly communicating. Instead, the third party negotiates separate shared values with the two participants (see Figure 7-2). When the original parties use the shared value they've derived, such as for an encryption key, the intruder can now decrypt the traffic, view, copy, or alter it, and re-encrypt it before sending it on. Neither of the original participants will be able to detect the intruder.

Figure 7-2

Diffie-Hellman man-in-the-middle attack

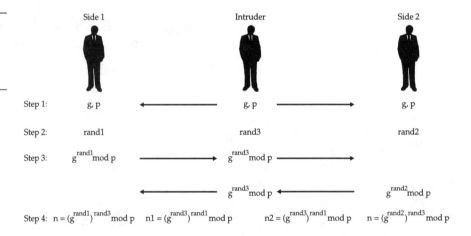

A number of variations strengthen the Diffie-Hellman algorithm by adding features to prevent man-in-the-middle attacks. One example is an authenticated Diffie-Hellman protocol, such as the Station-to-Station protocol developed by Diffie, Van Oorshot, and Wiener. The shared secret calculation is the same; however, the two parties also digitally sign the two public values g^{rand1} mod p and g^{rand2} mod p and then exchange the signatures. Each side verifies the digital signature to ensure that the communications have not been intercepted. Since an intruder does not have either side's private key, any signatures they try to insert will not verify.

Secure Sockets Layer

The *Secure Sockets Layer* (SSL) establishes a transport-level secure channel between two parties. SSL provides communications privacy through symmetric encryption and integrity through *message authentication codes* (MACs). SSL uses PKI primarily for authenticating the parties during connection establishment. Both the IETF's *Transport-Level Security* (TLS) (RFC 2246 1999) and the *Wireless Access Protocol* (WAP) Forum's *Wireless Transport-Level Security* (WTLS) protocol are direct descendants of SSL.

Netscape Communications Corporation originally developed SSL in the mid-1990s. SSL version 2 was the first version to be widely used. SSL version 3 improved the protocol's efficiency, flexibility, and feature set. TLS is a superset of SSLv3 with strengthened cryptographic functions.

SSL is a layered protocol with two layers. It runs on top of a reliable transport protocol, usually TCP. To give a feeling for how these protocols work, we'll describe SSL version 3 (SSLv3).

SSLv3's lower layer consists of the SSL Record protocol. This layer encapsulates data from higher-level protocols. The protocol data is protected with the cipher (encryption) and MAC algorithms negotiated in the SSL Handshake protocol. (A message authentication code uses cryptographic functions to provide a means of detecting a change in a message. SSLv3's MAC algorithm involves hashing a key together with the protocol data and the message sequence number.) This combination of cipher and MAC algorithms is called the current cipher spec. The record protocol transmissions include a sequence number so that missing, altered, or replayed messages can be detected. The record protocol optionally performs compression, if a compression algorithm was negotiated.

SSLv3's higher layer consists of the messages that are carried by the record level. These include the Change Cipher Spec protocol, the Alert protocol, and the SSL Handshake protocol. Before diving into the Handshake protocol, we'll cover the other higher-level messages.

The Change Cipher Spec protocol indicates a change in the ciphers used. The protocol consists of a single message that is encrypted with the current cipher spec. Both the client and server send the change cipher spec message to indicate they are about to begin using a new cipher spec and keys. The Alert protocol transfers messages about an event, including the event severity and a description of the event. These events are primarily error conditions, such as bad MAC, certificate expired, or illegal parameter. The Alert protocol is also used to share information about a planned connection termination.

The Handshake protocol is how a client and server negotiate the security parameters they will use for the secure channel. These parameters include the protocol version, the encryption algorithm, and cryptographic keys that will be used. In addition, the client authenticates the server, and optionally, the server authenticates the client. PKI comes into play in the client-server authentication.

To show how the Handshake protocol works, we'll step through an example (see Figure 7-3).

The client initiates the SSL connection by sending a Client Hello Message to the server. The Client Hello Message contains the client's desired security capabilities, including the protocol version, supported ciphers listed in preference order, and any compression methods supported. In addition, the client generates a random number and sends this in the hello message as a session ID.

The server responds with the Server Hello Message. If the server supports a protocol version, cipher, and compression method in the client's list, these are stated in the Server Hello Message. If the client and server have no protocol versions, ciphers, or compression methods in common, the connect fails. If the client and server had a preexisting session with this ID, the server returns the client's session ID value in the Server Hello. If not, the server responds with a different, server-generated random value that indicates a new session.

The server sends its certificate to the client. This is almost always an X509v3 certificate.

The protocol specification doesn't explicitly state what the client is to do with the server certificate. The client *should* verify the certificate's signature, check that a Certification Authority that the client trusts signed the certificate, and ensure that the certificate is within its validity period. Note that thorough signature verification would also require verifying the signer's entire certificate chain, as well as checking that the certificate was not present on the CA's latest *certificate revocation list* (CRL). Do clients actually implement these checks? Like most things, the answer is—it depends. In reality, the client is almost always a Web browser, and

Figure 7-3

SSL handshake

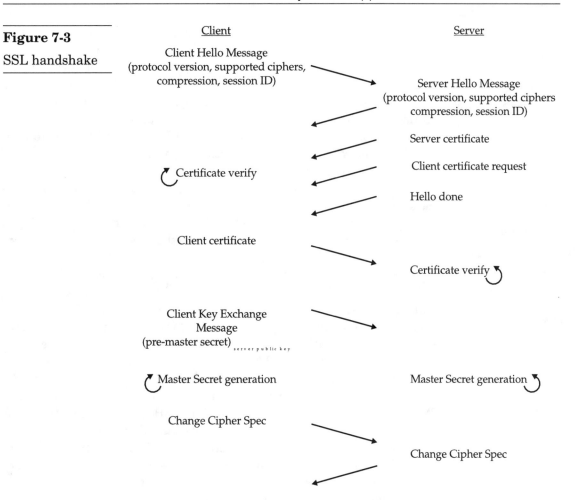

browsers are inconsistent in the level of checking they implement. No browsers currently check certificates against CRLs. Browsers do, however, check certificates against a set of trusted signers. If the server's certificate's signer is not in the trusted list, the user will see a pop-up window stating that the certificate is untrusted. Verifying the certificate would require that the user track down the CA's certificate and install it into his browser's trusted signer list. Most users have no idea how to do this and generally accept the certificate anyway.

The server requests the client's certificate. This protocol specification makes this optional, and in fact allows three options: the server does not request a client certificate, the server requires a client certificate or the connection fails, or the server requests a client certificate but continues connection setup if the client does not supply one. For this example, we'll assume that the server requires a client certificate.

At this point, the server sends the Server Hello Done Message to indicate it is done with its side of the initial negotiation.

The client sends its certificate to the server.

The server verifies the client certificate. The exact nature of this validation is up to the implementer. We'll assume the server validates the signature, checks the validity period, makes sure the certificate was signed by one of the CAs the server trusts, and that the certificate does not appear on the CA's latest CRL.

The client generates a pre-master secret value and encrypts it with the public key from the server's certificate. The client sends this encrypted value to the server in a Client Key Exchange Message. The SSLv3 protocol also permits other methods to be used for exchanging the pre-master secret, including Diffie-Hellman and Fortezza (hardware-based encryption systems used by the U.S. government).

The server decrypts the pre-master secret with its private key, and the server and the client convert the pre-master secret into the master secret. The conversion function uses both MD5 and SHA-1 hashes and the client and server random values previously exchanged. The master secret is used to generate keys for encryption and MAC computations. Alternatively, the client and server could use the Diffie-Hellman algorithm to generate the pre-master secret.

The client makes the pending cipher the current cipher and sends the Change Cipher Spec Message to the server. This message means that the server should make the just-negotiated cipher spec active.

The server sends the Change Cipher Spec Message to the server as confirmation.

At this point the handshake is finished and the two sides can exchange data using SSL's privacy and integrity services. Both sides convert the pre-master secret into the master secret by computing a series of hashes using the pre-master secret, the client's hello random value, and the server's hello random value. The master secret is then used to derive keys for the cipher and MAC algorithms, including a client write MAC secret, a server write MAC secret, a client write key, and a server write key, as well as a client write IV (if the cipher requires an initialization vector) and a server write IV.

A client can resume a session within a given timeout period by requesting a session with the same session ID as a previously negotiated session. The ability to resume a session was a new feature added in SSLv3 to reduce connection establishment overhead. Other features were added to improve the handshake efficiency and to add flexibility. For example, SSLv3 offers more ciphers than v2, adds support for the SHA hash and DSA algorithm, offers compression, and provides the ability to negotiate the protocol version. The number of messages needed to perform the handshake was reduced, and the Change Cipher Spec Message was added. The key generation method in SSLv3 is based on the master secret and random values, not the connection ID as in SSLv2.

TLS, the IETF's Transport Layer Security protocol, is very similar to SSLv3—so similar, in fact, that the specification text is identical in many sections. The differences between the two protocols are not huge, but they do make the protocols incompatible. The main differences are in the hashing functions and the cryptographic key generation functions. TLS uses the HMAC keyed message authentication function, which differs from the keyed MAC function specified in SSLv3. (For more information on HMAC, see RFC 2104, "HMAC: Keyed-Hashing for Message Authentication." HMACs are commonly used in IPsec.) TLS's master secret generation function is based on a pseudo-random function that uses HMAC. SSLv3's key generation function is different; thus, the two protocols will not generate the same keys given the same inputs and cannot interoperate. Some of the other differences include these changes in TLS: many more alert protocol messages, no Fortezza support, and the handshake finalization message is computed using different algorithms.

IPsec

IPsec defines a secure framework and a set of security services for network-level (IP) communications, parts of which employ PKI. IPsec can be used with both IPv4 and IPv6 environments. It operates in one of two modes: tunnel mode or transport mode. In tunnel mode, the entire IP packet is encrypted and becomes the data portion of a new, larger IP packet that has a new IP header and an IPsec header added (see Figure 7-4). If the IPsec *Encapsulating Security Payload* (ESP) service is used (more on this further in this section), the packet will also have an IPsec data trailer. In transport mode, the IPsec header is inserted directly into the IP packet (see Figure 7-5). Tunnel mode is primarily used by gateways and proxies (see Figure 7-6). The intermediate systems implement the IPsec services; the endpoints do not know about IPsec. In transport mode, the endpoints must both implement IPsec; the intermediate systems do not perform any IPsec processing on the packet (see Figure 7-7).

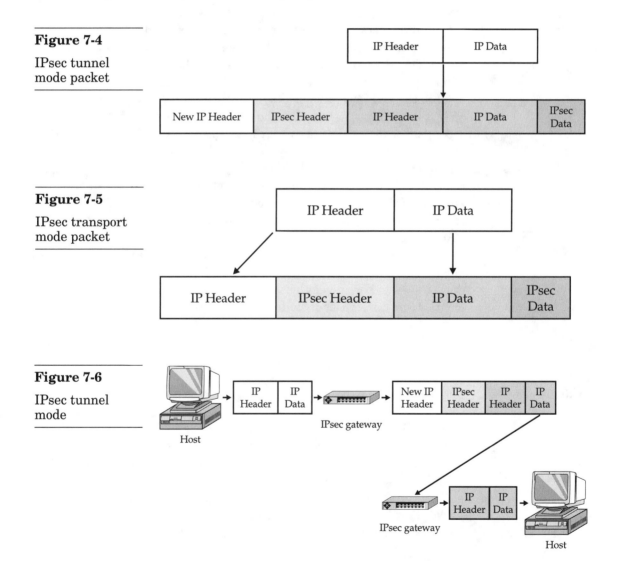

Figure 7-4

IPsec tunnel mode packet

Figure 7-5

IPsec transport mode packet

Figure 7-6

IPsec tunnel mode

Figure 7-7

IPsec transport mode

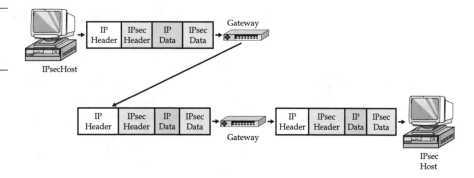

IPsec provides strong security and great flexibility. As a result, it is fairly complex to understand. We will use an example to show how two systems might use some of IPsec's options. In our example, a sales rep has IPsec-based *virtual private network* (VPN) client software installed on his laptop. When the sales rep connects to the Internet, the VPN client filters the traffic, watching for IP packets destined for the sales rep's headquarters office. It allows any traffic *not* going to the headquarters office to pass through normally (unsecure). When the client sees a packet that *is* addressed to the headquarters office, however, it intercepts it. It then uses IPsec services to transmit the packet securely to the headquarters office and to ensure that all traffic back from the headquarters office is also secure.

The first thing the VPN client does is to establish an IPsec security association with the headquarters office's communications server. A *security association* (SA) defines a security context between two parties. The *Internet Security Association and Key Management Protocol* (ISAKMP) is the framework that defines how the VPN client and server set up this association. With ISAKMP, they negotiate the encryption algorithm, the hash algorithm, the authentication mechanism, and the key establishment mechanism they will use for their IPsec services. Note that ISAKMP does not mandate particular algorithms or mechanisms so that it can provide maximum flexibility. It does, however, require the use of digital signatures within the authentication component. This means that the VPN client and server *must* have IPsec public key certificates to be able to establish a security association. It also means that the client and server need to know the security association options that the other supports; otherwise, the client and server may not be able to negotiate common security association settings.

The first part of ISAKMP SA entails the two parties negotiating a secure channel over which they will negotiate further SAs. Each subsequent SA is specific to a security protocol. By design, ISAKMP permits multiple security protocol SAs to be negotiated within the context of a single ISAKMP SA. ISAKMP is not limited to IPsec and can be used for other protocols, such as *Transport Layer Security* (TLS), although its current use is primarily for IPsec Authentication Header and Encapsulating Payload protocols (coming up below). ISAKMP consolidates the authentication and key negotiations that are commonly done in secure protocols, making security operations more efficient.

At this point, the VPN client and server have negotiated an ISAKMP SA for traffic from the VPN client to the server. They then negotiate a second SA. Why? Each SA is uniquely identified by the combination of a *security parameters index* (SPI) in each IP packet, the security protocol, and the destination IP address. As a result, each SA is one-way (one destination IP address, one SA). For the VPN client and server to exchange bidirectional IPsec traffic, they must therefore negotiate two security associations—one for traffic from the client to the server (the server is the destination) and one for traffic from the server to the client (the client is the destination).

The VPN client and server have now completed the first step in setting up IPsec communications. The SAs set the basic security context: the VPN client and server have agreed upon the algorithms to use and have authenticated each other. They then complete a second phase of SA negotiation specific to the IPsec services they will use. To apply IPsec's other security services to their communications, such as access control, connectionless integrity, data origin authentication, replay protection, or confidentiality, the client and server must negotiate the use of the *authentication header* (AH), the *Encapsulating Security Payload* (ESP), or a combination of the two.

The IPsec authentication header provides integrity, data origin authentication, and anti-replay services. The AH integrity service uses an *Integrity Check Value* (ICV) that is computed over the entire IP packet, except for header field values that may change during transmission (for example, time to live). The ICV can be a hash value, a keyed message authentication code (such as HMAC), or a digital signature. The ICV algorithm is specified in the IPsec SA. In general, a simple or keyed hash is used for point-to-point communications. Data origin authentication is done through verification of a keyed HMAC computed with a shared secret key or a digital signature. Replay prevention is based on a monotonically increasing sequence number. The sequence number is not allowed to "wrap"; thus, when a counter reaches its maximum value, it cannot cycle back to zero. IPsec mandates that a new SA must be created if a counter reaches its limit. The new SA will have a fresh counter and a new encryption key.

The *Encapsulating Security Payload* (ESP) protocol provides several features that are similar to AH, including integrity via an ICV, data origin authentication with keyed MACs, and replay protection through sequence numbers. ESP packets are formatted slightly differently from AH packets —with ESP, the ICV is added to the end of the IPsec packet, whereas AH places the ICV in the IPsec header. The biggest difference between the two, though, is ESP's confidentiality service: ESP provides confidentiality through encryption. The encryption algorithm is negotiated in the SA.

Returning to our example, the sales rep with the VPN client is sending sensitive contractual details back to the headquarters office, so the VPN client is configured to use ESP with origin authentication, integrity, and confidentiality services. The client and server use digital signatures during the authentication of their SA establishment. Since the VPN client is preconfigured with a shared HMAC key, the client and server agree to use keyed MACs and triple DES encryption to provide integrity, origin authentication, and confidentiality.

Other IPsec protocols can be used for key negotiation. Two of these protocols are the Oakley Key Determination Protocol and the *Internet Key Exchange* (IKE) protocol. OAKLEY uses Diffie-Hellman as the fundamental mechanism to negotiate a shared value, but adds address validation and authentication. OAKLEY's address validation uses 64-bit random "cookies" to deter denial-of-service attacks and to provide a weak peer address identifier. Authentication mechanisms include digital signatures, public key encryption, and symmetric key encryption with previously exchanged keys. OAKLEY participants negotiate a key name and a shared secret value that can be used as the basis from which other keys are derived. OAKLEY also enables the two parties to identify each other and negotiate three algorithms to use: an encryption algorithm, a hashing algorithm, and an authentication mechanism. The key exchange can be completed in as few as three messages; however, if the parties use the protocol's optional features, the number of messages will be larger.

IKE implements a subset of OAKLEY. As with OAKLEY, IKE authentication mechanisms include digital signatures, public key encryption, and preshared symmetric keys. IKE also supports negotiation of the Diffie-Hellman group. IKE can provide perfect forward secrecy of keys and identities, where the compromise of a single key only exposes the data protected with that key and does not affect any other keys used in the protocol.

S/MIME

The *Secure/Multipurpose Internet Mail Extensions* (S/MIME) add message authenticity, integrity, and privacy services to electronic messaging applications. S/MIME is not limited to electronic mail and can be used by other transport mechanisms that support MIME, such as HTTP. S/MIME can secure a single message part, multiple message parts, or an entire message. S/MIME uses *Cryptographic Message Syntax* (CMS) encoding to envelop, sign, or sign and envelop messages.

Mail user agents can automatically add cryptographic security services to mail being sent and interpret cryptographic services that have been applied to received mail. S/MIME messages are usually transmitted in Base64 encoding to facilitate the transmission of binary data. The S/MIME cryptographic service specification gives SHA-1 as the preferred digest and DSA as the preferred signature algorithm. If RSA is used, the minimum RSA key size should be 768 bits.

The MIME type application/pkcs7-mime is used to carry CMS objects of several types including envelopedData and signedData. For example, enveloped-only messages are formatted as CMS envelopedData objects. A copy of the content encryption key is encrypted for each recipient and for the originator. The CMS object is then inserted into an application/pkcs7-mime MIME entity. Enveloped-only messages do not provide message integrity. Signed-only messages provide message integrity, but not confidentiality. Signed-only MIME formats are application/pkcs7-mime and multipart/signed. Recipients without S/MIME clients cannot view application/pkcs7-mime messages, but may be able to view multipart/signed messages. Signed and encrypted messages are created by nesting signed-only and encrypted-only messages. The messages can be nested in either order.

The following mini-table shows the relationship between MIME types, applicable CMS objects, and S/MIME types. The file extension helps receiving agents determine how to handle and decode received messages.

MIME Type	CMS Objects	S/MIME Type	File Extension
application/pkcs7-mime signedData signed-data	envelopedData	enveloped-data	.p7m
application/pkcs7-mime	certs-only message	certs-only	.p7c
multipart/signed application/pkcs7-signature	SignedData (Detached signature CMS object)	Not used	.p7s

Time Stamp Protocol

The *Time Stamp Protocol* (TSP) provides proof that data existed at a particular time through the services of the *Time Stamp Authority* (TSA). TSP is currently under development in the PKIX working group.

The TSP is a simple request/response protocol. The entity requesting a timestamp sends a TimeStampReq message to the TSA to request a timestamp. The TimeStampReq message contains the hash of data to be timestamped. The TSA returns the timestamp in a TimeStampResp message. The TimeStampResp includes the status of the request (that is, granted or rejected) and the timestamp in the form of a signed data message formatted in accordance with CMS.

The PKIX work levies a number of requirements on a TSA. For example, the TSP server must use a trustworthy time source, timestamp only a hash of the data, and not include any identification of the requesting entity in the timestamp.

WTLS

Wireless Transport-Level Security (WTLS) is the WAP Forum's specification for security services that provide privacy, data integrity, and authentication between applications. WTLS provides similar functionality to TLS, but is adapted to the wireless environment. For example, WTLS adds handshake optimization and dynamic key refreshing to improve performance in low-bandwidth wireless networks with relatively long latency.

Unlike TLS, WTLS can function with either connection-oriented or datagram networks.

WTLS uses the same protocol concepts as TLS and SSL, with a record protocol and handshake protocol. Using the handshake protocol, the client and server agree on the protocol version, select mutually agreeable cryptographic algorithms, authenticate each other, and generate the shared master secret. WTLS supports performing the handshake protocol with datagrams; in this case, all messages going in one direction must be concatenated into one transport service data unit. WTLS also supports a shared secret handshake if the client and server have already established a shared secret. This facilitates an abbreviated handshake, providing better performance for wireless networks.

Formatting Standards

Interoperability between PKI applications requires knowing what the bits of data received from another application are supposed to mean. Standards provide common agreements for data syntax and meaning. The most prevalent formatting standard for PKI applications is the X.509 standard, since it defines the basic structure for public key certificates. The PKCS standards from RSA Laboratories are the main standards that define what those bits of data mean. These standards define such things as how to properly format a private key or a public key. Other important standards are the PKIX certificate and CRL profile, the IEEE P1363 project's work in defining cryptographic algorithms, and the IETF's working group in XML digital signatures.

X.509

X.509 is the *International Telecommunications Union-Telecommunication* (ITU-T) Standardization Sector and the *International Organization for Standardization's* (ISO) certificate format standard. Defined as part of the ITU-ISO's series of standards on directory services, X.509 is the fundamental standard that defines public key certificate structure. First published in 1988, the X.509 was revised in 1993 and again in 1996. The current version, X.509 version 3, added support for extension fields that greatly increase certificate flexibility. An X.509v3 certificate includes a mandatory set of fields in a predefined order, as well as optional extension fields (see Chapter 5 for more details). X.509 permits considerable flexibility even within its mandatory fields, as it provides multiple encoding options for most fields.

PKIX

The *Public Key Infrastructure* (PKIX) working group in the IETF's security area is defining a series of standards for public key certificate usage in the Internet. The PKIX working group was formed in October of 1995 to develop Internet standards necessary to support interoperable PKIs. The group's first work item was to create a profile limiting certificate data structures, extensions, and data values to a specific set of options. The X.509 standard's great flexibility makes interoperability difficult; by restricting the options allowed, the PKIX group hopes to increase the ability of one PKI to interoperate with another.

The PKIX working group has defined profiles for public key certificates and for CRLs. In some cases, it has defined additional certificate extension fields or certificate attributes, as well as object identifiers for these attributes. PKIX is also developing new protocols to facilitate the management of PKI information throughout the PKI's life cycle. Many of these protocols are discussed in this chapter, including the *Certificate Management Protocol* (CMP), the *Secure Multipurpose Mail Extensions* (S/MIME), and the *Online Certificate Status Protocol* (OCSP).

IEEE P1363

IEEE project P1363 began in 1994 to develop cryptography standards, including the Standard Specifications for Public Key Cryptography. The project started with specifying mathematical primitives and cryptographic techniques for the RSA and Diffie-Hellman algorithms and has since broadened its work to include elliptic curve cryptosystems. Although not limited to formatting standards, the P1363 group's work is important to ensure PKI interoperability since it provides a reference specification for a range of common public key techniques, including key agreement, public key encryption, digital signatures, and identification from several families, such as discrete logarithms, integer factorization, and elliptic curves. It also covers related cryptographic considerations, such as key management and secure random number generation.

PKCS

The *Public Key Cryptography Standards* (PKCS) were initially developed by RSA Laboratories in collaboration with industry, academia, and government representatives to further public key cryptography interoperability. Still spearheaded by RSA, the PKCS work has expanded over time to cover a growing set of PKI formatting standards, algorithms, and APIs. The PKCS standards provide fundamental definitions of data formats and algorithms that underlie virtually all of today's PKI implementations.

The PKCS standards are as follows:

- **PKCS #1 RSA Encryption Standard**   PKCS #1 defines basic formatting rules for RSA public key functions, specifically digital signatures. It defines how digital signatures are to be computed, including the format of the data to be signed and of the signature itself. It also defines the syntax for RSA public and private keys.

- PKCS #2 covered RSA encryption of message digests and was incorporated into PKCS #1.

- **PKCS #3 Diffie-Hellman Key Agreement Standard**   PKCS #3 describes a method for implementing Diffie-Hellman key agreement.

- PKCS #4 originally specified RSA key syntax but was subsumed into PKCS #1.

- **PKCS #5 Password-based Encryption Standard**   PKCS #5 describes a method for encrypting an octet string with a secret key derived from a password to produce an encrypted octet string. PKCS #5 can be used for encrypting private keys for secure key transport, as described in PKCS #8.

- **PKCS #6 Extended Certificate Syntax Standard**   PKCS #6 defines a syntax for X.509 certificates extended with attributes that provide additional information about an entity. (When PKCS #6 was first published, X.509 had not been revised to support extensions. These extensions have since been incorporated into X.509.)

- **PKCS #7 Cryptographic Message Syntax Standard**   PKCS #7 specifies a general syntax for data that may have cryptography applied to it, such as digital signatures and digital envelopes. PKCS #7 provides a number of formatting options, including formatted messages with no encryption or signature applied, enveloped (encrypted) messages, signed messages, and messages that are both signed and encrypted.

■ **PKCS #8 Private Key Information Syntax Standard**   PKCS #8 defines private key information syntax and encrypted private key syntax, where the private key encryption employs PKCS #5.

■ **PKCS #9 Selected Attribute Types**   PKCS #9 defines selected attribute types for use in PKCS #6 extended certificates, PKCS #7 digitally signed messages, PKCS #8 private key information, and PKCS #10 certificate-signing requests. The certificate attributes defined include e-mail address, unstructured name, content type, message digest, signing time, countersignature, challenge password, and extended-certificate attributes.

■ **PKCS #10 Certification Request Syntax Standard**   PKCS #10 defines a syntax for certification requests. A certification request consists of a distinguished name, a public key, and optionally a set of attributes, collectively signed by the entity requesting certification. (The PKIX Certification Request message in CMP is a PKCS #10.)

■ **PKCS #11 Cryptographic Token Interface Standard**   PKCS #11 or "Cryptoki" specifies an *application programming interface* (API) for single-user devices that hold cryptographic information (such as encryption keys and certificates) and perform cryptographic functions. Smart cards are typical devices that implement Cryptoki. Note that Cryptoki defines the interface to cryptographic functions and does not specify how the device is to implement the functions. Furthermore, Cryptoki only specifies cryptographic interfaces and does not define other interfaces that may be useful for the device to have, such as for accessing the device's file system.

■ **PKCS #12 Personal Information Exchange Syntax Standard** PKCS #12 defines a format for personal identity information, including private keys, certificates, miscellaneous secrets, and extensions. PKCS #12 facilitates transferring certificates and associated private keys so that users can move their personal identity information from device to device.

■ **PKCS #13 Elliptic Curve Cryptography Standard**   PKCS #13 is currently under development. It will cover elliptic curve parameter generation and validation, key generation and validation, digital signatures, and public key encryption, as well as key agreement, ASN.1 syntax for parameters, keys, and scheme identification.

■ **PKCS #14 Pseudo-Random Number Generation Standard** PKCS #14 is currently under development. Why does random number generation deserve its own standard? Many fundamental cryptographic functions used in PKI, such as key generation and Diffie-Hellman shared secret negotiation, use random data. However, if the random data is not random but is actually selected from a predictable set of values, the cryptographic function is no longer fully secure since its values are constrained to a reduced range of possibilities. Secure pseudo-random number generation is therefore critical to the security of PKI.

■ **PKCS #15 Cryptographic Token Information Syntax Standard** PKCS #15 promotes interoperability for cryptographic tokens by defining a common format for cryptographic objects stored on token. Data stored on a device implementing PKCS #15 will appear the same to any application that uses the device, although the data may actually be implemented in a different internal format. The PKCS #15 implementation acts as an interpreter that translates between the card's internal format and the format expected by applications.

XML

The eXtensible Markup Language is a flexible means of defining digital data formats. A natural use of XML is to define formats for signed data objects. Realizing this, the IETF XML Digital Signatures Working Group is defining XML elements that will facilitate signed data object interoperability.

The basic concept in the IETF work is that XML signatures can be applied to arbitrary data objects. The signer first computes a digest of the data object (containing virtually any type of digital data). The digest is then placed in an XML element that is itself digested and cryptographically signed. The XML signature elements delimit the data that is signed and can also contain other information related to the signature, such as a timestamp.

Application Programming Interfaces

One way to add PKI capabilities to new or existing applications is to use a set of APIs that already implements PKI functions. Microsoft's CryptoAPI, the Open Group's *Common Data Security Architecture* (CDSA), and the IETF's *Generic Security Service API* (GSS-API) each provide a standardized set of interfaces for PKI and related security functions. Any PKI application will need to access public key certificates—the *Lightweight Directory Access Protocol* (LDAP) has become the de facto standard for certificate storage.

Microsoft CryptoAPI

Microsoft's CryptoAPI is a broad set of security functions that are part of the Windows operating systems. CryptoAPI abstracts cryptographic functions and hides their actual implementation. In fact, CryptoAPI permits multiple implementations of the same cryptographic functions via *Cryptographic Service Providers* (CSPs). A CSP is an independent module that implements cryptographic functions accessible through CryptoAPI's common interfaces. In other words, a CSP wraps or hides the cryptographic implementation so that the user need not worry about it. Microsoft provides a base CSP; other vendors provide CSPs that contain their own implementation of some or all of CryptoAPIs functions.

CryptoAPI provides functions in these general areas:

- Base cryptography functions support selecting, initializing, and terminating a CSP. These functions also include cryptographic key manipulation functions for generating, exchanging, and storing cryptographic keys. Other functions include object encoding and decoding, data encryption and decryption, hash generation, and digital signature creation and verification.

- Certificate and certificate store functions manage certificate collections, certificate revocation lists, and certificate trust lists.

- Certificate verification functions support manipulating *certificate trust lists* (CTLs) and certificate chains, such as placing a CTL into a signed message and validating certificate chains.

- Message functions manipulate PKCS #7 messages, where message functions specifically operate on message constructs. The message functions include encrypting and decrypting messages and message data, signing messages and message data, and verifying signed messages. Low-level message functions operate directly on PKCS #7 messages. CryptoAPI also includes a higher-level set of message functions that wrap several low-level functions, such as CryptSignAndEncryptMessage, which performs PKCS #7 formatting, encryption, and signing in one API call.

■ Auxiliary functions cover additional functions that do not fit into other categories. These include manipulating certificate extensions and comparing certificate attributes, and object ID manipulation functions.

A brief example will show how CryptoAPI works (see the encrypt.c example in the Microsoft SDK for the full program). encrypt.c is a simple program that takes a plain-text file as input, encrypts it, and creates an encrypted file. The main CryptoAPI functions used in encrypt.c are as follows:

■ **CryptAcquireContext**   encrypt.c first sets up a cryptographic context that specifies a CSP using the CryptAcquireContext function. This function returns a handle to the CSP.

■ **CryptGenKey**   Using CryptGenKey, the name of the desired encryption algorithm, and the CSP's handle, encrypt.c next generates an encryption key and obtains a handle to the key. The key's value is hidden within the CryptoAPI key object.

■ **CryptEncrypt**   Using the CryptEncrypt function and the key handle, encrypt.c then encrypts the file's data. The encrypted data is then written to a file.

Another CryptoAPI feature (either a minus or plus, depending on your viewpoint) is that applications can specify few, if any, details of cryptographic algorithms. This can make implementing cryptographic functions simpler, but can make interoperability with other CSPs or other cryptographic toolkits extremely difficult.

Common Data Security Architecture

The *Common Data Security Architecture* (CDSA) from the Open Group is based on work originally submitted from Intel Architecture Labs. CDSA is a layered security architecture that features extensibility and interoperability. It provides flexibility through plug-in security modules and APIs for security services. CDSA is available from the Open Group as an open source implementation. CDSA features trust services based on public key certificates.

The *Common Security Services Manager* (CSSM) is the core of CDSA. CSSM manages security services and add-in modules, defines APIs for accessing security services, and defines service provider interfaces for security service modules (see Figure 7-8). CSSM's internal services provide integrity assurance and security context management, where the integrity services verify internal integrity of CSSM components and the integrity, identity, and authorization of other CSSM components. The security context management services manage the parameters needed for cryptographic operations.

Figure 7-8

CDSA layered architecture

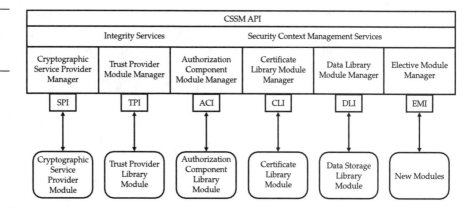

CSSM has six main module managers:

- Cryptographics Services Manager provides a common API for accessing all of the CSPs used in the system.

- Trust Policy Services Manager processes requests for security services that require policy review and approval.

- Certificate Library Services Manager manipulates certificates and certificate revocation lists. Its functions include creating, signing, verifying, and extracting fields from certificates. The add-in libraries facilitate certificate processing.

- Data Storage Services Manager provides secure, persistent storage for security objects, including certificates and CRLs. It supports querying information about security objects, such as the object's creation time, size, and modification time.

- Authorization Services Manager is a general authorization service for determining if an operation is permitted on a specific object based on a set of submitted credentials.

- Elective Module Manager provides the flexibility to extend the architecture with additional managers.

Generic Security Service API

The *Generic Security Service API* (GSS-API) provides general security services while hiding the services' implementation. The ITEF's Common Authentication Technology working group designed GSS-API to be used for peer-to-peer exchanges that require security, such as communications protocols. The GSS-API specifications were originally published in the early 1990s and have been revised several times to accommodate new technologies, such as Java. The main GSS-API functions are as follows:

- Initializing security contexts.

- Authenticating peers.

- Credential management.

- Message security functions, including message signing, verifying, sealing, and unsealing. GSS-API supports per message integrity and data origin authentication, as well as message confidentiality.

GSS-API is probably most widely used with Kerberos environments, but also supports public key functions, including key establishment and digital signatures for integrity checking.

Lightweight Directory Access Protocol

The IETF developed the *Lightweight Directory Access Protocol* (LDAP) as a simplified front end to the X.500 Directory Access Protocol. LDAP reduces the complexity of using X.500 directory services by providing approximately 90 percent of the full X.500 protocol's functionality at 10 percent of the processing cost.

For PKI environments, LDAP servers have become the preferred means of storing certificates. Since LDAP products are widely available, LDAP gives a standard method for storing and retrieving certificate and CRL data. Furthermore, development kits are readily available to develop LDAP applications.

Interoperability between LDAP directories is the next challenge to tackle. The IETF is working to standardize LDAP schemas pertaining to certificates and CRLs, which should further interoperability between LDAP products, such as certificate servers and authentication products that base authentication or authorization on certificate contents and directory structure. As a further complication, individual LDAP directory implementations may use schemas tailored to the corporation's structure. Some companies design their corporate LDAP schemas to match their corporate structure—for example, one schema may have *organizational units* (OUs) for each corporate subsidiary, and another may have OUs for each geographic location or each corporate functional area (marketing, sales, and so on). In some schemas, users are identified with a unique user ID, in others, by their e-mail address. If PKI products cannot customize their publication schemas to match the corporate schema, adding certificates to an existing LDAP directory can be difficult.

Application and PKI Implementations

Browsers and e-mail clients are the most prevalent examples of public key technology today. Netscape and Internet Explorer browsers have supported public key technology virtually since their inception. Both browsers support key pair generation and certificate request creation, as well as private key and certificate storage. With Internet Explorer, most of this support comes in the form of ActiveX controls that invoke Microsoft CryptoAPI functions, while Microsoft keys and certificates are commonly stored in the registry. With Netscape browsers, the functionality is built into the browser itself. Netscape browsers, for example, maintain their own private key and certificate repository. Essentially all major e-mail clients today support S/MIME. A user can sign, encrypt, or sign and encrypt e-mail messages with only a few mouse clicks.

Despite the work of standards bodies such as the IETF, interoperability between products is still an issue. For example, Internet Explorer keys and certificates will not work with Netscape browsers. Microsoft private keys are stored in a Microsoft-specific "pvk" format that is incompatible with PKCS-formatted keys.

Products are also inconsistent in their approach to securing their public key implementations. Netscape requires password protection for private keys; Microsoft makes passwords optional. The Netscape keygen browser function for generating key pairs in a Netscape browser lets users pick the length of the key to generate. Developers cannot limit users' behavior since keygen has few options. Since Internet Explorer's key generation functions are actually based on CAPI, they allow considerably more developer control.

User features are another area where public key applications are maturing. If a user loses his private key (or the password to unlock the private key), most current products force the user to generate a new key pair and obtain a new certificate. Installing a private key and certificate in multiple products or on multiple computers can be a challenge even for the technically knowledgeable. Most products support the capability to export and import keys and certificates; however, the formats they support differ as do the import and export procedures.

Signed Data Application

To show how PKI applications work, we conclude this chapter with an example of PKI at work. This example shows how PKI might be used in a business-to-business e-commerce application for automotive parts wholesaling. The main players in this example are an automotive buyer for a large automaker, the e-commerce site's catalog and wholesale order site, and the parts manufacturers who fulfill the parts orders.

1. The automotive buyer connects via HTTPS to the e-commerce site. The site's Web server requests client authentication, causing the buyer's browser to pop up a window listing the buyer's certificates. The buyer selects the parts warehouse client certificate. The Web server validates the buyer's certificate during SSL connection establishment, including validating the user's certificate, checking that the certificate is not expired or revoked, and validating that its signer is on the site's trusted signer list.

2. To determine the user's purchasing authorizations, the e-commerce application retrieves the user's identity from the client certificate and checks that the user ID named in the certificate is authorized to access the e-order application. It then retrieves the user's purchasing authorization limits by querying the site's central LDAP repository for the user's group membership. The user is a member of a group authorized for purchases up to $20,000.

3. The buyer selects three types of bolts from the parts warehouse online catalog. When the buyer clicks Done on the Web order form, the auto parts manufacturer Web site downloads an ActiveX control signed with the warehouse site's software publisher certificate.

4. The user's browser verifies that the ActiveX control is signed by a trusted software publisher, the control's certificate is valid, and the signature verifies correctly.

5. The signed ActiveX control calls Microsoft CryptoAPI functions to access the purchaser's private key. The browser pops up a window informing the user that he is signing the order. The buyer clicks OK. The ActiveX control then generates a hash of the order data and signs the hash with the buyer's private key. The signature and the order form are posted to the parts warehouse Web site.

6. When the parts warehouse receives the order, it first requests a secure timestamp from its external timestamp service. The secure timestamp includes a hash of the order data, the date and time, and a signature calculated with the timestamp service's private key. The parts warehouse logs the order and the secure timestamp in its log. It then verifies the signature on the transaction, records the transaction in its order database, and processes the order to determine which parts manufacturers need to fulfill the order. It generates new order notices for these manufacturers and sends the order notices in signed and encrypted S/MIME e-mail messages. Finally, the parts warehouse generates a signed and encrypted e-mail with a confirmation receipt of the transaction and sends it using S/MIME to the parts purchaser.

Summary

This chapter covers a wide range of ground, surveying the services, protocols, formatting standards, and APIs that can help you build PKI applications. Some of these are well-established technologies, such as SSL and HTTPS; others are emerging, such as timestamp or notary services. To show how a PKI application might actually use a combination of these enabling technologies, we concluded with an example that showed a PKI application for auto parts purchasing.

CHAPTER 8

Trust Models

This chapter examines the concept of establishing trust relationships. Trust relationships between multiple certification authorities are necessary to ensure that all subscribers to a PKI do not have to rely on and trust a single CA, which would be impossible to scale, administer, and safeguard. The goal is to ensure that identities created by one Certification Authority can be trusted by relying parties that have a different issuing authority. We will examine the models used to build these trust relationships and the provisions within X.509 that allow trust relationships to be established and controlled.

What Is a Trust Model?

Trust models provide a framework for creating and managing trust relationships. However, before we become too involved with trusted identities and relationships, we should start with a definition of trust.

Trust

The 2000 version of X.509 defines trust this way (X.509, Section 3.3.54):

> "Generally an entity can be said to 'trust' a second entity when the first entity makes the assumption that the second entity will behave exactly as the first entity expects."[1]

NOTE:

This definition is nearly as effective as the definition of a network node in one architectural model, which was defined as a "named collection of user expectations."

The concept of trust defined here involves a relationship between two parties and a set of expectations placed on that relationship.

The confidence level that can be applied to these assumptions or expectations (that is, the degree of trust) is directly related to the *locality* of the two parties. Locality is a sense or "measure" of the "closeness" of the two parties. If you know the other party well and have experience that supports your expectations, you will have a higher confidence level in the trust you establish. The further removed the two parties are from each other, or the less experience you have with the way the other party operates, the lower the confidence level.

NOTE:

The exception to this rule (the one that proves it, according to my English teacher) is that in a community such as the military, the most trusted individual is the commander in chief, from whom all trust flows.

At some point, the other party is so far removed and your resulting confidence level is so low, it may be necessary to introduce a third party. In this model, you defer to a third party you trust, who can assure you of trustworthiness of the other party and raise your confidence level. This, of course, is the concept of the Certification Authority, described in Chapter 3.

The use of a third party to establish trust invokes a *transitive* trust relationship. The CA trusts a *subscriber*. You, the *relying party*, trust the CA, and as a result impute trust to the subscriber.

Trust Domains

The concept of whom you can trust is affected by the community in which you operate. Within an enterprise, for example, you are likely to have a higher confidence level in the other people who work for the same organization than you have for people who work outside of it. Within a community, there are established relationships and modes of operation that allow you to place a high level of confidence in the trust relationships. Provided all of the individuals in a community abide by the same rules, the community can be said to operate within a single domain of trust. A trust domain can be practically defined for an organization as the set of systems under common control or subject to a common set of policies (policies can be explicitly stated or can be implied by the operational procedures implemented).

Recognition of trust domains and their boundaries is important when constructing a PKI. The use of certificates issued by a CA from another trust domain is typically much more complex than using certificates issued by a CA within your own trust domain.

It is possible, and at times desirable, to build a CA using one of the trust model mechanisms described in this chapter within a single domain of trust. For example, an enterprise can choose to establish a *hierarchical* trust model to allow partitioning of the users into manageable subsets, or because the network topology requires geographic distribution of the registration authorities or the certificate servers. However, any of the alternate trust models described can be used just as effectively.

NOTE:

The hierarchical trust model was introduced in Chapter 4.

Within an enterprise, trust domains can be partitioned along organizational or geographical lines. For example, the company may be split into separate operating entities or divisions, each holding significant autonomy.

It is entirely possible that multiple trust domains will exist within the organization, some of which may overlap. When the various trust domains begin to assert specific policies and operating procedures, things become much more interesting—particularly when the different parts of the organization need to interoperate. In most cases, a high-level set of policies that establish common operating requirements will tend to draw together the trust domains into some kind of working whole. For the purposes of an IT infrastructure, including the Certification Authority, the creation of an overarching trust domain that establishes broad policies for local trust domains can make the difference between success and failure in your PKI deployment.

As establishment of trust is essentially rooted in human relationships, it should not be surprising that politics, rather than technology, often plays a more significant role in defining trust boundaries and relationships. Within a single enterprise, the needs of separate divisions to maintain their own autonomy can mean they are not prepared to use a hierarchical structure that requires them to subordinate themselves to any other entity within a trust model. To meet these needs, you must be able to facilitate trust relationships within a *peer-to-peer* trust model, where the decisions that impact a trust relationship can be more autonomous.

When you extend the requirements for trust relationships across organizational boundaries, however, the question of how to build trust relationships becomes more vexing. The goals, aspirations, and cultures of different organizations make it much more difficult to establish trust relationships with high confidence levels. Establishing trust models across organizations or trust domains becomes a problem of quite a different degree.

As part of this chapter, we want to describe the use of trust models and their mechanisms to establish relationships between domains of trust.

Trust Anchors

In any trust model, the certificate user or relying party must use some criteria to decide when the requirements for establishing a sufficiently high level of confidence in an identity have been met. In short, when can you decide that you trust an identity?

In the trust models we will examine, the decision to trust an identity is made when it can be determined that an identity, or the issuer of an identity, was certified by a sufficiently trusted entity. This trusted entity is the *trust anchor*.

How you conclude that a trusted entity is sufficient for this purpose can be decided in several different ways. Let's consider how you might identify trust anchors in your world of nondigital relationships.

You may have direct knowledge of the individual being identified and can satisfy yourself (by asking some pertinent questions) that they are who they say they are. In this case, you are directly verifying the identity so there is no requirement for an external trust anchor. Another way to describe this is that the trust decision is *local* to you. So you and the trust anchor are one and the same.

If the individual comes from outside your immediate circle of acquaintances, life becomes a little more difficult. If one of your acquaintances knows him, you can use a form of imputed trust—you trust the individual because you trust your acquaintance and the relationships he has established. The trust anchor here is the acquaintance who attests to the identity of the individual and possibly also certifies you to other people. Note that this trust anchor is located very close to you.

NOTE:

If none of your close acquaintances knows the individual, but a large enough group of people you know vaguely are all prepared to certify the identity, that may be sufficient in some models. PGP provides a mode of operation that supports this notion. As a technique for establishing trust, it is not generally well thought of, as it leaves you open to collusion among the certifiers of the identity.

Finally, you may decide to rely on a highly trusted but well-removed entity that you do not know directly, but you consider has a sufficiently trustworthy reputation. An example here might include the Department of Motor Vehicles for drivers' licenses. If this entity has certified the identity, you are prepared to trust it. In this case, the trust anchor is well removed from you, but its reputation provides sufficient confidence for you to have confidence in the identity.

Trust Relationships

As we discussed in Chapter 3, it may be necessary to establish a series of trust relationships that allow a certificate user to find a path from the certificate issuer that leads to a trust anchor. For a Public Key Infrastructure, this trust relationship is established between two issuing authorities when one or both issue a certificate for the other's public key. In addition to attesting to the identity of the Certification Authority, the certification process has the added aspect of certifying or declaring that a *trust path* can be established through the participating certification authorities. This path allows a user validating an identity to trace the trust relationships back to her trust anchor.

Trust models describe how those relationships are built and what the rules are for finding and traversing trust paths.

It is worth mentioning that trust relationships can be bidirectional or unidirectional. In most cases, they are bidirectional—if you decide to trust someone, he will probably return that trust. This is also the simplest case for constructing trust models, as chains of trust can be constructed or verified in either direction. Some special cases exist where trust is only extended in a single direction. For example, when crossing from a top-secret to an open trust domain, it may be appropriate for the trust to be extended only to authorities within the top-secret trust domain.

Earlier, we considered some of the political issues associated with trust domains and establishing trust relationships within and without an organization. Just as establishing trust becomes more difficult when you cross the boundaries of a trust domain, you also encounter problems such as scaling effective trust solutions. A trust domain tends to be bounded by the very fact that, as it grows, it becomes increasingly difficult to have high levels of trust in the participants. This leads to the sense that keeping the distance between participants short is more likely to lead to higher levels of confidence in the relationships established. For example, you have a high level of confidence in the identities of your immediate family or co-workers. For a very extended family relationship, or for establishing the identity of an employee in another location, you may need to rely on a network of intermediaries who can establish this trust for you.

NOTE:

We are talking about a confidence level in the identity, not what your immediate family member might do. You may not be prepared to trust a particular family member further than you can throw him, but you will still have a high level of confidence in who they are. This emphasizes the distinction between authentication *to establish an identity that you can trust, and* authorization, *which defines what you are prepared to allow the holder of an identity to do.*

For practical electronic commerce to become a reality, it is necessary to establish trusted identities for a worldwide population that are certified by many different trust domains. Even if identities for the general populace are ignored and only the subset of certificate users within enterprises is considered, you are still dealing with hundreds of thousands of trust domains and potentially many millions of identities.

This leads to a tension between the need to establish trust relationships among a very large population and the need to keep the number of intermediaries necessary to establish a relationship small (the fewer intermediaries involved, the greater the locality of trust and the higher your confidence level in the ultimate relationship). The number of intermediaries required to establish a path between a certificate owner and a trust anchor must be kept small if practical verification of identities is to be achieved. The promise of PKI is that it can facilitate establishment of trusted identities for huge populations.

To resolve this tension, you must be able to construct trust models that allow partitioning of the population and identification of well-defined points for building trust relationships that allow minimal paths for trust validation to be constructed.

General Hierarchical Organizations

To begin, we will consider a general model for partitioning a large population. In this model, two types of certification authorities will be considered. A *leaf Certification Authority* issues certificates to end-entities (users, network servers, application code segments, and so on). An *intermediate Certification Authority* issues certificates for leaf CAs or other intermediate CAs.

Let us consider the general hierarchical structure shown in Figure 8-1 as a method for organizing a set of relationships between a partitioned set of users or identity space.

For the purposes of this example, we will consider that any leaf CA is capable of issuing 10,000 end-entity certificates. In addition, an intermediate CA can certify up to 100 other CAs. An intermediate CA forms a root to this hierarchy or inverted tree structure with the same properties as other intermediate CAs, and with no other special properties assigned to it.

In this case, where we provide four levels of certification authorities—one level of leaf CAs providing end-entity certificates and three levels of intermediate CAs—we can accommodate a total population of 10 billion end-entity certificates (this assumes an even distribution of CAs, each running at full capacity). If we were to reduce the number of levels and use only two levels of intermediate CAs, we can still accommodate 100 million certificates. This certainly allows a significant identity space to be constructed.

What about the certificate path lengths for certificate validation? Let's look at an example.

In Figure 8-1, the arrows indicate trust relationships that have been established. In this case, all of the CAs, both leaf and intermediate types, have established bidirectional trust relationships.

Figure 8-1

General hierarchical structure

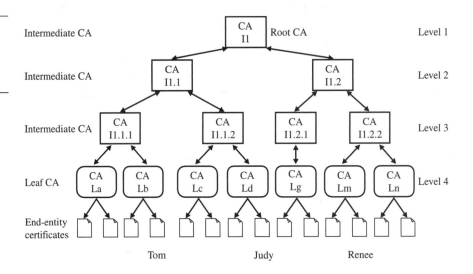

Consider a user—let's call him Tom—who owns a certificate and sends it to the owner of a different certificate to verify the digital signature Tom has placed on an electronic order form. In order to validate Tom's certificate, the second party—let's call her Judy—needs to validate the certificate chain associated with it. In order to validate the certificate chain, she needs to decide what she will use as her trust anchor. In this case, she has decided that the issuer of her certificate, the leaf CA designated as *Ld*, will be the trust anchor, for the perfectly sensible reason that if she could trust it to issue her own certificate, she should be able to trust the trust relationships it has established. We will refer to Judy's issuing CA as a *local trust anchor*.

In this case, when Judy receives a certificate from Tom, she is looking for a set of trust relationships that have been established between the leaf CA *Lb*, Tom's issuing authority and her own CA *Ld*. The path length, or number of CAs, that must have established trust relationships is five in this case (*Lb - I1.1.1 - I1.1 - I1.1.2 - Ld*).

If Tom now sends his certificate to Renee, who in turn uses the CA that issued her own certificate as a local trust anchor, the problem becomes how to find a set of trust relationships linking Tom's leaf CA *Lb* to Renee's leaf CA *Lm*. The path length in this case will be seven (*Lb - I1.1.1 - I1.1 - I1 - I1.2 - I1.2.2 - Lm*).

Seven is the maximum path length in this model where there are four CA levels as the path passes through the root CA. As a result, we can validate any relationship within this population of 10 billion users with at most seven trust relationships. The problem is that the majority of trust relationships will require a path that passes through the CA at the root of the hierarchy. This makes the root of the hierarchy a particularly sensitive security risk. The access to this CA and its signing keys must be controlled very carefully.

As you will see later, if you are prepared to live with some constraints on the general hierarchical model or if you allow more complex relationships, it is possible to shorten the maximum path length considerably.

Trust Models

In this section, we will examine some of the specific models that have been created to establish trust relationships. We will consider the three most common trust models, subordinated hierarchies, peer-to-peer, and the connected mesh models. To complete the discussion, we will consider some hybrid varieties that include aspects of each of the common models.

Subordinated Hierarchical Models

The generalized hierarchical model allowed bidirectional trust relationships and for certificate users to select trust anchors as they saw fit.

The subordinated hierarchy is a subset of the generalized hierarchy that applies some additional constraints (see Figure 8-2).

Figure 8-2

Subordinated
hierarchy

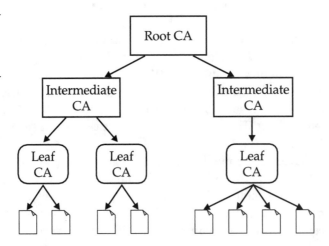

The root CA takes on particular meaning in the subordinated hierarchy model. It is designated as the common trust anchor for all end-entities. As such, by definition, it is the most trusted Certification Authority, and all other trust relationships devolve from it. It certifies the next lower set of subordinate CAs with a set of unidirectional trust relationships. In this model, only superior CAs issue certificates to their subordinates—subordinate CAs do not certify their superiors.

As the root CA in this model is the single trust anchor and as trust relationships are built from the most trusted CA, there is no other Certification Authority that can sign the root CA's certificate. As a result, the root CA creates a *self-signed* or *self-issued* certificate for itself. In this case, the certificate subject and the certificate issuer will be the same. The public key certified in the certificate corresponds to the private key used to generate the signature on the certificate. As a result, the public key in the certificate will be used to directly verify the signature on the certificate when the certificate is being validated. This is illustrated in Figure 8-3.

The subordinate hierarchy model can also apply *naming constraints* that limit the subordinate CA to certifying other CAs that correspond to specific forms of named subtrees. This is examined in more detail in the "NameConstraints" section.

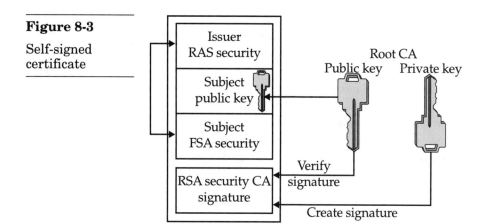

Figure 8-3

Self-signed certificate

As the sole designated trust anchor, the root CA certificate must be distributed to all certificate users. This places even more importance on the root CA signing keys than that required by the generalized model. In the subordinated hierarchy model, *all* paths will include the root CA certificate. Any compromise of the root CA keys will have disastrous ramifications for the entire trust model.

The loss of confidence in the operation of the trust model would encompass all certificate users. The root CA keys would of course have to be revoked, and a new root certificate issued and distributed to all certificate users. In addition, any subordinate certificates and keys that were suspect would need to be replaced—the flow-on effects would create major disruption in the operation of trust model.

The sensitivity of the root CA keys and the ramification of a compromise of key security are balanced by the fact that the root CA itself is used very infrequently. Its primary job is to certify subordinate CAs—a relatively rare event. The only other significant task it has is revocation of subordinate CAs it has certified—hopefully, an even more rare event.

The root CA certificate certifying the public component of the signing key is distributed to all certificate users. Provided that a repository containing the certificate is available, the root CA itself will seldom be directly encountered by anyone engaged in the operation of the trust model. As a result, the root CA can spend most of its operational life offline, with its signing keys securely locked away.

The subordinated hierarchy provides several benefits that have contributed to it becoming the most widely deployed trust model to date.

All certificate paths terminate with the root CA certificate, so only the certificate path toward the root CA must be traversed and validated. It is not necessary to build or validate the return path from the root CA to the certificate user's CA. As a result, the certificate paths will on average be approximately half the length of those required in the generalized hierarchy. If you consider the same parameters we applied to the generalized hierarchy case in the later section titled "General Hierarchical Organizations," we will always require a path length of four certificates.

As all certificate users rely on a common trust anchor, the result is that there will only be a single trust path used to reach a specific end-entity. This allows the end-entity to distribute the certificates for any intermediate CAs in the chain along with its own certificate to provide a path for the certificate user to follow to the root CA.

The most significant disadvantage of this trust model lies in the very reason for its simplicity and success: the existence of a root CA as the common trust anchor. For small communities, it may be possible to get agreement on a common root CA. The problem is, it is impossible to get all parties to universally agree on a single trusted root CA.

Subordinated hierarchies work most effectively when used in a context that supports a strongly hierarchical structure. The U.S. Department of Defense used a subordinated hierarchy in support of its Defense Messaging System (DMS).[2] The DOD PKI Roadmap currently specifies a hierarchical structure for deployment of its Public Key Infrastructure. In both of these cases, a subordinated hierarchy is a good fit, as the organizational structure of the DOD is hierarchical in nature. However, even within the DOD requirements, there are cases where a strict hierarchy is insufficient. This includes the case where a single user with a particular security rating must operate across trust domains with different security ratings. In the DOD trust model, each certificate with a different security rating is issued under a different hierarchy, and so the use of multiple distinct hierarchies and root CAs as trust anchors results.

The other well-known use of strict subordinated hierarchies was in the definition of the Internet Privacy Enhanced Mail (PEM) infrastructure.[3] PEM identified specific roles for intermediate and leaf CAs and defined policies that were applicable to their operation. The PEM model did have a number of interesting features, some of which have survived in current hierarchical deployments, even though PEM and its infrastructure did not.

PEM introduced a concept known as *name subordination*. Name subordination allows a CA to be certified to issue only certificates within a restricted subset (subtree) of the full X.500 name space that is subordinate to the name of the CA.

As an example, an engineering CA within RSA might have an X.500 name like:

```
{Country=US, Organization=RSA Security, Organizational
Unit=Engineering}
```

All certificates issued by a CA conforming to the name subordination rule would have to have a subject name prefixed with the same X.500 name as the CA. The result would be that the Engineering CA could not issue certificates where the subject name implied that the organizational unit for the user was "Marketing." For example:

```
{Country=US, Organization=RSA Security, Organizational
Unit=Marketing}
```

PEM also allowed some intermediate CAs to be certified by more than one superior CA. This means that more than one certification path could exist for an end-entity, which adds complexity to the certificate validation process. This led to the some simple policy constraints that are applied to determine which certification path should be evaluated for specific purposes.

PEM was ultimately unsuccessful. The reasons for this lie in the fundamental differences between the strict requirements for subordination in the PEM model and the need for more open and flexible operation within the Internet. In addition, there are some indications that secure e-mail was not as critical an application as was first expected.

Hierarchical trust models can work reasonably well within the confines of an enterprise—particularly if the enterprise has an organizational structure that is strongly hierarchical. The model tends to work badly when trust needs to be extended across enterprise boundaries. The two reasons for this are usually the lack of agreement on a trusted root CA (and its control) and the differences in operational policies instituted in different organizations.

Peer-to-Peer Models

A peer-to-peer trust model assumes establishment of trust between two certification authorities that cannot be considered subordinate to each other—rather, they are considered peers. The two CAs could be part of a single enterprise or trust domain, but more typically are in different enterprises or trust domains. In this section, we are going to consider a model where only a single set of certificates for cross-certification appears in a chain (see Figure 8-4). More complex variations will be discussed later.

Figure 8-4

Peer-to-peer cross-certificates

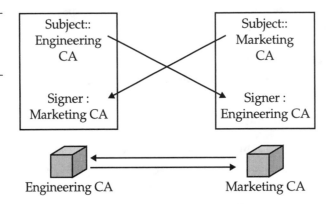

In this model, there is no root CA to act as a trust anchor. Certificate users will usually rely on their own local issuing authority to act as the trust anchor.

The certificate user will always validate a path running through the issuing CA, which in turn has had its public key certified by the certificate user's own CA. It is usual for each CA to certify the public key of the other creating bilateral trust. This process is often referred to as cross-certification.

The X.509 specification (section 8.1.2) defines a cross-certificate in this way:

"A Certification Authority may be the subject of a certificate issued by another Certification Authority. In this case, the certificate is called a cross-certificate."

This definition is equally applicable to hierarchical relationships as peer-to-peer relationships. Unfortunately, the term has historically held a broad variety of meanings for different communities. Cross-certification has often explicitly been linked to peer-to-peer relationships to distinguish them from hierarchical relationships. Here we will explicitly qualify the term cross-certification as peer-to-peer cross-certification.

Figure 8-5 illustrates a certificate path that has been constructed involving two CAs that have established a trust relationship using peer-to-peer cross-certification. It shows the cross-certificates issued between each of the CAs, as well as end-entity certificates that have been issued by the CAs. The issuer of one certificate is the subject of the other. The public key certified in one certificate corresponds to the private key used to sign the other. In this simple model, there is a maximum path length of two CA certificates.

Figure 8-5

Cross-certificate path

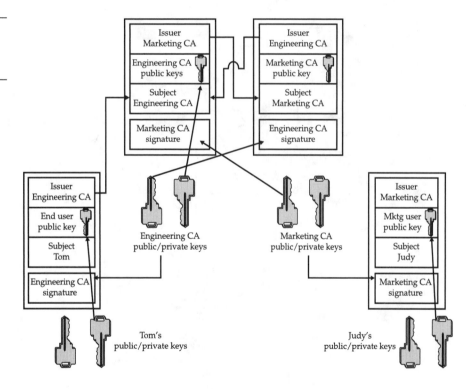

The simplicity of this peer-to-peer cross-certification model is offset by a lack of scalability if (for reasons of high assurance in the trust path) you restrict yourself to only allowing direct trust relationships. The result of this restriction is that every CA must directly certify every other CA that it wants to include in the trust model. If you want a fully connected set of trust relationships, the number of relationships that must be established is approximately equal to the square of the number of certification authorities. A fully connected mesh of this type is illustrated in Figure 8-6. The explosion in the number of relationships required quickly leads to a very unscalable trust model.

Figure 8-6

Fully connected meshes

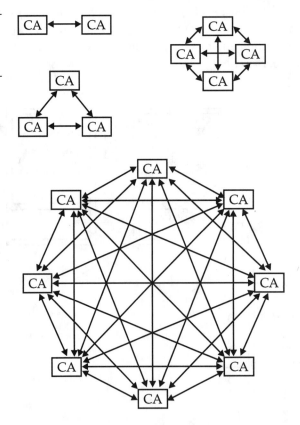

NOTE:

This is referred to mathematically as an "order n-squared" problem. The number of links required can be calculated as n*(n-1), where n is the number of certification authorities. Where bilateral trust relationships are established, each link will require the issuance of two certificates.

Note that each of the bidirectional arrows represents the establishment of two relationships. Two cross-certificates are generated and exchanged in this fully connected mesh.

Unlike the hierarchical model, a single trust anchor cannot be shared by all the certificate users. Instead, each certificate user must obtain the CA certificate for his local CA. This makes distribution of the CA certificates a little more complex. Existing distribution models often provide a list of trusted CA certificates as part of the Web browser or other application. Where local trust anchors are used, each kit would have to be tailored to include the CA certificate for the local user for each CA. In very large enterprises, this could be difficult.

Alternatively, the certificate user could obtain a copy of the issuing CA certificate when registering for her own end-entity certificate. Experience deploying PKI systems indicates that even a process as seemingly simple as providing a user with a Web page to download a CA certificate may prove to be too much overhead. If this process can be made a transparent part of the registration process, it is probably workable. However, the degree of transparency will be highly dependant on the applications that implement this support.

NOTE:

Currently, most Web browsers require (for very good security reasons) the user to step through a series of questions asking for verification of the trust of the CA certificate. For the vast majority of PKI users, these questions and their implications have no apparent meaning.

Automated pickup of the CA certificate does not adequately deal with the case of a certificate user who never registers for a certificate. A common example is the user who receives a digitally signed e-mail message but does not sign or encrypt e-mail herself. Within your own organization, you could decide to issue end-entity certificates to everyone or configure all applications with a "default" trust anchor to use in this case. This will not work when dealing with other organizations that do not have a matching trust model.

The most significant obstacle to deployment of peer-to-peer cross-certification today is the lack of application support for certificate chains containing cross-certificates. Currently, widely deployed PKI-enabled applications cannot process certificate paths that contain cross-certificates. Some programming libraries allow application developers to build support for cross-certificate chains, but the functionality has not yet been integrated into common applications. In addition, some PKI vendors provide application plug-ins that modify the behavior of the certificate validation logic to include support for construction and validation of paths containing cross-certificates. Wide deployment of trust models dependant on the use of cross-certificates will be hampered until application support for cross-certificates becomes common.

Earlier, we identified scalability problems with this simple peer-to-peer cross-certification model. If we relax the constraint that only a single set of certificates for directly cross-certified peers can appear in a certificate chain, more sophisticated models can be constructed that have better scaling characteristics. Unfortunately, as we will see in the next section, this sophistication introduces its own cost.

Mesh Models

The use of peer-to-peer cross-certification is useful, but somewhat limited while we are constrained to direct cross-certification of no more than a single pair of certification authorities. However, the same technique can be applied more generally to build sophisticated trust models. The trust model we will look at here is where a partial or fully connected mesh can be constructed by allowing more than two CA certificates in a certificate path.

To construct a set of trust relationships in this model, we allow each participant in a peer-to-peer cross-certified relationship to cross-certify with other peers. By allowing the certificate path to route through multiple CAs, we create a general mechanism for constructing long certificate chains. Using this mechanism, we could build a subordinated hierarchical structure by permitting only one-way certification from a superior CA to a subordinate CA. If we permit bilateral trust relationships and each CA in turn in a path has cross-certified each other, we could construct the generalized hierarchical structure.

Figure 8-7 shows an extended set of bilateral trust relationships based on cross-certification.

These extended cross-certified relationships are most useful across trust domains, or where subordination is not possible or reasonable. The problem that is introduced is that as pathways increase in length, it is difficult to maintain a uniform level of assurance across these different trust domains. For example, if the policies in one trust domain require stringent

Figure 8-7

Bilateral trust
relationships

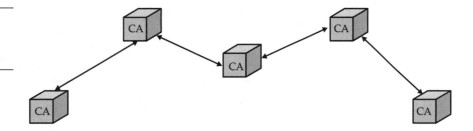

registration processes, including in-person verification of the identity of
the subscriber, while in another trust domain a simple e-mail request and
response process applies, there is unlikely to be agreement on the assurance level for the total certificate chain.

Long certificate paths also incur significant validation overheads, so it
is desirable to keep paths as short as possible. In situations where a trust
chain between two endpoints is frequently traversed, it can be worthwhile
to establish a direct relationship (see Figure 8-8).

Figure 8-8

Reducing path
lengths

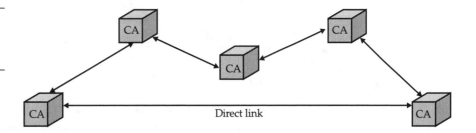

As a direct trust relationship has now been established, a higher confidence level in the trust chain can be maintained. The shorter path
requires less processing and resources to validate, and as a result, validation should be faster and more likely to succeed.

The disadvantage is that the number of relationships begins to
increase for each CA. Provided reduction in path lengths is used judiciously, this is a good thing, but in a highly connected electronic business
world, too many of these connections will push you back into scalability
problems. As we will see later, more sophisticated models are being developed that can reduce this problem.

In a mesh model, many alternate paths may need to be evaluated in order to determine what trust relationships to use. This is very similar to the processing that is required to traverse a series of network routers when sending a message from one location in the Internet to another. Unfortunately, we end up with all the same sorts of problems that need to be solved when evaluating network routes.

In the example shown in Figure 8-9, Renee can locate a path between her local CA acting as her trust anchor and Tom's issuing CA using multiple paths.

Figure 8-9

Cross-certificate mesh

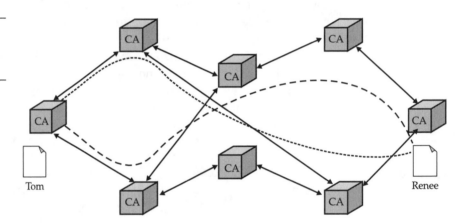

As trust relationships that extend through a large number of intermediate CAs are undesirable, we would like to select the best path between two endpoints. The best path will usually be the path with the smallest number of links; however, security policies implemented along a longer path may provide a higher assurance level. In general, we are looking for the shortest path that meets the policy constraints of the certificate user.

Remember:

The two endpoints are the issuer of the certificate being validated and the trust anchor, which is usually the Certification Authority that issued a certificate to the certificate user.

To eliminate paths with too many intermediate CAs, it may be desirable to limit the number of "trust hops" that you are prepared to take when constructing a path. However, it is very difficult to determine what a correct setting for such a hop count should be. As trust relationships outside your control are broken and established, the length of paths will vary, and too tight a limit on acceptable path lengths can result in previously acceptable paths becoming invalid.

In general, in a practical mesh network, you cannot be aware ahead of time of the paths that need to be traversed. The complexity of determining a valid path increases as the number of trust relationships increase. In addition, new trust relationships that are formed may provide paths you were previously unaware of. Those paths may be better or they may be worse as a solution to validating a trust chain. A side effect of new trust relationships may be that loops occur along some paths.

Dead ends are another possibility—until you have traversed a path, you cannot tell if it will be successful. Optimizations are possible, so you may be able to cache previously validated chains that meet your requirements. However, problems with stale cache information can lead to less than optimal or unworkable solutions.

As you can see, the increase in flexibility that we derive from using a trust mesh has a corresponding increase in the complexity level to handle operation of trust in a mesh model.

Figure 8-10 shows what can happen as a trust mesh grows. Unless the mesh is treated as some form of closed user group, it is entirely possible that some future choice made by a participant in the mesh will produce unexpected results. In this case, you may inadvertently extend trust to your evil and unscrupulous competitor. This emphasizes the need for an *authentication* or identity establishment system such as PKI as well as an *authorization* system. PKI will allow you to establish that you can trust the identities presented to you, but not what access rights you should accord to that identity. That is the domain of the authorization or privilege management infrastructure (PMI). Note that the 2000 edition of X.509 specifically proposes a standard solution to this problem.

NOTE:

A closed user group in this context would normally be determined by policies determined for the community and administered by a Policy Authority that controlled the construction of trust relationships.

Figure 8-10

Unexpected trust relationships

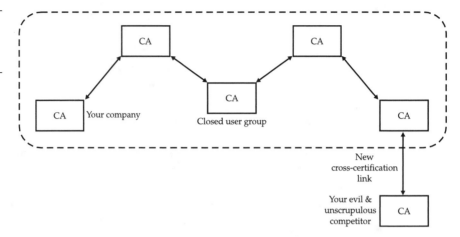

The difficulty in an unconstrained mesh model is that you do not have control over what actions your newly certified partner may take in the future. Will they be as careful performing due diligence in the next relationship they establish? Many of the issues that arise are not inherent in the trust model itself. Rather, crossing trust domains is a function of using peer-to-peer cross-certification. As a result, a community may need to establish a different type of authority to control actions taken by the various members or to limit membership in the trust model. This authority, discussed later, is generally referred to as a *Policy Authority*, as it addresses the construction and management of policies.

Path Construction

When constructing a path through a trust mesh, you may start with the certificate that is being validated and find a series of cross-certified peer-to-peer relationships that lead to the trust anchor—this is referred to as processing the path in the forward direction. Alternatively, you can process the path in the reverse direction by starting with the trust anchor and working toward the issuer of the certificate being validated. If you want, you could start at both ends and work toward the middle!

Note that the processing direction taken probably does not matter—workable solutions can be designed in any direction or combination (except possibly starting in the middle and working outward). What might constrain your choice of algorithm and processing direction is whether unidirectional or bidirectional trust relationships have been established between certification authorities. Unidirectional trust relationships are perfectly valid and may be a reasonable reflection of the business relationship they need to support. However, when it comes to establishing trust paths, they create many more problems. This is much like the increase in complexity caused when trying to navigate a downtown city area if a large number of one-way streets have been used. You never quite know when you will strike one and have to seek an alternate route around a one-way street leading in the wrong direction. (I have long held the belief that by changing a single one-way street sign in downtown Sydney, Australia, you could successfully trap the entire commuting public in a completely closed system.)

Locating the certificates used to establish cross-relationships is a significant issue in the mesh model. Unlike the subordinated hierarchy, it is not possible to predetermine the paths associated with each end-entity—they are all different, so the path cannot be sent with the end-user certificate. Construction of paths through a mesh relies heavily on the existence of and ready access to a repository such as an LDAP-compliant directory. For most practical deployments of a trust mesh, access will normally be required to multiple repositories (at least one per trust domain) during the iterative process of locating CA certificates.

X.509 (section 11.1.2 and 11.2.3) and the PKIX working group[4] have defined directory objects for certification authorities and cross-certificates. Cross-certificates are stored in a directory attribute named crossCertificatePair. Figure 8-11 illustrates the contents of the CA object and the cross-certificate pair attribute.

The cross-certificate pair contains certificates that have been issued as part of establishing a cross-relationship. The forward element is used to store a certificate issued to this CA by another CA. The reverse element is used to store a certificate issued to another CA by this CA. More than one instance of a cross-certificate pair attribute may be present, which allows a collection of paths through this CA to be listed. For a unidirectional trust relationship, only one of the forward or reverse elements needs to be present for each cross-certificate pair attribute. In a bidirectional trust relationship, where both elements are present, the subject and issuer names in one certificate must match the issuer and subject names in the other.

The forward entry of the crossCertificatePair attribute contains certificates issued to the CA because the process of starting at the end-entity certificate and progressing toward the trust anchor is considered constructing the path in the "forward" direction. Constructing a "reverse"

Figure 8-11

PKI CA directory object and cross-certificate pair attribute

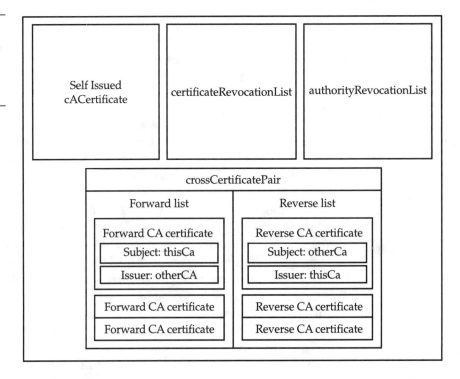

path requires starting at the trust anchor and working toward the issuer of the end-entity certificate using the reverse elements in the crossCertificatePair attribute. Figure 8-12 illustrates using three CA directory objects and the crossCertificatePair attribute to construct a path.

In the example shown in Figure 8-12, Andrew will receive a certificate from Tom. Tom's issuing CA is Company *abc*; it has cross-certified with the CA from Company *lmn*, which has in turn cross-certified with the CA from Company *xyz*. Company *xyz*'s CA issued Andrew's own certificate and is considered his trust anchor. The CA objects within each company's directory are shown.

X.509 also defines a directory attribute named PKI Path to be a sequence of cross-certificates. This ostensibly allows previously constructed paths from the CA to other CAs to be collected and saved. This is a subset of the possible forward paths from the named CA. This attribute has not been included by the PKIX working group in the X.509 directory schema for support of the Internet usage of PKI. Whether the PKI Path attribute will be used in actual PKI deployments remains to be seen.

Figure 8-12

Traversing cross-
certificate pair
attributes

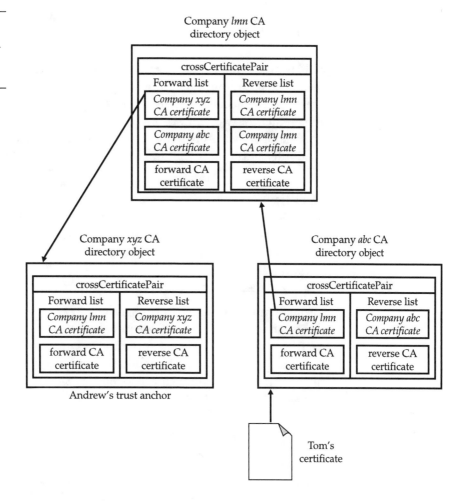

Access to directories to locate the component cross-certificates is a general requirement for the mesh solution. This raises some practical problems. Availability of the directory and network bandwidth must be sufficiently high to allow reasonable response time when constructing and validating paths. Latency associated with network topologies and throughput should be minimized to ensure that directory lookups and redirections can be serviced in reasonable time.

Mesh models will often be implemented to establish trusted identities across trust boundaries. This raises additional problems for the use of directories. Directories that reside in a different trust domain generally have significant access restrictions, if they can be accessed by external users at all. Directories contain much information that is proprietary or private, and some form of authentication is normally required before this information can be accessed. It is clear that wide-scale deployment of publicly accessible directories within each trust domain is necessary for a mesh model to succeed. These directories minimally need to provide access to CA objects providing cross-certificates and other PKI validation information. As we will see later, some practical deployments of cross-certification have proposed solutions to allow access to this directory-based information.

NOTE:

Presumably, these directories will employ publication techniques that will keep sensitive information private. This would include information that would expose company structure, such as the naming scheme used within the company.

Some implementations may choose other mechanisms to distribute or provide access to cross-certificate information. For some deployments, distribution of lists of trusted CA certificates to certificate users may be a reasonable solution. Some form of trust router could be built to distribute trust routing tables in much the same way that network routers distribute network routing tables today.

Hybrid Trust Models

The dynamic nature of business relationships makes it extremely unlikely that any static or narrowly bounded trust model will survive very long. Within a company, new blocks of end-entities will have to be added en masse as mergers or acquisitions expand the bounds of an enterprise. If a newly acquired company already has a certificate infrastructure in place, it will be necessary to integrate the new company's pre-existing trust model into the trust model for the enterprise. Divestitures of various kinds will require that some trust relationships be broken. Outside the company, associations between companies come and go, and with them, trust linkages that cross multiple trust domains.

Direct trust relationships may be required even when a subordinated hierarchy is used. This can facilitate a shorter, more direct path between a certificate issuer and a trust anchor for trust paths that are heavily used.

In some trust models, a different set of policies or constraints may need to be applied along that specific trust path. As a result, various combinations of hierarchical models with specific peer-to-peer cross-certification between nodes are likely, or even a complete overlay structure. We will consider a number of these hybrid trust models in the following sections.

Connecting Subordinated Hierarchies

Many enterprises and government agencies establish hierarchies for their internal use. Reasons for adoption of subordinated hierarchies include the following:

- Administrative overheads are small.
- The model scales well.
- Hierarchies match the internal structure of many organizations relatively well.
- Use of a common trust anchor makes distribution of the corresponding CA certificate simpler.
- Fixed pathways from end-entities to the trust anchor allow transmission of the pathway with the end-entity certificate possible.
- Application support for cross-certificate chains has been severely lacking to date.
- Until a trust model needs to cross trust domains, issues such as agreement on a common root are usually tenable.

An example of agencies with strong hierarchical support includes the various defense departments in each country. The U.S. DOD, for example, currently plans to support several hierarchies corresponding to the sensitivity level of information that needs to be transported across networks of differing security capabilities.

Enterprises or other organizations wanting to join trust models will resort to cross-certification if the different trust domains cannot agree on a common trusted root. Within the context of a treaty organization such as NATO, the national defense departments need to share identities. It is not reasonable to expect that each defense department will subordinate its trust model to a third party. The only realistic option is to use some form of direct certification of each other.

An example of the linkage of multiple hierarchies is illustrated in Figure 8-13.

Figure 8-13

Linked
hierarchies

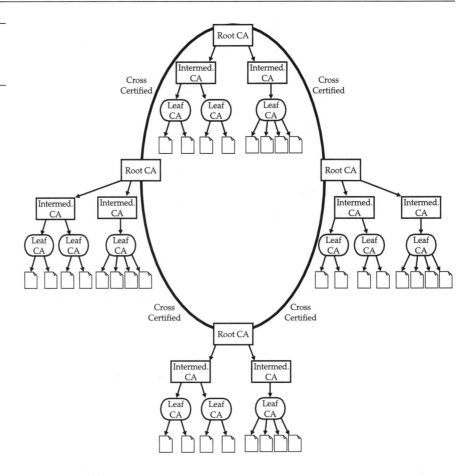

In this model, each of the root CAs cross-certifies with each of the others to form an inner ring or hub.

The initial trust structure implemented by most enterprises is usually some form of hierarchy to support internal applications. When an enterprise later needs to support business-to-business interactions with partners or suppliers, the challenge becomes how to share trusted identities. Cross-certifying the root CAs of each enterprise allows joining the trust models without the need to reissue certificates across each organization.

This solution is feasible for a relatively small set of businesses that want to adjoin trust models. It still has scaling properties that will cause problems in a large-scale e-commerce environment. We will examine some models that address these issues a little later in this chapter.

Cross-Links Within a Hierarchy

For hierarchies that are very large, the average length of certificate paths traversed can become too long. Heavily used trust paths may involve too many intermediate CAs. In either case, the paths become expensive to validate. Alternatively, it may become recognized that creating a "shortcut" between two endpoints in a trust path would optimize processing overhead for validation of a long path. Figure 8-14 illustrates the use of a certificate hierarchy with direct cross-certification.

Figure 8-14

Subordinate
hierarchy with
direct links

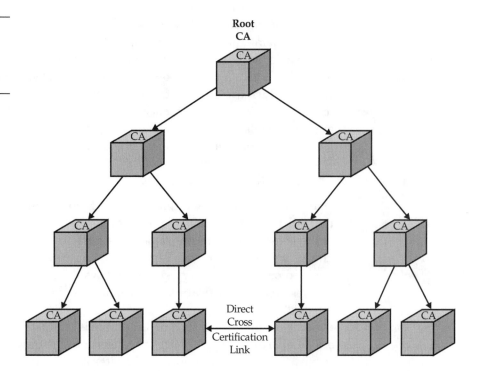

NOTE:

Of course, other alternatives exist. It is possible that within a hierarchy it may be less expensive to provide a caching scheme that stored preprocessed chains between the end-entity and the root CA. This can be a good alternative to the extra overhead associated with more complex decisions resulting from multiple paths.

Of course, the benefits of creating a direct link does not come free. Policies must be established now to define which path a certificate user should follow and under what circumstances. A single trust anchor no longer exists, so the trust anchor must be identified when validating any given path.

Provided this direct linkage scheme is used judiciously, it can bring the benefits of shorter path lengths. The complexity added by creating a large number of such links, however, is likely to quickly offset the benefits that a well-structured hierarchy brings. On the other hand, life is seldom well planned, and trust models are unlikely to remain well structured over time. Creating direct links is likely to provide a useful tool for dealing with problems that have grown up over time with the deployment of the trust model without requiring that it be rebuilt from scratch. If links are not added judiciously, it is possible that unintended relationships may be created, which are difficult to locate or understand. (My tenth grade history teacher, Mrs. DeVries, once observed that any political system (like any trust model) would work well in a perfect world. Of course, the problem is the world is a very imperfect place.)

Cross-Certification Overlay

One of the problems encountered with hybrid trust models is ensuring that all the information required to construct and validate certificate paths is available. Are the same trust anchors always used? Should you always try to find a root CA first, or should you look for a directly cross-certified path? Is the shortest path always the correct one to use? How do policies about certificate issuance or key usage constrain the path selected?

Some communities, such as the financial industry, have spent considerable effort constructing formal rules that allow hybrid trust models to coexist. This model described in the later section titled "The ISO Banking Trust Model" extends the use of cross-certification within a hierarchy. All CAs within a hierarchy are also directly cross-certified to form bilateral relationships between superior and subordinate CAs. The result is that any two CAs that need to establish trust will be able to construct a path using cross-certificates.

Who Manages Trust?

Management of trust relationships has two significant aspects. The first deals with issues specific to the management of trust anchors for certificate users. The second deals with management of the establishment of trust relationships between certification authorities.

The decision about who is the most suitable manager of these aspects of trust varies with the context in which you need to establish trust for relying parties.

User Control

An individual certificate user transacting business on his own behalf should be the arbiter of who or what he decides to trust. While using the Internet, he may encounter a Web site that provides a certificate asserting the identity of the company that owns the site. If the certificate has not been signed by a CA he knows, the user needs to decide whether to extend trust to the new certificate holder and its issuer.

Figure 8-15 shows the initial warning that would be provided by the Netscape browser.

Figure 8-15

"Unrecognized certificate issuer" warning

The user is then shown some high-level information about the certificate being presented (see Figure 8-16).

Figure 8-16

Site certificate

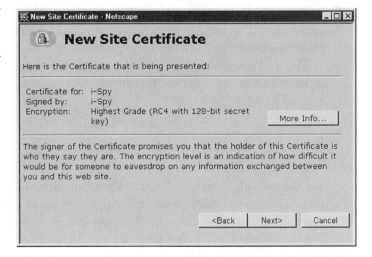

When the user clicks the button to view the certificate, additional information about the signer of the certificate is available, shown in Figure 8-17.

Figure 8-17

Additional
certificate
information

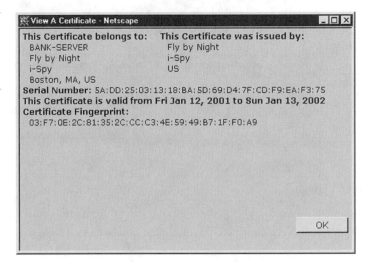

Finally, the user is asked to decide whether the certificate should be trusted or not (see Figure 8-18).

Figure 8-18

User decides on certificate status

It is desirable to have a service that would allow a certificate user to investigate the *bona fides* of the certificate issuer and its practices when making this decision. Such a service is unfortunately not generally available, so most PKI-aware users have come to rely on well-known public CAs such as VeriSign or Thawte and impute high levels of trust to server certificates issued by these services. Certificates issued by less well-known CAs are likely to be treated with more skepticism (as they should be).

NOTE:

This is analogous to a "Dun & Bradstreet" of the identity world. In some countries, such as Australia, the government may take a role in which it certifies CAs to provide some confidence level in the policies and procedures used for certificate issuance and life cycle management.

Applications that use PKI will usually store and manage a list of certificate issuers that are trusted by the application user. This is generally referred to as a *local trust list*.

Local Trust Lists

The CA certificates for all of the trusted root CAs for certificate hierarchies are generally stored in a trust list local to the user's Web browser or other client application (see Figure 8-19). This certificate list is described as local because it is generally only available to a single user (often for a single application on a single machine).

Figure 8-19

Web browser local
trust list

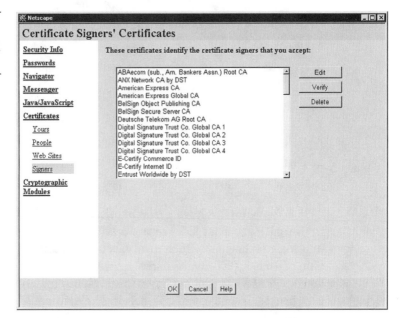

NOTE:

Any intermediate certificates can also be stored in the trust list, but are generally treated slightly differently from root certificates. In general, intermediate certificates will be accepted by most applications without querying the application user if they want to accept them. Root certificates, as trust anchors, require explicit acceptance by the application user.

The local trust list used in some applications is preconfigured with a very large set of root CA certificates that are provided by the application vendor. The CAs included are generally well-known public CAs. This is a wonderful ease-of-use feature, as most of the server certificates today are issued by the better-known public CAs. As a result, the certificates for many Web servers are automatically recognized when a user accesses the Web site. This is highly desirable from the perspective of providing the easiest possible secure access. After all, for the majority of people who are not aware of the wonders of PKI and its associated security services, hiding the use of PKI mechanisms is a good thing. (Fortunately, the world is full of such blissfully innocent people.) Being presented with a warning when validating a digital signature on e-mail (like the one shown in Figure 8-20) is not likely to encourage people to trust the contents of the mail message.

Figure 8-20

"Unknown signer" warning

The problem with ease-of-use features is that they are generally very bad for security. In this case, the collection of CAs provided in the local trust list is probably an excellent and trustworthy set. Quite possibly, application vendors are well placed to decide which root CAs should be trusted. On the other hand, these are not trust decisions made by the user in any conscious or deliberate fashion. As a result, application vendors predetermine the amount of trust extended initially on a user's behalf—often without the user being aware that it has happened.

This implicit trust problem becomes much more difficult if a CA on the list is compromised. To date, many applications have not been very diligent about verifying the validity of certificates, particularly revocation checking. Trusted CA certificate update mechanisms do not exist in many applications other than distributing a new version of the application. As a result, a compromised root CA could be blithely trusted by many users for quite some time before the application and its local trust list are updated.

A similar issue exists for root CAs that a user decides to trust directly. If a compromise of the CA occurs, how will the user find out about it? The Authority Revocation List (ARL) discussed in Chapter 5 is one solution, but there is very little support for this mechanism in most applications.

You potentially have a local user trust cache that can easily become stale and not a lot of options for refreshing it.

This remains a vexing question. In order for PKI to be successful, it is necessary to hide as many aspects of its operation as possible. However, fundamental issues such as "who will a user trust" should be exposed—and ultimately the decision should be made by the user. The challenge for PKI vendors is to make such security questions meaningful for non-technologists.

Managed Trust

Moving from an individual user on the Internet into an enterprise context, many of the mechanisms that were acceptable in a single-user environment are no longer credible. Fundamental issues like who is trusted and what identities should be used in a particular context need to be decided by the enterprise rather than individual users. Consistent administration of trust for all users across an enterprise becomes an issue.

Global/Dynamic Trust Lists

Trust lists are a very useful construct. They provide a mechanism that allows CAs from disparate hierarchies or other trust models to be specifically trusted.

Figure 8-21 shows a trust list in which a set of root CA certificates plus the associated intermediate certificates has been provided to the user. The presence of these certificates in the list carries the implication that the root CAs have been explicitly trusted.

Figure 8-21

Trust lists and multiple hierarchies

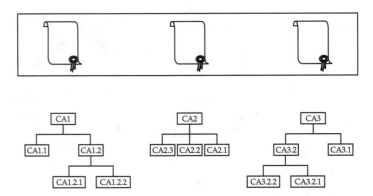

Trust lists have very practical benefits when dealing with different PKI solutions. CAs from different vendors select different trust models to support. Some provide only hierarchical support, others allow peer-to-peer cross-certification, and others allow mixed modes. Interoperability between PKI implementations and the trust models implemented becomes a problem.

One of the most difficult problems is distribution of trust anchors. Possession of a trust anchor that is designated as trustworthy for a particular use is central to establishment of trust from the certificate user's perspective. If the trust lists used to convey this information are not static and local to a client, but rather dynamic and centrally administered, the disadvantages of trust lists within an enterprise are mitigated.

Dynamic trust lists allow a central administrator within an organization to decide policy that defines the set of trust anchors that should be accepted by certificate users within the trust domain. New trust anchors can be added or deleted from the trust list by an administrator and the changed set downloaded to relying certificate users. An advantage of this approach is that it provides an adjunct to the normal certificate revocation process. Removal of a trust anchor from the trust list allows effective revocation of all certificates issued by that CA.

CA Trust Anchor Distribution

The Certification Authority that issues user certificates is a natural place to consider as a distribution point for CA certificates to use as trust anchors. It is already considered a trusted source, and the user has to interact with it during the registration process.

In most CA implementations using Web browser for registration, a link to a page on the Web server associated with the CA allows the CA certificate to be downloaded. Unfortunately, the additional steps required to load a CA certificate usually add more manual intervention to the registration process for the user, and it is not always obvious that this step is required. In addition, most Web browsers involve the user in a dialog designed to ensure that the CA certificate to be used as a trust anchor really should be trusted. The process as a whole is tedious and often confusing for the average PKI user.

New networking protocols used for certificate registration support transparent loading of CA certificates. One of these is examined in Chapter 5. As these protocols are used within client applications, the process of managing at least your local trust anchor should become easier.

Certificate Policy

We introduced the concept of a certification practices statement (CPS) in Chapter 3. This statement defines the procedures and policies that a Certification Authority uses during its operation. The CPS allows you to gauge the effectiveness with which identities are certified by a specific CA. This concept is examined further in Chapter 4.

Certification authorities can issue certificates for many different purposes. As we saw in an earlier chapter, certificates can contain information that is specific to some applications. For example, the certificate for an IPsec implementation requires the IP network address of a network component such as a firewall, while an e-mail application requires the e-mail address of a certificate subject.

In addition to certificate information required for an application to operate, there are also attributes that describe the way the identity was certified that make it more or less appropriate for a particular purpose. When a certificate user receives a certificate that has been issued by a particular CA, he needs to know if it is suitable for the use to which he will put it. For example, to access a system that handles highly sensitive information (particularly for systems operated by the military), you would prefer to use identities that have been certified with a very high assurance level.

X.509 creates the concept of a *certificate policy* to describe the information necessary to decide on the "fitness for use" of a certificate.

Section 3.3.10 in X.509 defines a certificate policy as:

"A named set of rules that indicates the applicability of a certificate to a particular community and/or class of application with common security requirements. For example, a particular certificate policy might indicate applicability of a type of certificate to the authentication of electronic data interchange transactions for the trading of goods within a given price range."

A certificate policy is described (in X.509 section 8.1.1) as a "document (usually in plain-language)." The policy has a unique identifier (known as an object identifier or OID) created for it, which is registered so the certificate issuer and certificate user can both recognize and reference the policy.

A certificate can be issued under multiple policies. Some may be procedural and describe the assurance level associated with creation and management of the certificate. Other policies may be technical and describe assurance levels associated with the security of systems used to create the certificates or where the associated keys are stored. Still others may be business policies defining the value of transactions for which this certificate should be used.

The list of OIDs identifying the policies under which a certificate has been issued are included in the certificate by the issuing Certification Authority.

The certificate user decides whether to accept a certificate based on the policy information. Generally, this would be implemented by configuring the set of policies that a user will accept into the applications that process the certificates. A profile maintained by the user (or on her behalf by an administrator) could list accepted policy identifiers.

X.509 introduces the concept of a *Policy Authority*, which is responsible for defining policies and issuing/registering policy identifiers. The set of policies issued by a Policy Authority is defined to be a policy domain. At the time of writing, few distinct policy authorities have actually been established, although some, such as the Policy Authority for the U.S. federal PKI, are under way.

Constrained Trust Models

In all of the trust models we examined, constraints on various aspects of the models began to intrude at different points in the discussion. Clearly, there is a sense in which the scope of the models seems too broad. For example, what can be done to protect yourself from third parties extending your trust to include your evil competitors in a trust mesh? This section looks at the various types of constraints that are possible within X.509 to allow better control on the trust models.

Path Length

The BasicConstraints extension in an X.509 certificate contains a field named PathLenConstraint. This field implements the "hop count" discussed when looking at the trust mesh model.

If BasicConstraints indicates that the certificate belongs to a CA, PathLenConstraint indicates the number of CA certificates that can follow it in a certification path. The absence of this field from any certificate in the chain indicates that the path can be any length.

A value of 0 indicates that the CA specified in the subject field can issue end-entity certificates only—it cannot issue certificates to other CAs. This creates the limited direct peer-to-peer model described earlier, allowing a CA to cross-certify with another CA and explicitly limit any future extension of trust by that CA. This results in a relatively bounded model to be constructed with future behavior reasonably controlled.

A non-zero value allows construction of mesh models, where successive CAs can extend trust by certifying other CAs. The impact of future decisions by third parties becomes much less clear at this point. Some models, such as the Federal Bridge CA, exercise some level of control over the activities of participants. At some point, however, coordinating and policy control activities begin to be indistinguishable from a trusted third-party model employed to support hierarchies.

The most difficult aspect of this extension is determining what value to set for it. There is a general sense in which long paths are likely to provide less assurance of attaining the level of trust required. The problem is, how long is that in relation to the average path length required to reach the other participants? This clearly mirrors the "network diameter" concept of a communication network.

When this value is set within a CA certificate, it is not clear if the setting will meet the requirements of all the subscribers to that Certification Authority.

Changes made by "downstream" CAs as they extend or prune trust relationships makes it difficult to predetermine what the correct value should be. If an existing set of CAs is just reachable, adding another layer to a hierarchy or integrating a new mesh will probably invalidate some set of paths.

Certificate Policies

This section discusses the certificate extensions that are used to identify and constrain use of the certificate based on the policies under which the certificate was issued.

CertificatePolicies

The CertificatePolicies extension contains a list of the OIDs identifying the certificate policies the Certification Authority used when issuing the certificate. Different applications using the certificate can rely on one or more of the policies that are listed.

If the extension is marked as non-critical, it specifies what policies the certificate was issued under, but does not constrain the certificate user to only use it for that purpose. Even if the certificate is used for other purposes, the certificate user can still require that a particular policy identifier be present in the certificates within the path.

If the extension is marked as critical, the Certification Authority has declared that the certificate can only be used for the purpose or under the constraints imposed by one of the listed policies. This effectively allows a limitation on liability, particularly in the case of public CAs. The CA can identify that it only warrants the use of the certificate for just the stated purpose and has no liability if it is used in any other context.

Any organization can specify its own policy OIDs for use in the Policy-Identifier field. Policy OIDs can be registered to ensure global uniqueness of the identifier and allow publication of the policy identifier. If a Certification Authority wants to explicitly certify that a certificate can be used to satisfy all possible policies, it can specify the special anyPolicy policy identifier.

NOTE:

Registration of policy OIDs can be made through national registration authorities in compliance with the Registration Authority Procedures Standard ISO/IEC 9834-1.

A PolicyQualifiers field defines additional information that may be useful to the certificate user evaluating the policy. These qualifiers are not processed as part of policy or certificate path validation, but are intended to help determine if a validated path is appropriate for the transaction. They can include references to human-readable information or possibly information that could be processed algorithmically. There is no mandated syntax for this field, so concern has been raised that its use might cause interoperability problems.

PKIX identifies[5] two qualifiers for use in the Internet:

- CPS Pointer is a URL that locates the certification practices statement issued by a Certification Authority.

- User Notice contains information that should be displayed to the certificate user. It may list the organization that issued the notification and the text to be displayed to the user.

PolicyMappings

The PolicyMappings extension allows the certificate issuer to indicate that a policy identifier in the issuer's domain corresponds to a policy identifier in the certificate user's domain. It allows for OIDs in use in the issuer's domain to be mapped or translated to OIDs in the certificate user's domain.

Policy mapping is useful where a certificate path crosses two policy domains. For example, it allows certificates used between defense departments in two different countries to identify equivalent certificate policies. Policy mappings of this type have been defined for use between the U.S. and Canadian governments, for example.

Policy mapping can never be used to map to or from the special policy identifier anyPolicy.

The use of such a policy mapping facility seems an obvious requirement when considering cross-certification between different trust domains. However, it can be difficult to locate corresponding policies across two domains for which all implications of policy statements will match. It also seems difficult to foresee what might happen when the constraints within a policy need to change or a policy is retired. The effectiveness of policy mappings in practice remains to be seen.

PolicyConstraints

This extension is a collection of constraints you may want to apply while performing processing that relies on the use of certificate policy fields.

The RequireExplicitPolicy indicator is used to specify that all certificates following the certificate being processed must explicitly include an acceptable policy identifier.

The InhibitPolicyMapping indicator is used to specify that policy mapping is not permitted for all certificates following the certificate being processed.

Each of the constraints can optionally specify a setting for a SkipCerts field. This field indicates the number of certificates in the path to skip before applying the corresponding constraint. Determining a meaningful setting for SkipCerts seems problematic, especially if cross-certification leads to later addition of paths that cross multiple domains.

InhibitAnyPolicy

The InhibitAnyPolicy extension specifies that the special policy identifier anyPolicy cannot be considered a match for certificates that follow this one in the path. Like the PolicyConstraints extension, the InhibitAnyPolicy extension allows a SkipCerts field to identify how many certificates to skip before applying this constraint.

NameConstraints

The NameConstraints extension allows a CA to identify what parts of a name space are covered when certifying another CA. The data type for the name forms covered by this extension is GeneralName, which covers a broad range of naming conventions. However, only GeneralName forms that support a well-defined hierarchical name space are valid. Directory name forms that comply with these requirements include X.500, Internet e-mail addresses, and Internet domain names.

The NameConstraints extension can only be used within a CA certificate. It provides a list of subtrees that define the parts of a name space to which other certificates in a path must conform.

The PermittedSubtrees field is a list of all of the name subtrees that are to be included in the newly defined acceptable name space. The subject of any certificate appearing in the certificate path after the certificate containing the NameConstraints extension must have a name within one of the listed subtrees.

Let's look at an example. RSA Security has engineering facilities in several different countries. Using an X.500 naming convention, the X.500 names might look something like this:

```
PermittedSubtrees:
{Country=US, Organization=RSA Security, Organizational
Unit=Engineering}
{Country=SE, Organization=RSA Security, Organizational
Unit=Engineering}
```

If the RSA Security CA were to be cross-certified by another CA, both X.500 subtrees could be explicitly included in the PermittedSubtrees field so that certificates with subject names preceded by either X.500 subtrees would be valid.

Alternatively, specific subtrees can be explicitly excluded using the ExcludedSubtrees field. For example, another company may decide to cross-certify with RSA Security but exclude access to the Swedish sales force. In this case, we might have a set of name space constraints that looks like this:

```
PermittedSubtrees:
{Country=SE, Organization=RSA Security }
ExcludedSubtrees:
{Country=SE, Organization=RSA Security, Organizational Unit=Sales}
```

where the international country code for Sweden is SE.

Where overlaps in the name space exist, the exclusion list takes precedence.

The NameConstraints extension also includes constraints that allow specification of which levels within a hierarchical subtree are considered significant.

NameConstraints is a very powerful mechanism for limiting the scope of trust relationships that are established using cross-certification.

Path Construction and Validation

Discovering a path leading from a certificate used to establish an identity to a trust anchor that establishes trust in the certificate issuer is a very complex problem. Simplifying assumptions, such as the constraints built into a strict hierarchical structure, allow the problem to be reduced considerably. Constructing certificate paths through a hierarchy contained within the bounds of an enterprise trust domain has been shown to be a tractable problem. However, as PKI is used to establish identities for large electronic commerce deployments, the simple hierarchical model and the luxury of a single trust domain are unlikely to be sufficient.

When links between intermediate CAs in a certificate path cross trust domains, access to information necessary to link from one CA to another becomes more difficult. Finding the correct repositories for linkage information referred to by preceding intermediate CAs and then determining what the next CA in the path should be are all difficult and time-consuming tasks.

To simplify the problem, it is normal to consider the process of establishing a trusted path in two stages. The first stage involves constructing one or more paths that meet constraints consistent with the trust model. This is referred to as certificate path construction or path discovery. The second stage is the process of validating the paths found to ensure that all the policies and constraints are satisfied to establish a trusted identity.

NOTE:

We will use the term path construction *here, if only for the reason that the term "construction" implies that we are executing a well-defined process, confident that we will achieve our goal of identifying a valid certificate chain. "Discovery," on the other hand, has an implication that if we are lucky we may find such a path, but it may be by accident as much as anything else. This is not to say that discovery is not a more accurate description of the process.*

Path Construction

Construction of paths in the subordinated hierarchical model is relatively simple. We considered this model in the earlier "Subordinated Hierarchies" section, where we discussed the fact that a single chain of certificates exists between the trust anchor (which is the root CA certificate in this model) and any end-entity certificate. Therefore, certificate chains can be directly transmitted along with an end-entity certificate, which is the way most PKI-enabled applications work today.

We introduced the concept of path construction in the "Mesh Models" section for establishing certificate paths in a peer-to-peer cross-certification model. The general case relied on forward and backward links located in CA objects. These CA objects are stored in a directory, and when processed successively, allow you to assemble the components needed to complete a path.

When dealing with paths where both hierarchical and peer-to-peer cross-certification models may be encountered, your path construction techniques need to allow for each. In addition, the existence of multiple peer-to-peer relationships to choose from means you need some heuristics to allow you to select optimal paths while avoiding routing loops and dead-ends.

While X.509 and PKIX describe rules for validation of certificate paths, they do not provide a lot of guidance on how to construct paths. The ISO Banking Trust Model described later in this chapter describes some path construction rules for that model. The next section describes one implementation of path construction logic and the rules used in the process.

Cygnacom Path Construction Heuristics

The heuristics used to guide selection of a path are sensitive to the constraints of the trust model being used. The Path Development Library developed by Cygnacom[6] is provided as an example of the heuristics used for path construction in the context of the U.S. federal government PKI.

The library's designers constructed the heuristics base on the assumption that although discovering a path through a full mesh network is hard, discovering a path through a cross-certified interconnected set of hierarchies is an easier problem. This weights the algorithms toward paths that follow a hierarchy. As a result, preference is given to the use of caCertificate (representing a hierarchical root) attributes over crossCertificatePair (representing peer-to-peer cross-certification relationships) attributes in a CA object in the directory to locate a path.

NOTE:

The caCertificate attribute within the CA directory entry is used to store a self-issued certificate for a CA.

Path construction works in the "forward direction" starting with the certificate for the end-entity and working toward the trust anchor. It implements an iterative process, successively working through each certificate using the issuer name in the preceding certificate as the subject name in the next. As each certificate is processed, the issuer of the certificate is checked to see if it is a trusted CA. Successive certificates are retrieved from the X.500 directory attributes for the issuer of the certificate being processed. If a dead end or a loop is encountered, backtracking is supported to allow further path development from a known point.

The library allows specification of certificate selection criteria based on key usage, validity period, and subject key identifier (which must equal the issuer key identifier of the previous certificate in the path).

The library prioritizes the set of available certificates for path construction and sorts them based on the following rules:

- Certificates retrieved from the caCertificate attribute should have priority over certificates retrieved from the crossCertificate attribute. (Hierarchic paths are preferred.)

- Certificates in which the algorithm used to sign the certificate matches the public key algorithm from the certificate should have priority. (This tends to simplify algorithmic processing.)

- Certificates that assert policies in the requestor's initial-acceptable-policy set should have priority.
- Certificates that assert policies should have priority.
- Certificates with fewer Relative Distinguished Name (RDN) elements in the issuer Distinguished Name (DN) should have priority.

NOTE:

The subject name in a certificate is described by a Distinguished Name, which is a qualified name construct comprised of a number of Relative Distinguished Name components. So, for example, organization (RSA Security) is one RDN, my location (Bedford, MA) is another. Taken together they create a fully qualified or Distinguished Name.

- Certificates matching more RDNs between the issuer DN and the relying party's trust anchor DN should have priority.
- Certificates that match more RDNs between the subject DN and the issuer DN should have priority.
- Certificates with validity periods extending furthest into the future should have priority.

Path Validation

Validation of each certificate in a path that has been constructed by the previous process includes the following criteria:

- The certificate must contain a cryptographically valid signature establishing that the contents of the certificate have not changed.
- The public key of the issuer must be used to verify the signature on the certificate.
- The validity period specified by the beginning and ending dates must show that the certificate is current.
- The subject and issuer names in successive certificates must match.
- The certificate must not contain fields that the certificate validator does not understand that are marked as critical to the interpretation of the certificate.

NOTE:
The issuing Certification Authority marks fields as critical, indicating that the presence and content of the fields must be understood by the certificate user before the certificate can be correctly interpreted.

- The certificate may only be used for the purpose for which it was originally created. For example, keys and certificates that are marked for use only in signing applications may not be used for encryption operations.
- The subject name must be consistent with any specified naming constraints.
- Certificates other than the end-entity certificate must be explicitly marked as CA certificates.
- The number of certificates following any CA certificate with a Path Length constraint must be consistent.
- Other policy constraints that specify usage conditions must be observed.

Finally, the certificate must not have been revoked. Even with all of the information internal to the certificate indicating that the certificate is valid, you must check to see if some exceptional external event has occurred requiring the certificate to be invalidated. So, revocation checking, using a certificate revocation list or some form of online verification check, must be performed.

Implementations

We have examined a number of theoretical trust models that can be used to establish trust relationships. The following sections discuss trust models that have been implemented within various application domains.

Identrus Trust Model

Identrus is a trust model built to allow participating financial institutions to act as certification authorities. These financial institutions provide services to verify and issue identities and then authenticate those identities for use in financial and nonfinancial transactions over the Internet.[7]

The Identrus trust model is a subordinated hierarchy, with the root CA administered by Identrus as a trusted third party on behalf of the participating financial institutions. The Identrus hierarchy implements up to four tiers, as illustrated in Figure 8-22. The first tier consists of the Identrus root CA. The second tier is made up of Level 1 financial institutions, which certify their business customers or Level 2 financial institutions. Level 2 financial institutions are generally considered smaller than Level 1 financial institutions as defined by Identrus criteria. Level 2 financial institutions can also certify their business customers. Certified businesses, which make up the third tier, issue certificates to their own employees, tier four.

Figure 8-22

Identrus
hierarchy

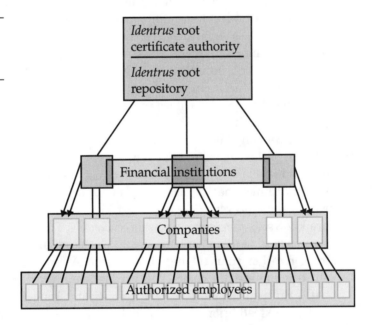

The Identrus model specifies many operational requirements for participating financial institutions and business customers. Included in these requirements is the provision of OCSP responders by the financial institutions for certificate validation. End-entity certificates and private keys are stored on smart cards or hardware storage modules.

ISO Banking Trust Model

The International Standards Organization (ISO) defines a profile for use of X.509 certificates and management in two draft standards:

```
DIS 15782-1, Banking - Certificate Management Part 1: Public Key
Certificates
FDIS 15782-2, Banking - Certificate Management Part 2: Certificate
Extensions
```

Annex G of 15782-1, entitled "Alternative Trust Models," is provided for information purposes and describes the principles chosen by this industry to construct hierarchical and peer-to-peer cross-certification models.

A third trust model—the Hybrid Trust Model—is also discussed, which is a much more interesting case. This is a variation on the generic hybrid trust models discussed earlier. This model, shown in Figure 8-23, starts by constructing typical hierarchies that contain root CAs, subordinate CAs, and end-entities. A variation on the theme is that CAs at all intermediate levels and the root CA can all issue end-entity certificates. Root CAs use peer-to-peer cross-certification with other root CAs to interconnect the subordinated hierarchies, forming conjoined hierarchies.

Where the model becomes more interesting is that additional peer-to-peer cross-certification is used to construct special relationships throughout the conjoined hierarchies.

Each of the subordinated CA relationships within the hierarchy is also overlaid with a complete set of peer-to-peer cross-certificates to allow bidirectional links that replicate the superior/subordinate links for all CAs within the hierarchy. The cross-certificates used to construct the overlay are known as *hierarchical cross-certificates*. The purpose of this parallel structure is to allow end-entities to choose their local CA as their trust anchor rather than relying on the root CA for their hierarchy. For end-entities making this choice, this arrangement provides them with a set of paths through the mesh to verify certificates issued by any other CA.

The next addition to the model is the specification of *general cross-certificates*. These are provided to create shortcuts to minimize the length of hierarchical certificate paths. As the context for the use of the certificates is to supplement the existing hierarchical structure, the trust derived from the use of this path is at least as restrictive as the least restrictive path that would have been traversed ordinarily.

The last type of certificate specified is the *special cross-certificate*. This is provided to allow direct cross-certification that is not constrained by restric-

Figure 8-23

ISO 15782-1
Hybrid Trust
Model

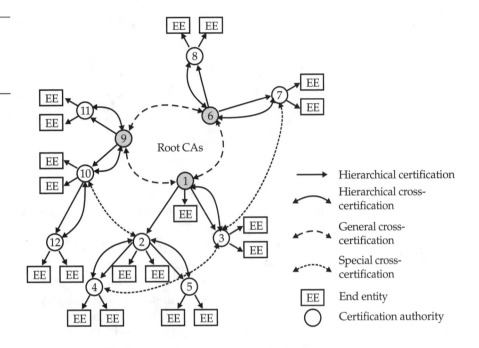

tions that exist along the hierarchical paths. Special cross-certificates can only be used between leaf CAs.

The rest of the definition for special cross-certificates is quoted verbatim from the standard:

> "Leaf CAs are defined as CAs that have a hierarchical certification path to the root CA, but have been issued a CA certificate with a Path Length Constraint of '0'. This permits further propagation of trust to another CA along the hierarchical certification path. Special cross-certificates are appropriate when each of the two CAs operate under policies that allow a higher trust level or less restrictions that would otherwise be permitted."

The treatment of the path length constraints when dealing with special cross-certificates creates some interesting problems. The normal path processing logic used by applications will require special case processing, as X.509 and PKIX explicitly prohibit any CA with the definition that a leaf CA has from issuing any certificates other than end-entity certificates. It is not clear how a special cross-certificate would be recognized or the exception to path length processing identified and authorized.

The hybrid model allows selection of hierarchical or mesh path certification schemes by all end-entities on an individual basis. This adds complexity from a management and operational perspective, but maximizes interoperability for the applications that use end-entity certificates.

Bridge CA

Interconnection of hierarchies using peer-to-peer cross-certification of the root CAs is a practical solution to providing interconnection of trust models without requiring consensus on a common root. The drawback is that a fully connected mesh network of root CAs is not a very scalable solution. The number of interconnections required to link all root CAs is approximately the square of the number of root CAs.

An alternative is to nominate a Certification Authority that will issue cross-certificates for all participants in the conjoined trust model. In this model, all CAs certify with the central CA—commonly known as a *bridge CA*. This model is illustrated in Figure 8-24.

A number of implementations of this model have been proposed. The bridge CA implemented by the U.S. federal government as part of the model for its federal PKI deployment has been defined most effectively.[8-10]

The certificates forming a path from the end-entity certificate to the CA certificate for the trust anchor are expected to be located in a directory. The processing of these paths is expected to be executed at the relying party client and are expected to use certificate policy attributes and name constraints.

The Federal Bridge CA is comprised of three elements:

- A federal Policy Authority (FPA)
- A Federal Bridge CA (FBCA)
- A bridge CA directory

The federal Policy Authority oversees the operation of the Federal Bridge CA. The member organizations that determine the policies of the FPA are agencies that have cross-certified with the FBCA. The Policy Authority is responsible for evaluating the certificate policies of agencies that apply for cross-certification. They also determine how to map agency policy settings into policy identifiers established for the FBCA.

Figure 8-24

Bridge CA model

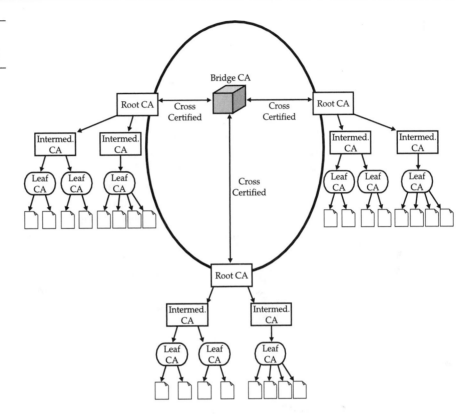

The bridge CA is not a root or a trust anchor; instead, it facilitates cross-certification between the participating CAs. The CAs cross-certified by the bridge CA are expected to be "principal" CAs within a government agency.

The directory implemented by the bridge is a full X.500 directory. The reason is the perceived lack of consistent features across LDAP directories, although the use of LDAP referral mechanisms is under consideration. The federal bridge implements a directory structure known as a border directory. The border directory is a set of directories distinct from any directory service operated by individual government agencies (individual agencies, like most enterprises, will not allow access to their internal directories). The border directory contains all certificates and revocation information issued under the FBCA.

Demonstration versions of the bridge CA have relied on path construction libraries like the one from Cygnacom described in the section titled "Cygnacom Path Construction Heuristics."

Summary

In this chapter, we have considered the use of trust models to describe the ways trust relationships are formed between certification authorities. Beginning with the general hierarchy, we considered the designation of trust anchors and how certificate users conclude that a particular certificate and its issuer can be trusted.

We refined the concept of general hierarchy by considering subordinated hierarchies and several forms of peer-to-peer cross-certification, including the general trust mesh and various hybrid models. The constraints that can be used within certificates to control the scope and applicability of the trust models were identified.

The methods and issues associated with constructing certificate paths and then validating those paths were described. As part of that description, we looked at some practical considerations that can be used.

Finally we looked at Identrus, the ISO Banking Trust Model, and the bridge CA as examples of how trust models can be deployed.

References

[1]ITU-T Recommendation X.509 | ISO/IEC 9594-8: "Information Technology—Open Systems Interconnection—The Directory: Public-Key and Attribute Certificate Frameworks."

[2]Defense Messaging System (DMS)-Public documents may be found at http://disa.dtic.mil/D2/dms/documents.html.

[3]Kent, S. "Privacy Enhancement for Internet Electronic Mail: Part II: Certificate-Based Key Management," RFC 1422, February 1993. http://www.ietf.org/rfc/rfc1422.txt.

[4]Boeyen, S. et al. "Internet X.509 Public Key Infrastructure LDAPv2 Schema," RFC 2587, June 1999. http://www.ietf.org/rfc/rfc2587.txt.

[5]Housely, R., et al. "Internet X.509 Public Key Infrastructure, Certificate and CRL Profile," RFC 2459, January 1999. http://www.ietf.org/rfc/rfc2459.txt.

[6]The Cygnacom Certificate Path Library can be found at http://www.cygnacom.com/cert/CPL_1_3_ICD.doc.

[7]The Opportunity for Financial Institutions in the Identrus System, 1999. http://www.identrus.com/.

[8]Bill Burr. Federal Bridge CA Concept (available at http://csrc.ncsl.nist. gov/pki/twg/y2000/presentations/twg-00-14.pdf).

[9]Report of the Federal Bridge CA Initiative and Demonstration, Electronic Messaging Association Challenge 2000 (available at http://csrc.ncsl.nist.gov/pki/twg/y2000/presentations/twg-00-19.pdf).

[10]X.509 Certificate Policy for the Federal Bridge Certification Authority, October 23, 2000. http://csrc.ncsl.nist.gov/pki/twg/y2000/papers/ twg-00-02.pdf.

CHAPTER 9

Authentication and PKI

Who Are You?

That is the eternal question.

It has been asked as long as people have been in existence. (It is frequently followed by such questions as "Have we met before?", "What's a beautiful person like you doing in a place like this?", and "Would you like to come up to my place and see my collection of cryptographic authentication devices?")

In addition to this question being the foundation of metaphysics, it also happens to be the foundation for most security.

Authentication

Authentication is the process of determining an identity to the necessary level of assurance. The need for authentication seems obvious, but mechanisms to prove an identity over miles of wire can be complex.

It makes no sense to have strong encryption of data unless you can identify the recipient(s) of that data. After all, the primary intent of encryption is to keep information private between communicating parties.

If you do not authenticate the recipient of the data, how can you know that inappropriate people did not decrypt the information?

When performing a digital signature, the purpose of the operation is to bind some form of identity to the object being signed. Unless that signature can be traced back to a specific identity, what good is it?

When accessing a protected Web page, the identity of the accessor must be determined before the right of that person to access the Web page can be evaluated.

Even in situations where privacy is desired, authentications typically must occur. Let's take a situation where you might want to purchase things online but are worried about the fact that data concerning your transactions is being collected. To get around this, you could create a new credit card account, backed by cash (which is inherently anonymous). This credit card account would not necessarily need to be tied to your identity. Further, you could open an anonymous post office box to accept the delivery of items. At this point, you might think that you have removed the need for authentication. If you look back a few paragraphs, you will note that I carefully defined authentication as determining an identity, not as determining a person. In this situation, each time the credit card was used, an authentication against the credit account occurs, even though this account is not tied to an individual. If an authentication against the credit account did not occur, the merchant would have no way of verifying that they would eventually get paid. As you can see, authentications can occur even in fully anonymous transactions.

NOTE:

Actually, I'm not sure if you can do this with a credit card, since by nature credit cards require an approval to extend credit, which in turn is tied to a particular person's credit history. I have seen this type of thing done using debit (also called cash) cards. In the case of a debit card, there needs to be adequate money deposited in an account before the transaction occurs. This is because the debit transaction debits the money in real time. Since the account is backed by deposited money, it does not need to be tied to an individual's credit history and hence can be anonymous.

Note that it is quite common that only one end of a conversation needs to be authenticated. Let's take the example of a company distributing a patch to their software. The company may not care who gets the patch, but it would be very important for the people using the patch to authenticate that the source of the patch was indeed the company who created the software, and not some evil-doer attempting to spread a virus or worm. In this case, a digital signature on the software can be used to authenticate the source of the software, even though no authentication of the recipient occurs.

There is one particular area where strong encryption is needed, but where authentication of the participants is not used. This occurs when you are attempting to perform an authentication! In this situation, you need a secure channel to transmit the authentication data, but since the authentication has not yet occurred, the secure channel must by definition be created without a prior authentication.

In most other cases, the use of strong cryptography is tied to authentication of the parties involved.

Authentication and PKI

There is a common misconception that PKI replaces the need for other forms of authentication. This is because most PKI protocols involve some mechanism to pass or gain access to a certificate. The distinguished name of a certificate identifies the owner of the public key contained within the certificate. Since mechanisms (such as those previously described in the SSL discussions) exist to cause the party you are communicating with to prove that they have the matching private key, you might think that everything is solved.

Herein lies one of the nasty little secrets of PKI. There has been much discussion in the industry about the need to have a trusted source issue the certificate, including the process of validating the owner of the public key before signing the certificate. As discussed before, this is where certificate practices statements come in. What is not discussed as thoroughly is the need to protect the private key from copying, and the need to strongly authenticate the owner against their private key.

The security of any solution is only as good as the weakest link in the security chain. The cryptography of PKI systems is strong. You can ensure that you have a certificate issued by a trusted source. You can check published CRLs to verify that a certificate is still valid. None of that is secure, if the private key is vulnerable to copying or can be easily accessed.

As a result of this, a strong PKI needs to be based on strong authentication of the owner against their private key. This chapter will discuss the major authentication techniques: passwords, authentication tokens, smart cards, and biometrics. For each of these authentication techniques, we will look at how they relate to PKI and what the various trade-offs are.

As with many things in life, there is no simple answer to the question, "What is the best form of authentication?" Each form of authentication carries with it different levels of security, different ease-of-use characteristics, different costs to procure, and different costs to manage. As we survey the authentication area, I will try to point out some of the more important considerations that can help you choose the best form of authentication for various problems.

Secrets

Electronic authentication is based on secrets.

Sometimes both you and the system attempting to authenticate you know the same secret. More commonly, you know a secret, and the system attempting to authenticate you knows something derived from your secret. In other cases, you know a secret, and the system attempting to authenticate you has ways of making you prove you have the secret.

Passwords

Passwords are the most common form of authentication, and in some ways the least understood. At first blush, they would appear to be the least expensive authentication option. There is no special piece of hardware the user must carry to use a password, and there is no special reader into which the password must be inserted. As we will see in a minute, this simplistic view is wrong.

Passwords in the Clear

In their simplest use, the system you are attempting to access knows your password. When you attempt to access the system, it presents a prompt, and you type in your user name and your password. The accessed system will look up your identity in some security database, and if the supplied password matches the stored password, access is granted.

In the early days of computing, before the Internet, before distributed systems, nay, before even PC LANs, this simple type of password processing was used to gain access to many standalone systems. Even today, this technique is widely used when the terminal you are entering your user ID and password into is directly connected to the system you are attempting to access. Since in these types of systems the actual clear-text password is stored in the system's authentication database, the actual process of performing the password validation can occur in a single line of C-code.

As you probably already realize, this is not a very secure solution. The fact that the actual clear-text password needs to be matched against the account database requires that the actual password be carried from the input terminal to the authentication software. This creates an opportunity for the password to be copied as it is being transmitted.

NOTE:

The term input terminal *is being used in a generic sense. This could be a client in a client/server relationship, a Web browser in a Web environment, or a keyboard and monitor in a desktop login environment.*

Obviously, the easiest way to protect against a compromise of the password as it is being transmitted is to encrypt the conversation between the input terminal and the system performing the authentication. This technique will work. In fact, there are many examples on the Web of sites that run server-side SSL sessions simply to protect the integrity of a simple password being sent by a user at a Web browser.

Despite the widespread use of this technique, it has many problems. First, setting up an SSL session just to encrypt a password is a bit of overkill. SSL requires the Web server to get a digital certificate from an authority that the Web browser will trust. This can cost significant money. In addition, the setup of the SSL session involves the transmission of many kilobytes of data and processor overhead on the client to perform the certificate validation, as well as the overhead of the whole key exchange protocol.

All that just to transmit a few characters securely.

Even if server-side SSL (or some similar technique) is used to protect the password as it travels from the input terminal to the authenticating system, there are other problems. Since the clear-text password is sent for matching, if there is a virus that has been inserted into the system you are trying to authenticate into, the virus could extract the clear-text version of the password after it was decrypted on the server-side of the connection.

Even more risky is the fact that the authentication database contains the passwords for the various users of the system. This makes the database an attractive target for an attacker, since gaining a single copy of the database will yield many user ID/password pairings.

Although this type of password system has seen wide use, it should only be used in environments that meet the following criteria:

- The authentication database is secure from tampering, and
- The input terminal must be directly connected to the system performing the authentication (in other words, not across a network);

or

- Encryption between the input terminal and accessed system must be used

Even if these criteria can be met, there has got to be a better way.

Something Derived from Passwords

One way to make this better is to remove the need to store the actual password at the accessed system. Instead of storing the actual password, you run some algorithm on the password, and then store the value derived from that algorithm. When the user wants to gain access, the input terminal can perform the same algorithm on the password the user supplies, and then send the new derived value to the accessed system to be compared to the previously stored derived value. In this way, the clear-text password only exists temporarily as input to the algorithm and can then be erased. The clear-text password never needs to be stored anywhere.

Obviously this algorithm must have some particular properties. Each time a particular password is input to the algorithm, it must produce the same output. If someone were to record the conversation between the input terminal and the accessed system, they could record the output of the algorithm, even if they could not record the original password that produced that output. As a result, it would be important that the output of the algorithm did not give any information about what the original password was. Additionally, it should be computationally infeasible for the attacker to create another password that would produce the proper output when fed into the algorithm. Hopefully by now you will recognize these as the properties of a cryptographic hash algorithm such as MD4, MD5, or SHA-1.

Take a look at Figure 9-1 to see this process pictorially.

Figure 9-1

Hashing
passwords

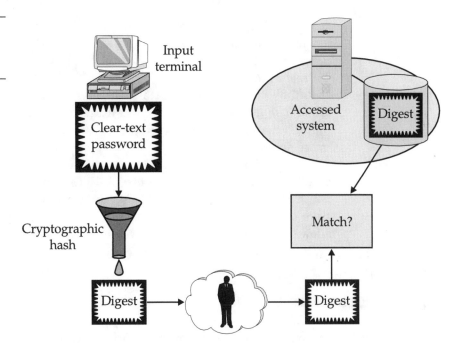

The user enters their password at the input terminal. A cryptographic hash algorithm such as MD5 is used to process the password and produce a digest. At this point, the clear-text password is erased from the memory of the input terminal. The digest is sent to the accessed system where it is compared with a previously stored digest of the same password. If the digests match, access is granted.

This system is an improvement from the previously described system:

■ The original clear-text password is not stored anywhere in this system and therefore is not vulnerable to being copied.

■ The clear-text password is not transmitted from the input terminal to the accessed system.

- Since the digest tells you nothing about the original password used to create the digest, the original password is protected even if an attacker sees the digest being transmitted by the input terminal.

- It is computationally infeasible for an attacker to discover a password that would produce the particular digest they have seen, and therefore the hacker cannot generate a password that could be used to log into the account.

With a properly selected cryptographic hash algorithm, the attacker will find it very difficult to gain access to the user's password. Despite the improvements, this system is still relatively vulnerable to one form of indirect attack.

Rather than attempt to attack the cryptographic hash algorithm, or attempt to guess the password, an attacker could take a more devious route. If the attacker can record the messages sent by the input terminal to the accessed system, they could replay those messages to the accessed system at a later time and gain access to the user's account. This type of attack is referred to as a *replay attack*. In this situation, the attacker will never know what the user's actual password is, but it does not matter since the accessed system will see the proper hash digest presented and allow the attacker access to the system.

Obviously, we are not quite there yet.

Adding a Little Randomness

To improve the security of the solution, we need to introduce some variability to the solution, so that each time an authentication occurs, the conversation will be different. In this way, the replay of an old authentication conversation will not allow the attacker access.

The easiest way to see how this works is to follow the message flow in Figure 9-2.

This figure assumes that at some time in the past, the user's password was hashed using a cryptographic hash such as MD5, and that a copy of the resulting digest was stored in the accessed system authentication database. We will talk about how this happened in a moment.

At the input terminal, the user enters their clear-text password. The password is then run through the same cryptographic hash to produce a new copy of the digest. Just as before, the clear-text password should be

Figure 9-2

Passwords with
challenge/
response using
encryption

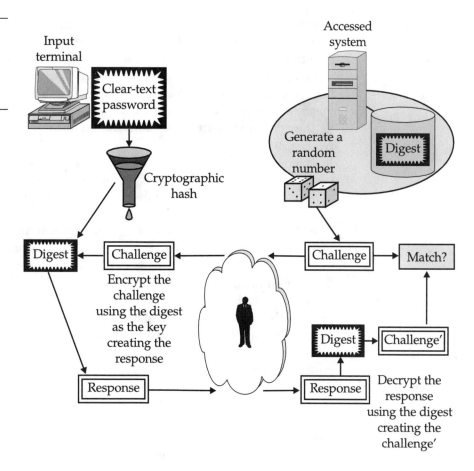

wiped from the memory of the input terminal. Unlike before, the resulting
hash is not sent to the accessed system.

Instead, the accessed system will create a new random number. In the
chapter on cryptography, we saw systems creating random numbers to be
used as symmetric encryption keys. The same process is happening here,
but the resulting number is not used as a symmetric encryption key. The
resulting random number is named *challenge* in Figure 9-2 because this
random number will be used to challenge the input terminal to prove that
the input terminal has the correct digest for the user.

The challenge will be sent in the clear to the input terminal from the
accessed system. At this point, one of two things could happen. We can per-

form an encryption at the input terminal and check the results via a decryption at the server; or we could run a parallel cryptographic function at both the client and server, and then verify both reached the same result.

Using Figure 9-2, let's explore the encryption/decryption model first. Once the challenge is received, the input terminal will perform a symmetric encryption of the challenge using the digest of the user's password as the symmetric encryption key. The resulting encrypted challenge is referred to as a *response*.

The response is then returned to the accessed system. The accessed system will then extract the saved digest for this user. That digest will be used as the symmetric key to decrypt the response, thus recovering the original challenge.

If the recovered challenge matches the random number originally created by the accessed system, the accessed system can be sure that the input terminal had the proper hash digest of the user's password. Since the user entering their password produced this hash digest, the accessed system allows the access.

The other method of challenge/response, which uses parallel cryptographic computations, is shown in Figure 9-3.

In this model, the input terminal will take the received challenge and perform some cryptographic computation involving the challenge and the digest of the user's password as a shared secret. The most common technique is to take the challenge and the digest of the user's password, and then hash them to produce the response. As before, this response is sent back to the accessed system.

In this case, the accessed system cannot reverse the hash, so it cannot recover the original challenge and compare it as before. Instead, the accessed system will take the original challenge and the stored copy of digest, and perform the same computation as was done by the input terminal. This will produce a second copy of the response. If the locally generated response matches the response sent by the input terminal, access is granted.

Note that both of these techniques have some nice features. The attacker monitoring the conversation between the input terminal and the accessed system will only see two random numbers flow between the systems. The original password is not passed between the two systems. Even the hash digest of the original password does not pass between the two systems. Note also that the accessed system does not contain a copy of the user's password, only a hash digest of that password.

Figure 9-3

Passwords with
challenge/
response using
parallel
cryptography

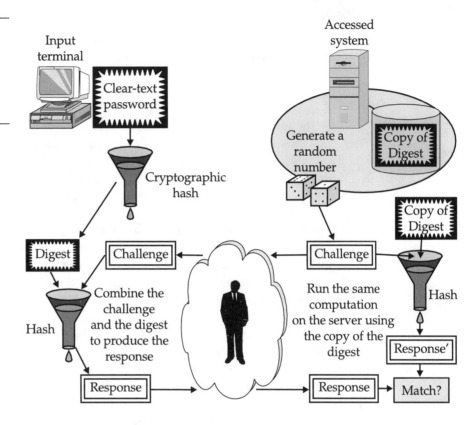

This challenge/response password process described above is the basis
for modern password-based authentication mechanisms. For example, the
process as described is essentially how Windows NT 4.0 password authentication works. Windows NT 4.0 uses the MD4 hash algorithm to produce
the hash digest of the user password. On Windows NT, the authentication
database is named the SAM (Security Account Manager) Database. Under
Windows NT, the challenge is a 16-byte random number. This type of solution is used as the basis for password authentication in a variety of products, including CHAP (Challenge Handshake Authentication Protocol)
RFC1994, in some Radius protocol extensions, and in Novell NetWare V3
authentication, as well as many others.

Notice that this system is immune to replay attacks. The reason the
replay type of attack fails is that the challenge is a new random number
generated uniquely for each login session. Since the recorded session and

the new session each started with a different challenge, the reply of the recorded session will fail to properly authenticate.

It is conceivable that a patient attacker could record the challenge and the resulting response. In fact, they could collect many of these challenge/response pairs for a particular user. They could then take these challenge/response pairs offline and perform a brute-force attack by searching for the proper symmetric key that would encrypt the challenge and produce the proper response. Since the output of the cryptographic hash is used as a symmetric encryption key, the way to deal with the brute-force attack is to choose a cryptographic hash function that produces a long enough digest that it becomes computationally infeasible to break the symmetric encryption. For example, if MD5 or SHA-1 is used, the estimated time to crack the encryption will exceed the lifetime of the universe. Even if the attacker were able crack the encryption, this would yield them the hash digest of the user's password, but not the password itself.

If an evil system administrator gained access to the authentication database and copied its contents, they would get a set of hash digests. The hash digests cannot be fed into the prompt of the input terminal to perform the authentication. The input must be the original clear-text password, because whatever is entered will be hashed, and the hash digest of a hash digest will fail to successfully authenticate.

It is possible that a determined attacker could build their own version of the input terminal software that would accept a hash digest rather than a clear-text password as input. This would be quite an undertaking, but far from impossible. If this were to occur, there would be a strong motivation for the attacker to get a copy of the hash digest of the user's password. Recall that it is computationally infeasible for the attacker to get this hash digest by cracking the symmetric encryption. In addition, if the attacker somehow brute-forced the hash digest for one user's password, they get that single digest. It is a more fruitful attack to go after the authentication database that has the hash digests for many users. This is the reason why the authentication database must be protected and why it is so important to trust your system administrators.

Although this type of system seems complex, high-quality toolkits that contain the necessary encryption and hash algorithms are readily available on a wide variety of platforms, including low-end embedded microcontrollers. As a result, it is pretty reasonable to expect that all modern systems, which are based on password authentication, should use a cryptographically strong solution such as challenge/response to protect the authentication from attack.

Password Update

We never talked about how the original copy of the hash digest got into the accessed system authentication database. Refer to Figure 9-4.

Figure 9-4

Password update

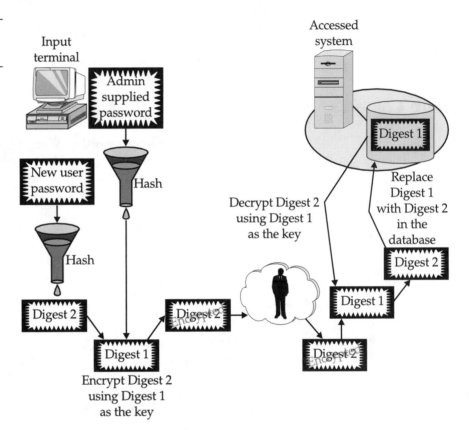

In most systems, the administrator assigns the user a temporary password that is hashed, and the digest of the temporary password is stored in the authentication database. The administrator will then tell the user what their password is through some out-of-band mechanism such as a letter or phone call. In addition, a flag is set on the user's account so that the user can only log into the accessed system once using the password created by the administrator.

When the user logs in for the first time, they will be presented with a dialog box that will force them to create a new password for the account.

The new password will be hashed on the client system. The hash of the new password will be encrypted using the hash of the original password as the key and then sent to the accessed system. The accessed system will decrypt the new hash digest using the old hash digest, and then replace the existing hash digest with the new hash digest in the authentication database. At this point, the user must use the new password to log into the system, and the administrator no longer knows the correct password to log into the user's account.

Here Come the Problems

As described, this is a fairly secure solution. When this design is applied to the real world, problems begin to appear. Let's go over the basic structures upon which the security of this solution is based:

- Clear-text passwords are never stored or transmitted.
- The hash digest of the passwords are stored on the accessed system's authentication database but are never transmitted.
- The only things that are transmitted between the systems are the original random challenge and the encrypted response.
- Because the challenge is different each session, a replay of a previous session will not work because the recorded response will not decrypt to the new challenge.
- At best, a determined attacker could find a way to get a copy of the authentication database which contains the hash digests. However, since a property of a good hash algorithm is that you cannot easily locate a particular clear-text that produces a particular hash digest, having a copy of the authentication database does not help the attacker get the passwords.

The weakness in this picture is the last bullet. The properties of a good hash are the ones I have described, but a good hash must be properly used if the features of the hash are to be preserved. In particular, cryptographic hash algorithms depend upon the assumption that the data being hashed is reasonably distributed. One way to understand this issue is to recall the discussion in Chapter 2 regarding random number generators being used for key generation. If you are relying on a 128-bit key for the security of your system, but your random number generator is not truly random and avoids picking numbers from a large part of the key space, you will effectively reduce the key space to a much smaller size, perhaps small enough that a brute-force attack can work.

A similar situation exists with hash algorithms. It is computationally infeasible to find a clear-text that hashes to a particular hash digest if, and only if, the attacker has a very large field of clear-texts to choose from. If enough of the possible clear-texts can be eliminated from the search, it will become computationally feasible to brute-force attack a hash algorithm by feeding all the remaining clear-text inputs to the hash and searching for the one that produces the correct digest.

This is the source of the problem with passwords. Let's assume we pick a robust cryptographic algorithm like MD5 to hash our passwords into a 128-bit digest. The chances that an attacker could discover, by brute force, a password that would generate a particular hash digest are very low. Unfortunately, people do not use passwords that are evenly and randomly distributed across the entire space of available alphanumeric characters.

For example, if we assume an eight-character password composed of only alphabetic or numeric characters (let's exclude special characters and lowercase characters for this example), each of the eight characters could be A-Z or 0-9. That is a total of 36 possible characters per position in the password. The resulting maximum number of passwords is 36^8, or 2,821,109,907,456. That's a bit larger than the number of keys in a 41-bit key space. In reality, the maximum number of passwords can be much larger because of the inclusion of lowercase and special characters.

It might seem that 8-character passwords are reasonably long. Unfortunately, human beings cannot seem to handle passwords like "ZQ6FV0J9" very well. When required to use passwords like this, we tend to write them down on yellow stickies that surround our monitor, or we write them on a slip of paper that we keep under our keyboard. (Quick, go move them before someone else reads this chapter and decides to check your monitor and keyboard.)

If, on the other hand, users are required to use long passwords but allowed to choose their own password, they tend to reduce the space of possible passwords from 2,821,109,907,456, to something on the order of 10. They pick the nickname they have for their loved one (SnookieWookums), or the names of their dogs, children, significant others, or (amazingly frequently) the word "Password" or "Secret." Let's get real—forget eight alphanumeric characters, most people have trouble remembering a couple of four-digit, numeric-only, ATM PINs. The most common PINs are "1234" or the same digit repeated four times.

Due to the fact that people choose passwords they can easily remember, the actual number of usable passwords within a certain password length is dramatically reduced. Because of this reduction in the size of the search space, and because readable words are typically used for the password, this opens the door for what is known as a *dictionary attack*.

A dictionary attack is pretty much what it sounds like. If an attacker can get the hash of your password, a dictionary attack program will take a dictionary of words and attempt to locate a password that generates the proper hash digest. These programs are smart enough to defeat the various techniques people use to try and obfuscate their password: things like alternating upper- and lowercase, appending numbers to the end of a readable word, substituting zeros for the letter O, and so on. In fact, the database of words and phrases underneath these programs has become quite sophisticated, and they are remarkably good at finding passwords from a hash digest.

Quite a number of password-cracking (actually hash digest-cracking) programs are available on the Web. If you do a search including terms such as "password cracking," you will easily discover entire sites dedicated to cracking the password databases of many systems, including Windows and UNIX variants. Some of the best-known tools are L0phtCrack, Crack, and NTCrack. These tools can easily process millions of passwords per second on modern PCs. If the password exists in the database of these tools, they will quickly find it. If the tool needs to try various combinations of letters, numbers, and punctuation, the process will take significantly longer. The Web is replete with Web sites and newsgroups describing how to exploit system weaknesses or operational blunders to gain access to authentication databases such as the SAM database, and then crack these databases.

Before we leave the discussion of password-cracking tools, I would be remiss if I left you with the impression that only attackers use these tools. A good security policy should include the periodic use of these tools to examine your own password files. It is only fair that companies should use the best attacker tools available, because you can be sure the attackers will. Note that it is important to let the user community know that these tools will be used, so they do not feel violated when a security officer in the company shows up on their doorstep with a list of their poorly chosen passwords. Actually, these tools only need to find the password to any privileged account and they have access to the whole system.

Part of a security officer's job should be to monitor the various newsgroups, hacker groups, and security industry watch Web sites to keep up with the latest in password-cracking tools and weaknesses in various operating systems.

The Costs of Passwords

It is a common misconception that passwords are the least expensive and easiest-to-use form of authentication. From the end-user point of view, there is some truth in this perspective. What could be easier to use—you just have to remember them and enter them as needed.

In reality, passwords largely fail to live up to their promise of low cost and ease of use. As the number of systems and services that we need to connect to grows, so does the number of passwords we need to remember. Increasingly, users are frustrated by their inability to remember all the passwords they need. This has lead to the growth of password storage devices such as electronic wallets or password caches on PDAs. This in turn leads to other issues around the security of these wallets, or concerns if the PDA is stolen. Many users resort to reusing the same password on multiple systems, another clear security violation.

Passwords may be problematic for end-users, but they are an absolute abomination for system administrators. There have been many studies done which show that the vast majority (over 40 percent in many cases) of time that system administrators or helpdesks spend has to do with the management of passwords for end-users.

NOTE:

Although I cannot cite a specific reference, I have been told by a reputable source that the percentage of time spent by administrators and helpdesk personnel is much higher than 40 percent on January 1 (presumably after the New Year's revelries kill all those valuable brain cells).

People forget their password (or their PDA with all their passwords) and need to call the helpdesk to get a temporary password reissued. In addition, when people forget their password, or accidentally repeatedly use the wrong password to access a protected resource, the repeated password failures trigger protection mechanisms that lock the resource and trigger security alarms.

Additionally, when administrators attempt to enforce a reasonably strong password policy, there is almost always a strong resentment from the user community.

It is not a pretty situation for the administrators.

Passwords Recap

Before we move on, let's review the good and bad attributes of passwords.

- Passwords are the most common form of authentication in use today.
- Modern password systems are based upon a challenge/response system and cryptographic hashes.

  - This means that clear-text passwords are not stored anywhere.
  - It also means that even administrators do not know the end-user's password.

- Password-cracking programs are readily available and should be used by security officers to test their installations.
- Passwords are actually one of the most expensive forms of authentication available.

Passwords and PKI

Now that you understand the strengths and weaknesses of password-based authentication, let's talk about the use of passwords in PKI systems to protect private keys.

By far, the most common private key storage in use today is a Web browser-based, password-protected file. In addition to Web browsers, many applications store private keys in a password-protected file. Lotus Notes, various mail clients, and various VPN clients are all common examples.

The first question to ask is whether password protection was even enabled when the private key store was created. Unfortunately, particularly with Web browsers, people frequently disable password protection on their private key stores. This is hardly surprising given the lack of understanding most people have regarding PKI in general, never mind the complexities of private key storage and the need for passwords.

If you are going to use a local private key store on a system, please protect it with *at least* a password. If you don't, anyone who walks up to your system can sit down and perform transactions that will be interpreted as coming from you. They could issue a bank transfer to move all your savings to their secret Swiss bank account. Or send a memo to your boss telling him that he is a bottom-dwelling, hydrogen sulfide-producing, single-cell plankton. Or they could order that new Lamborghini Diablo and have it shipped to their temporary address. You get the idea.

NOTE:

With Internet Explorer, you must set up the password on the credential store when you register for a certificate. The process of requesting a certificate triggers a key generation process, which in turn creates the database to store your private key. At that point, you are given the opportunity to create a password for controlling access to the private key. With Netscape Navigator, a similar process occurs, but you also can click the Security button, and then select Passwords to create a password or modify the behavior of the password authentication.

Given all the hard work the cryptographers and engineers went to in producing secure PKI systems (never mind the damage that could be done to you if someone were able to get your private key), you could at least pick a decent password while you are at it.

Pick something nice and long. Ram a few words, numbers, and special characters together. Misspell a word or two (on purpose). Toss in your favorite word from a foreign language. Add an umlaut. Do *something* to make it at least a *little* challenging for the password-cracking programs. After all, those attackers spent lots of time building those password-cracking programs, and it's kind of embarrassing if the program doesn't even have to work hard to get your password. And don't write it on the magic list under your keyboard!

Maybe you shouldn't use a password at all: remember Moore.

Moore's Law Has Got Us!

Most people are familiar with Moore's Law, which predicts a doubling of processor power roughly every 18 months. Unfortunately, human brain power does not progress at anything like this rate, and it is quite possible that cable TV and video games have reversed the growth in our brain power altogether. Graphically, I think the situation looks like Figure 9-5.

Figure 9-5

Moore's Law and brain power

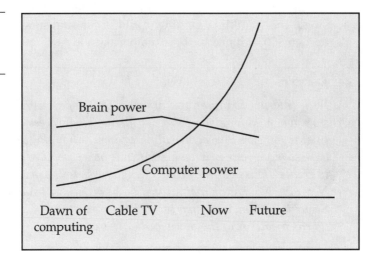

This graphic, although tongue-in-cheek, is actually kind of true. At this point in history, the processing power available to run password-cracking programs has pretty much reached a level where it can crack almost any password that a human being can remember.

This is the beginning of the death of passwords.

Already I have seen large corporate customers that have realized this, and who have instituted policies that forbid the use of passwords to protect administrator accounts or other critical resources. Even Microsoft has published papers that declare that passwords are evil. (Refer to the article "Password=Bad" by Paul Robichaux, on Microsoft's TechNet, February 2000.)

Once you realize this issue, you need to make certain decisions. Passwords must be used only in situations where they are protecting resources of moderate or low value. Even then, you must ensure that the password system is designed around a modern password system, such as a challenge/response system based on password digests. Administrators must be vigilant to ensure that the authentication databases are not available for attackers to copy and process with password-cracking tools. In addition, administrators should create a policy that enforces an acceptable minimum password criteria (minimum password length, mix of alphabetic and non-alphabetic characters, replacement interval, and so on). Password-cracking tools should be used to test your own authentication databases and make sure your users are using appropriate passwords.

In situations where resources of high value are being protected, stronger authentication techniques should be used.

Work to Strengthen Passwords

Before moving on to discuss tokens, smart cards, and biometrics, I should mention that new cryptographic techniques are being developed in an attempt to improve the security of systems based upon passwords.

Several protocols have been developed that combine passwords with Diffie-Hellman to produce a more secure password-based solution. Bellovin and Merritt of AT&T Bell Laboratories have developed EKE (Encrypted Key Exchange), which combined Diffie-Hellman with passwords known by both systems as a *shared secret*. EKE was later updated to AEKE (Augmented EKE), which replaced the passwords known by each system with the digests of the passwords.

Another protocol that combines Diffie-Hellman with passwords is SPEKE (Simple Password-authenticated Exponential Key Exchange), which was developed by Jablon of Integrity Sciences.

In addition to these Diffie-Hellman-based techniques, Ford of Verisign and Kaliski of RSA have developed a technique referred to as "password hardening." In this technique, a password hardening server helps to create a strong password from a user-supplied password, but this is done in such a way that even the server that helped to create the hardened password does not know what that hardened password is.

The details of these techniques go beyond what we will cover in this book; however, with a little Web searching you can find more information on these (and other) advanced password-strengthening techniques.

Passwords may be slowly dying, but they are far from dead yet.

Authentication Tokens

Easily the most common replacement for simple passwords is an authentication token. An authentication token is a device that generates a new value to be used for authentication each time it is used. These devices are small in size—many are similar in size and appearance to a small calculator, and others are roughly about the size of a remote control used to unlock a car.

Figure 9-6 shows a couple of example tokens.

Figure 9-6

Authentication tokens

Just about all authentication tokens have a processor, a liquid crystal display (LCD), and a battery. Depending upon the type of token, it may also have a keypad for entering information, a real-time clock, and perhaps other features. In some cases, the batteries are replaceable; in other units, the battery lasts the lifetime of the token. Some devices output numeric values, and others output hexadecimal values.

Each token is programmed with a unique value called a *seed*. The seed ensures that each token will produce a unique set of output codes.

Tokens generate pseudorandom numbers called *one-time passwords*, or *one-time passcodes*. These passcodes are called *pseudorandom* because if you collect the series of numbers produced by a token and plot the distribution of the numbers, the plot will look like the plot of true random numbers. In other words, the values will be evenly distributed across the space of values. However, passcodes are not truly random, because if you know how they are computed you can predict any particular value. This is important because the authentication server, which will verify the passcode, must be able to check that a particular token generated a particular passcode.

When logging into a resource, the user will enter their user ID, but instead of a password, the user will enter the passcode displayed on their token, as well as a PIN. Once a passcode has been used once, it cannot be used again (hence, "one-time"). In most systems, the accessed system does not verify the supplied passcode itself, but rather will ask a trusted authentication server to verify the code.

The authentication server must know the seed value programmed into each token. Since the authentication server knows the seed programmed into the token held by a particular user, the authentication server checks that the supplied passcode is the correct pseudorandom number for that user.

2-Factor Authentication

When authentication is being discussed, you will frequently hear reference to a number of "factors." An authentication process will involve one or more of these factors. The three most common factors are

- *Something you know,* such as a password or a PIN
- *Something you have,* such as a credit card
- *Something you are,* such as your voiceprint or fingerprint

Passwords are called *single-factor* or *1-factor* authenticators. This is because passwords only involve "something you know." If someone were to discover your password, they would be able to gain access to anything protected with that password.

Authentication tokens are *dual-factor* or *2-factor* authenticators. To use an authentication token, you must have the token itself (something you have) and must know the correct PIN (something you know). If an attacker were to get access to your authentication token—while you were at lunch, for example—it would be of no use to them unless they also knew your PIN. Similarly, if the attacker were to discover your PIN, it would be useless to them unless they also had your token.

Types of Authentication Tokens

There are two major classes of authentication tokens: challenge/response tokens and time-based tokens. Let's explore how each one works.

Challenge/Response Tokens

Hopefully, you will recall that we just discussed the use of challenge/ response authentication a few pages ago. In challenge/response password systems, the hash digest of the password is used as the shared secret to perform the authentication.

With tokens, the token and the authentication server also share a secret, namely the seed programmed into the token. The seed is nothing more than an appropriate-length random number that is unique to each token. If we replace the password digest with the seed, let's see how the process would work to create a challenge/response token. Recall that with passwords there were two ways to perform a challenge/response type of authentication. The first involved an encryption/decryption operation, and the second relied on parallel cryptographic computations. Let's look at the encryption/decryption model first. Refer to Figure 9-7 to follow the process.

As before, the seed programmed into the token is never revealed, but rather the authentication server uses a random number to challenge the token to prove that it has the correct seed value. Because tokens typically do not have an electronic interface to receive the challenge from the authentication server, the user will read the challenge off a prompt and enter it into the token. Using the encryption/decryption model, the token will then encrypt the challenge, using the internal copy of the seed as the key, producing the response. The response will be displayed on the LCD of the token. The user will then read the response off the token and enter it into the prompt where one would normally enter a password.

The authentication server will receive the response, and using the previously stored copy of the seed that was programmed into the token, will decrypt the response yielding challenge'. If the resulting challenge' matches the original challenge, the authentication server can say with assurance that the token was in the possession of the user authenticating.

Figure 9-7

Challenge/
response
encrypting token

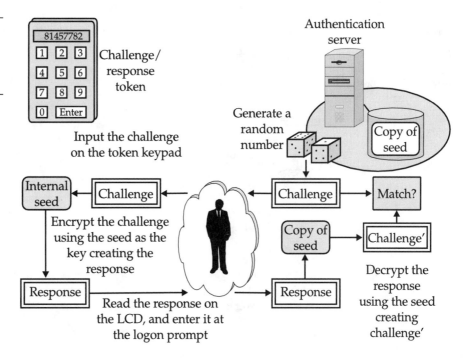

Sounds great! Now that you are experts in challenge/response authentication, this should seem pretty simple to you. Unfortunately, there is a big problem. Conceptually, this process as described will work, but it is not usable. The problem lies in the output of the encryption. Let's assume for a moment that the token is using a 128-bit seed. The size of the value output from the encryption operation will vary with the encryption algorithm, but it must be at least as large as the block size of the symmetric cipher. In this example, let's assume the symmetric cipher has a block size of 128 bits. A 128-bit value would require 32 hex characters to represent. People simply do not tolerate having to read and properly type long strings of characters. In fact, most tokens sold today use six or eight characters in the display.

To get around this problem, you cannot simply truncate the result of the encryption operation to six or eight characters and throw away the rest. If you tried to do this, the decryption at the authentication server would fail. As you can see, you end up needing to build the token around a parallel computation model. Refer to Figure 9-8.

Figure 9-8

Challenge/
response parallel
encryption tokens

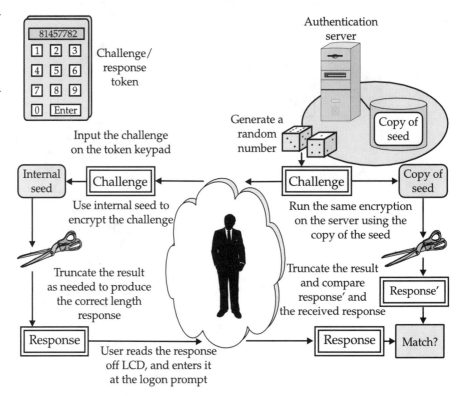

Recall that a good encryption algorithm will produce an output that gives no information about the original clear-text. Essentially, this means that the output of an encryption will have the same properties as a random number. If you take a random number and discard a portion of it, the remainder will be a random number. This means that you can take the output of the token encryption algorithm, decide how many digits you wish to display, and throw away the excess bits without leaking information about the seed. Obviously, you do not want to go to a value that has too few characters, or the probability that an attacker can just pick a number at random and have it properly authenticate will start to increase. That is why passcode lengths in the range of six or eight characters are good. They are usable by people, but still long enough to make the probability that a guess will work low.

Once the output of the encryption is truncated to the desired number of characters, it is displayed on the LCD of the token. The user enters the displayed value where a password would normally be used. The truncated response is then sent to the authentication server for verification. By truncating the response, we have of course destroyed any chance of decrypting the response and recovering the challenge. As a result, the authentication server validates the response via the parallel computation method described above.

The authentication server takes the original challenge and encrypts it using the stored copy of the seed. The resulting response will be truncated in precisely the same way as was done in the token. The authentication server will then compare the truncated response received from the token with the truncated response just computed. If they match, the authentication is granted.

As you can see, no real encryption and decryption is happening here. We are simply running parallel cryptographic algorithms in both the token and the authentication server. Although some tokens have used an encryption algorithm as we just discussed, most opt for a simpler solution. Namely, they use some form of a cryptographic hash algorithm instead of an encryption algorithm. Refer to Figure 9-9.

Figure 9-9

Hash-based challenge/response tokens

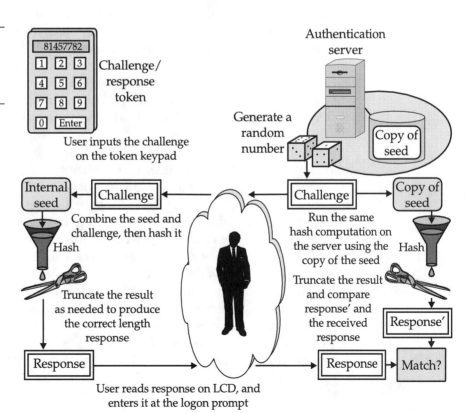

In this scenario, the challenge would be input into the token as before. At this point, the seed and challenge could be appended together, and the resulting value run through a cryptographic hash then truncated as needed. The resulting digest would be displayed on the LCD as the response.

At the server end, the server could take the stored copy of the seed, combine it with the challenge, and run the resulting value through the same cryptographic hash and truncation process. If the response from the token matched the truncated digest just produced by the server, it would know that the correct token was used to authenticate.

Using a hash rather than an encryption has several advantages. Hashes are easier to implement and use less CPU power than an encryption algorithm. This makes them ideal for the low-end processor of the token. The use of a smaller processor results in lower cost and longer battery life. The hash is easier for the server to run as well, resulting in an increase in the number of authentications per second that the server can perform.

Time-Based Tokens

Up to this point, we have been discussing challenge/response tokens. A simpler-to-use form of token has evolved, which at this point has become the dominant form of authentication token.

The problem with challenge/response tokens is that they are somewhat cumbersome to use. Recall that many (perhaps most) users of tokens are not highly technical and find the sequence of events somewhat confusing. In addition, they may not be accessing protected systems frequently, and therefore may tend to forget the sequence of events because they are not practiced in performing that sequence. Lastly, in this process the user must read two different values (the challenge and the response) without error; they must also enter three different values (PIN into keypad, challenge into keypad, response into prompt) without making a mistake. People frequently make a mistake somewhere in that process and fail to be authenticated. This increases user frustration with the process.

Time-based tokens address many of these issues. Refer to Figure 9-10 and let's look at how they work.

The first thing to notice about this graphic is that the token does not have a keypad. Additionally, the authentication server does not need to generate a challenge and transmit it to the user for entry into the token. The reason for this is that time is used as the variable input to the authentication, not a random challenge. This is where the term *time-based* comes from.

Figure 9-10

Time-based
tokens

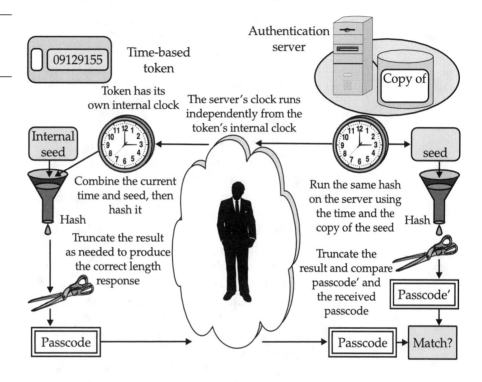

As can be seen from the figure, the process is fairly straightforward. As
with challenge/response tokens, each token is programmed with a unique
seed, and a copy of that seed must reside at the authentication server. At
the time of token manufacture, the internal real-time clock in the token is
started and programmed with its initial time value. In addition to this,
the actual clock frequency may be measured and an adjustment factor
programmed into the tokens to cause the tokens to keep accurate time.

Unlike challenge/response tokens that produce passcodes only when a
challenge is entered into the token, time-based tokens continuously generate passcodes. Typically, the token will compute a new passcode every
60 seconds. The current time is combined with the seed and fed through a
cryptographic computation such as a hash. The output of the computation
is a pseudorandom number, which is then truncated to the desired number of digits. The resulting truncated pseudorandom number is displayed
on the LCD of the token as the passcode.

NOTE:

It is not necessary that the current time be used. The only requirement is that the server must know what time the token was programmed with, and when. This information could be stored in the same record that contains the copy of the seed that will eventually be loaded into an authentication server.

When logging into a resource, the user will enter their user ID, but instead of a password, the user will enter the passcode displayed on their token. Once a passcode has been used once, it cannot be used again (hence one-time).

The authentication server also has a clock that maintains the current time. When the authentication server receives the passcode, it independently takes the current time, combines it with the copy of the seed, and performs the same cryptographic computation as the token. The resulting pseudorandom number is truncated in the same manner as is done in the token, producing an independently generated passcode. If the passcode received from the token matches the passcode generated by the server itself, access is granted.

If you think about this process for a while, some timely questions will come to mind. In some cases, the server must compute more than one passcode to authenticate a user. There are a couple of reasons for this. If the token's clock is exactly synchronized with the authentication server's clock, but the 60-second interval is just about to change when the user types in their passcode, the delay in transmitting the message to the authentication server would cause the passcode to arrive in the next 60-second interval, and therefore the passcodes would not match.

The situation where the clocks do not match actually can occur more frequently. The clock inside the token is continually ticking away. If you visit the Ice Hotel in Northern Sweden for a night, and happen to have your token with you, the low temperatures will cause the clock in your token to run slightly slow. If you take your token to Singapore, the heat will cause the clock in your token to run slightly fast. Over time, it is inevitable that the clock in the token will drift out of synchronization with the authentication server.

NOTE:

The Ice Hotel only exists for a few months each year in the Swedish town of Jukkasjarvi in Swedish Lapland. The entire hotel is constructed from solid blocks of ice from the frozen Torne River, which are carved by artisans. Guests sleep in rooms made of (and on beds made of) solid ice. In the hotel bar, drinks are served in cups formed by drilling a hole in a solid cube of ice. For obvious safety reasons, no electric blankets are allowed.

These issues with time and the clocks mean that a time-based authentication server must work a little harder than a challenge/response-based authentication server. If the time-based authentication server fails to match the passcode on the first try, it will not immediately reject the authentication. It will advance its clock one minute into the future and try again. If that fails, it will retard its clock one minute into the past and try again. If that fails, it will try plus or minus two minutes, and so on. Typically, an authentication server will try and locate the passcode within a window of plus or minus a few minutes of the center time on the server clock. If the server locates a matching passcode within this interval, it will successfully authenticate the user, but it will also remember how far off the token clock is from the server clock (clock offset). On the next authentication, the server will use the clock offset to first adjust its clock to match the token's clock, and then attempt to verify the passcode.

If the authentication server fails to locate the correct passcode within the inner windows of time (plus or minus a few minutes), it can open the windows up to a larger range—say, plus or minus 10 minutes—and try and locate the passcode. If the passcode is not found within the inner window, but is located within the outer window, the authentication server may ask the user to enter the next passcode just to be sure that the user really has the correct token. If the second passcode works, the new clock offset is saved and the authentication is granted. Figure 9-11 shows these windows graphically.

These techniques allow the authentication server to track the gradual drift of the clocks embedded in each token. As a result of this clock drift tracking, passcodes are usually authenticated on the first or second try.

Figure 9-11

Time drift

  Time-based token

Authentication server

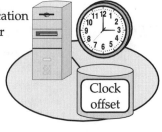

Clock offset

 The hardware real-time clock in a time-base token can drift due to ambient temperature changes. As a result, the generated passcode may not be the same passcode as the server would generate at this instant

If after adjusting the server clock by the previously stored clock offset, we find the passcode within the inner window, allow the user in, and store the new clock offset

$\left.\begin{array}{c}+2 \\ 0 \\ -2\end{array}\right\}$

If we cannot locate the passcode within the inner window, search within the outer window. If the passcode is located, ask the user for the next passcode. If the next passcode is correct, let the user in and store the new clock offset

$\left.\begin{array}{c}+10 \\ \\ \\ \\ -10\end{array}\right\}$

If we cannot locate the passcode within the outer window, reject the authentication

One other safety guard is implemented within the time-based authentication server. After each successful authentication, the computed token clock center time is recorded. Any new authentication must be based on a time later than the remembered token clock center time. In other words, the authentication server does not allow time to run backward on the token.

As you can see, time-based servers must work harder than their challenge/response counterparts. This is a trade-off done to allow the tokens to be easier to use. Users do not need to read and properly type a challenge into the token, and then type the resulting response. They only need to type the passcode, and a PIN. In addition, because there is no need to enter a challenge, time-based tokens can do away with the keypad, allowing a small authentication token that can be attached to a key-chain. This makes it less likely that the user will forget their token.

The time-based key fob token is by far the most successful authentication token ever produced. At the time this chapter was written, approximately 10 million of these devices had been shipped, and by the time you read this millions more will probably be in customers' hands.

PIN Management

You may have noticed that I have not yet discussed the use of the PIN with an authentication token. Without the PIN, a token is another 1-factor authentication device. It is only "something you have." If an attacker borrowed your token off your desk while you were at lunch, they would be able to compute the appropriate responses to authenticate into the system. We need to introduce the PIN to change the 1-factor authentication into a 2-factor authentication. I've avoided discussing the PIN until now because the operation of tokens was complex enough without having to introduce PINs, which can be used in a couple of different ways. The two primary ways I would like to discuss are PIN activation of the token and PIN factoring into the response computation.

PIN Activation of the Token

You could imagine a token designed so that it would be inactive until the appropriate PIN was entered. The entry of the correct PIN would activate the token, allowing a challenge to be entered. This is not an optimal solution from a security point of view. The reason for this is that an attacker who has access to the token needs to find the PIN. If the attacker enters a PIN and the token remains inert, the attacker will know it is the wrong PIN. To avoid disabling a token by entering too many bad PINs, the patient attacker would try a couple of PINs, and then return the token to the owner's desk. Presumably, the owner would enter the correct PIN the next time the token is used, resetting the bad PIN counter inside the token. The next time the owner is away from his or her desk, the attacker would try a few more PINs.

Although this is admittedly a tedious process, and not likely to be successful, there is an easy way to avoid giving the attacker any information about the PIN. The token could be constructed to accept any PIN and allow a passcode to be generated. If the correct PIN were used, the token would operate correctly and produce the correct passcode using the internally programmed seed. If the incorrect PIN was used, the token could switch to a different seed within the device, generating a passcode, but a passcode that would fail to authenticate.

To help catch the attacker, we could go one step further. Assume that when the incorrect PIN was entered, all tokens would use the same special seed value; let's call it the "bad PIN seed." It would be a simple change to the authentication server to first see if the response could be authenticated using the correct seed. If so, the authentication would succeed. If not, then attempt to authenticate the response using the "bad PIN seed." If this operation works, the authentication server would know that a bad PIN was entered onto the token keypad (as opposed to the user just fat-fingering either the challenge or the response). The authentication server could then perform some appropriate response such as generating an event log warning the administrator that bad PINs were being entered into the token, or perhaps locking the user's account if several of these bad PINs happened in a row. During this process, the attacker would see the token behaving properly until the account was disabled.

So far, we have talked about using the PIN to activate the token. One downside to using a PIN to activate the token is that the token will need to internally store the PIN for comparison. This implies that the token will need mechanisms to allow the user to change the PIN if the user becomes concerned that their PIN may be known. This adds complexity to the design of the token.

In addition, having the PIN processed on the token may create situations where the token will lock itself if too many bad PINs are entered. This in turn creates the need for a PIN management procedure that can be used to unlock a locked token. This may involve requiring that the token be sent back to the administrator for re-initialization.

Lastly, since the PIN would need to be stored within the token, there is a chance that an attacker could borrow a token, carefully pry it open, and use sophisticated tools to read the memory of the microprocessor within the token. If this could be accomplished, the attacker would gain all factors. They would be able to obtain the seed value, the PIN, and presumably the algorithm used to generate the response. If they could then carefully glue the token back together and place it on your desk, you might never know that your token had been compromised. The attacker could at this point create a token that generated the exact responses your token generates, and they would know the correct PIN to use. In effect, they have stolen your digital identity.

There are ways to make this process very difficult for the attacker, and we will discuss them below in the "Tamper Resistance" section.

On the upside, one benefit of having PIN processing on the token is that the server does not need to know users' PINs, which may make users feel more secure.

Before I leave the topic of PIN activation of the token, I should mention that this is a very common method of handling PINs. Authentication devices we will discuss in a moment such as smart cards and USB dongles are PIN-activated devices.

The PIN as Part of the Computation

There is another way to deal with PINs. Rather than use PINs to active the token in some manner, or alter the token's behavior, a PIN can become part of the cryptographic computation that occurs within the token. For example, the PIN could be combined with the seed before the cryptographic computation is performed. Another solution would be to combine the PIN with the pseudorandom number in some way. If the PIN is included as part of the pseudorandom number computation, the server needs a copy of the PIN. This is so the server can perform the same PIN processing computation before the returned passcode is compared with the locally generated passcode.

In this model, the PIN is not stored in the token. This means that if an attacker has access to the token, they will be unable to extract the user's PIN, even if they dismantle the hardware. It also means that the token does not need PIN management functions that can be complex to implement in low-end processors. Lastly, it means that there is no need to develop a PIN-unlock procedure and a process to get the token to an administrator to perform the PIN-unlock.

However, the PIN management functions must now occur at the authentication server. This implies that there is support in the protocol between the token and the authentication server to support PIN management functions such as requesting the user to enter a new PIN and pass that back to the server. A user interface to perform the PIN management functions must also be provided.

You might wonder how a key fob-sized, time-based token can be used as a 2-factor authenticator if it does not have a keypad to accept the PIN. When using the key fob-sized tokens, the PIN is entered into the login prompt as a prefix to the passcode. The software prompting for the passcode knows how to perform the final combination of the PIN with the passcode before it is sent to the authentication server for validation. Note that there are time-based tokens that do have keypads for those situations where the additional security of entering the PIN into an external hardware device is desired.

Authentication Token Recap

Before we move on, let's review the important points about authentication tokens:

- Authentication tokens come in two major types: challenge/response and time-based.

- Authentication tokens introduce the concept of 2-factor authentication: something you have (the token) and something you know (the PIN). One factor without the other is useless.

- Challenge/response tokens typically look like a small calculator, with an LCD and a keypad. A challenge is passed to the user who enters it along with a PIN into the keypad. The token computes the response and displays it on the LCD. The displayed response is entered into the login prompt.

- Internally, the challenge/response token will typically hash the seed, challenge, and PIN together and produce a pseudorandom number. That number is truncated to a reasonable number of characters and displayed on the LCD.

- Challenge/response tokens work differently than password-based challenge/response solutions due to the need to truncate the generated pseudorandom number.

- Time-based tokens typically look like a small key fob, with an LCD display but no keypad. The user simply types the displayed pseudorandom number preceded by their PIN into the login prompt.

- Internally, the time-based token maintains a real-time clock whose output is hashed with the seed to produce a pseudorandom number. That number is truncated to a reasonable number of characters and displayed on the LCD.

- Although we haven't discussed them here, there are software-only implementations of authentication tokens that run as an application on PCs, PDAs, cell phones, and so on, converting these devices into authentication tokens.

Authentication Tokens and PKI

Authentication tokens primarily relate to PKI in one of two ways. Tokens can act as the client-side authentication mechanism in conjunction with server-side PKI, and tokens can act as the initial authenticator to grant access to private keys.

Tokens as Client-Side Authenticators

We have used SSL to demonstrate the establishment of a secure communications channel, as well as the implicit authentication of both the Web server and the user at the Web browser. These techniques involved the transmission of X.509 certificates in both directions during the SSL session setup, as well as mechanisms to probe each side to prove that the private keys that match the public keys in the certificates were indeed present.

As we discussed before, these concepts are seen in many different protocols, including WTLS in the wireless space, in various VPNs including IPsec, and of course in SSL for Web sessions. In order to authenticate the user (client) side of all these different protocols, public key client software, digital certificates, and private keys must be distributed to each client. If the user will be performing operations other than authentication that require PKI, such as digital signatures, the cost and complexity of distributing and maintaining desktop software, as well as managing the life cycle of digital certificates, may well make sense. In these situations, using a PKI method to authenticate the user is the right thing to do.

There are many cases where this is not the case. If the only function that the client-side PKI will be used for is to authenticate the user, the cost and complexity of distributing and maintaining the desktop PKI software and/or the digital certificates may be overkill. In addition, there are some cases where it is not practical to manage desktop software, or it is undesirable to manage certificates. Many business-to-consumer environments may fit this description. It may just be impractical for eBay to manage PKI software and/or certificates to all bidders and sellers.

Due to these issues, an interesting hybrid of PKI and authentication tokens has emerged. Let's use secure Web transactions as an example. Let's say that your favorite bank wanted to allow its customers to do secure online banking. (By secure, I *don't* mean the solution that exists in the U.S. today where you access your bank account with only a PIN.) In this situation, the bank may not be interested in issuing, qualifying, or distributing X.509 certificates to each bank member who desired to bank online. What they could do instead is to purchase a certificate for their banking Web server and turn on server-side SSL. As you have already seen, server-side SSL will cause an encrypted session to be created between the Web browser and the Web server, and an implicit authentication of the Web server will occur. So far, so good. The communications are secure, and the user knows they are in communication with the bank. Without digital certificates issued to all the bank members, you cannot enable client SSL authentication, so what many banks have done is to issue their customers authentication tokens to perform the client-side authentication. This solution requires no desktop software and does not require the distribution of certificates to the bank customers. When the user connects to the secure Web server running over a secure server-side SSL session, they will be prompted to enter their user ID as well as the current passcode from their authentication token. If the passcode is correct, the user is authenticated, and they are allowed to do online banking. This exact solution has been deployed to thousands of bank customers in Europe.

This type of solution is a great combination of PKI and authentication tokens. Due to PKI, you get strong authentication of the Web server and strong encryption of the communications. Due to the authentication token, you get strong authentication of the user.

Although we have used a secure Web session as the example, precisely this type of solution is also used to set up secure IP sessions with VPNs, including IPsec. Again, the VPN server will have a digital certificate and matching private key. The server-side certificate is enough to establish the encrypted VPN session and is also used to authenticate the VPN server. The user attempting to connect to the VPN server authenticates using an authentication token.

Authentication Tokens to Protect Private Keys

One other solution that has evolved is the use of authentication tokens to protect software private key stores.

As we discussed above, most private keys are stored in password-protected files. This reduces the security of the user's private key to the strength of their password—assuming they even use a password!

An interesting solution has evolved that allows an authentication token to be used to protect the private key (and other security information) with strong 2-factor token-based authentication. In this solution, the user's private keys are stored in an encrypted container held at the back-end server. To gain access to their private keys, the user authenticates using an authentication token. After a successful authentication, the encrypted container for that user is downloaded to their system and decrypted. At this point, the private keys become enabled for use with the cryptographic service providers.

This is a much better solution than password-protected private key containers, because it strengthens the security and trust of the private key from a 1-factor password level to a 2-factor authentication token level. In addition, it moves the control of the security from the end-user, who is typically unaware of all the issues, to the security administrator.

Smart Cards

Smart cards are basically a small microprocessor with memory embedded inside a piece of plastic the same size as a credit card. Their use ranges from simple phone card styles of applications to complex PKI devices that support cryptographic acceleration.

Smart cards are built to a set of standards, with the ISO7816 being one of the most important. The ISO7816 standards define the shape, thickness, contact positions, electrical signals, protocols, and some operating system functions to be supported by smart cards.

Smart cards are recognizable by the fact that they typically have what looks a bit like a small gold seal on one side of the card. As we will see in a moment, this is actually a set of gold electrical contacts to connect to the smart card. In fact, a microprocessor is hiding underneath those gold contacts. Figure 9-12 shows a smart card and some of the key features.

As you can see in the figure, smart cards are small data processors that can accept data, process it with programs stored in the smart card memory, and then emit the processed result out the communications port.

Smart Card Construction

To make a smart card, a microprocessor chip is bonded to the back of the metal contact that you see on the front of a smart card. Wires are then attached from the contact points on the chip to the metal contacts on the front of the smart card. A blob of epoxy is then layered on top of the chip and wires, and the whole mess is inserted into a cavity milled out of the plastic card. The whole thing is only 0.8mm thick and looks like the one shown in Figure 9-13.

Figure 9-12

Smart card fundamentals— smart cards can be considered small data processing systems

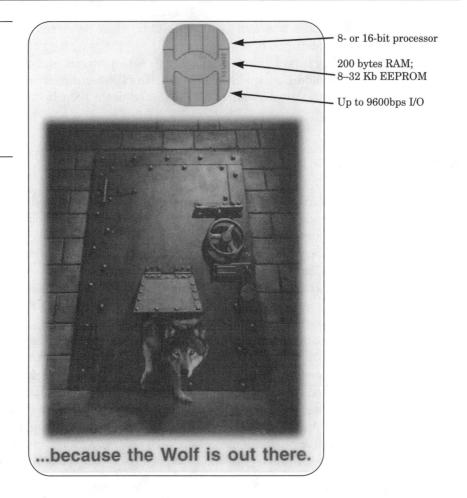

8- or 16-bit processor

200 bytes RAM; 8–32 Kb EEPROM

Up to 9600bps I/O

...because the Wolf is out there.

The only circuitry on a smart card is a single integrated circuit. Power is supplied to the card via one of the contact pads on the smart card surface, typically 5 volts. The clock for the processor is also supplied via a contact pad, typically 3 to 5 MHz. All communications with the smart card are carried out through a single contact pad. This means that all communications with the card are serial and half duplex by nature, and typically limited to 9600bps. The smart card reader does the connection to the contact pads supplying the power, clock, and I/O.

Figure 9-13

Smart card
cutaway

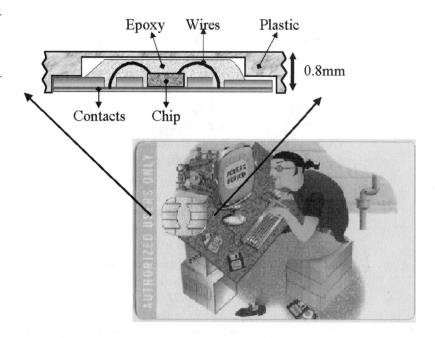

NOTE:

*Actually, we should soon start seeing multichip smart cards. To be secure,
all communications between the chips inside a smart card will need some
form of security such as encryption to protect the data from being
snooped by attackers.*

One interesting thing to note. On all the various smart cards, the actual
pattern made by the gold contacts on the front of the card looks different.
Even though these all look different, in reality where the fingers in the
reader touch the contacts on the card is always the same.

Talking to a Smart Card

Since smart cards are small microprocessors embedded in plastic, they
need some mechanism to get power to run and to communicate with the
outside world. As a result, all smart cards require a *smart card reader*.

The reader creates the electrical signals needed to reset a smart card, power it up, provide communications, and provide a system clock. In some cases, there are direct electrical connections between a smart card and the reader; in other cases, the connection is over an RF (radio frequency) connection.

Smart cards that have contact pads, and which have a direct electrical contact with their reader, are known as *contact cards*. Contact cards are typically inserted into a reader, where small metal springs will sit down onto the contact pads, completing the electrical connection with the smart card. Until now, most smart card readers have been a separate device from a computer system and plugged into a serial port or, increasingly, into a USB port. FireWire readers are probably not far away. Increasingly, there is interest in embedding readers directly into a PC, PDA, or other device. In the bulk of the world outside the U.S., where GSM cell phones dominate, almost all cell phones have a built-in smart card reader for a miniature GSM smart card. Most people tend to refer to the miniature GSM smart card as a *GSM chip*. Keyboards and notebook computers with embedded smart card readers have been available on the market for several years, but are not shipped in large quantities. By far, the most common type of reader is a serial- or USB-connected external reader.

Smart cards that do not have contact pads, and which have an RF connection between the smart card and the reader, are known of course as *contact-less cards*. Contact-less cards have a wire loop embedded inside the plastic of the smart card. The wire loop acts as an inductor for two purposes. First, when the card is introduced into the RF field created by the card reader, a current is induced in the wire loop. This current is used to power the smart card. Secondly, the same wire loop is used for communications between the smart card and the reader.

The readers for contact-less smart cards may or may not contain a slot for a smart card to be inserted. This is because some contact-less cards can be separated from their reader by distances of several feet or more, while others need to have the smart card positioned within a few millimeters of the reader electronics, and therefore need the slot to properly align the smart card.

Just to make things interesting, there are smart cards that have both contacts and a wire loop. These types of smart cards are called *combi-cards*. Typically, the wire loop is used for one set of applications, such as a door access system. The contact portion may be used for different applications, such as accessing your PKI credentials.

In this chapter, I will use the generic term "smart card" to cover contact, contact-less, and combi-cards. It should be noted that the most common forms of smart cards you will see for electronic security and PKI are the contact card and combi-card. Contact-less cards dominate the transportation and toll industries.

Smart Card Classifications

Despite the various ways in which smart cards and readers communicate, smart cards can be classified into some broad categories.

Stored Value Cards

The most primitive, most common, and least expensive type of smart card is a *stored value card*. These cards contain EEPROM (electrically erasable programmable read-only memory)—in other words, memory that can be erased to store different data. EEPROM is used because it is non-volatile. Unlike the memory in a PC, when the smart card is removed from the reader and power is cut off, EEPROM does not lose its contents. The EEPROM is a simple file system used to store such things as telephone credits, electronic cash, or other simple values. These cards also contain a simple microprocessor, typically an 8-bit microcontroller. Access to these cards is via a PIN that is usually in the range of four to eight digits. The microprocessor handles accepting the PIN and controlling access to the stored files.

These cards are not much more than memory on a card. They are best thought of as an electronic version of a magstripe card.

The security in a stored value card comes from the encryption of the data on the card, not from elaborate protection of the encrypted data. Due to the limited security of these types of cards, they are not commonly used in electronic security.

After simple stored-value type smart cards, the taxonomy of smart cards gets a bit more complex. Since we are examining smart cards from a security and PKI point of view, I tend to split smart cards into two broad categories, each with many subcategories. The two main categories are cryptographic smart cards and non-cryptographic smart cards. I will admit right up front that the line between the two is getting a little blurred.

Non-Crypto Cards

The second type of smart card is a *non-crypto card*. These cards contain a more advanced microprocessor, as well as expanded EEPROM memory. All communications with the memory must go through the microprocessor, and the microprocessor can enforce PIN protection or other security features. These cards typically have a more complex processor (typically an 8- or 16-bit processor) and additional tamper-resistance features to protect against attackers. You'll see more discussed in the "Tamper Resistance" section later in the chapter. Refer to Figure 9-14 for an internal view into a non-crypto card.

Figure 9-14

A non-crypto smart card

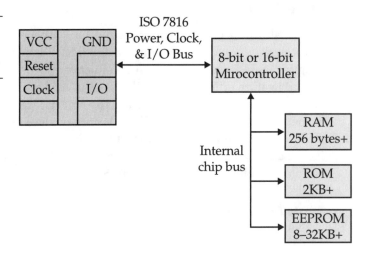

In this picture, the RAM is temporary storage where the processor performs computations, the ROM is permanent memory where the operating system for the smart card lives, and EEPROM is rewritable memory where the application data (and in some cases, code) lives. The amount of RAM, ROM, and EEPROM is highly variable from one smart card to another.

Note that all communications with the memory must go though the microprocessor; there is no direct connection between the memory and the contacts. It is the responsibility of the operating system that runs in the smart card to properly control access to the data that resides in the EEPROM. The operating system is provided by the smart card manufacturer and also ranges quite a bit in functionality from one card to another. We will discuss some of the smart card operating systems in a moment.

Crypto Cards

As I mentioned before, crypto cards and non-crypto are beginning to blur into each other's territory. The original distinction between these two cards was that a crypto card could perform asymmetric cryptography (in particular, RSA encryption), whereas a non-crypto card could not. This distinction was significant because the RSA algorithm was sufficiently complex that it could not be implemented in software in the simple 8-bit and 16-bit processors inside a smart card—at least not at the 3MHz-to-5MHz clock rates fed to smart cards by the reader. An 8-bit or 16-bit microcontroller running at 3MHz or 5MHz has a speed that is positively glacial when compared to any desktop PC.

As a result, these cards needed a hardware accelerator to help perform the complex mathematics needed to run the RSA algorithm at a reasonable speed. Reasonable usually is defined as RSA signatures taking less than one second to complete. Let's look inside a crypto card, like the one shown in Figure 9-15.

Figure 9-15

A crypto card

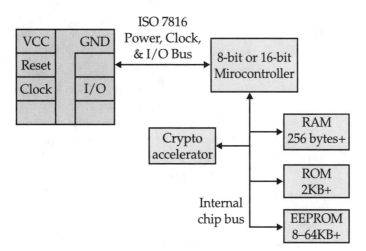

As you can see, the only difference between the crypto card shown here and the non-crypto card shown in Figure 9-14 is the presence or absence of the cryptographic acceleration hardware.

The most common smart card processors have traditionally been based on tried and true microcontroller architectures such as the 8051 series of processors originally developed by Intel, the 68HC05 series of processors originally developed by Motorola, or the H8 series developed by Hitachi (among others). These venerable 8-bit and 16-bit workhorses of the computer world are literally everywhere. They run your toaster, TV, thermostat, mouse, car engine controller. They are like little digital bugs: for every one you see, you know there are 10 more hiding somewhere. The stability of their architecture and the wide availability of fabrication facilities to make these chips have made them ideal to help keep smart cards reliable and inexpensive. Unfortunately, the age of their architectures and their slow clock speeds rendered them unable to run RSA encryption without some hardware assistance. The addition of the hardware acceleration unit added cost to these chips, and in some cases took away valuable EEPROM memory. As a result, a clear distinction grew up between crypto (read: more expensive and less EEPROM) and non-crypto (read: cheaper and more EEPROM) chips.

Unfortunately, or fortunately depending upon your point of view, the changes in smart card architectures and operating systems are removing this clear distinction. As more modern operating systems for smart cards have evolved, they are hungry for processing power and memory. Most of these new operating systems run some form of interpreted bytecode. The performance of the processor chip must be dramatically upgraded if an interpreted bytecode-oriented smart card is to compete with a traditional smart card programmed with a hand-crafted assembler.

This pressure has driven smart cards toward more advanced architectures, all the way to where we are beginning to see 32-bit RISC-based ARM processors in smart cards. In addition to the higher power processors, some very clever tricks have been played to allow these advanced smart cards to be put into an existing reader that supplies a 3MHz-to-5MHz clock, but then internally generates a synthetic clock to run the processor at speeds of up to 25MHz or possibly more. These advances are beginning to create the next generation of smart cards. Smart cards based on these modern chips from companies such as Atmel and Infineon are just appearing on the market. They are ideal for running the new generation of smart card operating systems.

One other factor is eroding the distinction between crypto and non-crypto smart cards. Due to the overwhelming acceptance of RSA as the open de facto standard for public key cryptography, smart cards that are used in open systems must be able to support the RSA algorithm. However, if a smart card is used in a system where the application provider can control both ends of the conversation, other asymmetric cryptographic algorithms such as ECC (or a second generation asymmetric algorithm such as NTRU) could be used. ECC, for example, can run in a non-crypto smart card to perform strong asymmetric cryptography, without the need for a hardware acceleration unit. This situation further blurs the distinction between a crypto smart card and a non-crypto smart card. In truth, crypto and non-crypto cards are converging on a new generation of smart cards based upon advanced chip architectures and modern open operating systems.

When Are Smart Cards Not Smart Cards?

Before I move on to smart card operating systems, I should mention one important point. When smart cards are discussed, one's mind immediately forms the image of credit card-like pieces of plastic.

That format of a smart card is convenient. Our wallets are designed to hold them; they can be printed on with our picture and become an employee badge; we can add magnetic stripes or wire loops to these cards to create a door access device in combination with a smart card. It is easy to forget that the plastic is just a holder for the smart part of a smart card—that is, the microprocessor with tamper-resistant features.

These same tamper-resistant microprocessors exist in other form factors. Several manufacturers make devices referred to as *USB dongles*. USB dongles are small pieces of plastic about the size of your thumb. Internally, they contain a microprocessor similar to a smart card, and some of these devices contain cryptographic accelerators just like crypto cards. When inserted into a USB port on a system, these USB dongles behave similarly to a smart card, and can emulate the behavior of a smart card from a cryptographic point of view. Early versions of these devices were not particularly tamper-resistant, but I believe that the manufacturers of these devices will improve the security of their devices over time.

In addition to USB dongles, there are other devices. One of the most interesting is the Dallas Semiconductor iButton. The iButton is essentially a smart card chip, with tamper resistance, and it comes in crypto and non-crypto versions just like a smart card. Instead of mounting the chip in a piece of plastic, Dallas Semiconductor mounts the iButton in a small metal can that acts not only as the case for the electronics, but also as the contact to communicate with the device. There are iButtons that have real-time clocks, iButtons that have internal batteries, iButtons that hang on your keychain, iButtons that run JavaCard, and even an iButton crypto ring (sort of like a Cap'n Crunch™ decoder ring—but for real!).

When considering the impact of smart cards, be sure to broaden your definition to include these and other smart card-like devices.

Applications on a Smart Card

Smart cards can support a variety of applications. For example, a security-related smart card may contain your public and private keys, and certificates for use by Web browsers via a cryptographic service provider. Another smart card-based application might be a password cache used to store the various user IDs and passwords used to gain access to various resources. Yet another smart card application might contain information needed to fill out shipping and credit card information for purchases made online. Many such applications exist, including loyalty points (such as frequent flyer points), cash cards, electronic tickets, and so on.

Traditionally, these various smart card applications used the smart card as a portable data store, with the application software running in a host system or an intelligent smart card reader. The software was generic, and it took the context and data for its execution from the inserted smart card. One notable exception is the crypto card, where in addition to the storage of public/private keys and certificates, the crypto card also performs cryptographic operations inside the smart card as an extension of the smart card operating system.

A different model is emerging with modern smart card operating systems. These modern operating systems not only support data storage on a smart card, but also allow applications to be written that will execute within the processor on the smart card. In some cases, the application software is loaded into a smart card and remains resident in the card. In other cases, the application software can be dynamically loaded into the card as needed.

Smart Card Operating Systems

One class of smart card, which is gaining in popularity, is the Java-based smart card. Java-based smart cards run the *JavaCard* operating system, which was developed by Sun Microsystems and is promoted by the Java-Card Forum. The reason that JavaCard-based smart cards are gaining in popularity is because as JavaCard becomes more mature, smart card manufacturers and smart card applications developers see JavaCard as a means to allow the portability of applications across multiple JavaCard-based smart cards from different vendors.

Most smart cards today run proprietary operating systems developed by the various smart card vendors. To produce truly useful applications on these cards, it is usually necessary to use features of the card operating system that go beyond the simple functions specified in the ISO7816 specifications. As a result, once an application is developed for one smart card, it is very difficult to port that application to a different smart card. It is frequently difficult to port the application to a new smart card from the same vendor.

JavaCard promises to break this tight coupling between smart cards and smart card operating systems by defining a richer set of functions and an abstraction from the details of the smart card and smart card operating system. One other important feature of JavaCard is that it allows for the concept of *post-issuance* application loading. This means that smart cards can be upgraded with new applications after they are deployed to end-users. This is very important because most people looking at using smart cards have some set of applications that they know they need to run on the smart card, but they also know that there will be other applications which they have not realized they need yet.

In the long run, the card independence promised by JavaCard is good for applications developers because it broadens the set of smart cards their application can run on. It is good for the end-user because it gives them a choice in selecting the best price/performance smart card for their application from a variety of vendors. And it is even good for the smart card manufacturers because it allows them to gain access to more applications that can run on their card.

JavaCard is not the only card-independent operating system. The *Windows for Smart Card* operating system from Microsoft also promises to allow applications to be easily developed for smart cards, and then deployed on a variety of Windows for Smart Card-based smart cards. In addition, Windows for Smart Card also promises to support the concept of post-issuance application loading.

MULTOS is another card independent operating system developed by a consortium led by Mondex and MasterCard. Like JavaCard and Windows for Smart Card, MULTOS is a multi-application smart card operating system. One unique feature of MULTOS is that the operating system was designed specifically with high-security and financial transactions in mind. In fact, MULTOS has achieved a high-level European security rating named "ITSec E6 High" in several countries, making it the first open smart card operating system to achieve this level of certification.

Smart Card Tamper Resistance

All smart cards have some form of protection against hackers attempting to extract secrets from the integrated circuit inside the smart card. As has been seen in the press, some of these techniques are not sufficient to protect against modern attacks. In addition, and like all areas of security, the definition of what is sufficient tamper resistance changes each year as new silicon techniques become available, and as the experience and tools available to attackers increases.

We can thank the European satellite TV system for training some of the most educated smart card hackers. In these systems, the smart card is used to store decryption keys used to decipher scrambled satellite TV broadcasts. A lucrative black market in blank smart cards and cheap electronic smart card programmers has grown up around the Internet, including many Web sites that publish the details of how to defeat these smart cards. As satellite TV has caught on in the U.S., so has smart card cracking.

I thought that it might be fun to go over some of the typical—and some of the most interesting—tamper-resistance techniques used in smart cards.

Physical Tampering

Perhaps the most direct attack one can perform on a smart card is to expose the surface of the integrated circuit embedded within the smart card. Once exposed, microprobes can be affixed to the chip surface, and then memory can be read out or other direct tampering of the chip can occur.

To expose the integrated circuit, several physical layers must be breached. First the card plastic itself must be removed. This is done by scraping away the plastic or by applying chemicals that attack plastic.

The next barrier is the epoxy that surrounds the chip itself. The epoxy is typically removed with a strong acid or other chemical solvent. Ironically, the chemicals that are used to clean chips at the end of the chip manufacturing process work quite nicely for this purpose. Lastly, a layer of protective silicon oxide, called the passivation layer, must be removed to probe the chip. This last barrier requires some specialized equipment, but this equipment is common in the semiconductor test and repair industry.

One common technique used by smart card manufacturers to prevent this type of attack is to use different types of epoxy coverings over the chip, but to leave strategic holes in each of the layers of epoxy. In this way, when a solvent strong enough to dissolve a certain layer of epoxy is applied, the next layer of epoxy will still protect most of the chip, but certain areas of the chip will immediately be exposed to the chemical solvent. The epoxy solvent destroys the exposed areas of the chip. When these areas of the chip are destroyed, the chip ceases to function.

I have also heard rumors that some manufacturers have light detectors of some sort in the chip silicon. In theory, if the epoxy surrounding the chip is removed, these light sensors will detect ambient light and somehow deactivate the chip. Personally, I don't see how these would work. In the first case, there is no power source to activate these monitors if the chip is under attack. Secondly, all silicon detectors I am aware of have limited ranges of light frequencies that they can detect. It would be a simple matter to work under infrared light or perhaps UV light to avoid such a light sensor.

Out of Range Clock Frequency Detect

Recall that the operating clock for a smart card is supplied from the smart card reader via one of the smart card contacts. This can be used as an attack point by decreasing the clock frequency to the point where the processor begins to operate erratically. This occurs because most of the smart card processors in use today cannot be run as a static part—that is, they must have a continual clock to operate properly. The attackers drop the input clock, or vary the input clock between normal speed and a speed too slow for the processor in the hope that the processor will become confused and start to do something interesting, like transmitting all of its memory out the I/O pin. A similar attack can be mounted by sending the smart card clock frequencies that are too high.

The tamper-resistance techniques used to protect against this type of attack are simple and what you might expect. In the simplest case, the input clock is monitored via a phase-locked loop or other simple technique, and if the clock is found to be out of range, a non-maskable interrupt is generated, forcing the processor into a known safe state. A somewhat more sophisticated technique is for the processor to have its own internal clock source (a synthetic clock) that is marshaled by the externally provided clock. In this technique, the real clock is internal, and the external clock is simply a reference. Since the real clock is generated internally, tampering with the external clock will not interfere with the processor, and detection circuits like those discussed above will shut down the processor if the external clock is tampered with.

I should mention that no modern smart card takes drastic action (like destroying memory) if the external clock source appears to be out of range. There were some early smart card designs that erased all of the internal EEPROM (key storage, for example) when they detected an external clock out of range. This might seem like a reasonable thing to do because a flaky clock is a sign of tampering. In practice, this turned out to be a really bad idea. When smart cards are inserted or removed from a reader, the little metal fingers that touch the contact areas on the smart card bounce up and down thousands of times before settling down onto the smart card contacts. This bouncing of the clock contact was interpreted by the early smart cards as a tamper attempt, which caused the EEPROM to be erased. As you can imagine, the failure rate of these cards was tremendous. All modern schemes that detect an abnormal clock simply reset the smart card into a secure mode that requires that the smart card to be restarted.

Clock Jitter

A similar, but more clever attack is to run the clock at the correct frequency, but at a precise interval from the initial smart card reset, insert a high-frequency burst hidden in the normal clock stream. It was found out by the satellite TV hackers that this technique, when used on certain smart cards, would cause the processor to miss an instruction or two. By carefully injecting this high-frequency pulse at exact intervals, the hackers were successful in causing the smart card to skip a specific instruction—they could do this with amazing repeatability. Although they did not have the source code to see which instruction they should clobber, they just started at the beginning and hit one instruction after another.

This was a very clever attack. It was not an attack on the crypto or the key store; it was an attack on the basic nature of the processor. What they were looking for was the instruction that loaded the counter of how many bytes to transmit out the I/O pin. If they got it right, they could get the I/O routine to dump all of EEPROM. Cute.

Fortunately, there are two simple techniques to protect against this. The first is to put a low-pass filter on the clock pin that will remove the high-frequency pulse. The second is the technique mentioned above where the real clock is internally generated, so the high-frequency pulse is ignored.

Out of Range Power Voltage Detect

If one drops the supply voltage for a microprocessor below a certain critical level, the processor will start to fail to execute properly. This is primarily due to the dynamic memory losing its state; in effect, the memory and register bits are randomly changing from zeros to ones (or vice versa). An attack based on dropping the processor voltage is similar to the clock jitter attack, where the hacker hopes that something interesting will happen when the processor begins to act erratically. I am not aware of any reported attack using this technique, but I think that this attack has been successfully applied. The reason I suspect this is because almost all smart cards I have looked at have some form of detection for supply voltage out of range. In almost all cases, the processor is designed to detect low supply voltages.

Structural Tamper Resistance

Most of the simple attack protections listed above are to detect or prevent a fairly straightforward attack. The protection techniques listed below typically assume that the hacker will be able to physically get at the chip. These techniques are designed to make it hard for the hacker to do anything useful once they get to the chip itself.

Bus Scrambling

If a hacker can get to the chip itself, they can place microprobes on the address and data lines going to EEPROM; then they either passively monitor the data crossing the bus or insert specific addresses on the bus and see what data shows up.

The first level of protection is to scramble the address and data lines, so it becomes difficult for the hacker to figure out what address is being touched or what data lives at that address. A simple static scrambling of the address and/or data lines can be broken with patience, so manufacturers have moved to more advanced techniques (some actually based on cryptographic techniques) to mix up the addresses and data. A simple example of this would be to use the last data returned to form an offset for the next address and for data to be accessed. This would make it extremely difficult for the hacker to figure out what is going on.

Fake Bus Transactions

Remember that *Star Trek* episode "The Ultimate Computer" (the original series), when Dr. Daystrom's M-5 multitronic unit kept sending signals down a dormant circuit to fool Scotty and Spock into wasting time disrupting a circuit that was actually dead?

Well, never let a good idea go to waste. This same technique is used on some smart cards to send random addresses and data down the microcontroller bus mixed in with the real data and addresses (which are of course scrambled as described above). This really depresses the hackers because they have no external way of telling what is real data and what is a decoy.

Scotty didn't like it either. Of course, in the *Star Trek* episode, Dr. Daystrom impressed his brain pattern on the M-5 circuits, which caused M-5 to go berserk. Let's hope the smart card manufacturers haven't tried this yet.

Bus Layering

In this technique, the address bus lines are laid on the "outside" of the chip. Stated another way, the address lines are the lines the hacker will first see when they get the epoxy off the smart card microcontroller. Buried underneath the address lines are the data lines and the EEPROM storage area. With this technique, the hacker would have to cut the address lines to get to the data (either the EEPROM or the data traveling over the data bus). Cutting the address lines would render the chip inoperative.

Flattening the Chip

The two bus-related attacks have one basic assumption behind them. The assumption is that the chip is physically laid out like almost all integrated circuits today. If you take a picture of the chip surface, you can see clearly identifiable subsystems connected via bus structures. The CPU is here, the EEPROM is there, the crypto accelerator is in that corner, the I/O logic is in that corner, and so on. The chip is laid out this way for two primary reasons: one is the result of ASIC design, and the other is because of human beings.

Many semiconductor manufacturers allow customers to select microcontroller subassemblies from an ASIC library (I'll take one CPU, two timers, one I/O module, some EEPROM . . .) and stick them all on the same chip. The ASIC compiler basically glues the various subassemblies together without significantly changing their physical architecture. This leads to chips that have clearly identifiable subsystems that are connected by tiny buses.

The second reason this type of layout occurs is when human beings are directly involved with the chip layout or chip testing. The complexity of even these little microcontrollers is so high that the system needs to be partitioned into smaller units easily handled by the designer or tester.

Computers are not so picky. In fact, strict partitioning of the microcontroller functions may lead to less than optimal use of the chip silicon. If a computer is used to lay out the chip, it will frequently optimize the layout on the silicon so that the functional blocks are split across the surface of the chip. Bit 0 of the accumulator may be in the lower left, bit 1 may be in the upper right, and so on.

Taken to its extreme, the chip becomes a uniform sea of gates properly interconnected to create the microcontroller. The concept of chip flattening is exactly this. This makes probing the resultant chip almost impossible since there are no landmarks to help the hacker know where to attach the microprobes.

Differential Power Analysis

I would be remiss if I did not mention an important, but relatively new form of attack on smart cards. A statistically based attack on smart cards named *differential power analysis* (DPA) has evolved as a powerful attack. It has particular use against cryptographic smart cards.

With DPA, the attacker needs to gain access to your reader. Without your knowledge, the attacker will insert a small resistor in the wire that provides power for your smart card. They will also install some sort of meter to record voltages present across that resistor.

As the smart card is happily performing its functions—such as encrypting information—the smart card processor will draw varying amounts of power from the smart card reader. Some instructions draw more power than others. The execution of some algorithms leaves a visible trail in the record of power consumption. The number of bits in a key that are a 1 versus a 0 will determine how much power the smart card will need to read the key from memory to perform an encryption.

If the attacker can record enough repeated operations (such as encryptions), a statistical analysis of the power consumption record can not only reveal the algorithm being used within a smart card, but it can actually expose the keys that are hidden in tamper-resistant memory inside the smart card.

Obviously, this attack requires access to reader hardware, and in its most effective forms requires some information about the cryptographic algorithms being executed within the smart card. Nonetheless, this is considered a powerful attack, and the smart card industry is just beginning to develop protection mechanisms against DPA. Some of the proposed solutions involve scattering the cryptographic computations so that information about the algorithm does not leak out of the smart card. Other solutions involve splitting the key handling and cryptographic operations into smaller operations that can be scheduled with varying random computations to confuse the data gathering. Some hardware solutions involving smoothing the power consumption through on-chip capacitors have also been proposed.

Paul Kocher of Cryptography Research is perhaps the best-known cryptanalyst in this area. Search the Web for "DPA," "Kocher," and "smart card" if you would like to read more about DPA.

Smart Card Recap

Before we move on to the relationship between smart cards and PKI, let's recap the high points of smart cards:

- Smart cards contain small microprocessors embedded in credit card-sized pieces of plastic.
- There are three major classes of smart cards: stored value, crypto, and non-crypto.
- Most smart cards are contact cards where cards are inserted into a reader that electrically makes contact with the smart card.
- Some smart cards are contact-less cards where the connection between the reader and the card is over an RF channel.

- Some smart cards have both contact and contact-less portions; they are called combi-cards.
- Smart cards are evolving to higher-end processors such as 32-bit RISC engines and are evolving toward open operating systems such as JavaCard, MULTOS, and Windows for Smart Card.
- A high-tech cat and mouse game exists between smart card manufacturers and hackers attempting to break a smart card. The tamper-resistance techniques used on smart cards are increasingly ingenious and high-tech. So are many of the attacks.
- We should never imprint our brain patterns on a computer.

Smart Cards and PKI

Smart cards are 2-factor authenticators: something you have (the smart card) and something you know (the PIN). In addition to this, smart cards have secure, tamper-resistant memory to store sensitive information such as private keys. Lastly, smart cards can perform cryptographic computations entirely within the tamper-resistant microprocessor.

These factors make smart cards an ideal companion to PKI. In addition to these issues, many cryptographic smart cards also support the ability to perform key generation within the smart card. Performing *on-card key generation* with early smart cards was not a particularly good idea. Almost none of these early crypto cards had hardware support for generating good random numbers. As we discussed in the chapter on cryptography, good random numbers are the basis for strong keys. Poor random numbers are the basis for weak keys. Without the hardware to generate good random numbers, many of these smart cards generated weak keys. In these situations, it was better to generate strong keys external to the smart card, and pass the strong private key into the smart card to be held in tamper-resistant memory.

With newer smart card chips, such as those from Atmel and Infineon, hardware support for random number generation has been added to the chips. Assuming that the operating system runs on top of these chips takes advantage of this hardware support, it is now better to ask the smart card to generate the public/private key pair within the smart card, and store the private key in tamper-resistant memory. The smart card can then emit the public key so that it can be sent to a Certification Authority to have a digital certificate created. With this type of smart card-based PKI solution, the user will never see or know what their private key is. The private key will never leave the smart card, and all cryptographic functions that require the use of the private key (such as wrapped key unwrapping or digital signature creation) will occur within the crypto card.

Note that not all cryptographic functions should exist within a smart card. For example, when performing a digital signature across a document, which is a megabyte long, one of the first steps in the process is to produce a hash digest of the document. If we decided to perform the cryptographic hash inside the smart card, we would have to send a megabyte of text to the smart card through the half-duplex 9600bps reader interface to the smart card. This would take over 15 minutes to just move the data before the hash could be computed.

Another example of things you should not do on a smart card includes bulk symmetric encryption. The reason is the same. If, for example, the symmetric encryption for an SSL session were to occur within a smart card, all your traffic to Web sites protected by SSL would be slowed down to the equivalent of a 4800bps line as the data to be encrypted was first sent to and then retrieved from a smart card at 9600bps.

Other PKI-related operations are appropriate to perform in the smart card. You would run the cryptographic hash across the megabyte document in the PC, but then send the hash digest to the smart card to be signed by the private key. Similarly, you would perform the SSL symmetric encryption in the PC, but you would pass the wrapped key to the smart card so it could decrypt the wrapped key using the private key within the smart card, and emit the unwrapped symmetric encryption key. As discussed above, key generation is appropriate to perform on a smart card, if the smart card is generating strong keys.

One other reason why smart cards are ideal for use with PKI is that a smart card is very portable. As a result, you can carry your private keys and digital certificates with you in your wallet, and wherever you go, there are your private keys!

Cryptographic smart cards typically support two or more private keys. One private key is used for digital signatures, and the other is your key unwrapping private key. In situations where some form of key recovery system is in place, it is important to be able to archive a copy of your key unwrapping private key. On the other hand, you never want to release a copy of your private key used for signing. To resolve this issue, most crypto cards support both the ability to perform on-card key generation for the signing private key, and external key generation for the key unwrapping key so that a copy of that key can be archived before it is written into the smart card. Refer to Figure 9-16 to see how this works.

Figure 9-16

Smart card
private keys

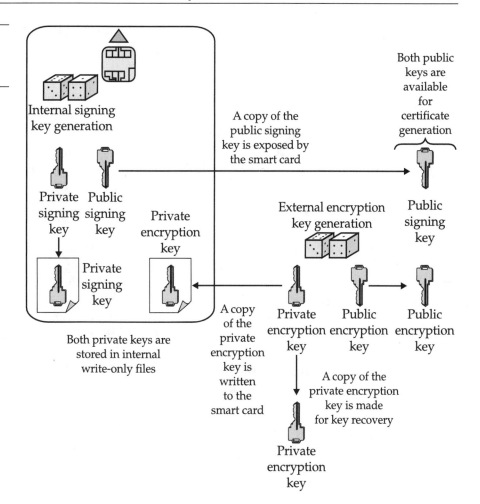

As you can see from the figure, the key pair used for digital signatures is generated inside the smart card. The private key is directly written to a file inside the smart card and cannot be read. The mating public key is transmitted out of the smart card, allowing a request for a digital certificate to be made. As discussed above, the owner of the smart card cannot read their private key, and all cryptography involving the private key must occur within the smart card. This is the ideal way to deal with the generation of your private key used for signing, because it is not possible for two copies of your private signing key to exist, and therefore it is possible to trust that the signatures signed by that private key are authentic.

The situation is a little different with the key unwrapping private key. In many cases, you would like to keep a copy of a person's key unwrapping private key for recovery purposes. If that person's dog ate their smart card, and the only copy of the key unwrapping private key resided on the smart card, it would be impossible to decrypt the symmetric encryption key needed to recover encrypted data sent to that person. This is not the case with the private signature key, since the certificate of the user is all that is needed to check a signature, and that is both publicly available and usually appended to the signed document.

NOTE:

I never know just what to name this private key. It is commonly referred to as your key encipherment key, your key wrapping key, or your private encryption key. I even called it the private encryption key in the figure because it fit a little better. In reality, all of these terms are a little wrong when talking about key wrapping. When using a combination of symmetric bulk encryption with asymmetric key wrapping, the symmetric encryption key is encrypted (wrapped) with the public key of the recipient. As a result, the private key of the recipient is actually used to decrypt or unwrap the symmetric key. That is why I tend to call the private key involved the key unwrapping key.

As a result of this need to keep a copy of the key unwrapping private key, it should not be generated inside the smart card. If this key were generated inside the smart card, the smart card would refuse to divulge a copy of the key, thus preventing the archival operation. Instead, the key pair for key wrapping operations is generated outside the smart card, the private key is copied for recovery purposes, and then the private key is written to the write-only memory in the smart card. The partner public key is then sent off to get a certificate made.

In addition to storing your private keys and performing private key operations, crypto cards typically have storage for your digital certificates. Smart cards are frequently used to store other security-related information that may not be directly related to PKI, including things such as file encryption keys, or perhaps a wallet of your various passwords so you can do away with all those yellow stickies.

For all their good points, there are a few problems with smart cards when used with PKI. The first problem is that most systems do not yet come with embedded smart card readers. This will limit the use of your smart card to those systems that have explicitly installed smart card readers. A related problem is that smart card reader drivers, and smart card-aware cryptographic service providers (such as CAPI and PKCS11 providers) must be installed on systems before smart cards can be used.

Over the last few years, these problems have become less severe. Microsoft now ships the PC/SC smart card framework as an integral part of Windows 2000. Most smart card reader manufacturers now ship PC/SC-compliant reader drivers that make the process of adding a reader a plug-and-play operation. The cost of smart card readers has dropped dramatically over the last few years, so it is fairly easy to find readers at price points less than $20 per unit.

I believe we are at the leading edge of when smart card technology will become ubiquitous, and the security of our PKI systems will benefit immensely from widespread adoption of smart cards.

Biometric Authentication

It would also seem that biometrics are a compelling security device. After all, they are the ultimate way to prove that you are really you. As we will see later in this chapter, it is not quite that simple. It is not easy to compare the security issues of biometrics with other types of authentication. Biometrics have the promise of being one of the best authentication methods, but if not properly used, they can be worse than passwords.

Without a doubt, biometrics capture people's attention and imagination. I have been using several biometric authentication devices for about a year, and they are just plain cool.

How Biometrics Work

All biometric systems measure some characteristic of the user. It can be your fingerprint, your voice, the pattern of lines in the iris of your eye, or something as wild as your body odor (not that you personally have body odor).

In all systems, a master template of the biometric characteristic must be created. When you attempt to authenticate to the system, you will be asked to present your biometric. The reader will take another recording of your biometric data (for example, your fingerprint) and then perform a comparison of the newly captured biometric data with the stored template. If there is a match, access is granted.

We need to examine each part of this process in a little more detail.

Biometric Data

The first thing you need to know about biometric data is that it is based on the idea of a "good enough" match. Every time a user presents their biometric, the data read is a little different.

Let's take the case of fingerprints. Fingerprints are read typically in one of two ways. One type of fingerprint reader takes an optical picture of your fingerprint (like a camera) and then processes the picture in order to create the biometric data. In the other major form of fingerprint reader, a capacitive sensor detects the minute difference in electrical signals from the ridges and valleys of your fingerprint. This data is then processed to create the biometric data.

Each time you present your finger to the fingerprint reader, a different set of biometric data will be created. This occurs for several reasons. First, it is unlikely that you will exactly position your finger on the reader at the exact same location each time. In addition, it is likely that you will rotate your finger slightly differently each time you present it. Sometimes you press harder on the reader than other times. Sometimes your finger is dirty. Sometimes you have cuts on your finger. Sometimes you have ink or other marks on your finger. Sometimes the reader itself causes the variability.

In any case, you can see that the data presented to the system will vary by some amount each time you present the biometric.

One other point you should know about biometric data is that a full record of your biometric is typically not recorded. Using the fingerprint example again, biometric authentication systems do not record the full picture of your fingerprint. Rather, these systems look for interesting characteristics of your biometric and record the position of these features. With fingerprints, these systems are looking for features such as where the lines in your fingerprint end or where loops occur. As a result, biometric data can be fairly compact. A fingerprint template, for example, is typically less than 500 bytes in size.

The issue of a "good enough"—but not exact—match is central to biometric authentication, and we will discuss it more below.

All biometrics share these basic concepts:

- Biometrics measure some physical characteristic of the user.
- The biometric data varies from presentation to presentation.
- As a result, biometrics are not exact matches.
- The full biometric pattern is not recorded, but rather the interesting features of the biometric are stored.

Registration

In all biometric systems, the user must register their biometric in order to create the master template, which can be compared against later. In some sense, you can consider the variability from one presentation of your biometric to the next a form of noise (in the electronic sense). Noise has the interesting property that it is somewhat random, whereas the signal is relatively constant. What this means is that if you take multiple readings of a biometric and then average them together, the noise will tend to cancel itself out, and the signal will reinforce itself.

In biometric systems, you would like to create the best master template possible. As a result, all biometric systems have a registration process where the user is asked to present their biometric multiple times to the system. The system will then average the readings and create the master template. The number of times you must present your biometric to a system varies with the type of biometric, and even with the vendor within a biometric type.

The registration process is one of the most critical stages in biometric authentication because, from a security and biometric matching point of view, you would like to collect lots of template samples to average together to create a wonderful master template. Unfortunately, from an ease-of-use perspective, you would like to collect as few copies of the template as possible so that the user does not find the registration process cumbersome.

Some biometric vendors seem to be getting into a second generation registration process. In some systems I have seen, the user has a fairly simple registration process, where they only present their biometric a couple of times. This will produce a template with significant errors. As the user uses the system, after a successful authentication, the biometric system will average the latest gathered biometric and the previously stored template. The new template then replaces the old stored template. In this way, the more the user authenticates to the system, the better the template will be. I would expect to see more of this type of registration process in the future.

FAR/FRR

Now that you understand that gathered biometric data varies from reading to reading, we need to talk about how the match actually works. Unlike the cryptographic systems we have been talking about up to this point, where we look for an exact mathematical match, biometrics reply on approximate matches. In a biometric system, the matching software compares the newly gathered biometric data with the previously stored template, and asks if the match is good enough. What determines "good enough" varies from system to system and is dependant upon the type of biometric as well as the internal biometric matching algorithms used in the system. In any case, all these systems have a configurable parameter called the *false accept ratio* (FAR) or the *false reject ratio* (FRR).

The FAR is a measurement of the likelihood that a user who *should be rejected* will be accepted by the system as "good enough." FRR is a measurement of the likelihood that the user who *should be accepted* is in fact rejected because the system thinks their match is not good enough.

FAR and FRR work against each other. If you loosen up the system to prevent inappropriate rejections of a valid user, you will make it more likely that an inappropriate user can get in. If you tighten up the system to make it less likely that an inappropriate user can get into the system, you will increase the chance that the valid user is rejected.

Biometric vendors are forced into a game of trade-offs. They need to trade off ease of use, security, FAR, FRR, cost, and performance. As a result, all biometric systems have a different set of characteristics, which to some degree forms their differentiation from other biometric vendors.

The Biometric Design Center

It is very important to understand that biometrics have two somewhat incompatible design centers for their use. Many vendors are introducing biometrics as an ease-of-use feature. Other vendors view biometrics as an authentication and security feature. Sometimes these two uses will conflict dramatically.

Ease-of-Use Biometric Solutions

A good example of a solution in the ease-of-use area is the use of biometrics to start a system like a PDA, cell phone, or notebook. In these systems, the vendors are typically trying to make their devices easier to use by replacing startup passwords with biometric authentication. One vendor I was working with was in discussions with a major notebook computer manufacturer about adding a fingerprint reader to the notebook. Instead of starting the notebook by depressing the power switch, the user would press their finger against the biometric sensor built into the notebook shell. If the match was good enough, the system would boot.

At first glance, you might think that this would increase the security of the system. I guess in some respects it might. But in reality, the security issues were subordinate to the ease of use issues in this design. As I considered this solution, I began to question how the power-up biometric verification would work. The problem is the storage of the template and the protection of the template. If the only action the user performs to start the system is to present their fingerprint, the bios software in the notebook will need to get access to the clear (not-encrypted) version of the template to perform the check for a match.

For this to work, the template must be stored either in the clear, or it must be encrypted with a static key derived from the hardware of the PC. This is because the user is not prompted for a password that could be hashed into an encryption key, nor does the user need to supply the key some other way such as via a smart card. If the user had to enter a PIN or password in addition to the biometric, they would lose the ease of use that was desired. Since the security comes from the PIN or password, you might as well do away with the biometric altogether. As it turned out, the biometric template was indeed stored in the clear as a bios extension. Hardly a secure solution.

In fact, if you think about it, in any biometric system where the template is stored local to the reader, and where the user need only supply their biometric to authenticate the system, the template is likely to be stored in the clear or with a static encryption key. There are some ways around this involving secure hardware. I will talk more about this in "The Holy Grail: Biometrics and PKI" section later in the chapter. As far as I can tell, none of the biometric solutions leverage secure hardware at this time.

Security-Based Biometric Solutions

Obviously, the other end of the spectrum is a security-based biometric design center. Typically in these cases, the biometric is combined with an existing form of authentication, such as a PIN, password, or smart card to create a multifactor authentication—something you are, plus something you have and/or know.

In most security-based biometric solutions, the template is stored in a trusted third party, usually a back-end authentication server. When the user presents their biometric at an agent (usually a PC), the template is passed over an encrypted session (such as server-side SSL) to the back-end server. The back-end server will then look up the user's master template, perform the biometric compare, and then pass back an "accepted" message to the agent if the match is good enough. In these solutions, the database of master biometric templates can be encrypted with a strong key stored, for example, on a smart card or other token. How well the master template database is protected varies considerably from system to system.

Many of these systems can also impose policy decisions at the back-end server. Examples include the need for additional factors of authentication for high-clearance users, or if a user is connecting to a resource protected by a high-clearance agent.

The most popular form of security-based biometric seems to be a 3-factor authentication involving a biometric (typically a fingerprint), a smart card, and the PIN to unlock the smart card. Note that while combining multiple factors together will increase the security of the system, it will also make the system harder to use.

Issues with Biometrics

Now that you have a good foundation in the basics of biometrics, I would like to address some of the problems that are unique to this area.

Coverage

In all biometric solutions, there is some portion of the user community that cannot use the biometric.

If we take fingerprint readers as an example, we can illustrate this problem. Obviously someone who has lost their fingers cannot use a fingerprint reader. But there are many less dramatic things that cause biometric readers to fail in capturing a biometric. A fingerprint reader that measures capacitance needs users whose hands have a certain amount of moisture and elastic skin in order to make a reading. If a user's skin is particularly dry or inelastic, the capacitive reader will be unable to determine where the ridges in the fingerprint are. Elderly people as a group tend to have problems with capacitive readers.

In another example, users who work in construction or machining jobs will also frequently have problems with fingerprint biometric readers. This is because these users tend to wear down their fingerprints or develop thick calluses that make it difficult for the biometric reader to read the ridges.

Other restrictions can occur because of the environment in which the user works. Some users must wear gloves as part of their work, and as such will be unable to use standard fingerprint readers. Examples of this would include healthcare professionals wearing latex gloves, or perhaps Homer Simpson handling reactor control rods.

Each type of biometric reader has issues in different situations. Iris readers may have problems with reflections from glasses or contact lenses. Voiceprint readers will have difficulty in noisy environments such as the floor of the NYSE. Voiceprint readers may reject you if you have a cold. For all I know, body odor biometric readers may reject you if you use a different deodorant.

Biometric vendors are striving to find ways around these problems. One recent example in the fingerprint area is the use of RF fingerprint readers (sometimes called radar readers). These devices do not read the surface layer of your skin, but rather look through your skin to vein, artery, and capillary structures beneath the surface of the user's skin. In theory, these readers should be more immune to effects like dry skin, or surface marks or cuts.

Agent-Side Spoofing

Another issue with biometrics is spoofing. Some biometrics are more resistant to spoofing than others.

One example is voiceprint biometrics. It is fairly easy for an attacker to get a high-quality recording of a person's voice. Most voiceprint biometrics are not like you see in the movies where someone says "My name is Bill Duane; my voice is my passport." (This is from the movie *Sneakers* with

Robert Redford and Dan Akroyd.) That type of system would be too easy to spoof by simply recording a person's voice and replaying it as needed.

In most voiceprint biometrics, the user is prompted to say a phrase that is different each time. The phrase is typically constructed from a series of words that the user uttered during registration. This does afford some protection, but since the vocabulary is typically limited, it is possible that an attacker could index a user's conversation enough to be able to replay the appropriate response. I have heard of some systems where the user must say words or phrases that are nonsense as a way to protect against a verbal spoofing attack.

It would seem that systems that rely on face or iris imaging are also vulnerable to a spoofing attack. None of the systems I have seen are stereographic (two cameras set some distance apart). As a result, the biometric reader (a camera) sees a flat field. An attacker should be able to supply the appropriate picture to spoof the system. Iris systems attempt to get around this problem by making the user move in certain directions (look left, look right, bark like a dog) so the biometric system can determine if the user is really present, or if the image it is seeing is a spoof attack using a photo.

Fingerprints are an interesting area when it comes to spoofing. You leave your fingerprints everywhere. If you don't believe me, just look at your monitor. As a result, it is pretty easy for an attacker who is near you to get a copy of your fingerprint. Once you have someone's fingerprint, it is very difficult to present that fingerprint to a system in such a way that the system would accept it. In the case of capacitive readers, the attacker would need to emulate the capacitance of living tissue and have the right fingerprint pattern on the emulated tissue. I think this is relatively hard to do, but the right kind of foam rubber might work.

Optical fingerprint sensors are somewhat more prone to spoofing attacks. Since an optical fingerprint sensor is basically a camera, if you can fool the camera in the sensor to see a picture of a fingerprint, you can spoof the reader. In practice this is hard, but not impossible to do. Most optical fingerprint readers are based on the angle of total reflection created by the differences in the index of refraction between the glass surface of the reader and the air. See, you should have been listening more carefully in that high school physics class instead of dreaming about that cute person two seats ahead of you. And you thought that you would never use concepts like angle of total reflection and index of refraction ever again. Techniques like sticking a fingerprint image to double-sided transparent tape can partially fool many optical readers, but to completely fool one of the readers would take some work.

I have spent time explaining attacks on fingerprint readers, mainly because they seem to be the most popular form of biometric authentication on the market today. Similar client-side spoofing issues exist for almost any form of biometric; some are significantly more vulnerable to spoofing than fingerprint readers, and others are less. As you evaluate potential biometric solutions, be certain to explore the issues of replay attacks and spoofing so that you have a good understanding of where the use of that particular biometric authentication is appropriate and where it is not.

Server-Side Attacks

An entirely different form of attack occurs if someone can insert their biometric template into the biometric server under somebody else's name. In this situation, the attacker would be able to authenticate as somebody else and inherit that person's privileges.

Replay Attacks

In some biometric systems, it would seem that replay attacks would be a better way to attack the system. If an attacker can get into the reader hardware, or can get into the PC and intercept the conversation between the reader and the agent software on the PC, replay attacks are possible.

If the attacker can record the digital data stream between the reader and the agent software, and then replay the recorded session, they will get into the system.

Many biometric systems attempt to prevent replay of the master template. The matching software in these systems relies on the fact that biometrics will vary from one presentation to the next by some small amount. If the matching software gets an exact match between the master template and the newly recorded biometric data, these systems will reject the authentication.

Unless these systems keep an audit trail of all the biometric data supplied to the system (perhaps a hash of the data), they will not be able to detect when a previously captured biometric (other than the master template) is being replayed at the agent.

Iris pattern biometrics and fingerprint biometrics are systems where the templates are just supplied to the reader, and a match is performed. In some ways this is like supplying a password. Since there is no challenge involved in the authentication, this means the authentication process itself is prone to replay attacks. Since the underlying system architecture does not defend against a replay, other techniques are needed. Most of the proposed techniques involve attempting to perform some sort of *live-detection*.

Live-detection means that in addition to collecting the supplied biometric, the reader will attempt to ascertain if there is also a live person providing the template. Fingerprint readers, for example, could look for a pulse, or perhaps measure some other characteristic of a living fingerprint such as temperature, skin transparency, and so on. If they could integrate a chi detector, we would be all set.

Other systems, like faceprints or voiceprints, where the user reacts to some sort of instruction, are inherently less prone to replay attacks. In some sense, the instruction to say a specific phrase or to make a certain face is like a challenge, and the fact that you properly did it is like the response.

I don't have a clue how easy it is to spoof a body odor, but I would guess that the attacker might be able to raid your clothes hamper and use an appropriate article of clothing to emit your body odor. The mind boggles . . .

Unfortunately, it almost seems that if a biometric is resistant to spoofing, it is more vulnerable to replay attacks. Conversely, if a system is resistant to replay attacks, it seems more vulnerable to spoofing!

Social Issues

You may have noticed that I have yet to talk about laser retinal scans. Those of us who are *Star Trek* fans will recall scenes of Kirk using a laser retinal scan to access the Genesis project data. In addition, there have been James Bond movies where SPECTRE emulated the President's retinal pattern to a laser retinal scanner in order to gain access to atom bombs.

Laser retinal scans are technically a reasonable biometric. They have similar properties as the RF (radar) tissue reader. They read the unique pattern of veins and nerves in the retina of the eye. Nevertheless, you don't see laser retinal scanners on the market. The reason is entirely social. Nobody in their right mind would willingly stick their head into a device that shoots a laser beam into their eyeball. It does not matter what level of UL testing you have, or what the power level of the laser is in picowatts, people won't do it.

Similar social issues exist with the other forms of biometrics. People associate fingerprints with criminals. People don't like the idea that a facial recognition system is recording the image of their face. Speaking to your computer is unacceptable in some settings.

Given the diversity of the world, I also wouldn't be too surprised if there were some cultural or religious taboos regarding the capturing of someone's voice, eye, or face.

Cross-System Replay

Biometrics are different than any other form of authentication you know in one extremely important way. Biometrics have some similarities to an imaginary world where you had to use the same password for everything you tried to do. Let's imagine for a minute that fingerprint biometrics become the biometric of choice (not that far-fetched).

Even today, you can use fingerprint biometrics to gain access to an ATM cash machine—one set of ATMs that supports this is the Purdue Employees Federal Credit Union. At Disney World, they are using hand geometry biometrics for season ticket holders instead of paper tickets—but let's assume it is a fingerprint for this example. New York, Maryland, and Connecticut all use fingerprint biometrics to prevent welfare fraud.

So let's say that I have for one reason or another registered my fingerprints with my local bank, with Disney, and with the state government. The first thing you need to think about is that I only have one set of fingerprints, and my fingerprint is acting like a password. As a result, I have now effectively registered the same password (my fingerprint) with three different agencies. To make this more fun, let's assume that we install a fingerprint biometric system to protect access to your company's computer systems.

While I might be willing to trust that my bank is interested in protecting my master template to a high level of security, should I have the same faith in the state government, or perhaps Disney? Recall that in this example, Disney and the state government are using biometrics for ease of use. It would be entirely reasonable that within the scope of their environment they would protect the master template with an adequate level of security from an ease-of-use point of view, but that this level of security would be insufficient from a security point of view.

It is conceivable that the state government or Disney may happen to buy the same system as we used at your company. In the simplest case, the attacker could spend the morning at Space Mountain and then spend the rest of the day breaking into the system at Disney to steal a copy of their master template database.

They could then try and find a way to slip their master template into your company's biometric authentication system in order to create an account for themselves.

Another possible attack is that the attacker could break into the state master template database and steal a copy of your master template. The hacker could then replay your template and get access to your company as you. Note that the master template from the state would not exactly match the master template registered at your company, so the check for an exact match with the master template would not catch this attack.

This attack works basically because you are using your biometric as a common authenticator across different systems.

Revocation

Biometrics have one other difference compared with any other form of authentication you are used to. Biometric credentials are not revocable.

With passwords, tokens, and private keys, if someone cracks your authenticator, you invalidate the old credential and get a new one. If an attacker gains access to a biometric template of yours, there is absolutely no way to issue a new credential. We don't have the technology to lop off fingers and issue new ones with different fingerprint patterns.

If this isn't bad enough, once a biometric is compromised at one place, all places where that biometric has ever been used are at risk. With passwords, you (usually) don't use the same password at different places (I hope that the PINs for your bank cards are all different). With PKI, CRLs can be used to revoke certificates when a private key is compromised.

With biometrics, if a compromise is detected, there is no way to notify all other holders of master templates for that biometric.

It is foolish to assume that attackers cannot compromise a security system. Proper security design must deal with the possibility that an attacker will succeed in extracting master templates. This is all the more likely when some master templates are stored in the clear or are stored in systems designed for ease of use rather than security.

The inability to perform revocation of a compromised biometric is a serious issue. There is some research in the industry around *revocable biometric templates*. One example of this idea involves morphing the master template before it is stored in the biometric authentication system. For example, let's say that I am using faceprints as my authentication technique. At work, my face recognition system could take my master template and merge it with an image of Barney. The resulting horrifying image could be my master biometric template at work. Each time I authenticated with my faceprint at work, it would capture the image, merge it with Barney, and then attempt the biometric match.

At the local government office, my master template might be merged with one of Big Bird. If an attacker successfully compromised the work master template database, they could not replay that template at my local government office, because the morphs are different. Once it was discovered that my work template had been compromised, I would reregister my face using Lassie as the morph, and never use Barney again as the morphing key. In this way, by revoking the Barney morphing key I have also revoked my morphed template. In addition, I have never stored the original raw template so I don't need to worry about a compromise of my fundamental biometric. To see how this might work, refer to Figure 9-17.

Recommendations

Despite all the technical issues we have discussed with biometrics, people are willing to proceed with the use of biometrics on the basis that (even with the problems) biometrics are more secure than passwords and are easy to use.

In addition, the biometric vendors have subtly moved away from strongly pushing the security aspects of their solutions. They are more aggressively pushing the ease of use aspects. Consequently, I think they will be successful in getting biometric solutions deployed in the marketplace. The presence of ease-of-use biometric solutions in the market will create a pressure to use biometrics as a security authentication solution.

Fortunately, there are some possible biometric solutions which I think deal with many of the issues raised above and allow a secure biometric solution to be developed.

Figure 9-17

Revocable
biometric
templates

 →  →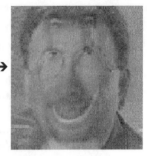

The original image is not
used as a template

It is first morphed with a
master "key"

The resulting horrific,
morphed image becomes
the master template

The Holy Grail: Biometrics and PKI

In solutions where master templates are stored in a back-end server, the templates should be stored encrypted, and the encryption keys should be kept on some form of tamper-resistant memory such as a smart card. It would be good if the templates were protected by some form of revocable template mechanism. Due to the inability to revoke a biometric, this database becomes a highly attractive point of attack. The server can be engineered as well as humanly possible, but we all know that social attacks are frequently more effective, and in this case the motivation to mount a social attack can be high.

I think that a much more secure solution is to remove one of the root problems. If biometrics are used to unlock some secondary but revocable credential, I am much happier.

My favorite example of this is to store your master template in the tamper-resistant memory of a crypto smart card, or a smart card-like crypto device. The user would then have a reader attached to their PC, which has some intelligence, and which is both a smart card reader and a biometric reader. When the smart card is inserted into the reader, the reader would cut itself off from any communication with the PC, prompt the user to supply their biometric, and then pass that biometric directly to the smart card. The smart card would accept the biometric data and compare it to the stored master template. If the match is good enough, it would unlock the smart card as if a PIN had been entered by the user.

At this point, the user's private keys are enabled for crypto, and a normal PKI authentication can occur. From this point on, PKI authentication is used; the biometric is not used again.

To my mind, this solution is close to the ideal biometric solution. It has the following attributes:

- The biometric master templates are not stored in a central location.
- The biometric master template is carried around with the owner, avoiding privacy concerns.
- Since the template-matching process happens in the tamper-resistant smart card, it is not possible to intercept the master template.
- The PC never sees the biometric data (master template or supplied biometric data).
- Spoofing is pretty much defeated because attackers would have to gain access to the smart card in order to replace the master template.
- Replay is pretty much defeated because the attackers would now have to place a hardware interceptor inside the intelligent smart card reader in order to capture the biometric data and replay it.
- Once the smart card is enabled, PKI credentials are used from then on. Since certificates can be revoked, you have essentially replaced a irrevocable credential with a revocable one.

The solution as described is sort of the holy grail of secure biometrics. It is not available on the market yet, although solutions that approach this nirvana are beginning to appear. The reason this type of solution is not yet available is that the processing of biometric templates to determine if the match is good enough is quite CPU-intensive. Until 32-bit processors with high-speed synthetic clocks become more available, this type of solution will be hard to implement. Some interim solutions are beginning to appear where some template processing happens in the PC, and then a reduced template is passed to the smart card for a final match.

Biometric Recap

Here are the major points surrounding biometric authentication:

- Biometric authentication is based on something you are—your fingerprint, your voice, your iris pattern, your body odor.
- Biometrics can be used as 1-factor authenticators all by themselves. This is frequently how biometrics are used in a solution targeted at ease of use rather than security.

- Biometrics can be combined with other factors to create 2-factor authentications. Examples of a 2-factor solution might include entering a password (something you know) along with your biometric (something you are). Another example might be a smart card (something you have) that is unlocked by a biometric (something you are).

- Biometrics can be combined with other factors to create 3-factor authentications. One example would be that you could insert a smart card (something you have) into a reader, then enter a PIN (something you know), and then present your biometric (something you are). The choice of 1-, 2-, or 3-factor authentication depends upon the trade-off desired between security and ease of use.

- Biometrics have issues with spoofing, and need some form of protection such as live detection or requiring the user to perform a different action at each authentication.

- Biometrics are irrevocable credentials. The templates are very personal information and must be properly protected. Templates should always be encrypted, and techniques such as revocable biometric templates should be used wherever possible.

- The ideal solution is just beginning to appear: a combination of a biometric authentication against some local intelligent device such as a smart card, which then releases a secondary revocable credential such as a digital certificate.

- Biometrics are cool.

Wrapping Up Authentication

Before closing this chapter, I would like to reinforce a few key points:

- PKI does not replace the need for authentication, but rather makes strong authentication even more important.

- The strength of a PKI system depends on the trust you have in the Certification Authority as well as the strength of the user's authentication to gain access to their private key. Weak authentication to the private key weakens the entire system.

- We are entering a time where passwords should not be used to protect critical resources. Stronger 2- and 3-factor authentications are necessary.

- Authentication tokens, particularly time-based tokens, are the dominant form of strong authentication. Hybrid PKI-token solutions are currently very popular. In these solutions, PKI is used to authenticate the server and encrypt the session. The token is used to authenticate the client. These hybrid solutions are likely to make tokens a major form of strong authentication for the foreseeable future.

- Smart cards are an ideal place to hold private keys and perform secure PKI operations. Modern smart cards have excellent performance, lots of memory, good on-card key generation support, and run rich multi-application environments. We are at the leading edge of a huge growth in the use of smart cards.

- Biometrics are complex. As single-factor authentication devices, they are easy to use but lack strong security. In combination with other factors, biometrics can help create strong 2- and 3-factor authentication solutions. There is a tension between the use of biometrics for security and the use of biometrics to make systems easier to use. The holy grail combination of using a biometric to unlock a smart card, which then enables your PKI credentials, is not quite here yet but is fast approaching.

CHAPTER 10

Deployment and Operation

Operating a PKI entails a lot more than just generating certificates. Since your certificates will provide a binding statement about a public key and the identity associated with the key, you will need to make sure your PKI is secure. And since installing and running a secure application can be an expensive commitment, you must be sure your business warrants the PKI. Predeployment PKI planning needs to consider a number of issues, including identifying business drivers, application migration to PKI, acceptable user impact, and more. If you decide to go ahead with the PKI, deploying and operating the PKI bring additional concerns. This section covers the major issues to be considered in PKI planning, deployment, and operation.

PKI Planning

This section delves into the issues a PKI planning effort should consider. As you will see, there are quite a few of these issues. We suggest that you don't shortchange the planning effort. If these issues aren't considered before deployment, they are quite likely to arise during deployment, when making changes is much harder. For each planning issue, we describe the major concerns to be addressed, then summarize the decisions a typical company will have to make during its planning process. Although most of the discussion emphasizes user certificates, similar issues can arise for other types of certificates, such as VPN or server certificates.

Business Drivers

The business problem being solved will define the extent to which PKI should be integrated into the corporation. The business drivers for PKI deployment need to be clearly understood or the PKI deployment won't happen. For example, if the business drivers only affect a small percentage of users, the PKI deployment will, at best, be limited. If the business drivers affect most users, the PKI deployment will receive enough corporate attention to succeed on a much larger scale.

Typical business drivers for PKI include the following:

- **E-business** The company wants to expand its e-commerce business and must make sure its transactions are secure. For large transactions, the risk of fraud or theft can spur the company to use PKI to limit its potential losses. For small transactions, the company may want to reduce the costs of resolving disputed transactions.

- **Information privacy, integrity, and authenticity** The company wants to use the Internet as a communications channel between its different locations, or between itself and its partners and customers. These communications may be in a variety of forms, such as e-mail, documents, or drawings, and frequently contain corporate confidential information and intellectual property. Having the communications pass without exposure or tampering is a high priority for the company. The company would like to ensure that the communications are genuine and have not been spoofed or altered by an intruder.

- **Paperwork reduction** The company has to process signed documents and then archive the documents for an extended period to satisfy legal regulations. To reduce its paperwork processing and archival storage costs, the company wants to replace physically signed documents with electronically signed documents.

- **Lower user support costs** Corporate computer users use a large number of applications, each requiring a separate user account ID and password. Dealing with user account administration and forgotten passwords is consuming a growing percentage of helpdesk resources. The company is also experiencing an increased number of security incidents because users write down their passwords or because they leave their accounts continuously logged in so they won't have to reauthenticate.

- **Government regulations** In the United States, the *Federal Drug Administration* (FDA) within the *Department of Health and Human Services* (DHHS) has regulations governing electronic record submissions and the use of electronic signature regulations, under CFR21 Part 11. These regulations specify electronic record guidelines for drug companies that submit electronic records to the FDA. The DHHS is also mandating healthcare regulations for patient information protection under its *Health Insurance Portability and Accountability Act* (HIPAA). Electronic signatures are one mechanism that can be used to protect transactions containing HIPAA information.

- **Increased security** The company has had several security incidents where unauthorized users have accessed sensitive information. The company feels it needs stronger mechanisms for authentication, authorization, and access control.

PKI adoption generally requires a corporate champion to drive the budget process and planning efforts. Preliminary planning may require a committee to evaluate the impact of PKI on the business and the cost-effectiveness of PKI enabling different applications now and in the long term. Gaining corporate buy-in may require having a cross-section of key business units participate in the decision-making process. Making the final go/no-go decision on PKI may require pilot studies to determine the impact on different business functions or to determine the highest payoff applications.

Decisions

- What are the main business drivers for PKI? How will these change in the future?

- Who will be the corporate PKI business sponsor(s)?

- Who will allocate the budget funds for PKI planning? If the decision is to go ahead with PKI, where will the funding come from?

- Who will be the PKI planning focal point?

- How will PKI cost-effectiveness be determined? Pilots? Consultant studies? Who will pay for these?

Applications Planning

Once the business drivers are understood, the company can analyze the applications that will have the biggest payoff with PKI. Some of these may have an immediate fall-out from the business drivers. Other applications may be less obvious—they may not be first-priority business drivers, but if the PKI is in place, they could take advantage of it.

The most common PKI applications are the following:

- **Secure e-mail** PKI can provide integrity, privacy, and authenticity for e-mail messages. If the sender signs an e-mail message with her private key before the message is sent, the recipient can verify the signature to ensure the message was not altered en route and to check that it did actually come from the sender. If the sender encrypts a message with the recipient's public key, only the intended recipient can decrypt the message with her private key. This makes the message private to the two parties.

- **Secure communications** PKI can secure communications over the Internet and other open communications channels. For example, SSL is widely used to secure e-commerce Web communications; its security is based on public key authentication and key negotiation mechanisms. *Virtual private networks* (VPNs) that are based on *IP security services* (IPsec) provide similar capabilities.

- **Secure e-commerce transactions** Digitally signed transactions can provide assurance that the signer did in fact originate the transaction and that the transaction has not been altered en route.

- **Signed software files** Software publishers can sign their files to prove that the files legitimately came from them and that the files have not been altered since publication.

- **Single sign-on** Users can reduce the number of passwords they must remember using single, or reduced, sign-on techniques. Instead of individually authenticating to each separate application, the user authenticates to a PKI credential store, such as a smart card. Authentication client software on the user's computer then transparently intercepts subsequent authentication requests and supplies the correct credentials for each application. Single sign-on is more realistically called reduced sign-on since truly achieving single sign-on is difficult.

If the desired set of PKI applications means changes to existing applications, the company will have to determine how to PKI-enable these applications. Creating a new version that intrinsically supports PKI provides the best integration, but the cost can be high to rework existing software. Other options include inserting a PKI agent or proxy that intercepts legacy communications and transparently adds PKI functions, or adding PKI to the underlying communications infrastructure, such as with IPsec, and not touching the application at all. Finally, the application can be revised to use middleware that supports PKI. This can take the form of secure channel support, such as with SSL.

Decisions

- Which applications will use PKI? Which applications have the highest priority?

- How will existing applications be migrated to PKI? What will be the migration order? How will PKI be added to the application?

- Will new applications have to support PKI? What guidelines will determine which applications must support PKI? Which corporate entity will oversee and enforce these decisions?

Architecture Planning

Regardless of the PKI applications, some base PKI elements are always required. These are a registration authority, a *Certification Authority* (CA), and a certificate repository. Some vendors combine these into a single server; others support separate services. During the PKI architectural planning process, your company will decide how to use these elements in your environment. These decisions will likely be revisited as you gain experience with PKI and as the number of PKI applications and users grows.

You will need to make at least one pass through the other planning topics in this section before you can come up with a first cut at a PKI architecture. For example, the PKI architecture will have to fit with your existing infrastructure. Your support center locations will be a major consideration in placing the PKI servers, as will the applications that will be PKI-enabled and the centers of user population.

The CA architecture is a primary consideration. The simplest architecture is to have the root CA directly issue all certificates (see Figure 10-1).

Figure 10-1

Flat CA
architecture

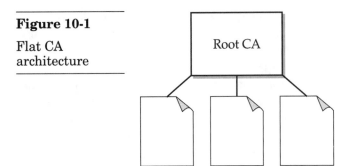

This means that all certificate requests will go directly to the CA. Making
the root CA this accessible, however, is a security concern as it increases
the risk that the root CA's signing key could be exposed or stolen. For this
reason, a hierarchy that removes the root CA from direct access is common (see Figure 10-2). The root CA only issues certificates to its subsidiary CAs and then can be taken offline. The issue then becomes the
number and location of subsidiary CAs. Cost is certainly one factor—the
more CAs, the higher the software, hardware, and operational costs will
be. You may need separate CAs, however, if your corporate locations are
widely separated or if autonomous corporate groups insist on controlling
their own PKI. A more complex CA hierarchy may be needed if you participate with multiple external business partners, such as a group of geographically dispersed banks or merchants. This group may have its own
CA hierarchy established, and you will have to determine how your CA
will fit into this architecture.

Determining whether to separate the registration function from the CA
is another architectural issue. Security is frequently the driving factor,
since having certificate applicants interact directly with the CA opens a
path for intrusion attempts. If these attempts are successful, the trustworthiness of your CA is blown and you will be faced with reissuing all of
your certificates (after locking down the server!). If you only issue certificates internally, direct CA accessibility may not be a concern, but as soon
as external users enter the picture, the security complexion changes.
You're now faced with making your CA accessible from outside the company. If this doesn't make you uncomfortable, it should! Separating the
registration function from the CA and running it on a separate RA server
will let you make the RA server directly user-accessible, whereas the CA
can be tightly locked up behind your firewall. You can also set up different

Figure 10-2

Hierarchical CA architecture

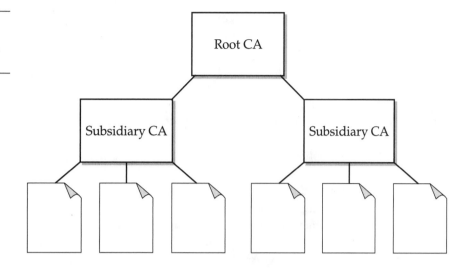

RA servers for internal and external registration and only make one RA server externally accessible. RA servers can also help reduce the traffic to the CA. Figure 10-3 shows an example of architecture that uses regional RA servers. The regional RA servers offload registration traffic from their CA, and can be collocated with the main certificate user populations to improve responsiveness. The RA servers only forward final certificate request messages to their respective CAs. With this architecture, the CA

Figure 10-3

Distributed CA and RA architecture

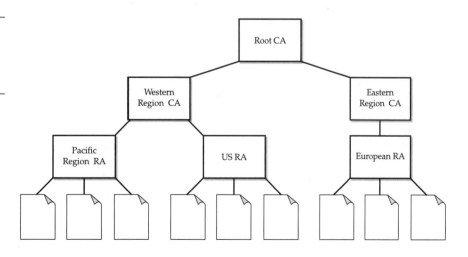

can reside in a secure server facility remote from the user population. The root CA can even be offline as it only has to issue certificates to the subsidiary CAs. Once this job is done, it can be offline until new subsidiary CA certificates are needed.

For added security, many CA products maintain an internal database that is the definitive certificate repository. Permitting direct queries to this database, however, is a security risk. Fortunately, all major CA products publish certificates and CRLs to a separate LDAP directory. PKI applications commonly include capabilities for LDAP queries to retrieve certificate information as part of certificate verification. If your company is widely geographically dispersed, you may need multiple LDAP servers to improve performance. Most LDAP servers support a replication feature to facilitate this. If external certificate query support is an issue, placing an LDAP server on an externally accessible DMZ is a simple answer; however, the external database should only contain data that is acceptable for public access. This may require adjusting the replication process to only copy a subset of the LDAP data to the external server.

Decisions

▦ How many levels should the CA hierarchy have?

▦ Will there be any external certificate users?

▦ Will the CA, RA, and certificate repository functions be consolidated or separate elements? If separate, how many of each element will be needed? Where will these be located?

User Impact

Changing how applications work or adding new applications always impacts end-users. They will have to enroll for a user certificate, a process that is likely foreign to them. If an application that currently requires user ID and password authentication changes to PKI-based authentication, users have to be trained in the new functionality: *The Web site you want to view requests authentication. Select the certificate to use.* Huh?

Users who couldn't remember their passwords before are just as likely to forget the PINs or passwords needed to unlock their PKI credential stores. The helpdesk is going to need training to deal with locked-out PKI users.

Mandating that users have to physically present themselves at a registration authority with their ID in hand may not be possible if 10,000 users have to register in a month. If users are widely scattered at different geographic locations, are the registrars prepared to rack up frequent flier miles? For external certificate applicants, in-person registration may be totally infeasible. If different types of certificates will require different user background checks, users will have to know exactly what identity proofs they must provide to the RA. How will RAs establish that a user does in fact belong to a particular category? Is there a corporate database the RA function can reuse?

Mobile users are invariably a concern. Physically presenting themselves to an RA may be close to impossible for some road warriors. If you have multiple CAs, which one should mobile users obtain their certificates from? Will this certificate be usable everywhere the user travels? Will he or she need more than one?

If the PKI deployment timeframe is immediate, user training and registration will have to be done on a compressed schedule. If deployment can be spread over time, the impact on users and the support infrastructure can be lessened, plus lessons learned can be factored in to smooth the process.

If an RA process seems too complicated for your users, many CA products support a streamlined enrollment process. The enrollment function accesses a database of approved certificate enrollee information. If the user can prove his or her identity, such as with a preassigned password, the enrollment process queries the user's information and automatically generates a certificate request for the enrollee. In many products, the certificate can be automatically approved and installed into the user's system. The user information and passwords can frequently be drawn from existing information repositories.

What does the user do with the certificate once he receives it? PKI applications are not consistent in the type and amount of configuration they require to install a certificate. Browser certificate installation has become fairly painless, but e-mail client configuration can be a challenge even for technically skilled users. If the user wants to use the same certificate in multiple systems, certificate export and import capabilities are unique to virtually every PKI product.

Decisions

- How many users will receive certificates? How many of these users are internal to the enterprise? External?

- Are there different types of users, such as employees, contractors, or temporary employees, customers, suppliers, or partners? Will any of these user categories require different forms of identity verification before they can be issued certificates?

■ What impact on end-users is acceptable to achieve the business goals? New features in existing applications? New applications? How much time can users spend in training without affecting their job performance?

■ Where are these users located? Within a single location, region, or nation?

■ Do users share systems? Do they move from system to system during the day? What percentage of users are mobile?

Support and Administration

Certificate administration will be a new function that an administration group will have to take on. The new certificate administration group will handle initial certificate enrollment, certificate approval, and certificate life cycle management, including revocation, renewal, and replacement. If users have problems with their certificates or with PKI applications, the helpdesk will need additional training and possibly more staff. Since the budget is always tight for these groups, how will the expanded support needs be paid for? Will the additional cost be squeezed out of the existing support budget? Will it be a new budget item? What will ongoing costs be once users adjust to the new applications?

The location of the support group versus the user population is another issue. If users must download certificates and then configure their applications to use the certificates (as with most mail clients), some users will likely need hands-on support. If the helpdesk is remote, how will this be handled?

Eventually, issuing user certificates may become part of user account administration. When a new user account is created, the user is automatically enrolled for a certificate. Behind the scenes, the user account administration function is integrated with the certificate enrollment function. This level of integration may also be desirable for other PKI applications. For example, when the user receives the remote access software, it has already been registered to her and has her VPN certificate preinstalled.

Decisions

- Which support organizations will be involved with PKI support? How well does the location of these organizations map to the population of users, servers, and devices that will receive certificates?

- Will new organizations be needed for certificate registration and identity verification? How much staff and funding will be needed for these functions initially? For ongoing support?

- Will the existing helpdesk support PKI users with certificate usage and PKI applications? If the helpdesk is currently outsourced, will this mean a contract change? If the helpdesk is internal, will more staff or training be needed?

- Will user certificate management be integrated with other user account administration functions? For example, when a new user has accounts created, will he automatically be enrolled for a certificate? If users leave the company, will their certificates automatically be revoked? What level of integration will this require between administrative systems?

Infrastructure Impact

The PKI will add a minimum of one new server, the CA server, to the corporate infrastructure. If the CA, RA, and certificate repository functions are separated, the number of new servers will be larger. The certificate server, in particular, has special requirements, as it must be physically secured.

PKI applications will increase the load on network resources. Certificate enrollment, for example, will be a new application with new network resource requirements. The certificate repository will see increasingly heavy traffic as PKI users and devices query certificates and check certificate expirations. Digitally signed messages are larger than unsigned messages; the same is true for signed transactions. As PKI applications become more pervasive, signed traffic will increase. The end result will be that network resource consumption will increase, even though the business functions being performed may be the same. Infrastructure planning must evaluate the network capacity to the main PKI servers versus the likely population of certificate users and PKI application servers. PKI alone may not require network upgrades, but when other changes planned to the network or other applications are factored in, the network impact may be substantial.

If PKI is used for authentication, the certificate repository server and the network connectivity to it must be highly reliable. Any downtime would mean no authentication service. The CA server and the RA server are less time-critical services. Certificate enrollees can try again later, generally with minimal impact. Certificate issuance, revocation, and CRL generation are usually not real-time functions, although this may not be true for all environments. Financial institutions dealing in large transactions, for example, need to know whether the certificate signing a multi-million dollar transaction is indeed valid at the precise instant the transaction is processed.

If the infrastructure support team is not used to running secure servers, they will need training. The facility in which the CA server will operate must also be physically secured. The PKI platforms must be hardened. (Hardening means turning off unnecessary services, closing all communications ports except those strictly needed for the PKI functions, applying all current OS security patches, and so on.) The CA, RA, and certificate repository servers all should be hardened to prevent attacks that would permit bogus certificates to be issued or false answers on certificate validity checks. The RA, for example, could be altered to put incorrect information into certificate requests or to generate completely false requests. The certificate repository could replace legitimate certificates with false ones. If authentication will be based on the certificate repository's contents, this would amount to changing the authentication credentials.

Backup and recovery processes and procedures are critical for PKI servers and have special security requirements. For example, if a CA server fails, its restoration process must ensure that the certificate database is the correct one and has not been altered.

Decisions

- Where should PKI servers be placed relative to the population of PKI users or devices? Are there secure server facilities in these locations?

- Is the network connectivity sufficient to the preferred server locations? Is extra bandwidth available if PKI traffic grows?

- If network changes are needed to accommodate increased load, whose budget will pay for the changes? Who manages the network infrastructure in the affected locations? Is the network operations group internal or outsourced?

- If PKI functions are used for authentication, are the affected network segments reliable?

- Is the support staff capable of operating a secure server? Will new procedures be needed to describe secure operations? Secure server backup and recovery? Handle security breaches?

Certificate Content Planning

Certificates are just a string of binary data (octets in standards-speak). For an application to be able to use a certificate, it must have some idea of how to parse the binary data. The *International Organization for Standardization* (ISO) originally defined the identity certificate format as part of its X.500 series of standards for directory services. All certificate standards in use today derive from this X.500 base standard, with X.509 version 3 now the fundamental standard for certificate content. According to this standard, certificates must contain certain elements in a specific order to be a valid certificate. The X.509 standard, however, provides choices for how certificate data can be encoded and also has optional extensions. Thus, if corporation A and corporate B choose different optional extensions and different ways of encoding the same information in their certificates, neither will be able to accept and use the other's certificates without extra translation processing. If corporation A then partners with corporation C, D, and E, the problem rapidly escalates and corporation A's software development staff is busy writing certificate translators instead of developing applications.

The concern for certificate interoperability has led to the development of certificate profiles. A certificate profile defines the way that specific certificate elements must be encoded. If a CA states that it issues certificates that follow a specific profile, PKI-using applications have a good idea how to decode that CA's certificates. Example profiles include the Internet X.509 Public Key Infrastructure Certificate and CRL Profile (commonly called PKIX after the name of the IETF working group that is developing it), the *Secure Electronic Transaction* (SET) profile, the *Data Over Cable*

Interface Specification (DOCSIS) profile for cable modems, and the U.S. Federal PKI X.509 Certificate and CRL Extensions Profile.

Adopting a profile may still not provide enough certificate definition, however. Profiles such as PKIX do define basic certificate fields that must appear in certificates, but still provide encoding options for some fields. A subject name, for example, must be encoded as a "directory name," but a directory name can be a teletexString, a printableString, universalString, a utf8String, or a bmpString. PKIX also does not constrain what goes into these strings, stating, "This specification does not restrict the set of attribute types that may appear in names." This can lead to interoperability difficulties between PKIs if each defines different subject name content or applies the encoding options differently. For example, suppose users in corporation A are uniquely identified with a user ID, and corporation A certificates place the user ID in the certificate subject name. Corporation B also identifies users with a user ID, but puts the user ID in the certificate's SubjectAlternativeName extension (this is perfectly legitimate by PKIX rules). When a PKI application tries to extract the user identifier from the certificate, it now needs to handle two cases, both of which are profile-compliant.

Certificates may need to contain specific information depending on the applications that will use them. User or device identifiers are common. Certificates used for signed e-mail must contain the user's e-mail address. Professional attributes such as job title or professional certification may also be required if the user is signing as an official function of her office. PKIX allows considerable flexibility for certificates to contain custom, private extensions.

If users will be issued a single certificate for signing and for encryption, the profiles state that the certificates must contain specific extension values. The Certification Authority may permit some flexibility in the algorithms and key lengths possible in its certificates. You will need to determine which algorithms and key lengths provide the best trade-off between security and performance for your environment. Your corporate security policy may come into play here (if your company is seriously considering PKI and doesn't have a security policy, you will need to develop one to document your corporate security roles and responsibilities. Reconsider hiring that security consultant!). If the keys will only be used internally and your company security policy is lenient regarding internal-only cryptography, you may be able to use shorter keys and save some processing cycles.

Publishing certificates to an existing directory structure can be an issue if the CA's determination of the directory *distinguished name* (DN) for publication doesn't match the DN for existing directory entries. One case might be if your corporate structure is reflected in your internal directory schema but not in your certificates. You may need customization software from the CA vendor to adjust the DN that their product will use for publication.

Determining the certificate format requires knowledge of the current status of certification standards as well as CA product capabilities. This may be a good area to use consultants with specialized expertise.

Decisions

■ Are any certificate profiles applicable to your PKI? How well do these align with your other PKI application needs?

■ Which encryption algorithms and key lengths will be used in the certificates?

■ Will certificates be used for both signing and encrypting? Will separate signing certificates be issued?

■ What certificate fields are needed for your PKI applications? To support partners? Which optional extensions will you use? For example, will you include the *uniform resource identifier* (URI) for your certificate policy?

Database Integration

Most large companies are moving to centralized repositories of user data, such as LDAP directories. Others have centralized their user account administration. The certificate repository may need to be integrated with these existing user data repositories.

If certificates must be published to an existing directory or database, you will need to determine how well the existing schemas map to the default CA publication schema. For this discussion, we assume you'll be publishing to an LDAP directory, since that's the most common directory for certificates. First off, you'll have to determine if your certificates will be published to a new part of the directory or added to existing entries. For example, will a user certificate be added to the user's existing LDAP record? If the directory and CA schemas are widely different, or the CA doesn't support directory publication, this can require CA product customization.

If you don't have an existing directory and are using certificate registration to build up your user database, you may need the certificate registration process to collect information that will be published to the directory, but not put in the certificate. Not all CA products support this capability out of the box, so you may need to pay for customization.

On the other hand, existing directories can be leveraged to streamline certificate enrollment. The RA can retrieve data about an enrollee from the central database and prepopulate enrollment forms. These queries can even be done behind the scenes, turning certificate enrollment into a one-step, transparent process for enrollees.

Revoked and expired certificates are another database issue. Revoked certificates need to be stored so that signatures on old documents can still be verified. These certificates, however, will consume storage space. You will need to decide how long to store certificates and when old certificates can be archived. If the database stores multiple certificates for a user, you must determine how to make sure certificate queries return the correct certificate. One option is to let expired and revoked certificates remain in the directory, but with a different object type that marks them as invalid.

If certificates are used for authentication and will be integrated with a centralized authentication function, you will need to consider how certificates relate to user accounts. You may want to synchronize the certificate and user account databases so that a user automatically receives a certificate when she is issued a corporate account. Terminated users are another consideration. Ideally, the user's certificate should be automatically revoked when her corporate accounts are closed. If the company has layoffs or sells part of the business, you may need to perform these functions on a large scale in a short period of time. Integrating certificates with user account management may require custom software integration between the CA and your account administration products.

Decisions

- Will existing corporate databases be used to streamline certificate enrollment?

- How well does the CA's default directory publication schema map to the existing directory schema? Can the CA product be tailored to match your schema? Will this require customization?

- Will revoked and expired certificates be left in the database?
- Will a certificate repository be integrated with user account management? Will this include new user accounts? Terminated employees? What about layoffs? Will this require custom software? Is this software in the planning budget?

Legal and Policy Considerations

A certificate is a Certification Authority's statement that the public key in the certificate is valid and that other information given in the certificate, particularly the identification data, is bound to that public key. If your company is going to issue and rely on certificates, the CA's statements have to be trustworthy, where trustworthiness is determined in large part by the CA's operational practices and the policies it implements. For CAs that issue certificates to external parties, these are spelled out in the CA's *certificate policy* (CP) and its *certification practices statement* (CPS) (see Chapter 7, "Application use of PKI," for a detailed discussion). For internal usage certificates, you still need to address these topics, but you may decide to document your procedures in your corporate security policies. Recall that the CP and CPS documents state the CA's legal warranties and its limitations on liability. These documents are not required by law (yet) for commercial CAs, but you will have a far stronger case in any disputes if you have them. Your corporate lawyers should be involved in creating your CP and CPS, and will want to review your business partners' documents if you engage in PKI-based transactions with them. RFC 2527 provides content descriptions for CPs and CPSs. You may want to hire a consultant who specializes in this area to help guide your document creation.

CPs and CPSs are important considerations for cross-certificates (see the "Trust Models" section for more on cross-certification). Before issuing cross-certificates, each company must determine how well its policies and practices match those of the other company. Assuming that both sets of lawyers can be satisfied, the certificate mapping is technically implemented with the policy mapping certificate extension, covered in detail in Chapter 7. Your planning analysis must determine if you will need to use this extension to define one or more mappings between pairs of policy object IDs between your policies and policies in the other company.

Certificate registration procedures will likely be an important consideration in your legal concerns. The registration procedures must spell out how a certificate applicant will authenticate to your CA or RA. These concerns will be different if your CA is a public CA versus a private, corporate CA. Some of the areas these procedures must cover include:

- What identity proofs are required for the different certificate categories you may issue? For example, will external users be identified differently from internal users? What identity proof is required for server certificates? Device certificates? Software publisher certificates? How much user impact is acceptable before users refuse to comply?

- How will the CA or RA validate these proofs? Will a human RA have to examine a company ID, a driver's license, a memo on corporate letterhead? Will an automated RA query information from an internal database?

- Will your RA or CA require proof of possession? *Proof of possession* (POP) means the applicant proves that he does in fact have the private key that goes with the public key in the certificate request. In general, this means that the requestor performs a function with the private key that matches the key type in the request. Or, in plain English, if the request is for a signing key certificate, the requestor signs the request with her private key. If it's for an encrypting key, the requestor encrypts some data that the CA or RA provides. The PKIX standards require POP but allow some leeway on how it is determined. Your RA or CA will need to consider how to meet this requirement for the different types of certificates it will issue and for each different way in which it accepts certificate requests. If the applicant does not have the key at the time of the request (for example, the private key is on a smart card that will be assigned to the user), POP will not be possible.

The validity period of your certificate is another issue with legal ramifications. Since your CA is making a legal statement about the entity named in each certificate, you may want to limit your exposure by making certificate validity periods short. That way, if the certificate is misused or its associated private key stolen, your risk is reduced. On the other hand, issuing and reissuing certificates increases overhead costs, so you may want to limit these costs (and user angst) by lengthening validity periods. One approach is to define certificate categories and make the certificates used for more sensitive functions have shorter life spans. This reduces the risk associated with private key theft for those certificates. The most sensitive keys are the CA signing keys, with the root CA signing key being the most sensitive of all. Expiring CA certificates frequently, however, is not a good idea since transitioning CA keys is complex. Other mechanisms, such as storing the signing keys in hardware and physically securing CA access, are more viable options. Your validity periods and any other means you will use to reduce private key exposure risk should be stated in your CPS.

Since certificates have finite lifetimes, they will expire periodically. Will certificate users be able to renew their certificates? What will this process entail? Will it be a repeat of the initial registration procedure? A simpler scheme is to have the applicant present some form of re-authentication data, such as a challenge phrase. What about Certification Authority certificate renewal? How will certificate users obtain the new CA certificates? Cross-certification certificates will also expire. Given the complexity of cross-certification, you will need to decide if you must revalidate the other company's CP and CPS for each renewal.

What happens if someone forgets the password to unlock his or her private key? What if the laptop storing the private key is stolen? What if they think someone has tampered with the laptop and might have copied the private key? In these cases, you will want to revoke the certificate that goes with the private key. You will therefore need a policy defining how certificate revocation will be handled. Who will have the authority to revoke certificates? What is the process? Since reissuing certificates can require lengthy background checking, will you implement the capability to suspend a certificate while an investigation decides if the certificate really should be revoked? If you do revoke a certificate, you will need to create an audit record of the requestor, the revoker, and the reason for the revocation in case of disputes. Once you revoke a certificate, you will need to generate a *certificate revocation list* (CRL) entry to notify other certificate users that the certificate is now invalid. This also means that you will have to decide how often to issue CRLs. Weekly CRLs are common; however, if risk from using a revoked certificate is high, you may need to issue CRLs more often. High-value transactions, for example, can require virtually real-time revocation checking.

Digitally signed data doesn't add any security value if the recipient doesn't validate the signature and the certificate associated with the signature. Full validation (covered in Chapter 4, "PKI Services and Deployment,") means performing the mathematical operations to verify the data signature, check that the certificate is within its validity period, check that the certificate has not been revoked, and verify the signing certificate's signature as well as all of the CA certificates in the signing certificate's trust chain. This is obviously a lot of computation. You must make a policy decision on whether to require full validation each time a signature must be verified. An alternative is to cache information about certificates that you have successfully validated within a specific time period. How long to make this period will depend on your risk from accepting an invalid signature.

Checking whether a certificate has been revoked means checking the certificate's serial number against the issuing CA's certificate revocation list. You can obtain the CRL from the CA and check certificates against it locally. Alternatively, some CAs support a protocol called the *Online Certificate Status Protocol* (OCSP, discussed in Chapter 6). You can send the CA (or its designated responder) a protocol request about a particular certificate and receive a real-time response. Note that the OCSP responder may just be working off the same CRL you could have downloaded yourself. Using OCSP does not guarantee up-to-date revocation information, but it can save you from having to process the CRL. Note also what the presence of a certificate's serial number on a CRL means. Since CRLs are only issued periodically, if the certificate is listed on the CRL, it was revoked sometime between the last CRL issuance and the current one. The CRL does not state when in that time period the certificate was revoked. So, if you relied on that certificate during the period between CRLs, you may have actually accepted an invalid certificate! If your transactions require more precise granularity, you will need to arrange for more frequent CRL generation.

What if someone—a business partner, for example—disputes a transaction associated with a certificate from your CA? If the dispute requires legal adjudication, your company may be required to submit evidence about how its CA operates, how certificate keys are generated, and its policies regarding private key protection. What if the dispute occurs after the certificate has expired, although the certificate was valid at the time the transaction occurred? Will you maintain archival copies of certificates and CRLs? Your legal staff may need to provide guidance on the data that will need to be archived and the archival periods.

Decisions

- Your CA should comply with one or more certificate policies. It should operate in accordance with a certification practices statement. Who will develop these documents? Will you require outside assistance with them?

▓ Some of the topics that need to be covered in the certification practices statement include the following:

- Registration procedures for internal users, external users, and other certificate requestors, such as devices or servers. The registration procedure must spell out how certificate requestor identity will be verified.

- Renewal procedures for expiring certificates. These procedures must describe how identity will be assured for the new certificates.

- Certificate validity periods. How long will your certificates be valid? Will all types of certificates be valid for the same period?

- Certificate revocation. Who can revoke certificates? What should the policy be for when certificates must be revoked?

- Certificate revocation lists. How often will you generate these? Will you support an online query service such as OCSP? If not, how will you distribute your CRLs?

- Signature validity checking. Your PKI applications will rely on digital signatures for security. What are your corporate guidelines for signature validation? Does the entire certificate chain have to be revalidated each time a signature is verified?

Trust Models

A trust model defines the PKI trust relationships that meet your corporate security standards. Your PKI will accept certificates issued within the constraints of its trust relationships as valid. In short, the trust model says that by accepting certificates from a specific signer, you trust that signer. Chapter 8 provided an in-depth discussion of trust models; this section addresses the trust model issues you will need to address in planning your PKI deployment.

Trust models should not be taken lightly. If you decide to trust certificates from a CA who turns out to have poor security practices, you could open yourself to fraud (certificates that make bogus identity statements), theft (certificates that contain stolen identities), and attack (the CA's own identity is stolen, permitting man-in-the-middle attacks that appear completely genuine). Thus, trust models are a security policy and legal issue even more than a technical one. In general, if a company operates an internal CA and issues certificates to its employees, the company policy states that its users will trust the corporate CA. Before your company decides to trust certificates from an external CA, however, it should carefully review the CA's certification practice statement and certificate policies (see the "Legal and Policy Considerations" section). Your lawyers will need to review the CA's documents versus your own policies to see if the company will be exposed to additional liability by trusting the CA. Note that even individual users have trust models. Both Netscape and Internet Explorer browsers come with a number of root signer certificates already installed—an embedded trust model. You can choose whether to keep these signers or to delete them.

Trust models are of particular importance for companies who have their own internal CA and who then want to do business with other companies who also have an internal CA. Assuming the legal reviews go well, the companies have these main technical approaches to establishing trust relationships between their respective certificate authorities:

- Two sets of certificates, where each company issues a new certificate to the other company's users. Each user will thus have two certificates: one from their company and one from the other company. If the companies are large, the overhead alone may be too high to make this option realistic. Even if issuing a second set of certificates is feasible (and the users can deal with ensuring they will always use the correct certificate for each transaction!), the companies will likely have trouble verifying identities at the other company sufficiently to meet their CPS requirements.

- A hierarchical trust model, where the two companies establish a higher-level root that signs the public key of each company's root CA and acts as a trust anchor (see Chapter 8). For example, both companies may agree to participate in a consortium, such as a group of banks that agree to join in a common PKI.

- Multiple trusted roots installed into every application. In most cases, this means modifying each client to include additional trusted root certificates.

- A cross-certification model, where each company's root CA signs the public key of the other CA. Note that this model can be one-way or two-way. In a one-way trust, only one company trusts the other's CA; thus, only one cross-certification certificate is produced. In a two-way trust, both companies trust the other's CA, so each creates a cross-certification certificate.

An example will help explain the issues with trust models. Figure 10-4 shows a typical CA architecture that might be used within a company. This CA is autonomous since it is not related to any other CAs. This architecture has two levels of signers: a root CA and two subordinate CAs that sign user certificates. In PKI parlance, this CA architecture implements an autonomous, hierarchical trust model.

Figure 10-4

Hierarchical trust model

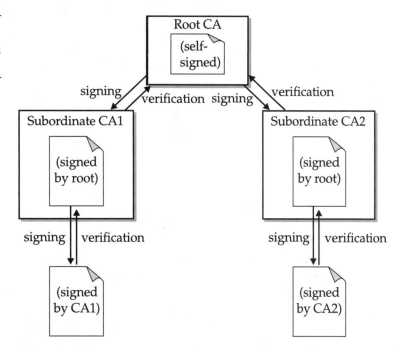

In Figure 10-5, we expand to two corporations, each with a separate, autonomous, hierarchical PKI architecture. In this example, corporation A and corporation B both have major offices in the United States and in Europe. Corporation A has 20,000 users in the U.S. and 5,000 in Europe. Corporation B has 15,000 users in the U.S. and 35,000 in Europe. The CA hierarchy for each company has a subordinate CA in the United States and another subordinate CA in Europe.

Assume that corporation A and corporation B become business partners. As part of their business arrangement, they want to exchange secure e-mail and submit digitally signed transactions to each other. Due to the number of client applications that would need to be revised if they chose

Figure 10-5

CA hierarchy
before cross-
certification trust

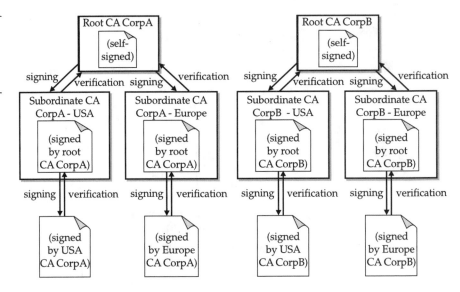

to install the other company's root as a trusted signer, they prefer to see if one of the other alternatives would have less IT overhead. Creating a new, common root CA isn't feasible for them—they are planning business partnerships with other companies, and establishing a common root with each partner will rapidly get out of hand. They want a strategy that they can use in this partnership that will also be expandable to other partnerships, and that can be easily severed if the partnership is dissolved.

They first consider issuing new certificates to the users in the other company. Each user involved in electronic commerce between the two companies would be issued a corporation A certificate and a corporation B certificate. For example, the corporation A employee would use its corporation B certificate if it were generating a transaction going to corporation B so that corporation B could verify the signature. If the two corporations decided to terminate their partnership, each company could simply revoke the certificates issued to the other company. In investigating the costs of implementing this option, corporation A finds that the license with their CA server vendor permits them to issue up to 35,000 certificates. To issue up to 50,000 additional certificates to corporation B will require a new license (and make the CA vendor very happy). Although the cost per certificate will be lower at the higher volume, the additional cost could be substantial. Corporation B's license allows them to issue an unlimited number of certificates. Their main helpdesk, however, is located at their

European headquarters. Supplementing this to accommodate registration and support for corporation A's largely U.S. user population will be expensive. Both corporations decide issuing new certificates is not a cost-effective option.

They next consider cross-certification. With cross-certification, each company would still control its own internal CA and issue certificates to its own employees. They would decide to trust certificates issued by the other company's CA. Since establishing this trust is primarily a legal issue, each company must review the other company's certificate policies and PKI implementation to determine if their own policies can be maintained with the trust. The technical issues are simpler: each CA would create a single new certificate, a cross-certification certificate for the other company. Corporation A would create a certificate containing corporation B's root signer's public key that is signed by corporation A's root signer. Corporation B would create a comparable certificate with corporation A's root signer's public key. In other words, each root CA would certify that the other company's root signer's public key is legitimate.

After completing their legal reviews, the two corporations decide to implement cross-certification. As shown in Figure 10-6, once the cross-certification is established, corporation A will verify a transaction signed with a corporation B certificate by treating corporation B's root signer as an intermediate corporation A Certification Authority. The transaction signature can be verified with the cross-certificate, then the cross-certificate itself can be verified with corporation A's root signer certificate.

Cross-certification can also occur within corporations. Assume that corporation A acquires another company, corporation C, which already has an established PKI. Corporation A will eventually issue new corporation A certificates to these new users. A short-term strategy would be to establish a cross-certification relationship with the existing corporation C PKI.

These models are founded on the concept of a root signer that is trusted. But what if a false certificate could be inserted that claimed it was a root signer? For this reason, many CAs create their root signing certificate, generate subsidiary CAs, then take the root signer offline, and move its signing key into protected storage. The root CA's public key certificate must be installed where it can be used to verify other certificates in its hierarchy. Many browsers come with signer certificates already installed. How do you know that these are legitimate? You will need to determine how to acquire and distribute root signer certificates securely to your certificate users.

Figure 10-6

Cross-
certification
architecture

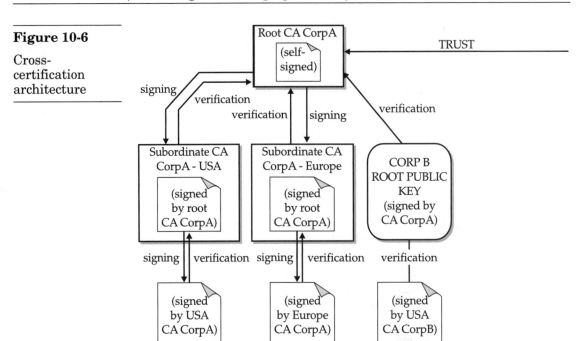

Note that not all PKI products currently support all of the trust alternatives outlined in this section. For example, not all applications easily support the addition of new trusted roots, and not all CA products can generate cross-certificates.

Decisions

- Do you need to establish trust relationships with other CAs? Is your legal staff capable of reviewing CPs and CPSs? Will you need to hire special expertise?

- Which trust model will your PKI use? Do the products you're considering support this model?

- Do PKIs exist elsewhere in your company that may need to be integrated in the future?

- How will you distribute your trusted root's signing certificate to your PKI users? Will any other trusted roots need to be deployed?

Figure 10-6

Cross-
certification
architecture
(cont.)

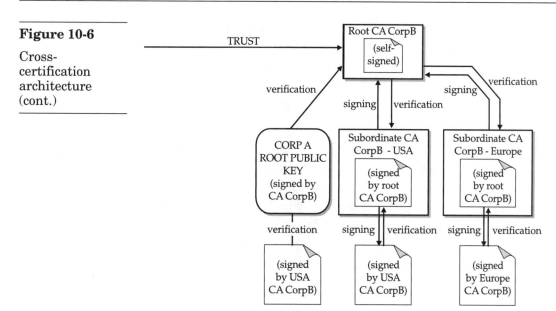

Deployment Considerations

You've completed your PKI planning and are ready to begin deployment.
The first PKI application will be a secure mail application. The lawyers
and your PKI consultant are busy writing your CP and CPS. What do you
do next? Since PKI is a complex undertaking (just consider all the planning issues!), most PKI adopters elect to deploy their PKI in phases. Here
are typical phase breakdowns:

- **Testbed** You bring in several leading vendor's products and kick
  their tires. You evaluate them for their ability to accommodate your
  user population, the types of certificates you will need, and your
  administrators' ability to understand their software. At the end of the
  testbed phase, you should have a preferred vendor and a backup
  candidate.

- **Vendor negotiations** Although not really a deployment phase,
  negotiating the final contract with the product vendor can take longer

than you expect. If your needs don't map exactly to the vendor's product capabilities, for example, you will have to negotiate customizations. Sometimes these can be bundled in with the product licenses; other times they will be an additional, and possibly substantial, charge. Your negotiations may take several iterations to smooth out the contractual details.

■ **Installation**   You set up the secure location for the CA server and install, configure, and test the CA product. If you are using a separate RA, this is also installed, configured, and tested, as are any directory and database integrations. Part of the CA installation will be signing key generation. You should have decided before installation whether to store the signing key on a separate, secure hardware device or in an encrypted file on the CA server. You can decide whether to harden the server platforms before installation and ensure that everything works before locking down the systems. Before you begin production, however, the servers should be fully hardened.

■ **Pilot**   A pilot phase will help your company gain operational experience with the CA product and the PKI application before full-scale deployment. In this phase, you will issue certificates to a limited set of users. These users will also install and configure the pilot PKI application. Feedback from these users will be invaluable for uncovering potential problems with the CA, RA, your integration software, training, support, the PKI application, and your deployment procedures. The users' response to this first application will be a telling indicator of how easily PKI will be adopted, particularly if the pilot user population represents a typical cross-section of the final population. Since pilots usually do have a few kinks, you may want your pilot certificates to have a short expiration and plan for reissuing certificates to pilot users in the full deployment phase. Be sure that all of the certificate types that you will deploy are covered in this phase, such as user signing certificates, device certificates, server certificates, and software publisher certificates.

■ **Limited deployment**   This phase begins production rollout, so it should begin with a security review of the PKI servers. You may even want to reinstall the server software on freshly hardened servers. The first wave of support staff should be trained, where training will include product operation and should encompass the issues that arose in the pilot. The certificate users may also receive formal training to help them understand the PKI functions they will be using. As the deployment begins, you will want to develop a procedure for capturing lessons learned so they can be factored into the full deployment.

■ **Full deployment** During this phase, you roll out the rest of the certificates and install the PKI application for the remaining users. The number of stages in full deployment will depend on the number of certificates to be issued, the geographic distribution of the certificate users, the support staff's ability to handle a growing population of certificates, and the speed with which the support staff and users can be trained.

Decisions

■ What will be the schedule and resource commitments for each phase? How long will each phase last?

■ Where will the production servers be installed? Do you have guidelines for operating secure servers?

■ Will training be purchased from vendors or created in-house?

■ Who will have the responsibility for product selection, vendor negotiation, hardware procurement? Where will the budget funds for these items come from?

Operational Considerations

The trustworthiness of your certificates will depend on the CA server's security. Your operational security policies must spell out administrator guidelines for ongoing secure CA server administration. The certificate administrators should be trained in operating and maintaining a tight-security server. The security guidelines should include reviewing the CA server's platform hardening on a regular basis. Part of ongoing administration should be keeping the server platform up to date with the latest operating system and security patches. Using security-scanning tools is a great way to find configuration flaws, as is running your own penetration tests.

Administrator access to the CA should be limited to the smallest possible number of staff. These administrators should use strong authentication to access privileged functions on the CA server. If the administrators are remote, their administration sessions should not only be strongly authenticated, they should also be encrypted. The administration interface, for example, should implement peer-authenticated SSL or use a VPN with additional application-level strong authentication. All administrator actions, including certificate approval, rejection, revocation, and server platform administration should be logged. This will give you an audit trail if you do have a security incident or if there's a question over which administrator performed an action.

Although certificates have a finite validity period, their legal life span may last longer. For example, transaction records or documents may need to be stored for several years to satisfy government regulations. If this is true, you will need to maintain an archive of expired certificates so that the transaction records can still be verified. This archive must be secure so that the certificates cannot be replaced with false ones. If that occurs, archived signed documents won't be verifiable or might even be altered. If you do archive old certificates, you will need to determine how long to keep expired certificates, how these certificates will be protected, and the procedures for accessing them.

The certificate server's database must be backed up just like any other database. Since this data is highly security-sensitive, however, special backup procedures are needed to ensure the data is not altered or corrupted. For example, if the database fails and is restored from a tampered backup copy, previously revoked certificates could be designated as valid. Or, even worse, valid certificates could be replaced with false certificates allowing impersonation. The backup media must be stored in restricted-access, fireproof, protected storage. The backup data should also be protected, such as with passwords or encryption. This will help prevent stolen backup media from being used or tampered with.

The CA's signing keys will need ongoing protection. If the keys are stored in an encrypted file, the CA server will likely require a password, PIN, or other authentication to access the key. Who is permitted to know the password? If the key is stored on a hardware device, who will know the data needed to unlock it? What if these staff leave the company, go on vacation, are out sick, or get hit by the proverbial bus? You should have a backup strategy for gaining key access. Another consideration is whether to trust individuals with this data. If your certificates are used for high-value transactions, you may want to consider a shared secret scheme. The key access data can be divided into shares, with each individual assigned a share. Thus, multiple people will be needed to restart the server. This provides more security at the cost of a more cumbersome procedure.

As more users and applications use PKI, you will need to determine how they will obtain the trusted signers they will need. Bootstrapping this process will likely be the hardest part (and should be addressed during deployment!). Once certificates can be obtained in a secure fashion from a known valid source, the process gets easier. You may want to consolidate your corporate trusted root signers into one location so they can be easily downloaded or packaged for application use.

CRLs will also be part of ongoing CA operations. Your planning process should have determined an initial schedule for CRL publication. As you gain experience with your CA, you may need to adjust this schedule. As more applications use PKI and require CRLs, you may decide to implement a certificate status checking protocol, such as the *Online Certificate Status Protocol* (OCSP), as described in the "Legal and Policy Considerations" section.

One of the most complex operational problems will be how to renew or replace root CA keys. With certificate expiration, you can plan the changeover and spread the new certificate installation over time. Current practice is to issue a new certificate with a validity period that overlaps the expiring certificate. That way, both certificates will be valid during the transition period. The worst case will be if the root CA's signing key is revoked. In this case, all certificates relying on this certificate must be revoked and reissued with the new CA signing key. If you have a large number of certificates, this can be a massive effort. You will have to determine how to send your CA users the new root CA key securely. The upheaval associated with a CA key revocation could provide opportunities for hackers to introduce new signers that appear legitimate.

Summary

This chapter takes a different perspective on many of the concepts introduced in earlier chapters; it looked at the decisions that you would have to make to put an actual PKI into place. The issues examined covered planning, deployment, and operations. Since PKI deployment must consider a number of technical, budget, and support issues, the emphasis here is on careful consideration before jumping into a deployment. Each topic has a summary list of questions that should help guide your PKI planning.

CHAPTER 11

PKI and Return on Investment

This chapter is not about technology; it's about time and money. That is, organizations often ask for help with not only the technology case, but also the business case for their investments in Public Key Infrastructure—in other words, what is the *return on investment* (ROI) for PKI?

This is not always an easy question to answer—PKI is an e-security *infrastructure*, after all, and the ROI for infrastructure of any kind can be extremely difficult to quantify. Some don't try and have implemented based more or less on a leap of faith. At some point, however, we can observe that the ROI for infrastructure often becomes *unnecessary* to quantify, because the capabilities it enables are both mission-critical and well understood. For example, when is the last time any large business required a return on investment analysis to determine whether or not it should invest in enabling infrastructure such as telephones, facsimile machines, or e-mail? This chapter is developed from the present perspective that ROI for PKI is somewhere between too difficult and not necessary, somewhere between a leap of faith and a matter of course.

The objectives of this chapter are to provide reasonably fine-grained frameworks for both the "investment" and the "return" components of the PKI ROI equation, to advance the level of practical detail in discussions about the business case for PKI, and to generate specific ideas for PKI ROI analysis. It is not an objective—nor is it possible, given the innumerable e-business processes that can potentially leverage PKI as their e-security foundation—to provide a single set of formulas or templates into which one can simply plug numbers and compute the one right answer.

Total Cost of Ownership: The "I" in ROI

How much does Public Key Infrastructure really cost? When the financial returns are difficult to quantify, the investment side of the ROI equation—that is, the *total cost of ownership* (TCO) for a particular implementation of PKI—is naturally the initial subject of focus. In 1998, when commercial PKI products and services were first coming to market, a competing pair of reports from respected industry analyst firms attempted to address the question of TCO for PKI. Fanned by marketing hype, these reports initially received a considerable amount of attention, but ultimately lost credibility on at least two major counts. First, their frameworks for listing all the potential cost elements for licensing, deploying, and managing a PKI were inconsistent and incomplete. Second, and related to the first, they were generally perceived as being overly biased toward their respective vendor sponsors, although undoubtedly this was simply a remarkable coincidence.

Here we provide a general, comprehensive, and unbiased framework for capturing the various elements of cost currently involved with implementing a PKI. In considering this framework, however, there are three obvious but important caveats to keep in mind:

- *Use incremental analysis.* TCO calculations should include only those investments that are incremental to those which have already been made. For example, if directory services have already been purchased and deployed, these sunk costs should *not* be included in the TCO calculation for a new investment in PKI. If, however, the deployment of PKI were to require upgrades, expansions, or other incremental costs associated with directory services, these incremental costs *would* be included in the TCO calculation.

- *Use the line-item veto.* PKI is a sophisticated technology with many available options, and obviously not all options are required for every business process. If the TCO framework lists a particular cost element that doesn't apply to the particular business environment under analysis, simply cross it out. For example, some deployments will install client software at the end-user desktop; others won't.

Some deployments will include smart cards (and associated readers, drivers, and so on); others won't. Some deployments will involve significant resources for the integration of back-end applications; others won't. Your mileage may vary.

■ ***Keep things in perspective.*** TCO is a perfectly appropriate metric for PKI ROI calculations, but cost is certainly not the sole criteria for selecting a PKI vendor. Other important vendor selection criteria include product functionality, technical architecture, strategic vision, financial strength, reputation and trustworthiness, and service and support. According to one industry analyst, in fact, cost should be given only 8 percent of the total consideration in the selection of a strategic PKI supplier.

With these points in mind, there are four high-level categories for capturing the total cost of ownership for PKI: products/technologies, plant (facilities), people, and process. Cost estimates should be captured for a reasonable period of time, typically three to five years. This is helpful at a minimum for time-based budgeting and expectation-setting, and it provides the foundation for (optional) more detailed investment analysis such as net present value as well. The worksheet in Figure 11-1 lays out examples of specific cost elements for each of these high-level categories in more detail.

Products/Technologies

This category should capture the costs of all the products and technologies that make up the PKI architecture under analysis, whether they are acquired through traditional license agreements, or if they are provided as part of a managed service. Since product/technology costs are typically a function of the number of users, this exercise presumes that a model can be identified for the total number of users and how they will be rolled out over a period of time.

When there is client-side software or Web-based plug-ins, this category should include all licensing/acquisition costs as well as the cost of ongoing maintenance, upgrades, and support. For configurations that include client-side hardware (such as smart cards, tokens, or biometrics), it should include licensing/acquisition costs for the hardware, any other incremental product/technology requirements (readers, cables, software drivers, and so on), and ongoing maintenance, upgrades, and support. Some

Figure 11-1

Total cost of ownership

			Year 0	Year 1	Year 2	Year 3	3-Year Totals
Products	Clients	PKI Client Software/Licenses					
		Desktop software					
		Web plug-ins					
		Maintenance / Support					
		PKI Client Hardware					
		Strong Authentication (e.g., smart cards, tokens, biometrics)					
		Maintenance / Support					
		Subtotal					
	Servers	PKI Server Software/Licenses					
		Certificate Server					
		Security Server					
		Directory Services					
		Authentication Server					
		Other Server Functionality					
		Maintenance / Support					
		PKI Server Certificates					
		PKI Server Hardware					
		PKI Server Maintenance / Support					
		Subtotal					
Plant	Facilities	Secure Facilities					
		Disaster Recovery Facilities					
		Subtotal					
People	Core Team	Project Manager					
		Security Manager					
		PKI Architect					
		PKI Server Administrator(s)					
		PKI Client Administrator(s)					
		PKI Certificate Administrator(s)					
	Extended Team	Trainer(s)					
		Application integration developer(s) (when required)					
		Application system owner(s) (1 per application) (when required)					
		Network specialist(s)					
		Server specialists(s)					
		Enterprise communication specialist(s)					
		Help Desk specialist(s)					
		Desktop configuration / installation specialist(s)					
		Desktop support specialist(s)					
		Subtotal					
Process	Prepare	Train Core Team					
		Validate PKI Requirements & Goals					
		Develop Certificate Policy and Certification Practice Statement					
	Plan & Organize	Organize Project & Work (standards, etc.)					
		Develop Operations & Support Plans					
		Develop Pilot & Deployment Plans					
		Develop Communications & Change Management Plans					
	Design	Define Certificate Architecture					
		Design PKI Server Architecture					
		Determine Client Architecture & Delivery Mechanism					
		Design Application Integration Architecture (when required)					
		Design End-User Administration & Support processes					
		Design Communications & Change Management processes					
		Evaluate & Test technology components					
	Develop	Assess IT System Infrastructure					
		Install PKI server(s)					
		Develop custom application integration components (when required)					
		Integrate with other IS and Security systems (when required)					
		Build production PKI database					
		Install and test custom application integration components					
		Develop and test End-User administration process					
		Develop and test Server Operation process					
		Develop Communications & Change Management Tools					
		Prepare Help Desk & End-User Support organization					
	Deploy	Pilot - Core Group (Security team)					
		Pilot - Extended Group (Security team + Support team)					
		Pilot - End-User production group					
		Production rollout - Phase 1					
		Production rollout - Phase 2					
		Production rollout - Phase N					
	Manage	Help Desk					
		PKI Admin					
		IT Admin					
		Application Admin					
		Subtotal					

configurations may simply include the cost of digital certificates for the specified number of users.

On the server side, this category should similarly include the licensing/acquisition cost of all software and hardware for the architecture under analysis (which may include a number of application- or architecture-specific features), plus ongoing maintenance, upgrades, and support.

Plant (Facilities)

This category should capture the cost of all facilities required to operate the infrastructure components of the PKI, plus the cost of any disaster-recovery facilities. Most large organizations have their own data center, but existing capabilities are not always sufficient in terms of physical security, redundancy, fault tolerance, and off-site recovery appropriate for a large-scale, mission-critical PKI. If additional facilities are required, their costs should be included here.

People

This category is meant to capture the cost of all people—either in-house staff or external professional services, or a combination of both—involved in planning, organizing, designing, developing, deploying, training, managing, and supporting a PKI (see the "Process" section that follows). The detail in Figure 11-1 shows a typical approach consisting of a core team (architect, administrators, security manager, and project manager) and an extended team (trainers, developers, network and server specialists, communication specialists, helpdesk, and desktop specialists). The involvement over time and associated cost of the core team and extended team are a function of the specific application(s), architecture, and rollout schedule.

Process

Implementing a PKI involves many steps, including preparation, planning, organizing, designing, developing, deploying, training, and ongoing management and support. PKI technology must be integrated with the existing computing infrastructure, and the operational and support processes required for a production system must be developed and deployed. This is not to say that PKI is uniquely complex or difficult, however. On the contrary, in this sense the process for implementing PKI is no different than that which is required for any other "enterprise" infrastructure. Good planning, technical expertise, attention to process, and proactive project management are the keys to successful implementations. Figure 11-1 shows a typical list of tasks in each of the major process categories.

Total Cost of Ownership: Summary

The most important point for developing a meaningful total cost of ownership for PKI is to *consider all relevant costs* in the categories of products/technologies, plant (facilities), people, and process. The long list of potential cost elements in Figure 11-1 can seem daunting, unless you remember to keep the concepts of incremental analysis and the line-item veto in mind! You should also remember that people with hands-on experience in these matters are now generally available—if not you, then someone in your organization; if not someone in your organization, then someone from a trusted e-security supplier or a respected professional services organization. Get them involved.

With the denominator of the ROI equation on firm ground, we can now turn our attention to the part that tends to generate the most enthusiasm in the corner offices: the financial returns made possible from PKI-enabled business processes.

Financial Returns: The "R" in ROI

What financial returns does Public Key Infrastructure really provide? As PKI becomes more widely deployed, and as more hands-on experience makes the total cost of ownership for PKI more accurately understood, our focus turns inevitably to the more exciting but previously elusive "R" side of the PKI ROI equation.

Here we provide a general framework for unlocking the financial returns that are made possible by implementing PKI-enabled applications. In considering this framework, the following simple, step-by-step approach should be kept in mind:

■ *Focus on the business process.* It's worth repeating that PKI is an e-security *infrastructure*, and infrastructure in the absence of a specific business process returns nothing. For example, if you invest in telephones, facsimile machines, and e-mail systems, but never place a call, transmit a document, or send a message, what have you gained? Moreover, returns from e-security infrastructure are generally difficult, if not impossible, to separate from the returns from the business processes themselves. The primary focus—once it has been determined that authentication, data privacy, data integrity, digital signatures, or other e-security capabilities provided by PKI are important business requirements—should therefore be on the financial returns from the successful implementation of a particular (security-enabled) business process. This approach also accommodates the reality that financial returns are typically application-specific, company-specific, industry-specific, and so on. The next section ("Business Process") discusses this topic in more detail.

■ *Establish appropriate metrics.* With a proper focus on security-enabled business process, the next step is to establish the appropriate metrics for determining potential financial returns. The metrics chosen will logically be a function of not only the particular business process under analysis (that is, is it an internal process? a customer-facing process? a partner-facing process?), but also the specific business objectives you have in mind (are you aiming to increase revenues? lower costs? improve efficiency?). A subsequent section ("Metrics") discusses this topic in more detail.

■ *Establish a baseline for the current state.* Having established an appropriate set of metrics, the next step is to use them to establish a baseline for the business process under analysis, based on the way things are today. This is the "business as usual" scenario.

■ *Compare to the desired future state.* The same metrics can then be used to compute the financial impact of implementing a new or improved business process that meets the specific business objectives you have in mind. This is the "business as a result of" scenario: the desired future state that will result from the successful implementation of a new or improved PKI-enabled business process.

If this straightforward approach sounds familiar, it should come as no surprise. It's a time-honored method for establishing value, a process we've all gone through (consciously or otherwise) countless times before.

Once again, we can observe that PKI is not uniquely complex or difficult to analyze in this regard. On the contrary, this approach for computing financial returns for PKI-enabled applications is the same one used for virtually any other significant investment. All you need, given the relatively early stage of PKI market development, is a general framework to help organize the attack and jump-start a detailed discussion of potential financial returns.

With this in mind, the next two sections present a high-level model for categorizing various business processes that can be positively affected by PKI, followed by several examples of potential metrics of interest. The remaining sections then explore the four high-level categories through which the financial returns made possible by PKI-enabled applications can be unlocked: revenues, costs, compliance, and risks.

Business Process

Again, this approach is suitable for virtually any new or improved business process that is made feasible by the enabling e-security capabilities provided by PKI: authentication, data privacy, data integrity, digital signature/non-repudiation, authorization/personalization, large scale, and so on. Given the innumerable e-business processes that can potentially leverage PKI as their e-security foundation, a simple model such as the one shown in Figure 11-2 can be helpful to organize them into a reasonable number of discrete categories.

At the most general level, Figure 11-2 depicts three major categories of e-business applications: internal, customer-facing, and partner-facing. If it helps you to think of these as enterprise, *business-to-consumer* (B2C), and *business-to-business* (B2B), respectively, please feel free to do so. Note that this is a traditional enterprise-centric, one-to-many model that should therefore seem quite familiar, but may not necessarily accommodate a number of emerging e-marketplace, many-to-many scenarios such as auctions, B2B exchanges, and so on. If it can be useful to you in spite of this limitation, please read on.

At the next level of granularity, Figure 11-2 suggests that the universe of e-business applications can be further segmented by function, using the following six categories: collaborative, informational, transactional, payment/funds transfer, distribution, and relationship.

Figure 11-2

E-business
application
categories

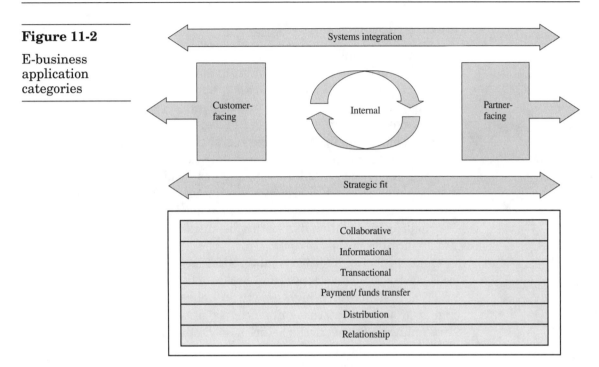

Collaborative

The design/development business function, which is often carried out through a traditional customer-supplier relationship, is one example of a collaborative e-business application. In this case, the protection of valuable intellectual property may be a primary e-security concern, such as to ensure that new product plans or customer lists are not disclosed to competitors. The authenticity of users, an encrypted communications channel, the ability to control access based on identity, and the ability to protect information at its source and/or destination may therefore be critical e-security requirements. E-mail applications are also collaborative in nature, although to date only a small percentage of business environments have determined that digitally signed and encrypted messages are truly required.

Informational

For customer-facing applications, this category includes traditional functions of search, discovery, and offering such as the online provision of product information, customer service information, and ordering information; the ability to customize products and services online; the ability to personalize the online shopping experience; and so on. For partner-facing applications in this category, examples might include the online provision of supply information (inventory, schedules, product roadmaps, and the like), quality information (such as incidence reports), and relationship management information (contact lists, frequently asked questions, discussion forums, and so on). The typical corporate intranet, which is primarily informational in nature, is an excellent example of an internal application in this category.

Outward-facing informational applications are often critical to business concerns such as reputation and brand, particularly from the perspective that projected high growth in online sales is dwarfed by even higher growth in Internet-influenced sales—sales in which research is done online and then purchases are made in traditional channels. For this reason, the authenticity and integrity of the online information can be key e-security concerns. To the extent that any informational application deals with high-value information (for a discussion of "high value," see the subsequent section on "Risks"), the authenticity of users, an encrypted communications channel, the ability to control access based on identity, and the ability to protect information at its source and/or destination may also be critical e-security requirements.

Transactional

Examples of customer-facing applications in this category include the ability to open accounts, submit orders, modify orders, track order status, and so on. Partner-facing examples are similar, although in this case it might be more appropriate to say transmit purchase orders, transmit invoices, process invoices, and track order/invoice status, since the majority of B2B transactions are still currently conducted with these traditional mechanisms. Security concerns for transactional applications include the authenticity of both parties in a transaction, the privacy and integrity of transmitted data, the ability to authorize users to perform certain actions based on their identity, and the authenticity and non-repudiability of the transactions themselves.

Payment/Funds Transfer

Payment and funds transfer applications have a natural affinity with traditional e-security functions (such as authentication, data privacy and integrity, authorization, non-repudiation, and audit). Apparently, fraud and theft will be with us as long as real money is at stake, and bank robbers will always rob banks "because that's where the money is." In the B2C world, the volume of electronic payments is rapidly increasing, driven as much by the parties involved in processing electronic payments (merchants, merchant banks, card-issuing banks, and third-party payment processors) as by consumer demand. Why? First, because processing paper-based transactions costs significantly more than processing transactions based on credit cards, debit cards, point-of-sale check conversions, and so on. In addition, electronic payments yield significantly more information about customers and transactions in terms of preferences and buying patterns, which both merchants and card-issuing banks would like to mine. This creates a personal privacy issue, and recent legislation such as the Gramm-Leach-Bliley Financial Services Modernization Act has begun to regulate all financial services companies who collect customer data. In general, both traditional security-related issues of fraud and theft, and newer issues of consumer privacy will drive the use of PKI-based technologies in the payment/funds transfer category.

Distribution

For physical goods, the shipping/receiving function is perhaps less affected by e-security concerns, except to the extent that logistics information might be compromised and used to help steal goods in transit. For digital goods, which can be perfectly and infinitely copied at virtually zero cost, electronic distribution can be either a godsend (for example, the opportunity to gain significant reductions in publication cost and faster delivery time, through online publishing) or a constant concern (such as with the issues of piracy and intellectual property protection). In either case, e-security technologies based on PKI can play a key role in the controlled distribution of digital content.

Relationship

Few would disagree that management of the customer/supplier relationship is a critical business function, and in recent years there has been increasing attention on the importance of attracting and keeping profitable customer relationships. Customers want to use and maintain a product or service more effectively, and suppliers are constantly striving to provide faster, better, and cheaper levels of service and support. Here lies a fundamental tension, between the end-user desire on the one hand to receive customized, personalized service based on his unique relationship and preferences versus his desire on the other hand to protect the privacy of his personal data, preferences, credit card information, and such. Indeed, with major government privacy regulations—such as the *Health Insurance Portability and Accountability Act* (HIPPA) regulating the treatment of patient records, and the Gramm-Leach-Bliley bill regulating financial services companies who collect customer data—already coming into effect, plus additional federal privacy initiatives on the horizon, personal privacy is a hot issue. Digital signatures should prove invaluable for requirements such as the "chain of trust" in HIPAA, which requires that patient information shared with partners maintain the same level of security it enjoyed with the initially responsible party. In general, compliance with personal privacy legislation should stimulate significant demand for PKI-based technologies over the next several years.

Finally, although they are not application categories per se, Figure 11-2 also references two additional topics that can have a direct impact on the ROI equation: systems integration and strategic fit. *Systems integration* refers to the degree to which customer-facing, internal, and partner-facing systems and applications are integrated with each other—where tighter integration is generally correlated to higher financial returns. *Strategic fit* refers to the alignment of customer/partner business process with internal business process (are the respective business processes compatible with one another?), and the readiness (comfort level, technological capabilities, and perceived importance) of customers/partners to adopt e-business applications. For example, digital certificates on smart credit cards might provide highly beneficial authentication and digital signature capabilities for transactional B2C applications, but not until (1) online merchant systems actually have the capability to accept and leverage digital certificates, and (2) consumers are willing to embrace and use the new technology on a widespread basis.

Even with this very basic level of categorization, we can now quickly frame the ROI discussion in the context of the key e-security enablers for a particular e-business application. The next step is to establish an appropriate set of metrics for determining potential financial returns.

Metrics

As noted, the most appropriate metrics are a function of both the business process under analysis and one or more specific business objectives. Table 11-1 lists a number of potential metrics for certain example business objectives, and provides examples of "impact statements" in the form of questions that set up a comparison of the current state with the desired future state in terms of one or more specific metrics. Quantifying the answers to these questions is the key to unlocking the financial returns made possible by PKI-enabled applications.

As noted above, quantifiable financial returns made possible by PKI-enabled applications tend to fall into one of the following four high-level categories: revenues, costs, compliance, and risks. The remaining sections of this chapter explore these four categories in more detail, and include several case studies and examples of quantifiable results.

Revenues

Business processes that generate new or increased revenue streams create perhaps the most compelling justifications for investments in enabling infrastructure such as PKI. Because revenue enhancements are generally more strategic than tactical in nature, however, they can also be somewhat more difficult to quantify.

Based on metrics such as those found in Table 11-1, we can reasonably quantify any number of incremental revenue streams for PKI-enabled applications. For example, suppose two-thirds of your online customers currently end up abandoning transactions that require them to print, sign, and mail paper documents rather than allow them to complete the entire transaction online. What would it mean in terms of incremental revenue if you could substantially reduce this drop-off rate to only one-third by using digital signatures to complete the transaction immediately while simultaneously minimizing the risk of subsequent repudiation? For many document-intensive industries (including financial services, insurance, healthcare, and so on), this would have an enormous impact on revenues, not to mention the potential for reducing the related costs associated with paper, printing, postage, and the processing of traditional paper forms.

Other possibilities for quantifiable revenue-based financial returns include cross-selling or up-selling opportunities with established customers,

Table 11-1	Business Process	Example Business Objectives	Potential Metrics	Example Impact Statements (The Key to Unlocking Financial Returns)
Example Metrics and Impact Statements	Customer-facing	Maximize online revenues from existing customers	% of revenue generated online, % of existing customers doing business online, % of customer wallet spent online, % dropoff rate, Repeat business rates, % of up-sell, cross-sell conversions, Lifetime revenue per customer	"Two-thirds of our online customers don't complete transactions that require them to print, sign, and mail paper documents. What would the financial impact be if we could reduce this drop-off rate to one-third by using digital signatures to complete the entire transaction online, as well as eliminate the cost of paper, printing, postage, and processing?"
		Minimize costs of finding and acquiring new customers	% of new customers acquired online, Cost of new customer acquisition, Brand perception, brand awareness	"What would the financial impact be if we could leverage 50% of all established online account relationships with Line of Business #1 to create an online account relationship with Line of Business #2?"
		Maximize customer satisfaction; reduce helpdesk and suport costs	# of incorrect order incidents, Service levels used, # of service/ helpdesk requests, % of service/ helpdesk requests resolved online	"What would the financial impact be if authorized customers could resolve 80% of helpdesk calls directly, online, rather than by live agents over a toll-free number?"
	Internal	Increase responsiveness to changing market conditions	Order cycle/ delivery time, Product time-to-market, Product time-to-change	"What would the financial impact be if we could reduce our process cycle time from X days to Y hours, while preserving the integrity and authenticity of documents and transactions?"
		Reduce costs, improve productivity	Cost of materials, Cost of services, Productivity per employee, # of service/ helpdesk requests, % of service/ helpdesk requests resolved online	"What would the financial impact be if we could improve employee productivity and eliminate helpdesk calls caused by password resets, by using PKI-based authentication with our virtual private network or with our Reduced Sign-On initiative?"

	Partner-facing	Tighten degree of system integration with strategic partners	% of production goods procured online, % of maintenance/ repairs/operating supplies procured online	"What would the financial impact be if we could shorten delivery times and reduce inventory by enabling authorized users to procure 80% of all maintenance, repairs, and operating supplies through a Web browser, mobile phone, or wireless personal digital assistant?"
Table 11-1 Example Metrics and Impact Statements (cont.)		Reduce partnership costs, improve partner reliability	Comparative prices, Cost/Uptime of partner connections, Cost/Rate of partner repairs, replacements, returns, Cost, time commitment scorecard	"What would the financial impact be if we could provide authorized strategic partners with increased access to sensitive information, without compromising security or giving up control?"

an increased number of transactions per customer, and higher rates of repeat business. Important but less quantifiable examples in this category might include competitive advantage, strategic positioning, and corporate brand/image. A transactional financial services example is provided in the next sidebar.

Costs

Reductions in cost are perhaps the most reliable driver of financial returns for PKI-enabled applications. Although cost reductions are generally more tactical than strategic in nature, they are also generally the easiest returns to quantify (hence their popularity). Cost-based financial returns are typically expressed as some combination of the following:

- *Cost savings*   The new or improved business process is less expensive; we can spend fewer dollars than we did before.

- *Cost avoidance*   The new or improved business process scales to higher levels; we can avoid spending as many additional dollars in support of new capabilities or expanded scale.

Example: Online Brokerage Transactions

Organization: Online brokerage firm servicing self-directed individual investors.

Application: Instant account opening using an online, paperless process to open an online brokerage account and fund the account electronically using the ACH mechanism.

Business benefits: The time to open a new account reduced from three to 10 days to less than three minutes, a critical factor in accelerating revenues from new account growth and from converting prospects more quickly to active traders—an impact of tens of millions of dollars. Cost avoidance compared to manual account processing and helpdesk calls related to new account openings, as well as cost reductions from reduced mailing and storage costs—an impact of more than $2 million.

Benefits of PKI: Account activity acknowledged and authorized by electronic signatures; reduced risk from stronger user authentication; higher integrity of stored customer data.

- ■ *Efficiency*   The new or improved business process saves time; we can increase the velocity at which we conduct e-business.

- ■ *Effectiveness*   The new or improved business process increases productivity; we can do more or different things with the resources we already have.

Although it is impossible to generalize about the best sources for cost-based financial returns, at present three areas seem to be particularly fruitful: helpdesk costs, telecommunications costs, and costs associated with the processing of electronic forms and electronic records.

The numbers in Table 11-2 illustrate why so many companies target the helpdesk as a rich and easy source of cost-based financial returns: end-users can usually experience faster, more convenient service at a reduction in cost of up to two orders of magnitude. Common PKI-enabled applications that can obtain substantial leverage from reductions in helpdesk costs include corporate intranets, reduced sign-on initiatives, virtual private networks, and one-to-many extranets. A secure extranet case study example is provided in the sidebar.

Example: Secure Extranet

Organization: Mutual funds, trust and investment services company.

Application: Secure extranet for 5,000 independent financial advisors. 24/7 self-service access to high-value financial and client information.

Business benefits: Annual cost savings of approximately 40 percent compared to phone-based, agent-based system. Largest driver for cost savings is 3x reduction in toll calls and direct agent assistance compared to previous process.

Benefits of PKI: Privacy and integrity of data; authentication of users; user accountability to data; customized content; reduced risk of data loss/theft; centralized control of trust policies and parameters.

Table 11-2

Example Cost
Reduction Target:
Helpdesk

Type of Customer Service	Average Cost per Transaction
Agent (phone-based)	$5.00
Agent (Web chat)	$2.50
Agent (e-mail)	$2.25
E-mail (auto-reply)	$0.75
Web (self-service)	$0.05

Telecommunications costs also represent low-hanging fruit for cost-based financial returns, and are often used in particular to justify investments in virtual private networks. Many organizations implementing VPN technology overlook authentication as a critical e-security requirement, however, on the mistaken assumption that an encrypted communications channel has fully addressed the problem of secure remote communications. Replacing a VPN's weak password-based authentication with stronger authentication technology such as PKI not only improves overall security (by more strongly establishing who's on the other end of your VPN), but also takes aim a major source of helpdesk costs. (According to some studies, up to 60 percent of helpdesk costs are related to lost

Example: VPN

Organization: Technology consulting and services firm.

Application: Site-to-site VPN connecting multiple firm offices. Secure server-to-server connections for sensitive intra-firm collaboration and information exchange.

Business benefits: 6x increase in bandwidth, 3x reduction in annual communications costs compared to previous frame relay.

Benefits of PKI: Stronger authentication than username/password; easier management and administration of users and devices; e-security infrastructure can be leveraged for additional applications.

or forgotten passwords.) A VPN case study example is provided in the sidebar.

A third area ripe for harvesting cost-based financial returns has to do with the cost of processing paper forms, documents, and business records. This is most relevant in document-intensive industries such as financial services, insurance, and healthcare, where enormous financial returns are possible from cost reductions in the "four Ps" of paper, printing, postage, and processing.

The cost of manual document processing is very high. The average paper document is copied nine to 11 times at a cost of approximately $18 and filed at a cost of approximately $20, plus the additional cost of storage, electronic media, physical plant, postage, and other distribution. And mistakes are expensive: the cost of finding and retrieving misfiled paper documents is approximately $120. Of course, there are other business benefits to electronic forms processing in addition to lower costs, including wider, easier access, better quality, higher data integrity, and the ability to avoid cost by containing growth in headcount.

As an illustration of the magnitude of financial returns of this type, Table 11-3 compares the average distribution cost of Internet-based channels with that of traditional channels for term life insurance, bill payment, and banking, respectively. An electronic mortgage case study example is also provided in the sidebar.

Example: Electronic Mortgage Transaction

Organization: Home mortgage services.

Application: Online mortgage transaction.

Business benefits: 30-45 day cycle time reduced to five hours. Reduced risk of mishandled documents, errors, and omissions. Reduction in administrative staff and training costs. Improved customer service. Savings of approximately 20 percent in total loan life cycle costs compared to previous process.

Benefits of PKI: Provable chain of evidence as to the authenticity of documents; authorization to access documents based on user authentication.

Table 11-3

Example Cost Reduction Target: The Four Ps of Forms/Document Processing

	Traditional Distribution	**Internet-Based Distribution**
Term Life Insurance	$5.50	$2.75
Bill Payment	$2.75	$0.75
Banking	$1.08	$0.13

Compliance

By *compliance* we mean some business process that we are required to implement, or some e-security requirement that we are obligated to meet. Compliance generally refers to things about which we have very little choice—that is, things we must do in order to stay in business as we know it. In some cases, compliance may be related to cost avoidance (such as to avoid a fine); in others, it may be related to protecting an existing revenue stream. In any event, compliance-based business cases tend to be somewhat binary: above a certain threshold, we just do it. As it relates to e-security infrastructure, compliance-based arguments tend to come from one of the following four categories: regulatory, partner, customer, and competitive.

- ***Regulatory compliance***   Failure to implement could mean fines, loss of revenues, jail terms, and so on, such as HIPAA regulations for the U.S. healthcare industry, or the Gramm-Leach-Bliley bill for the U.S. financial services industry.

- ***Partner compliance***   Failure to implement could mean losing the ability to participate with a key partner or group of partners, such as a segment of the financial industry moving to the Identrus model for cross-certification.

- ***Customer compliance***   Failure to implement could mean the loss of a business relationship with a key account, such as "all General Motors suppliers who wish to have their contracts renewed must implement technology X by a certain date."

- ***Competitive compliance***   Failure to implement could mean the loss of competitive advantage and likely revenue loss—"our competitors are eating our lunch!"

Compliance-based business cases tend to be made not so much on the basis of precisely quantified financial returns, but on the basis of "the cost of doing business" or as a means to avoid "what will happen if we *don't* implement."

Risks

Until only recently, risk-based arguments were probably the most frequently used approach to justify investments in e-security infrastructure. Marketing campaigns and business cases alike were commonly based on arguments of *fear, uncertainty, and doubt* (FUD). Selling security through fear can be reasonably effective up to a point—for example, the big bad wolf certainly sold fairy tales in volume for the Brothers Grimm—but it also tends to marginalize e-security as an operating expense, subject to being trimmed at the first round of budget cuts. Today, happily, there is beginning to be significantly less emphasis on FUD and more on the systematic management of risk.

Risk is an inescapable fact of e-business, and there are only four things we can do about it: accept it, ignore it (which is the same as accepting it), assign it to someone else, or mitigate it. Investments in e-security infrastructure that are made with prevention in mind are usually not all that visible (unless there's a problem), which tends to make risk-based justifications the least glamorous of the four categories in our model.

It seems obvious, but risk mitigation investments should be focused on things that are worth protecting, such as high-value information and high-value transactions. For examples of "high-value" information, consider the following:

- Information that generates revenue, either directly or indirectly: information, programs, services, and so on

- Information essential to the smooth running of the company: operational information, administrative information, and so on

- Information pertaining to future revenue streams: research, new product plans, marketing plans, customer databases, and so on

- Information that must be protected by law: personnel records, student records, patient records, and so on

Once high-value information has been identified, you can then make a reasonable attempt to quantify the impact of various security-related risk scenarios, using the familiar "impact statement" approach. For example:

- ***Productivity loss***   What would the financial impact be if a security breach caused a sustained disruption of internal processes and communications? If you lost the ability to communicate with customers? (Keep in mind that 99.5 percent uptime still translates to 3.6 hours of downtime per month, and look at the average cost per hour of downtime for various businesses in Table 11-4.)

- ***Monetary loss***   What would the financial impact be if there were a security-related corruption of your accounting system which led to delays in shipping and billing? If there were a diversion of funds? What would be the expense of recovery and emergency response?

- ***Indirect loss***   What would the financial impact be if a security breach caused the loss of potential sales? The loss of competitive advantage? The impact of negative publicity? The loss of goodwill and trust? (Indirect losses are among the most difficult to quantify, but also among the most compelling in the risk-mitigation category, especially for businesses built on the fundamental foundation of trust.)

- ***Legal exposure***   What would the financial impact be, due to failure to meet contractual milestones? Due to failure to meet statutory regulations for the privacy of data? Due to illegal user or intruder activity on company systems? (Your corporate counsel can potentially be an excellent source of justification for PKI-enabled business process.)

The answers to these risk-oriented impact statements can be difficult to quantify, but as shown in Table 11-4, the financial implications can be extraordinary. And the risks themselves are very real—it seems that not a month goes by without a highly publicized security breach, and undoubtedly the vast majority of security breaches go unpublicized. The annual FBI/Computer Security Institute survey on computer crime and security shows that over 80 percent of respondents now answer "yes" or "don't know" (which is probably the same as "yes") to the question "Have you experienced some kind of unauthorized use of your computer systems in the previous year?" Unauthorized access by insiders is twice as frequent as unauthorized access by outsiders—and growing—and the Internet has rapidly replaced internal systems and remote dial-up as the most frequent point of attack.

Financial Returns: Summary

The most important points for developing meaningful financial returns for PKI-enabled applications are to focus on the business process, establish appropriate metrics, and look for all relevant returns in the following high-level categories: revenues, costs, compliance, and risks.

As we have seen in the example metrics and impact statements provided in Table 11-1, by properly framing the ROI discussion in the context of the key e-security enablers for a particular e-business process, we can very quickly begin to quantify financial returns using a straightforward, widely accepted approach.

Table 11-4	**Business**	**Average Cost per Downtime Hour**
Example Risk Mitigation Target: Productivity Loss	Pay-Per-View Television	$150,000
	Home Shopping Television	$113,000
	Catalog Sales	$90,000
	Airline Reservations	$89,500
	Teleticket Sales	$69,000
	Package Shipping	$28,000
	ATM Fees	$14,500

With the numerator of the ROI equation well established, all that remains is to put it all together, that is, to compare the investment represented by our TCO analysis with the sum of the financial returns made possible by PKI-enabled applications.

PKI ROI: Summary

What is the return on investment for PKI? The only credible response is "it depends," but Figure 11-3 provides a high-level summary of the frameworks developed in this chapter that can help us generate a more definitive answer. On the one hand, we have a framework for capturing the various elements of cost currently involved with implementing a PKI. It presumes a particular application architecture, and aims to include all relevant costs for products, plant (facilities), people, and process. On the other hand, we have a widely accepted methodology for quantifying the potential financial returns from a particular PKI-enabled business process, including all relevant returns from higher revenues, lower costs, better compliance, and mitigated risks. On balance, your personalized comparison of the two halves of the ROI equation will determine your own ROI for PKI. In general, however, we believe that the benefits from PKI-enabled applications significantly outweigh the costs of PKI implementation. Yes, Virginia, there is a strong ROI for PKI.

As we said at the beginning, this is not about technology; it's about time and money. To put things in perspective, consider the parallels between current thinking about e-security infrastructure and the thoughts about various quality initiatives in manufacturing in the 1980s (just-in-time manufacturing, Total Quality Management programs, and so on). A common business issue for pragmatic, nontechnical executives at that time was the "cost of quality," as in, "Sure, these quality programs sound great, but how much will they really cost, and will there really be a return on my investment?" Then, a provocatively titled little book, *Quality Is Free*, helped business people to better understand and quantify the financial effects of poor quality: scrap, rework, longer cycle times, product returns, poor word of mouth, higher customer support costs, and so on. So the phrase "Quality Is Free" was really a concise, provocative summation of the concept that the cost of implementing quality programs was significantly less than the financial returns made possible by producing high-quality products in the first place.

Figure 11-3

PKI ROI
summary: "e-
Security is free"

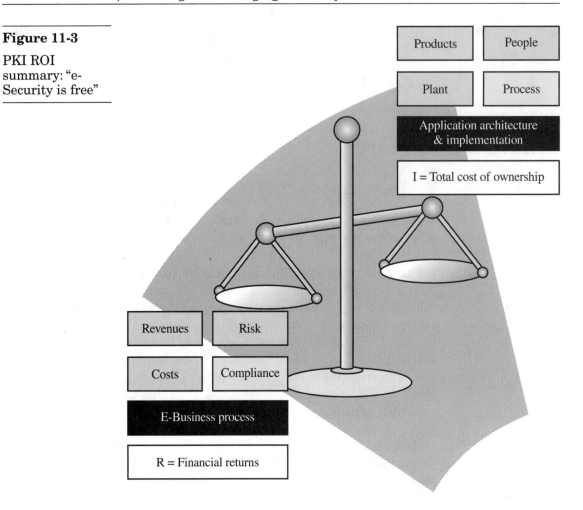

And so it is with e-security: the total cost of ownership for implementing and enabling e-security infrastructure such as PKI is significantly less than the financial returns made possible by PKI-enabled applications. In other words, "e-Security Is Free." *Plus ça change, plus c'est la même chose.*

References

Aberdeen Group, "Evaluating the Cost of Ownership for Digital Certificate Projects," July 1998.

Computer Security Institute/FBI Computer Crime and Security survey, 1996-2000.

Crosby, Philip B., *Quality Is Free: The Art of Making Quality Certain.* McGraw-Hill/Mentor Books: 1992, Phil Crosby.

Enterprise Management Associates, "Security Strategies" survey, April 2000.

eOriginal, "Applying PKI to Business Applications," presentation at PKI Forum members meeting, September 2000.

Forrester Research, "Measuring eBusiness Success," September 2000.

Gartner Group, "Calculating Potential CRM Benefits," September 2000.

Gartner Group, "Justifying Consolidated Security Administration Tool Costs," May 2000.

Gartner Group, "PKI Selection Criteria: The Decision Drivers Approach," February 2000.

Gartner Group, "Resolving PKI Issues," conference presentation, June 2000.

Gartner Group, "Virtual Private Networking," conference presentation, June 2000.

Giga Information Group, "A Total Economic Analysis of Two PKI Vendors: Entrust and VeriSign," September 1998.

Giga Information Group, *IdeaByte*, December 1999.

Hurwitz Group, "The e-Business Advantage: Making the Most of PKI," February 2000.

Organization for Economic Cooperation, presentation by Gen3 Partners, May 2000.

Renaissance Worldwide, Inc., "Choosing a PKI Vendor: A Total Cost Management Analysis of Entrust, VeriSign, and Equifax," March 2000.

RSA Security Inc., "Keon PKI Implementation Guide," July 2000.

The Science of Selling, marketing integration workshop, November 2000.

University of Texas at Austin, "E-Business Value Model," October 2000.

APPENDIX A

X.509 Certificates

In Chapter 3, we looked at the content of a real world certificate and compared it to general format and content of an X.509 certificate. Chapter 4 discussed key and certificate life cycle management and considered the certificate revocation list. In this appendix, we will describe in detail the contents of X.509 v3 certificates and v2 certificate revocation lists. This appendix is intended primarily as a reference. Descriptions of the use of these fields will be found in the relevant chapters elsewhere in the book.

This appendix is primarily targeted at the X.509 description of the use of these fields. Where appropriate, PKIX usage variations will also be noted.

Certificate Types

Two major types of certificates exist: end-entity certificates and CA certificates.

End-entity certificates are issued by a Certification Authority to an entity that does not in turn issue certificates to another entity.

CA certificates are issued by a Certification Authority to an entity that is also a Certification Authority and so may issue end-entity certificates (and possibly other certificate types). A CA certificate is distinguished by the presence of a certificate field named *Basic Constraints*, explicitly set to indicate that a CA certificate has been issued. Basic constraints will be discussed later in the section "Certificate Extensions."

Several cases of CA certificates can be identified:

■ **Self-issued certificates** The self-issued certificate has both the issuer and subject names set to the name of the Certification Authority that issued the certificate. This form of CA certificate may be used to allow special operations such as the validation of a new public key pair when a key rollover event occurs for the CA. In this case, the new key is contained in the certificate, and the old key is used to sign the certificate, allowing the new public key to be trusted.

■ **Self-signed certificates** A self-signed certificate is a special case of the self-issued certificate. In this case, the public key certified in the certificate issued by the Certification Authority corresponds to the private key used to sign the certificate. The use of self-signed certificates was examined in Chapter 8 when we discussed trust models.

■ **Cross-certificates** In a cross-certificate, the subject and issuer are different certification authorities. Cross-certificates are used by one Certification Authority to certify the identity of another Certification Authority. The use of cross-certificates to construct trusted relationships between certification authorities was discussed in detail in Chapter 8.

Certificate Format

The Certification Authority creates a certificate by signing a collection of information about the entity. This information includes the public key and distinguished name of the entity and may include an optional unique identifier that holds additional information about the entity.

X.509 defines the form of a certificate issued by a Certification Authority with a name of CA for a subject with a distinguished name of A using the following symbolic form:

$$CA<<A>> = CA\{V, SN, AI, CA, UCA, A, UA, Ap, T^A\}$$

In this case, the certificate contains the following information:

V   The version number of the certificate

SN   The serial number

AI   Identifies the signature algorithm used to sign the certificate

CA   The distinguished name of the issuing CA

UCA A unique identifier for the issuing CA (optional)

A   The distinguished name of the subject identified by the certificate

UA   A unique identifier for the subject (optional)

Ap   The public key of subject A

T^A The validity period of the certificate described by a start date and an end date for which the certificate is valid

X.509 also describes the format of a certificate using an ASN.1 description that is even less readable than the symbolic form used above.

The general format of an X.509 certificate is shown in Figure A-1 in a graphical form.

The standard fields defined for each certificate include the following:

- **Version number** Indicates the format and allowable content defined within a certificate of a particular version. The latest release of X.509 certificates is version 3. Although some version 1 certificates may occasionally be seen, version 2 certificates were a short-term aberration, quickly replaced by version 3.

- **Serial number** The serial number for each certificate issued by a particular CA is unique.

- **Signature** Identifies the type of hash function and signature algorithm used to sign the certificate. In the diagram, the signature field represents the description of the algorithm used as well as the actual signature generated for the certificate.

NOTE:

A typical signature algorithm identifier might be md5WithRSAEncryption, *indicating that the hash algorithm used was md5 (Message Digest #5, defined by RSA Labs) and the encryption algorithm used was RSA.*

Figure A-1

General X.509
certificate format

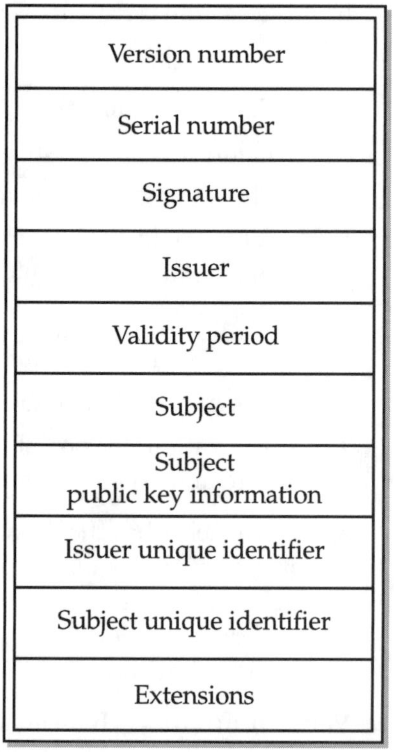

| Version number |
| Serial number |
| Signature |
| Issuer |
| Validity period |
| Subject |
| Subject public key information |
| Issuer unique identifier |
| Subject unique identifier |
| Extensions |

- **Issuer** Identifies the Certification Authority that issued and signed the certificate.

- **Validity** Defines the start and end dates for which the certificate can be considered valid.

- **Subject** Names the individual or entity being identified by the certificate corresponding to the public key contained in the certificate.

- **SubjectPublicKeyInfo** Contains the public key being certified for the subject of the certificate. In addition to the public key, it also identifies the algorithm for which the public key can be used.

- **IssuerUniqueIdentifier** Allows the issuer of the certificate to be identified where the issuer name may have been reused. This is an optional field and may only be used if the version number of the certificate is v2 or v3.

- **SubjectUniqueIdentifier** Allows the subject of the certificate to be identified where the subject name may have been reused. This is an optional field and may only be used if the version number of the certificate is v2 or v3.

- **Extensions** Allows additional information to be encoded in a certificate without requiring modification of the certificate format. Standard extensions are defined by X.509 and are described in the next section. In addition, private extensions may be defined by any organization. An example of a private extension defined by the PKIX working group within the IETF for Internet use of certificates is described in the next chapter.

Certificate Extensions

Certificate extensions allow additional information to be specified for a certificate. The set of extensions defined or accepted by a particular community may vary. Profiles may be defined describing the set of extensions that are used by participants within the community and what interpretation should be placed on the use of an extension. For example, the PKIX working group has defined unique extensions for use within the Internet. The U.S. government has defined its own profile for users of the bridge CA.

In this section, we will discuss the difference between critical and noncritical extensions and then move on to describe different classes of extensions. Detailed discussion of some extensions may be deferred to specific chapters, such as the treatment of trust establishment in Chapter 8.

Criticality Indicators

Certificate extensions contain a flag that indicates whether the extension must be considered critical.

The general meaning of the criticality flag is that when it is set to true, it indicates that the extension must be processed. If the user of a certificate does not recognize or cannot otherwise process a certificate containing a critical extension, the certificate must be considered invalid.

Processing rules for the semantics of some extensions may also be affected by the use of the critical flag.

If an extension is not marked as critical, the certificate user may ignore the extension. This allows for extensions defined in one community to be used in another even if the meaning of the extension type is not recognized by the second community.

Key Extensions

This class of extensions includes information about the keys used by certification authorities and end-entities. It also includes constraints on how keys may be used.

Authority Key Identifier

The AuthorityKeyIdentifier extension, shown in Figure A-2, is a non-critical extension used to specify which of multiple public keys owned by a Certification Authority be used for verification of a signature on a certificate. This allows a Certification Authority to operate using multiple sets of keys, and allows a certificate user to identify which key set should be used.

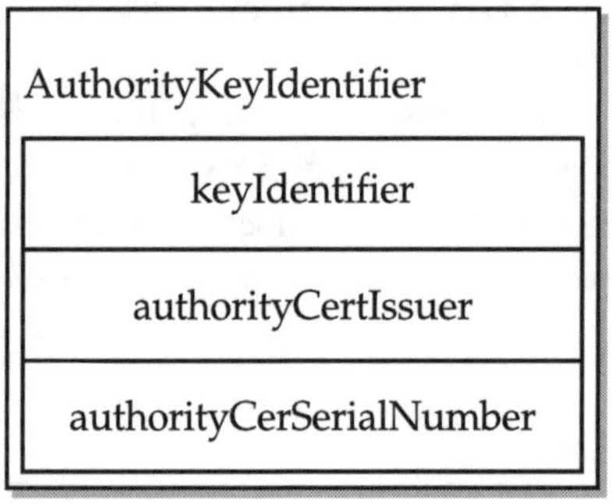

Figure A-2

AuthorityKey-
Identifier
extension

AuthorityKeyIdentifier
keyIdentifier
authorityCertIssuer
authorityCerSerialNumber

PKIX NOTE:

The AuthorityKeyIdentifier must be included in all CA certificates to assist in certificate chain building, except where the CA certificate is self-signed.

Explicit specification of the keys to be used allows CAs to handle cases such as key rollover for the Certification Authority, where multiple CA certificates and keys are in active use. It is also useful for locating expired keys for long-term signature verification purposes, where chain validation is required for signing certificates where possibly all certificates and keys in the chain may have expired.

The specific CA key may be identified by specifying a value for the keyIdentifier field of this extension, or by using a combination of the CA certificate serial number (authorityCertSerialNumber), and the CA name (authorityCertIssuer) fields. Both mechanisms may be used, but the keyIdentifier form allows more specific identification when constructing certificate paths.

Subject Key Identifier

The SubjectKeyIdentifier extension identifies the specific key set a public key belongs to when the subject of the certificate has more than one key set in use. Unlike the AuthorityKeyIdentifier, only the keyIdentifier form is used. This extension is always marked non-critical.

PKIX NOTE:

The SubjectKeyIdentifier must be included in all CA certificates to assist in certificate chain building. It is optional but recommended for end-entity certificates.

Key Usage

The KeyUsage extension defines the purpose for which the public key can be used. It has the following possible settings:

- **KeyCertSign** The key is used to verify signatures on certificates. This setting is only valid in CA certificates.

- **CRLSign** The key is used to verify the CA signature on a certificate revocation list.

- **NonRepudiation** The key is used when providing a non-repudiation service. This key may be used by a third party providing some form of notary service where an end-entity's signature is verified and signed to prevent later denial that the signature was used.

- **DigitalSignature** This identifies keys used for digital signature purposes other than the signature key types previously listed.

- **KeyEncipherment** This key is used to encrypt other keys or security information. It might be used for securely transporting keys. When specified, it may be constrained to indicate that the encipherment key may only be used to EncipherOnly or DecipherOnly.

- **DataEncipherment** This key is used for encryption of user data. Keys or other security data are not covered by this key type—the KeyEncipherment key must be used for those purposes.

- **KeyAgreement** This key is used in the process of establishing or agreeing on what key should be used for further operations. The Diffie-Hellman algorithm is an example of a key agreement protocol.

The KeyUsage extension may be marked as critical or non-critical.

PKIX NOTE:

It is recommended that the extension be marked as critical.

If the extension is flagged as critical, the key must be used only for its designated purpose. When flagged as critical, the CA is indicating that the key is being certified for that purpose only, an important concept if issues of liability are raised when a key is used for other purposes.

If the extension is flagged as non-critical, it takes on the status of an advisory field. The key may be used for other purposes at the discretion of the certificate user. The field may also be set to non-critical if the primary purpose of the setting is to select the correct certificate and key pair where a user may have more than one.

Extended Key Usage

The ExtendedKeyUsage extension is to allow additional usage information to be specified for the key. The key usage is defined as a list of key usage identifiers. Any organization can define specific key usage information and corresponding identifiers (the same rules apply for registering these identifiers as other objects). For example, Microsoft adds *Object Identifiers* (OIDs) that include specification of:

■ Smart card logon usage

■ Client authentication usage

■ Secure email usage

And many other application specific extended key usage identifiers.

The extension may be marked as critical or non-critical. If it is marked critical, the key must be used only for the specified purpose. If it is marked non-critical, the key usage indications are advisory.

Private Key Usage Period

When using digital signature keys, there are cases where the validity period for the private key may be different from the validity period for the certificate. It is often necessary to validate digital signatures using the certified public key long after it is no longer valid to use the private key to generate signatures. The PrivateKeyUsage extension is always marked as non-critical.

The private key has a validity period specified by a notBefore field indicating the earliest date that a private key can be used to generate a digital signature, and a notAfter field indicating the latest date the private key can be used. The treatment and use of this extension varies with different PKI communities and should be defined by relevant PKI and security policies.

Policy Extensions

Policy extensions allow specification and constraint of the policies that are used to define the use of certificates.

Certificate Policies

This is a list of the policy identifiers and qualifiers that pertain to the use of the certificate. The policy identifiers may be used in the process of certificate path validation. If the policy extension is specified within a CA certificate issued by another Certification Authority, it identifies the policy conditions under which that certificate path may be used.

The list of policy identifiers is contained in the policyIdentifier field of the extension and is an identifier of a particular certificate policy. Policy identifiers can be created as required by any organization and can be registered with your favorite national standards body (ANSI in the United States) to allow unique identifiers. Qualifiers may be optionally applied to each specific policy identifier. Qualifiers are intended to carry human readable information or pointers such as a user notice or a URL pointing to a human readable version of the policy.

When path validation is being performed, policy identifiers can be used, but policy qualifiers cannot. Policy qualifiers encountered during the process can be presented to certificate users to determine the applicability of path that was validated.

If the extension is marked as critical, the certificate may only be used in compliance with the requirements of the specified policies. The interpretation of any qualifiers may be defined by applicable policy.

If the extension is marked as non-critical, the use of the certificate is not necessarily constrained by the listed policies. Policy qualifiers may be interpreted or ignored at the discretion of the certificate user.

The special policy identifier anyPolicy may be referenced by a CA to indicate that the certificate may be trusted for use with all possible policies.

Policy Mappings

The PolicyMappings extension is only valid within CA certificates. Policy mapping is used to create a correspondence between certificate policies (specified by policy identifiers) defined by policy authorities in different policy domains.

It indicates that the issuing Certification Authority has recognized that the subject CA it is certifying has a policy identifier that is considered equivalent to a policy identifier recognized by the issuing CA. The extension consists of a list of certificate policy identifier pairs. The special policy identifier anyPolicy is not valid for policy mapping.

The extension may be marked as critical or non-critical. It is recommended that the extension be marked as critical, as it is not entirely clear what the meaning of a non-critical policy mapping extension means.

PKIX NOTE:

This extension must be marked as non-critical.

Subject and Issuer Information Extensions

These extensions support the use of alternative forms of names for certificate subjects and issuers. Different naming schemes are implemented for the use of Internet e-mail or domain names, X.400 addresses, and EDI names. Uniform resource identifiers (World Wide Web resource names) and IP addresses are also valid names. In general, it is possible to use any structured naming scheme.

Subject Alternative Name

The SubjectAlternativeName extension carries a list of different name forms that can be used to identify the subject of the certificate. If the extension is marked as critical, the Subject field may contain a null name and at least one of the names in the SubjectAlternativeName list must be understood and processed by the certificate user. Any names that are not recognized may be ignored.

PKIX NOTE:

If the Subject name field is null, this extension must be marked as critical.

Issuer Alternative Name

The IssuerAlternativeName extension carries a list of different name forms that can be used to identify the issuer of the certificate. If the extension is marked as critical, the Subject field may contain a null name, and at least one of the names in the list must be processed by the certificate user. Any names that are not recognized may be ignored.

PKIX NOTE:

This extension should not be marked as critical.

Subject Directory Attributes

The SubjectDirectoryAttributes extension is a non-critical extension that allows the inclusion of directory attributes that are applicable to the subject of the certificate.

Certification Path Constraint Extensions

CertificationPathConstraints are used when processing certificate paths. The constraints apply to the types of certificates a certified CA may issue or the types that are allowed in subsequent certificates in a certification path. These extensions are considered in greater detail in Chapter 8 in the discussion on trust models.

Basic Constraints

The BasicConstraints extension allows CA certificates to be identified. This extension carries the CA and PathLenConstraint fields. An entity whose public key is certified in a certificate with the basic constraints CA field set to true is permitted to sign certificates.

If the CA field is set to true, the PathLenConstraint field may also be set to indicate the maximum number of CA certificates that may follow this one in a certification path. If the path length is set to 0, the subject CA may only issue end-entity certificates—it may not issue certificates to other CAs.

X.509 recommends that the extension be flagged as critical, otherwise end-entities may inadvertently be authorized to issue certificates. If the CA field is set to false, the public key contained in the certificate may not be used to verify signatures on other certificates. If the CA field is set to true and the path length is specified, certificate users must verify the certification path according to the path length value.

If this extension is absent or marked as non-critical, the certificate must be considered an end-entity certificate, and the public key cannot be used to verify signatures on other certificates.

PKIX NOTE:

This extension must be marked critical in a CA certificate.

Name Constraints

The NameConstraints extension defines the name spaces with which a Subject or SubjectAlternativeName must comply in subsequent certificates. The extension allows the specification of name trees a name must be included in or excluded from. Further discussion on the use of this field may be found in Chapter 8. The extension may be marked critical or non-critical.

PKIX NOTE:

This extension must be marked as critical.

Policy Constraints

The PolicyConstraints extension allows the issuer to use the requireExplicitPolicy field to indicate that subsequent certificates in a certification path must contain acceptable policy identifiers.

The inhibitPolicyMapping field in the extension allows the issuer to prevent the use of mapping between different policies for subsequent certificates in a certification chain. This is usually implemented when certificate chains cross policy domains, and it is considered unlikely that any sensible corresponding policy mapping operation will result in a meaningful result.

The extension may be flagged as critical or non-critical, but is recommended to be set to critical.

PKIX NOTE:

CAs must not issue certificates where the policy constraints is a null sequence—one of inhibitPolicyMapping or requireExplicitPolicy must be specified.

Inhibit Any Policy Constraint

The InhibitAnyPolicyConstraint extension allows exclusion of the use of the anyPolicy policy identifier. This allows control over a CA using any policy as opposed to an explicit policy. It may be set to critical or non-critical.

PKIX NOTE:

This extension is not supported.

Certificate Revocation List Format

In Chapter 5, we discussed certificate revocation in some detail, where a certificate is invalidated by an issuing authority prior to its normal expiration for reasons such as key compromise or a change in the status of the certificate owner. A status mechanism must be provided to allow certificate users to check the revocation status of the certificate. X.509 allows for three cases:

- The certificate cannot be revoked.
- The certificate is revoked by the Certification Authority that issued the certificate.
- The certificate is revoked by another authority to which the issuing Certification Authority has delegated the responsibility for revocation.

The revocation mechanism specified by X.509 is the use of *certificate revocation lists* (CRLs), although the specification allows for alternate schemes to be utilized.

X.509 makes a distinction between the date and time when a certificate is revoked by a Certification Authority and the date and time when the revocation status is first published. The date of actual revocation is specified along with the certificate entry in the CRL. The revocation notice date is specified in the header of the CRL when it is published.

The location of revocation information may vary for different certification authorities (the different locations for CRL information are elaborated in Chapter 5). The certificate itself may contain a pointer to where revocation information is located, or some form of indirection may be implemented where a revocation list may point the certificate user to a different location. The certificate user may know of a directory or other repository or mechanism where revocation information may be obtained based on configuration information established during initialization (see Chapter 5 for more details).

In order to maintain consistency and auditability, the Certification Authority is required to:

- Maintain an audit record of certificate revocation
- Provide revocation status information
- Publish CRLs even when the CRL is an empty list (assuming it uses CRLs at all)

Figure A-3 graphically describes the content of a certificate revocation list.

Figure A-3

Certificate revocation list format

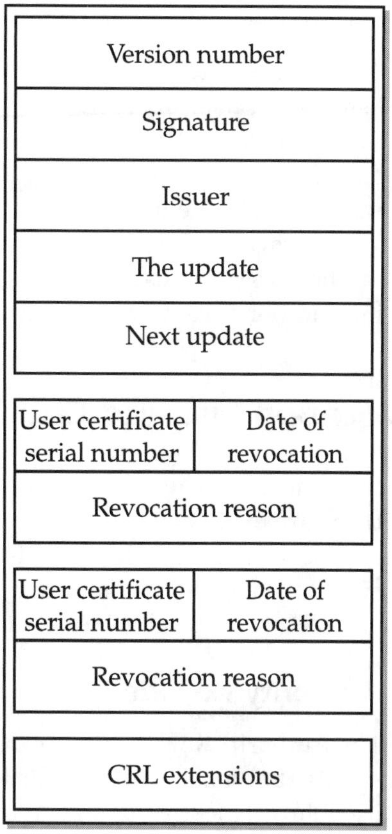

The standard fields defined for the certificate revocation list include the following:

- **Version number**   The latest version defined to date is v2. CRLs that contain critical extensions must be marked as version 2.

- **Signature**   Identifies the type of hash function and signature algorithm used to sign the revocation list.

- **Issuer**   The name of the authority that issued and signed the revocation list.

- **ThisUpdate**   Defines the date and time the revocation list was published.
- **NextUpdate**   Defines the latest date and time by which the next revocation list will be issued.

Certificates that have been revoked by the Certification Authority are listed as a series of revokedCertificates. Each entry identifies the certificate by its serialNumber and includes the revocationDate specifying the date and time when the certificate was revoked by the Certification Authority. Each entry may optionally specify extensions (crlEntryExtensions) providing additional information about the revoked certificate.

The revocation list may also optionally provide extension fields providing additional revocation information.

Certificate Revocation List and CRL Entry Extensions

In addition to the standard fields defined for a CRL described earlier, there are extensions that apply to the CRL as a whole and to individual entries within the CRL. The following sections define these extensions and list what they are used for. A more complete explanation of the various CRL types can be found in Chapter 5.

Authority Key Identifier

The AuthorityKeyIdentifier extension is a non-critical extension used to specify that a particular public key owned by a Certification Authority be used for verification of a signature on a CRL. This allows a Certification Authority to operate using multiple sets of keys, and allows a certificate user to explicitly identify which key set should be used to validate the signature on the CRL.

PKIX NOTE:
This extension must be included in all CRLs and must be set to critical.

The same justification for using the AuthorityKeyIdentifier is applicable to certificates and may be found in that section.

When this field is used for a certificate, the specific CA key may be identified by specifying a value for the keyIdentifier field of this extension, or by using a combination of the CA certificate serial number, authorityCertSerialNumber, and the CA name, authorityCertIssuer fields. Both mechanisms may be used, but the keyIdentifier form allows more specific identification when constructing certificate paths.

Issuer Alternative Name

The IssuerAlternativeName extension carries a list of different name forms that can be used to identify the issuer of the CRL. If the extension is marked as critical, the Issuer field may contain a null name, and at least one of the names in the list must be processed by the certificate user. Any names that are not recognized may be ignored.

PKIX NOTE:

This extension should not be marked as critical.

CRL Number

The CRLNumber extension is a CRL extension that contains a sequence number that allows a CRL user to determine whether all CRLs prior to the current CRL have been seen. The sequence number increases sequentially. The extension is always marked non-critical.

PKIX NOTE:

This field must be included in all CRLs but is marked as non-critical.

Reason Code

The ReasonCode extension is a CRL entry extension that identifies the reason for the certificate revocation. The reason codes currently defined include the following:

- **KeyCompromise**   The private key of the certificate subject is believed to have been compromised. This reason code is applicable to end-entity certificates.

- **CACompromise**   The private key of a CA is believed to have been compromised. This reason code is used when revoking CA certificates.

- **AffiliationChanged**   The name of the subject or other information in the certificate has been changed. This reason code does not imply that the private key has been compromised.

- **Superseded**   The certificate has been superseded by a newer certificate. This reason code does not imply that the private key has been compromised.

- **CessationOfOperation**   The certificate is no longer required for the purpose it was issued. This reason code does not imply that the private key has been compromised.

- **PrivilegeWithdrawn**   A privilege that was specified within a certificate has been withdrawn.

- **CertificateHold**   The certificate has effectively been suspended or put on hold. If this reason code is used, the HoldInstructionCode extension may be specified. Certificates that have been suspended may later be revoked or released and the entry removed from the CRL.

- **RemoveFromCRL**   This reason code is explicitly used for delta CRLs to indicate that a certificate has expired or has been released from the hold state.

The ReasonCode extension is always marked non-critical.

Hold Instruction Code

The HoldInstructionCode extension is a CRL entry extension that allows an instruction code identifying how to process a certificate that has a reason code of CertificateHold. There are no standard instruction codes identified in X.509, although some have been specified by the PKIX working group. The extension is always considered non-critical.

Invalidity Date

The InvalidityDate extension is a CRL entry extension that identifies the date at which it is known or suspected that a private key was compromised. The extension is always non-critical.

CRL Scope

The CRLScope extension is a CRL extension that defines the scope of various types of CRLs, including:

- *Simple CRLs* that provide revocation information about certificates issued by a single Certification Authority
- *Indirect CRLs* that provide revocation information from multiple certification authorities
- *Delta CRLs* that update previously issued revocation information
- *Indirect delta CRLs* that provide revocation information that updates multiple base CRLs issued by one or more certification authorities

The different types of CRLs are described in Chapter 5.

PKIX NOTE:

This extension is not supported.

Status Referral

The StatusReferral CRL extension is used to provide linkage information that will lead certificate users to a source for revocation information. If the StatusReferral extension is used, the CRL does not contain revocation notices. In addition, certificate users are required to ignore this CRL as a source of revocation notices. The information contained in the extension (or some other out-of-bounds mechanism) must be used to locate an actual source of revocation notices.

The StatusReferral extension may contain a list of CRLs and information about the state of each CRL. This mechanism might be used to publish information about the CRLs (such as the last update time) that allows users to judge the applicability of CRLs that have previously been cached. The information might result in a download request for a CRL containing revocation notices.

Alternatively, the StatusReferral extension may be used as a redirection mechanism. For example, due to configuration changes, the original source of revocation information identified in a certificate may have changed. The StatusReferral extension allows a new source to be pointed to by substituting it for the original CRL at that location.

The extension has been designed to be extensible, which could allow for revocation schemes that do not use CRLs to be referenced (or possibly upgraded to) in the future.

This extension is always marked critical to prevent certificate users who cannot interpret the extension from mistakenly relying on the content of the CRL for revocation notices. Certificate users who do not recognize the extension are required to ignore the CRL—preventing its use as a source of certificate notices.

PKIX NOTE:

This extension is not currently supported.

CRL Stream Identifier

The CRLStreamIdentifier extension is a non-critical extension that allows a Certification Authority to issue multiple certificate revocation lists. Each Certification Authority must allocate a unique identifier for each CRL stream it wants to maintain. The combination of the CRLNumber and the CRLStreamIdentifier extensions allows a unique identifier to be created for any CRL from any Certification Authority.

PKIX NOTE:

This extension is not currently supported.

Ordered List

The OrderedList extension is a non-critical extension that allows the order of certificates within the RevokedCertificates list to be specified. Certificates can be listed in ascending sequence using AscSerialNum to list based on the SerialNumber field of each list entry or by using AscRevDate to order the entries based on the RevocationDate field.

If this extension is not present, no assumptions may be made as to the ordering of entries in the RevokedCertificates list.

PKIX NOTE:

This extension is not currently supported.

Delta Information

The DeltaInformation extension is a *non-critical* extension that identifies that delta CRLs are also available corresponding to the CRL containing the extension. The extension may only be used in CRLs that are not delta CRLs, and it identifies the location where the delta CRLs may be located. In addition, the extension may optionally specify the time that the next delta CRL will be issued.

CRL Distribution Points and Delta CRL Extensions

Since a standard CRL contains all unexpired revoked certificates, it is likely to become very large. Loading large certificate revocation lists to certificate users may be slow over low bandwidth network connections. Memory requirements may constrain certificate users to the extent that it may not be possible to process a large revocation list.

Two alternatives have been created to allow for more flexible revocation information. Delta CRLs allow distribution of revocation updates where lists of changes are propagated rather than publishing the full list of revocation notices. CRL distribution point CRLs may be used to identify a location where revocation information may be found for each certificate. This may be a directory where each certificate entry contains a CRL attribute indicating the revocation status for the certificate or a location where a CRL may be found.

The topic of certificate revocation—and CRL distribution points and delta CRLs in particular—is discussed in more detail in Chapter 5.

Of the extensions discussed here, the following are certificate extensions:

- CRLDistributionPoints
- FreshestCRL

The following are CRL extensions:

- IssuingDistributionPoint
- DeltaCRLIndicator
- BaseUpdate

The remainder is a CRL entry extension:

▤ Certificate Issuer

Certificate Extensions

The following are extensions that are specific to certificates.

CRL Distribution Points

The CRLDistributionPoints extension is a certificate extension that identifies CRL distribution points the certificate user should reference to verify the revocation status of this certificate. The extension can be marked critical or non-critical. If it is marked critical, the certificate user must retrieve and check a CRL from one of the listed distribution points.

The distribution points are identified as a list of entries containing a DistributionPointName that specifies the names of the distribution points that may be used to look up a CRL. The name of the CRL issuer is also provided in the CRLIssuer field, and this is the default name used to look up the CRL if no explicit DistributionPointNames are provided.

Each entry also identifies the types of revocation information supported by the referenced distribution point. If the ReasonsFlag field is omitted, the CRL provided by the distribution point will contain a revocation entry for this certificate when it is revoked, irrespective of the revocation reason. The ReasonFlag field supports the following revocation reason indicators:

▤ Unused

▤ KeyCompromise

▤ CACompromise

▤ AffiliationChanged

▤ Superseded

▤ CessationOfOperation

▤ CertificateHold

▤ PrivilegeWithdrawn

▤ AACompromise

PKIX NOTE:

Use of this extension is recommended, but it should be set non-critical.

Freshest CRL

The Freshest CRL extension is a certificate extension that identifies the freshest CRL that should be used when checking the revocation status of the certificate. If it is marked as critical, the certificate user must obtain and check the indicated CRL before the certificate is used. If it is marked non-critical, the certificate user can make use of any locally available scheme to verify the revocation status of the certificate.

PKIX NOTE:

This extension is not currently supported.

CRL Extensions

The following are extensions that are specific to CRL.

Issuing Distribution Point

The Issuing Distribution Point extension is a critical CRL extension that identifies the distribution point that issued this CRL—see Figure A-4 for how these extensions tie together. In addition, the extension identifies the type of revocation information that is carried in the CRL. This allows a subset of revocation information to be carried at the distribution point. If the field is omitted, the CRL contains all revocation information applicable to the distribution point.

The possible revocation information represented in the CRL is identified in the IssuingDistributionPointsSyntax field and includes the following indicators:

- **OnlyContainsUserCerts** Revocation information is carried only for end-entity certificates.
- **OnlyContainsAuthorityCerts** Revocation information is carried only for CA certificates.

Figure A-4

Distribution point extension relationship

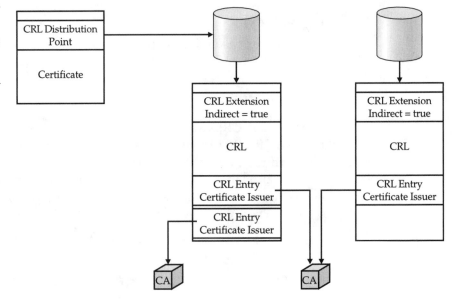

- **OnlySomeReasons** The OnlySomeReasons indicator is a list, which if present includes the set of revocation reason codes used in the CRL.

- **IndirectCRL** If set, this indicates that the CRL may contain revocation notices from authorities other than the issuer of the CRL.

- **OnlyContainsAttributeCerts** The CRL is used to carry revocation notices for a special type of certificates used in privilege management systems known as attribute certificates. Attribute certificates are discussed in Chapter 3.

Delta CRL Indicator

The Delta CRL Indicator extension is a critical CRL extension that identifies this CRL as a delta CRL rather than a base CRL. The corresponding base CRL is identified using a CRL number issued by the Certification Authority. It must contain all of the revoked certificates for a particular scope that form the base context for subsequent delta CRLs that are issued.

Base Update

The Base Update extension is a non-critical CRL extension that is used within delta CRLs. It indicates the starting date for which the delta CRL contains revocation information.

CRL Entry Extensions

The following are extensions that are specific to CRL entry.

Certificate Issuer

The CertificateIssuer extension is a critical CRL entry extension that identifies the certificate issuer responsible for the entry in the CRL. It is used when the IndirectCRL indicator is set in the IssuingDistribution-Point extension (in the CRL) to specify that indirect CRLs are supported. In the case of indirect CRLs, contributions are provided by multiple CAs so it is necessary to explicitly identify the responsible CA.

APPENDIX B

Solution to the Test

The Answer

In Chapter 2, I asked you to show how to apply your knowledge of symmetric and asymmetric cryptography to help my sister send my Mom's recipe so that it meets the following constraints:

- The solution must be secure.
- Encryption of the recipe must be fast.
- The encrypted cipher-text must be compact.
- The solution must scale to large populations.
- The solution must not be vulnerable to key interception.
- The solution must not require a prior relationship between the parties.
- The solution must be able to guarantee the source of the recipe.
- The solution must be able to detect if the recipe was modified in transit.

Let's start by looking at the sending side:

Starting with Mom's secret peppermint stick pie recipe, my sister's software will first generate a *random symmetric encryption key*. That key will be used to *encrypt the recipe*, yielding the encrypted form of the recipe:

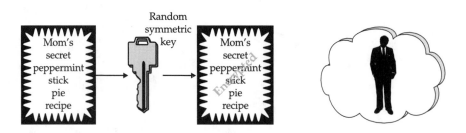

In order to get the symmetric key to the recipient, we will need to perform a *key wrapping operation*. With key wrapping, we use the *public key of the recipient* (in this case, me) to encrypt the symmetric key, producing the wrapped key:

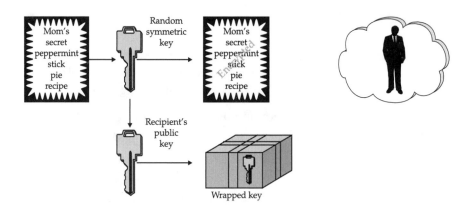

The next step is to begin the process of creating the digital signature. The first step in this process is to *hash the clear-text recipe and produce the original digest*:

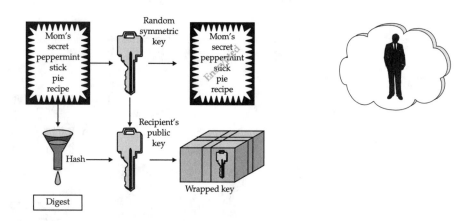

To create the signature, we take the *sender's private key* (in this case, my sister's private key) and *encrypt the digest* we just created:

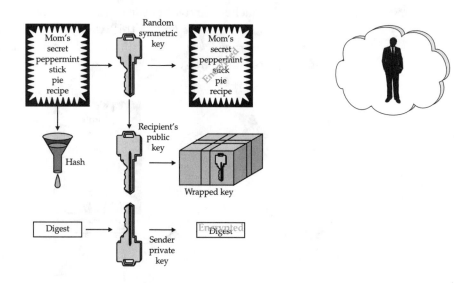

Last, we take the cipher-text, the wrapped key, and the encrypted digest, and put them together into the *digital envelope* and send it to the recipient. Note that to be nice guys, we should really attach our digital certificate with our public key, but to simplify things I have left this off:

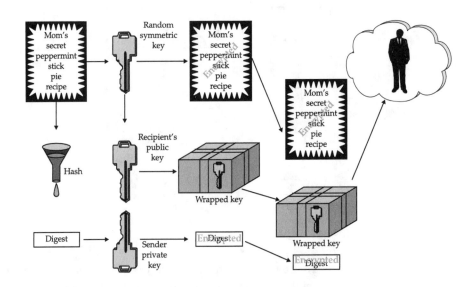

When the package arrives at the destination, the first process will be to use the *recipient's private key* (in this example, this is my private key) to *decrypt the wrapped key*. This will yield the symmetric encryption key used to create the cipher-text:

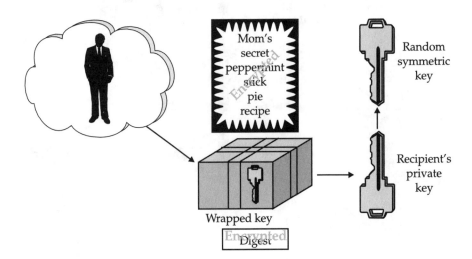

Now that we have the symmetric key, we can use it to *decrypt the cipher-text* and recover the original clear-text recipe:

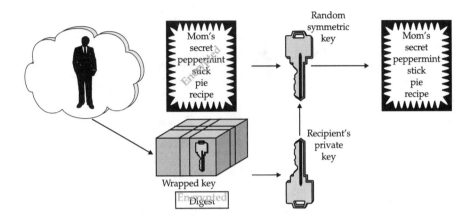

The next step is to use the *sender's public key* (my sister's public key) to *decrypt the encrypted digest* attachment. Normally, the sender would help out by sending her digital certificate so we could verify the certificate and extract the public key. Otherwise, we would need to look up the certificate in a directory and perform the same checks.

For the sake of clarity, I've left out the steps involved with certificate validation processing. Refer to Chapter 2 if you want the details:

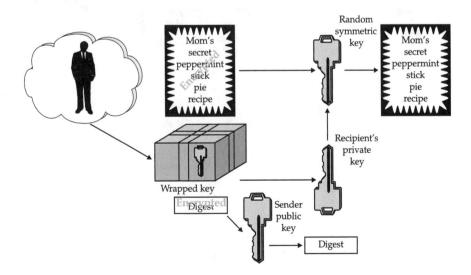

Next, we take the clear-text recipe and run it through the same hash algorithm that was used by the sender to create the original digest. This produces a *second copy of the digest,* which I have labeled Digest:

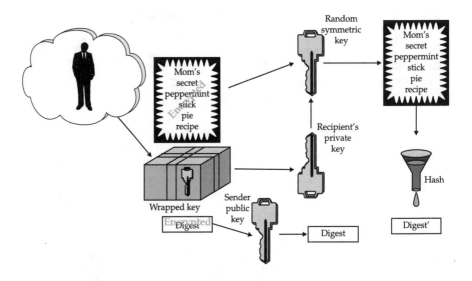

The last step in the process is *to compare the two digests*:

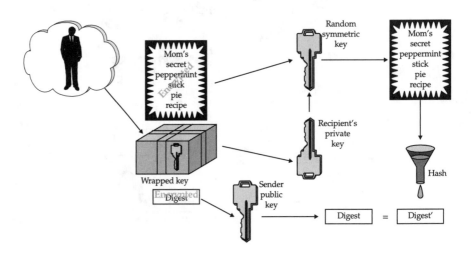

If the digests match, we know with assurance that:

- The recipe came from my sister.
- The recipe was not tampered with in transit.

Additionally, we have used the symmetric cipher to perform a fast, compact, and secure encryption of the recipe. The encryption protected the recipe so that hackers on the Internet could not see it. Public/private key cryptography was used to wrap the symmetric encryption key, allowing us to have a scalable solution that is not vulnerable to interception, and which did not require a prior relationship.

The Reward

Now that you have successfully completed your final exam in cryptography, I feel that you deserve some reward for all your hard work. Here is Mom's actual peppermint stick pie recipe. This is a particularly fun recipe to do with kids, since it involves several smashing operations and lots of stuff to make a big mess with. Here are the ingredients:

5 chocolate wafers (or chocolate graham crackers)

1/4 stick butter or margarine

25 marshmallows (extra will be needed if you have little helpers)

1/2 cup milk

1 teaspoon vanilla extract

1/8 teaspoon salt

Peppermint extract

1 cup whipping cream

A couple of candy canes (or peppermint candy)

Red food coloring (optional)

The Crust

Heat the oven to 350° F. Crush (or smash, if you prefer) enough chocolate wafers to make about 1 1/2 cups of crumbs. Chocolate wafers make a better crust, but chocolate graham crackers can be substituted. Melt the margarine and mix it into the crumbs. Press the mixture firmly into the bottom and sides of a 9″ pie plate.

Bake the crust for 10 minutes, and then set aside to cool.

The Filling

Place the marshmallows and milk in a saucepan and heat over low heat, stirring constantly until the marshmallows melt. Remove from heat, and stir in the vanilla, salt, and 6 drops of peppermint extract. Refrigerate for about an hour, until the filling begins to thicken.

Take the candy canes and crush, smash, or grind them up well. Peppermint candy works well too. It is best if the candy is pretty well ground up, without large chunks. Fold into the chilled filling. Some people like to add a few drops of red food coloring to enhance the color of the filling.

Beat the whipping cream until stiff. Fold the whipped cream into the filling until mixed well. Pour the filling into the cooled crust and chill thoroughly (overnight).

APPENDIX C

Privilege Management Infrastructure

We have touched briefly on the differences between *authentication* and *authorization* in several places in this book. By this time, it should be clear that authentication is the process by which you prove who you are—if you make use of some unique identifier, the process also involves *identification* and establishes the identity of the user. In the case of *Public Key Infrastructure* (PKI), this is the subject of the certificate.

Authorization, on the other hand, relies on authentication to prove who you are—it needs to know your identity. Rather than identify you, authorization describes what it is you are allowed to do. So it considers the rights or privileges you have to perform some task. As an example, consider the security system you use to get access to the building you work in. Just because the door access system recognizes you and lets you into the building does not mean that you can do the same things as the CEO (unless of course you are the CEO). In Chapter 3, we used the example of the passport and the visa. The passport identifies you to the immigration officials, but your visa describes what it is you are allowed to do (visit, work, study, and so on).

The system that manages your rights or privileges falls under the general heading of a *Privilege Management Infrastructure* (PMI). The 1997 edition of X.509 introduced the concept of an *attribute certificate* (AC) to describe a certificate that handled attributes about what you were authorized to do. However, the concept was fairly ill-defined, and there was little to help anyone who wanted to implement such a system. The 2000 edition of X.509 dedicates nearly half of the specification to discussing attribute certificates.

The subject of a PMI is at least as large as a PKI, so the intention in this appendix is to introduce this topic so you are aware of where this technology is moving.

Attribute Certificates

Why do we even need a separate certificate type to represent attributes? That is the topic of this section—so it was a good question to ask.

The Motivation

What is wrong with using a standard X.509 certificate (for the rest of this chapter, known as an *identity certificate*)? Well, in fact, it is possible to use an X.509 identity certificate to carry attributes specific to privilege management. The field used for this purpose is the *subjectDirectoryAttributes* extension. However, just because you can do it does not mean you should.

The problem with identity certificates is that they are relatively long lived. Relative to what? Relative to the frequency with which your access rights or privileges change. For example, if you are working on a production line as a general worker, and your supervisor goes on leave for two weeks, if you are lucky you may be temporarily given the role of line supervisor during that time. As a result, you need to access the payroll system in order to log the hours that each worker on the line worked. When the supervisor returns, you lose this privilege or access.

If you use an identity certificate for this purpose, you need to register for a new certificate to hold your new privileges and then revoke it when the privileges are withdrawn (or possibly suspend it until the next time you need it, if this functionality is supported by your PKI). In general, most privilege attributes change far more quickly than the validity period of identity certificates. In addition, it turns out that authorization has some annoying issues like delegation or impersonation. Delegation deals with issues such as a situation in which you are issued a particular privilege and wish to provide the same privilege or a subset of the privileges to someone who works for you. Impersonation allows someone to pretend to be you for a specific task (like the production line worker "impersonating" the supervisor in the previous example). Identity certificates do not support those sorts of capabilities very well.

One approach to this problem is to issue short-lived certificates that are constructed to hold attributes and link them to identity certificates. In this way, the identity of the certificate owner can remain relatively stable, while attributes associated with their identity can be changed. One of the interesting aspects of this short validity period is that you may not need revocation services (especially if the validity period is on the order of minutes). However, as we will see, to deal with longer validity periods (possibly weeks), there may be a need to revoke privileges associated with a user.

Attributes

What sorts of attributes are we dealing with? Some examples might include:

- Group membership
- Role identification
  - Collections of permissions or access rights
  - Aliases for the user's identity
  - Collections of roles (allow indirect roles to be updated without affecting the certificate that references them)

- Limits on the value of transactions
- Access times for operations (for example, never use the "destroy the entire system" function on the weekend—when no one else is around to stop you!)
- Security clearances
- Time limits (such as resource balancing systems—university student access to shared resources)

There may be multiple attribute certificates associated with the subject of the identity certificate. The attribute certificates do not all need to be issued by the same *Attribute Authority* (AA), nor do they need to be issued by the *Certification Authority* (CA) that issued the identity certificate.

Attribute Certificate Format

The attribute certificate, like its identity certificate cousin, is a signed structure. In this case, the signing or issuing authority will be an AA. The biggest difference is that there is no identity being established by the AA. The signature affixed to the attribute certificate is not attesting to the linkage between a public/private key pair and an identity, it is attesting to the privileges the holder of a certificate may possess. In fact, in the X.509 attribute certificate, there is no public key. Instead, there is a link back to the holder of the certificate.

Let's consider what type of information an attribute certificate contains (see Figure C-1).

Figure C-1

Attribute
certificate

Version number
Serial number
Signature
Issuer
Validity period
Holder
Attributes
Issuer unique identifier
Extensions

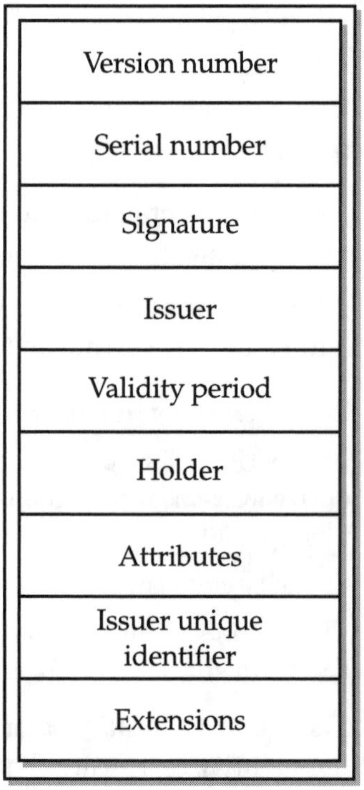

The standard fields in an attribute certificate include:

- **Version number**   Indicates the format and content of a certificate of a particular version. The current release is V2.

- **Holder**   The link to the identity of the holder of the certificate we referred to earlier. This may be a reference to the issuer and serial number of an identity certificate. It is possible to specify a general name, but this does not allow the identity of the certificate holder to be authenticated. The last alternative is the use of a message digest or cryptographic hash to allow authentication on the basis of comparing this with a corresponding hash provided by the user. This is shown in Figure C-2.

Figure C-2

Relationship between attribute certificates and identity certificates

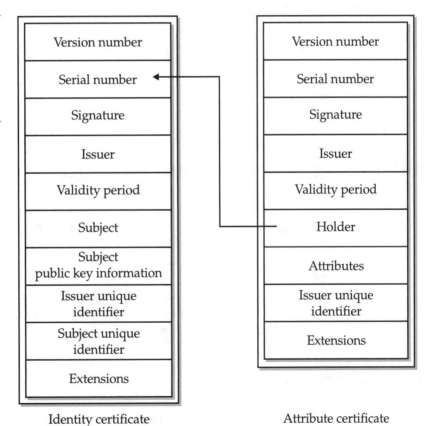

Identity certificate   Attribute certificate

- **Issuer** Identifies the Attribute Authority that issued the attribute certificate.

- **Serial number** A unique serial number that identifies this certificate among any others issued by the Attribute Authority.

- **Validity period** Specifies the start and end times during which the certificate is considered valid.

- **Attributes** Contains the attributes or privileges associated with the user that are being certified. With the exception of the role privilege attribute described later, X.509 does not specify privilege attribute types. Privilege attributes may be defined by the application or system using attribute certificates.

- **Issuer unique ID** An option that allows additional information about the issuer to be specified if the information in the issuer field is not considered sufficient.

- **Extensions** Allows additional new fields to be added to the attribute certificate without requiring that the certificate structure be changed.

- **Signature** The digital signature value calculated for the certificate including the information necessary to validate the signature (for example, an identifier of the signature algorithm used).

Privilege Management Infrastructure

Although a CA is the authority on identities within a domain, this does not imply that it is an authority on authorization. As a result, the normal case will be for an AA to be a separately administered privilege authority. Multiple AAs may issue attribute certificates against a single identity certificate issued by a CA.

X.509 also recognizes an entity known as a *Source of Authority* (SOA) that is trusted by the privilege verifier as "the entity with the ultimate responsibility for assignment of a set of privileges."

Attribute Authorities

An Attribute Authority is responsible for delegating privileges to end-entities or other Attribute Authorities. Before an AA can delegate a privilege, it must already be the holder of the privilege. This means that it in turn must have already been delegated the privilege, or it must be the source of the privilege.

The AA may be restricted from further delegating a privilege to another AA and may only be authorized to delegate the privilege to end-entities.

The AA can issue role certificates that specify the privileges associated with a named role or assign a role to an end-entity.

The Attribute Authority may also need to issue revocation notices for the certificates it issues. Revocation notices are not required, as for short-lived certificates they may not be deemed necessary. However, the AA is required to identify for the certificates it issues whether revocation information is supplied, and if it is supplied, where it can be located. For AAs that support attribute certificate revocation, they must publish an *attribute certificate revocation list* (ACRL). A separate directory object is defined to hold an ACRL.

Source of Authority

The Source of Authority is an AA and is analogous to the concept of a root CA or trust anchor. The SOA is considered the ultimate issuer of privileges. All privileges are delegated starting with an SOA. It is the termination point for attribute certificate delegation chains.

Attribute Certificate Revocation Lists

ACRLs are handled in the same way as for CRLs published by CAs. The same format is used to support CRLs for attribute certificates. An additional reason code is supported in the CRL entry extension to identify that an AA has been compromised.

PMI Models

This section discusses the various models used to operate a Privilege Management Infrastructure. The privilege management model describes how privileges are applied when making authorization decisions. The delegation model describes how privileges are delegated or allocated to entities. The role model describes how roles and the corresponding privileges are defined and how roles are assigned to end-entities.

Privilege Management Model

The privilege management model defines three entities:

- The *object* being accessed
- The *privilege asserter* seeking access to the object
- The *privilege verifier* that determines if access to the object should be permitted

The object being accessed may be a resource of some kind that has defined methods that identify ways in which the resource will be used. Most people would be familiar with a file object that supports access methods like read, write, execute, or delete. Some of the methods on an object are more sensitive than others—for example, you may allow read access to anyone on a file, but may wish to restrict write access to a small group of authors, and reserve the right to delete the file to yourself. The sensitivity of the method may also take into account attributes of the object. For example, the sensitivity could be affected by the dollar value of a transaction to be executed against a bank account. The sensitivity of the operation is also known as the context of use.

The privilege asserter is someone who holds a privilege and wishes to use or assert the privilege against an object with a particular context of use.

The privilege verifier considers the privilege that is asserted by the privilege verifier and the context of use, and determines whether that form of access will be allowed. In addition to the sensitivity of the object method used to access the object, a stated privilege policy is used to control access to the object.

A privilege policy identifies the minimum privilege necessary to access the object in different contexts. The policies must be protected ensuring integrity and authenticity. They may be stored in a directory for access by the privilege verifier.

Access control based on this privilege management model has five components:

- The privilege asserter (or privilege presenter)
- The privilege verifier

- The object method and its sensitivity
- Environment variables (dynamic state)
- The relevant privilege policy

The relationship between these components is described in Figure C-3. The privilege verifier combines the various inputs and determines if access should be allowed based on the security policy in combination with the other inputs.

Figure C-3

Access control model

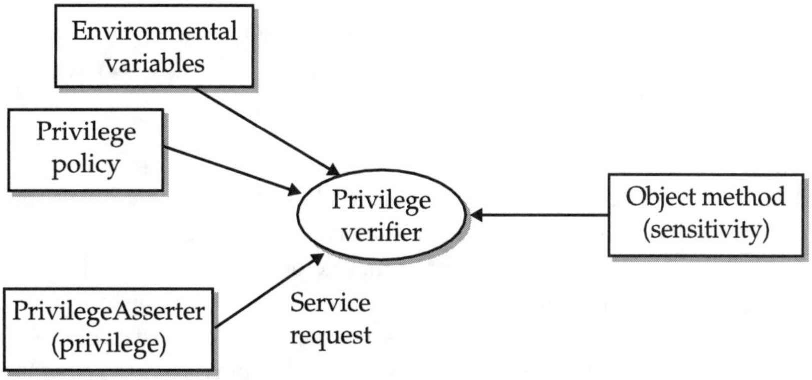

Delegation Model

The delegation model describes how privileges may be delegated.
The four components of the delegation model are:

- The privilege verifier
- The SOA
- Other AAs
- The privilege asserter (the end-entity holding the privilege)

The relationships between these components are shown in Figure C-4.
The SOA is responsible for the initial assignment of privileges to end-entities. In the simplest case, no delegation occurs and the SOA fills the role directly. However, in the delegation model, the SOA authorizes the privilege holder to act as an AA. The AA in turn may delegate the privilege it was assigned to end-entities or delegate its assignment to another AA. Whether further assignment to another delegated AA is allowed is

Figure C-4

Delegation model

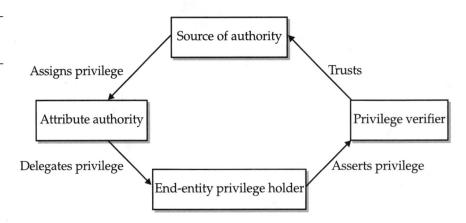

determined by the path length value set in the BasicConstraints extension in the attribute certificate issued to the AA.

An important principle of the PMI defined in X.509 is that an AA cannot delegate more privileges than have been issued to it. The downstream AA may be more restricted than an upstream AA. This may be based on constraints such as the name space that privileges may be delegated to.

A delegation path consists of a series of attribute certificates linked by holder and issuer names (see Figure C-5).

Role Model

In X.509, roles are a method of indirect privilege assignment. Roles are assigned privileges, and then individuals are assigned roles. The advantage of this mechanism is that roles may be updated to change the set of privileges assigned without the need to change the individuals assigned to a role.

Before going any further with this discussion, it must be stressed that roles are an optional feature of the X.509 PMI and are not required. The increase in complexity for the privilege verifier offsets the convenience and flexible management aspects of the privilege indirection.

Two types of attribute certificates are defined to support this model: *role specification* certificates and *role assignment* certificates. Assignment of privileges to role may take place without using role specification certificates provided some other mechanism is provided.

Figure C-5

Delegation path

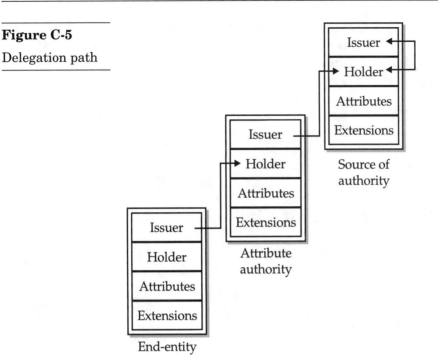

An end-entity asserting a privilege may provide a role assignment certificate rather then an attribute certificate containing privileges. The privilege verifier must recognize the name of the role presented and know the privileges associated with the role. The privileges may have been determined by some local method such as local configuration, or may have been discovered when a role specification certificate was presented.

A role assignment certificate may also include specific privileges in the attribute field, but they are not required. These privileges are assigned directly to the holder of the certificate, not the role to which she is assigned. Role specification certificates are a separate certificate type and may not be combined with any other purpose.

A role assignment certificate is identified by the use of a specific privilege attribute type. The role attribute is included in the *attribute* field of a role assignment certificate. The two pieces of information carried in the role attribute are the *roleName* and the *roleAuthority*.

The roleName is the identifier for the role to which the holder of the certificate has been assigned.

The roleAuthority is an option that identifies the name of the issuing AA for a corresponding *role specification* certificate. If it is included in the role attribute, the privilege verifier must use a role specification certificate with the same name in the issuer field.

A role specification certificate is an *attribute certificate* (AC) containing specified privileges in the attribute field where the name of the holder is a role name rather than an individual.

Role specification and role assignment certificates may be issued by different AAs.

Attribute Certificate Acquisition Model

A number of models exist for transfer of attribute certificates to the server that will be using them. These fall broadly under the headings of push models or pull models.

Push models assume that the client will send the AC to the server as part of the request for access to an object.

Pull models assume that the server will perform a lookup to access the AC that it needs corresponding to the identity in the identity certificate. This may be handled by publishing the attribute certificates to a directory, and relying on the server to perform a lookup of the information in the directory when the privilege holder presents herself. Alternatively, an online protocol could be used to perform a similar lookup, and PKIX currently has a proposal before it for such a protocol.

Privilege Management Certificate Extensions

Privilege management extensions are used to convey additional information about privileges that are carried in a certificate. They apply to attribute certificates or identity certificates that carry attributes in the subjectDirectoryAttributes extension described above.

The extensions fall into three classes:

- **Basic privilege management**   Carries information that is related to the assertion of a privilege

- **Privilege revocation**   Identifies the location of revocation status information

- **Source of Authority** Relates to the source that is trusted to provide assignment of privileges
- **Roles** Identifies the location of relate role specification certificates
- **Delegation** Allows delegation of privileges to be constrained

Basic Privilege Management Extensions

These extensions allow control over privilege assertion, such as the time when a privilege may be asserted, the application a privilege is applicable to, or policies that must be used when the privileges are used.

Time Specific

The TimeSpecific extension is used to restrict the time periods when a privilege may be used. For example, use of a privilege to activate an application may be restricted from 9:00A.M. to 5:00P.M., Monday to Friday. This could also be used to facilitate the delegation of privilege to your production line worker from his supervisor in the earlier example.

This extension must be marked as critical.

Targeting Information

The TargetingInformation extension may be used to specify a set of applications to which the privileges in the attributes field may be applied.

This extension must be marked as critical.

User Notice

The UserNotice extension allows user notices to be displayed to the holder of the attribute certificate when the privileges are asserted. This could be used to explain some constraint or condition under which the privileges are used (something like "all hope abandon, ye who enter here," or more likely a notice about the legal implications of using the privilege).

The extension may be marked as critical or non-critical. If it is marked as critical, the user notice must always be displayed each time the privileges are asserted.

Acceptable Privilege Policies

The AcceptablePrivilegesPolicies extension identifies a set of policies that must be used as part of the process of verifying the use of the privileges. This extension must be marked as critical.

Privilege Revocation Extensions

Attribute certificate revocation lists suffer from the same size and distribution problems as their identity certificate CRL cousins. These extensions allow control over where revocation information is found and indicate if revocation information will be present.

CRL Distribution Points

This is the same extension that is defined for use in identity certificates. It specifies where revocation information may be found for this attribute certificate.

No Revocation Information

The NoRevAvail extension explicitly identifies that revocation information is not provided for this attribute certificate. It may be used when the validity period for the certificate is very short.

This extension is always marked as non-critical.

Source of Authority Extensions

The extensions in this section are specific to the trusted sources of authority that originate the privilege definitions.

SOA Identifier

The SOAIdentifier extension indicates that the subject of the certificate may act as an SOA. The SOA is explicitly identified (or possibly licensed) as a trusted source of privilege information and management.

Note that this is not the only mechanism for identifying an SOA. Other mechanisms may be used.

This extension is always marked as non-critical.

Attribute Descriptor

The AttributeDescriptor extension provides a mechanism that may be used to define privilege attributes and the rules that apply to the privileges when they are delegated. This extension is only used in a special type of attribute certificate called an *attribute descriptor certificate*. The role of this certificate type is to convey the definition of a particular privilege attribute.

This attribute descriptor certificate is a self-issued certificate—that is, the issuer and holder fields are the same. This certificate is only used to convey definitions; the attributes field is empty, as it does not convey privileges.

Role Extensions

Attribute certificates can be used for assigning roles. If a privilege verifier receives a certificate in which a role is specified, it needs to be able to locate a certificate that contains the specification of privileges associated with the role.

Role Specification Certificate Identifier

The RoleSpecCertIdentifier extension may be used by an AA to point to a role specification certificate. This identifier may be used in a role assignment certificate. When the role assignment certificate is received by a privilege verifier, the identifier is used to locate the corresponding role specification certificate where the privileges associated with a role are defined.

The identifier used may be a role name corresponding to the holder name in a role specification certificate. Alternatively, the identifier may specify the name of the AA that issued the role specification certificate and its serial number. Finally, this extension may contain a locator that may be used to identify where the attribute certificate may be found.

This extension is always marked as non-critical.

Delegation Extensions

Delegation extensions are used to control the length of delegation paths and to distinguish end-entity attribute certificates from AA certificates (in the same way that end-entity identity certificates may not be used to certify other end-entity certificates). Otherwise, end-entities could establish themselves as an AA.

Similar issues for identity certificates exist with attribute certificates when dealing with name space control and policy control.

Basic Attribute Constraints

This identifies if the holder of the attribute certificate is in turn allowed to issue attribute certificates. This extension identifies that the entity has been certified as an Attribute Authority.

As with identity certificates and CAs, the BasicAttributeConstraints extension specifies a path length control that identifies how long a delegation path may be (the number of Attribute Authorities that may be in a delegation chain). As with identity certificates, a value of zero indicates that this is a leaf Attribute Authority that may only issue end-entity attribute certificates.

This extension must be present in AA certificates and it is recommended that it be marked as critical.

Delegated Name Constraints

The DelegatedNameConstraints extension operates within an attribute certificate the same way as the NameConstraints extension does in an identity certificate. It identifies what part of a name space all attribute certificates in the remainder of a delegation chain must comply with. It uses *permittedSubtrees* and *excludedSubtrees* to constrain the name space that the holder name of successive attribute certificates in the delegation path must comply with.

This extension may be marked as critical or non-critical.

Acceptable Certificate Policies

The AcceptableCertPolicies extension identifies the policies that must be used to issue the corresponding identity certificates to holders of attribute certificates. It is only valid in certificates issued to other AAs.

This extension must be marked as critical.

Authority Attribute Identifier

The AuthorityAttributeIdentifier extension is used to point to the attribute certificate of the issuing AA. This extension is a back pointer to the issuer's attribute certificate. It is necessary because an AA is not permitted to delegate privileges that it does not possess itself. A privilege verifier can use this pointer to check that the AA had enough privilege to delegate that privilege to the holder of this certificate.

A single certificate may be used to delegate multiple privileges when it is issued, or it may be done across multiple certificates. If multiple certificates were used, a list of identifiers would be included in this extension.

This extension is always marked as non-critical.

PKIX

The PKIX working group has a number of Internet Drafts under development that relate to the use of attribute certificates in the Internet. There is not sufficient space here to go into all of the details, but a number of qualifications of the X.509 recommendation are worth noting.

PKIX in the attribute certificate profiles makes the following recommendations:

- Attribute certificate chains or delegation chains are not currently supported.

- A single AA is responsible for issuing all of the attribute certificates for a set of privileges. Privileges from the one set must not be split among AAs.

- Multiple AAs may exist as long as they manage separate privilege sets.

- Support of both push and pull models for attribute certificate delivery is recommended.

- Although X.509 leaves open the possibility of a CA also being an AA, this is explicitly prohibited in the PKIX profile.

- PKIX adds support for a number of additional attribute certificate extensions including:

  - **Audit Identity** Allows an identifier other than the certificate holder to be used within audit trails when the privacy of the owner needs to be maintained

- **Service Authentication Information**   Allows a username and password to be transferred to a legacy application for authentication purposes
- **Charging Identity**   Identifies the holder of the AC for charging purposes
- **Group**   The AC carries group membership information

In order to support protocols for pull models in addition to the use of a directory, an Internet Draft entitled "Limited Attribute Certificate Acquisition Protocol" is under consideration.

Summary

This appendix introduced the world of privilege management infrastructure targeted at authorizing access end-entities may make to objects or services. The basic mechanism is the attribute certificate, which is linked to the identity certificate as a method for authenticating the user prior to identifying the privileges that are associated with the user.

Attribute certificates have a similar structure to identity certificates, but due to their short lifetime may not require the use of a revocation notification scheme. If revocation notices are required, they may be found using a variation of a CRL for attribute. If revocation notices are required, they may be found using a variation of a CRL for attribute certificate information known as an ACRL.

In general, although the current specifications create a basis for the use of attribute certificates for authorization, we can rely on little practical implementation experience. This is certainly one of the significant areas to watch in the near future as PKI and PMI vendors produce solutions based on these techniques.

Glossary

Algorithm A mathematical function, such as used to encrypt and decrypt information.

Asymmetric encryption A cryptographic approach that uses one key to encrypt a message, and a different key to decrypt the message. The foundation of Public Key Infrastructure. Compare to symmetric encryption. See *public-key encryption*.

Authentication The action of verifying information such as identity, ownership, or authorization. Authentication methods include passwords, hardware tokens, software tokens, smart cards, software smart cards, and biometric devices.

Authentication server A server that provides authentication services on a network.

Authentication token A device issued to authorized individuals that generates a code used to provide proof of their identity in a two-factor authentication system; can be a hardware token or a software token. Also called an *authenticator*.

Authorization The granting of appropriate access privileges to authenticated users.

Availability   The uptime of a computer system; some hacker attacks are designed to eliminate the availability of a key system.

Biometrics   User authentication based on unique physical characteristics, such as fingerprints, retinal scans, voice print, hand geometry or others.

Block cipher   A symmetric cipher that encrypts a message by breaking it down into blocks and encrypting each block.

Brute force   A hacking technique that uses sheer repetition rather than logic to overcome protection; used to test password alternatives, or to locate active modem lines.

CA   A Certification Authority (sometimes referred to as a certificate authority or a certifying authority). A trusted third-party organization or company that issues digital certificates used to create digital signatures and public/private keypairs.

CDSA   A CAPI developed by Intel and IBM and now owned by the Open Group; an emerging security programming standard.

Certificate   Also known as a *digital certificate*. A certificate is an electronic document binding together some pieces of information, such as a user's identity and public key. A *Certification Authority* (CA) typically issues certificates, but an enterprise, a government, or some other entity can sign its own certificate. This self-signed certificate is the root certificate for the entity and is used to sign subordinate certificates.

Certificate revocation list (CRL)   The Certificate Authority's listing of invalidated certificates. Revocation can be due to time lapse, employment change, theft of private key, or other reason.

Challenge/Response   An authentication approach where the authentication server provides a message (the challenge) that the user must process and enter correctly (the response) to prove identity.

Ciphertext   Information that has been encrypted into seemingly meaningless code.

Cleartext   A message that has not been encrypted.

Confidentiality   Limiting the communication of private content to known, authorized parties.

Crack   To overcome password protection or encryption. Crack is also the name of a popular password-breaking utility.

Cracker   Hacker term for a "principled hacker"; compare to hacker.

CRL   See *certificate revocation list.*

Cryptography   The art and science of using mathematics to secure information and create a high degree of trust in the electronic realm. See also *public key, secret key,* and *symmetric-key cryptography.*

Cryptographic Application Programming Interface (CAPI)   A standardized way of programming security features into systems.

Data integrity   Proof that a file or communication has been unchanged since origination.

Decryption   The rendering of ciphertext back into its original plaintext version.

Denial of service   A hacker attack designed to shut down or overwhelm a critical system, such as an authentication server or Web server.

DES (Data Encryption Standard)   The most common symmetric encryption method. Provides fast processing, and thus is often used with asymmetric encryption methods to encrypt lengthy text.

Diffie-Hellman Key Exchange   A key exchange protocol allowing the participants to agree on a key over an insecure channel.

Digest   A scrambled piece of data produced by a one-way hash function, which serves as a unique fingerprint of an original document; used in a digital signature to provide assurance of data integrity.

Digital certificate   A data structure used in a public key system to bind a particular, authenticated individual to a particular public key.

Digital signature   A technique for proving that a message has not been tampered with, using public key cryptography. Example: a hashed digest of a message is created, encrypted with the sender's private key, and included with the message itself (in essence, attaching a secret fingerprint of the original file). The recipient uses the sender's public key to decrypt the digest, which is then compared with a hash digest of the actual message received.

Directory In public key cryptography, a look-up table of user names and public keys based on standards such as X.509 or SPKI.

Distinguished name In public key cryptography, the concept that each individual must have a unique name in the directory. A distinguished name must be unique within a directory domain (set of names). A DN is a unique string comprised of multiple attributes that, when viewed as a whole, identify an entity (for example, a user or Certificate Authority).

DN See *distinguished name*.

DSA (Digital Signature Algorithm) An algorithm for use in digital signatures as defined by NIST in its *Digital Signature Standard* (DSS).

DSS (Digital Signature Standard) A standard for digital signatures defined by NIST.

Elliptic curve algorithm An alternative to the RSA algorithm and DSA for generating digital signatures; an elliptic curve is a more difficult mathematic problem to solve, giving a stronger cryptographic result with a shorter key.

Encryption The transformation of plaintext into an apparently less readable form (called ciphertext) through a mathematical process. The ciphertext may be read by anyone who has the key that decrypts (undoes the encryption) the ciphertext.

Encryption algorithm The mathematical formula used to encrypt information; based on the idea that factoring down a very large number (thousands of digits) is much more difficult than the task of generating it.

ESP (Encapsulating Security Payload) Encryption of an IP datagram. See also *IPsec*.

Extranet Making information on a private network available to authorized parties outside the organization, using Internet technology.

GSSAPI (Generic Security Services API) A standard for implementing security services in software that allows applications to pass user credentials between them, without forcing re-authentication.

Hacker A person who attempts to bypass computer security systems.

Hash-based MAC MAC that uses a hash function to reduce the size of the data it processes.

Hash code   A short piece of ciphertext created by a one-way hash algorithm; provides a unique fingerprint of the total keystrokes in a document, without the need to decrypt.

Hash function   Also one-way hash algorithm; the mathematical formula that turns a text block into a unique block of ciphertext of a fixed length.

HTTPS   A secure variant of the HTTP protocol. Under HTTPS, the connection between client and server is encrypted using a *Secure Sockets Layer* (SSL).

IKE   Part of the IPsec protocols; specifies how compliant devices share a public key when creating an encrypted tunnel. Formerly called ISAKMP/Oakley.

Integrity (Data integrity)   Refers to a duplicate or transmitted version that bears fidelity to the original in every way.

IPsec (pronounced "i-p sec.")   A set of protocols being developed by the IETF to build enhanced security features into the IP layer; used to implement secure connections, such as VPNs. See also *IKE, transport mode,* and *tunnel mode.*

ISO (International Organization for Standardization)   The standards body that defined the seven-layer Open Systems Interconnect (OSI) reference model for internetworking, among others.

Kerberos   A client-server authentication and authorization system developed by MIT in the late 1970s; uses symmetric encryption.

Key   The secret used to encrypt or decrypt ciphertext; the security of encryption depends on keeping the key secret.

Key exchange   A process used by two or more parties to exchange keys in cryptosystems.

Key pair   The two keys generated in asymmetric encryption; whatever one key encrypts, the other decrypts. Often used as public and private keys in PKI.

LDAP (Lightweight Directory Access Protocol)   Based on the standard X.500 LDAP directory. LDAP is a simple protocol that allows users to access and search disparate directories over the Internet.

MAC (Message Authentication Code)   A function that transforms a variable-length input, using a secret key, to produce a unique fixed-length output which serves as a kind of fingerprint for the original file. MACs can be hash functions, stream ciphers, or block ciphers.

Man in the middle   A hacker attack where the hacker positions himself between two unsuspecting parties in a communication session.

Masquerade   A hacker attack where the hacker fraudulently assumes the identity of another person.

Message digest   A unique fingerprint for a message or document created using a hashing algorithm, such as MD-5 or SHA-1. Tampering with the document will produce a different message digest.

MD5   A hash function developed by RSA Laboratories.

MIME (Multipurpose Internet Mail Extensions)   The standards for attaching additional files or information to e-mails.

Modulus   The integer used in cryptosystems as the base of cryptographic transforms.

Non-repudiation   The inability to deny actions. Non-repudiation of delivery prevents a recipient from denying receipt of a message; non-repudiation of origin prevents the creator from denying that he or she wrote the message; non-repudiation of submission provides proof of the time and date the message was sent.

PKCS   Public-Key Cryptographic Standards. A series of specifications developed by RSA Laboratories that define common cryptographic data elements and structures.

PKI (Public Key Infrastructure)   A system that uses asymmetric encryption to provide proof of identity, data privacy, non-repudiation and data integrity. Digital certificates and digital signatures are PKI elements.

PKIX   The IETF working group that articulates public key standards for use on the Internet.

Plaintext   Non-encrypted messages or data.

Policy   Business rules used to guide employee actions; security policy sets the framework for security technology.

Private key   In asymmetric encryption or PKI, the confidential encryption key held privately by the user. The private key can be used to encrypt a message, which provides proof of authentic message creation when decrypted by the corresponding public key; because the private key can also be used to decrypt a message, it protects the privacy of incoming communication from others, who use the public key to encrypt messages.

Public key   In asymmetric encryption or PKI, the encryption key posted publicly for communicating securely with the holder of a private key. The public key can be used to decrypt a message created by the user's private key, which provides proof of authentic message creation; the user's public key can be used to encrypt a private message for only that recipient.

Public-key encryption   This encryption scheme use two keys: a public key, that anyone may use, and a corresponding private key, that is possessed only by the person who created it. With this method, anyone may send a message encrypted with the recipient's public key, but only the recipient has the private key necessary to decrypt it.

Replay   A hacker trick of capturing an encrypted password and using it later to establish a fraudulent connection; including a timestamp in the passcode eliminates this risk.

RSA   One of the first public key cryptosystem, patented in 1983. RSA is a public-key cryptosystem based on the factoring problem. RSA stands for Rivest, Shamir, and Adleman, the developers of the RSA public-key cryptosystem and the founders of RSA Data Security (now RSA Security).

RSA Public/Private Key   The most popular asymmetric encryption algorithm implemented for the authentication of users.

Secret key   In secret-key cryptography, this is the key used both for encryption and decryption.

Session encryption   Encryption that is used for the duration of a communication session, such as during a secure connection to a Web server using SSL.

Session hijacking   A hacker approach of masquerading as one party in an existing communications session.

Shared secret   The key used in symmetric cryptography.

S/MIME (Secure MIME)   The IETF specification that defines a framework for the encryption and/or digital signing of an electronic message, or part of a message.

Stream cipher   A symmetric encryption technique that operates on one bit of data at a time; compare to block cipher.

Symmetric encryption   An approach that uses the same algorithm or key to both encrypt and decrypt information; compare to asymmetric encryption.

SSL   Secure Sockets Layer, an open standard proposed by Netscape Communications for providing secure (encrypted and authenticated) WWW services (as well as other applications, such as mail, FTP, and Telnet) over the Internet. SSL uses RSA public-key encryption.

SSO   Single Sign-On, the process by which a user authenticates once to gain access to multiple applications and resources without having to authenticate to each resource and manage multiple passwords.

SSSO   Secure Single Sign-On. This is SSO using strong authentication to identify the user initially. SSSO encrypts all application traffic and uses certificates to identify both clients and servers.

Subject Distinguished Name   Establishes a relationship between the named person or entity and the public key in a certificate. See *distinguished name*.

Symmetric cipher   An encryption algorithm that uses the same key is used for encryption as decryption.

Triple-DES   A technique used to make DES encryption stronger; a given message is encrypted three times using multiple DES keys.

Trust   In security technology, the definition of the relationship between two parties or computers, wherein certain rights or privileges are granted to the trusted party.

Trusted third-party   The reliance on a third party, such as a certificate authority, to vouch for the identity of one or both members in a transaction.

Two-factor authentication   A form of authentication that requires two distinct items to ensure user authenticity. Factors could include a token, personal identification number (PIN), biometric device, or smart card. A bank-issued ATM is the most common example of two-factor authentication.

Virtual Private Network (VPN)   The use of an encrypted tunnel over a public network, to provide privacy on par with a private network.

X.500   Generically, the ANSI standards that define directory services, including digital certificates.

X.509   The standard that defines the digital certificate.

X.509 certificate   Digital information signed by a certificate authority, an X.509 certificate contains subject-related information that links a specific user to his or her public key. The X.509 certificate contains, for example, the subject distinguished name, the RSA public key, the issuer name, and the digital signature.

Index

Symbols

A

INTERNATIONAL CONTACT INFORMATION

AUSTRALIA
McGraw-Hill Book Company Australia Pty. Ltd.
TEL +61-2-9417-9899
FAX +61-2-9417-5687
http://www.mcgraw-hill.com.au
books-it_sydney@mcgraw-hill.com

CANADA
McGraw-Hill Ryerson Ltd.
TEL +905-430-5000
FAX +905-430-5020
http://www.mcgrawhill.ca

GREECE, MIDDLE EAST, NORTHERN AFRICA
McGraw-Hill Hellas
TEL +30-1-656-0990-3-4
FAX +30-1-654-5525

MEXICO (Also serving Latin America)
McGraw-Hill Interamericana Editores S.A. de C.V.
TEL +525-117-1583
FAX +525-117-1589
http://www.mcgraw-hill.com.mx
fernando_castellanos@mcgraw-hill.com

SINGAPORE (Serving Asia)
McGraw-Hill Book Company
TEL +65-863-1580
FAX +65-862-3354
http://www.mcgraw-hill.com.sg
mghasia@mcgraw-hill.com

SOUTH AFRICA
McGraw-Hill South Africa
TEL +27-11-622-7512
FAX +27-11-622-9045
robyn_swanepoel@mcgraw-hill.com

UNITED KINGDOM & EUROPE (Excluding Southern Europe)
McGraw-Hill Publishing Company
TEL +44-1-628-502500
FAX +44-1-628-770224
http://www.mcgraw-hill.co.uk
computing_neurope@mcgraw-hill.com

ALL OTHER INQUIRIES Contact:
Osborne/McGraw-Hill
TEL +1-510-549-6600
FAX +1-510-883-7600
http://www.osborne.com
omg_international@mcgraw-hill.com

BSAFE ®

ENCRYPTION FROM THE MOST TRUSTED NAME IN e-SECURITY

Whether you need core cryptography routines, digital certificate management components, or fully implemented protocol for your application, the RSA BSAFE SDKs provide you with all of the components you need to make your applications absolutely safe and secure. By using RSA BSAFE products, your staff can save months of development time, enabling you to roll out mission-critical systems earlier and with more confidence. Contact RSA Security, your choice for authentication, encryption and PKI.

Products displaying this symbol contain or are compatible with the most trusted e-security technology

SECURITY™

The Most Trusted Name in e-Security®

www.rsasecurity.com/go/rsapress/PKI

How Do I Choose THE RIGHT PKI Solution?

Public Key Infrastructure (PKI) and digital certificates provide the best security foundation for e-business. But how do you choose the right PKI? The wrong decision could result in lost time and money. And put your reputation at risk in the process.

There's a lot at stake. That's why your best choice is PKI from the most trusted name in e-security, RSA Security. We've been the e-security industry leader for over 20 years. We pioneered public key cryptography and we know what you need in a PKI solution. That's why RSA Keon is the first truly interoperable PKI based entirely on open standards. And its modular approach allows for flexible implementation.

More than 7,000 organizations worldwide already trust us with their e-security. So for PKI you can trust, the right decision is RSA Keon. Contact RSA Security, your source for authentication, encryption and PKI.

www.rsasecurity.com/go/rsapress/PKI

SECURITY™

The Most Trusted Name in e-Security®

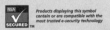

SECURITY™

The Most Trusted Name in e-Security®

The Company

RSA Security Inc. is the most trusted name in e-security, helping organizations build secure, trusted foundations for e-business through its two-factor authentication, encryption and public key management systems. RSA Security has the market reach, proven leadership and unrivaled technical and systems experience to address the changing security needs of e-business and bring trust to the new online economy.

A truly global company with more than 8,000 customers, RSA Security is renowned for providing technologies that help organizations conduct e-business with confidence. Headquartered in Bedford, Mass., and with offices around the world, RSA Security is a public company (NASDAQ: RSAS) with 2000 revenues of $280 million.

Our Markets and Products

With the proliferation of the Internet and revolutionary new e-business practices, there has never been a more critical need for sophisticated security technologies and solutions. Today, as public and private networks merge and organizations increasingly expand their businesses to the Internet, RSA Security's core offerings are continually evolving to address the critical need for e-security. As the inventor of leading security technologies, RSA Security is focused on three core disciplines of e-security.

Public Key Infrastructure

RSA Keon® public key infrastructure (PKI) solutions are a family of interoperable, standards-based PKI software modules for managing digital certificates and creating an environment for authenticated, private and legally binding electronic communications and transactions. RSA Keon software is designed to be easy to use and interoperable with other standards-based PKI solutions, and to feature enhanced security through its synergy with the RSA SecurID authentication and RSA BSAFE encryption product families.

Authentication

RSA SecurID® systems are a leading solution for two-factor user authentication. RSA SecurID software is designed to protect valuable network resources by helping to ensure that only authorized users are granted access to e-mail, Web servers, intranets, extranets, network operating systems and other resources. The RSA SecurID family offers a wide range of easy-to-use authenticators, from time-synchronous tokens to smart cards, that help to create a strong barrier against unauthorized access, helping to safeguard network resources from potentially devastating accidental or malicious intrusion.

Encryption

RSA BSAFE® software is embedded in today's most successful Internet applications, including Web browsers, wireless devices, commerce servers, e-mail systems and virtual private network products. Built to provide implementations of standards such as SSL, S/MIME, WTLS, IPSec and PKCS, RSA BSAFE products can save developers time and risk in their development schedules, and have the security that only comes from a decade of proven, robust performance.

Commitment to Interoperability

RSA Security's offerings represent a set of open, standards-based products and technologies that integrate easily into organizations' IT environments, with minimal modification to existing applications and network systems. These solutions and technologies are designed to help organizations deploy new applications securely, while maintaining corporate investments in existing infrastructure. In addition, the Company maintains active, strategic partnerships with other leading IT vendors to promote interoperability and enhanced functionality.

Strategic Partnerships

RSA Security has built its business through its commitment to interoperability. Today, through its various partnering programs, the Company has strategic relationships with hundreds of industry-leading companies—including 3COM, AOL/Netscape, Ascend, AT&T, Nortel Networks, Cisco Systems, Compaq, IBM, Oracle, Microsoft and Intel—who are delivering integrated, RSA Security technology in more than 1,000 products.

Customers

RSA Security customers span a wide range of industries, including an extensive presence in the e-commerce, banking, government, telecommunications, aerospace, university and healthcare arenas. Today, more that 8 million users across 7,000 organizations—including more than half of the Fortune 100—use RSA SecurID authentication products to protect corporate data. Additionally, more than 500 companies embed RSA BSAFE software in some 1,000 applications, with a combined distribution of approximately one billion units worldwide.

Worldwide Service and Support

RSA Security offers a full complement of world-class service and support offerings to ensure the success of each customer's project or deployment through a range of ongoing customer support and professional services including assessments, project consulting, implementation, education and training, and developer support. RSA Security's Technical Support organization is known for resolving requests in the shortest possible time, gaining customers' confidence and exceeding expectations.

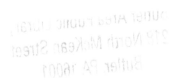

Distribution

RSA Security has established a multi-channel distribution and sales network to serve the enterprise and data security markets. The Company sells and licenses its products directly to end users through its direct sales force and indirectly through an extensive network of OEMs, VARs and distributors. RSA Security supports its direct and indirect sales effort through strategic marketing relationships and programs.

Global Presence

RSA Security is a truly global e-security provider with major offices in the U.S., United Kingdom, Singapore and Tokyo, and representation in nearly 50 countries with additional international expansion underway. The RSA SecurWorld channel program brings RSA Security's products to value-added resellers and distributors worldwide, including locations in Europe, the Middle East, Africa, the Americas and Asia-Pacific.

For more information about RSA Security, please visit us at:
www. rsasecurity.com.

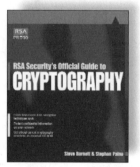
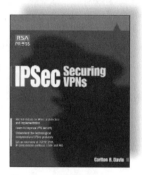